The Life of Christian Doctrine

The Life of Christian Doctrine

Mike Higton

LONDON • NEW YORK • OXFORD • NEW DELHI • SYDNEY

T&T CLARK
Bloomsbury Publishing Plc
50 Bedford Square, London, WC1B 3DP, UK
1385 Broadway, New York, NY 10018, USA
29 Earlsfort Terrace, Dublin 2, Ireland

BLOOMSBURY, T&T CLARK and the T&T Clark logo are trademarks of Bloomsbury Publishing Plc

First published in Great Britain 2020
This paperback edition published in 2022

Copyright © Mike Higton, 2020

Mike Higton has asserted his right under the Copyright, Designs and Patents Act, 1988, to be identified as Author of this work.

For legal purposes the Acknowledgements on p. viii–ix constitute an extension of this copyright page.

Cover design: Terry Woodley
Cover image © Dinodia Photos / Alamy Stock Photo

All rights reserved. No part of this publication may be reproduced or transmitted in any form or by any means, electronic or mechanical, including photocopying, recording, or any information storage or retrieval system, without prior permission in writing from the publishers.

Bloomsbury Publishing Plc does not have any control over, or responsibility for, any third-party websites referred to or in this book. All internet addresses given in this book were correct at the time of going to press. The author and publisher regret any inconvenience caused if addresses have changed or sites have ceased to exist, but can accept no responsibility for any such changes.

A catalogue record for this book is available from the British Library.

Library of Congress Control Number: 2020932415

ISBN: HB: 978-0-5676-8720-3
PB: 978-0-5676-9783-7
ePDF: 978-0-5676-8721-0
eBook: 978-0-5676-8722-7

Typeset by Deanta Global Publishing Services, Chennai, India

To find out more about our authors and books visit www.bloomsbury.com and sign up for our newsletters.

Contents

Acknowledgements	viii

Part One Doctrine in the life of the church

1	What is doctrine?	3
	Beginning in the middle	3
	Questions and concerns	4
	The path ahead	6
	Contexts	9
	Terminology	12
	Final comments	14
2	The story of doctrine in the Church of England	16
	Introduction	16
	Doctrinal diffidence?	19
	Inventing Anglican diffidence	22
	A contested inheritance	28
	Empire and exclusion	31
	The integrity of Anglicanism?	36
	Conclusion	41
3	Locating doctrine in the Church of England	45
	Introduction	45
	Ordinary belief	46
	Circulations	53
	Formal theological education	58
	Ecclesiastical deliberation	64
	Conclusion	72

Part Two The nature of doctrine

4	The emergence of doctrine	75
	Introduction	75
	The life of the church	75

	The emergence of doctrine	86
	Conclusion	93
5	Doctrine and intellectualism	95
	Introduction	95
	The lure of intellectualism	96
	The knowledge and love of God	101
	Conclusion	109
6	Doctrine and belief	111
	Introduction	111
	Doctrine as second order	111
	Belief	118
	Doctrinal theology and ordinary belief	130
	Conclusion	137
7	Doctrine and scripture	140
	Introduction	140
	The unchained word	141
	Reading settlements	144
	The call to Christian reading	149
	Reading differently	156
	Conclusion	168
8	Doctrine and disagreement	170
	Introduction	170
	Christian disagreement	171
	Beyond separation	180
	Facing disagreement	191
	Conclusion	201
9	Doctrine and change	203
	Introduction	203
	Reforming the sinful church	205
	Diligence and disruption	209
	Cries, feasting and intimacy	215
	The dynamics of change	222
	Conclusion	230
10	Coda: Serving the church	234
	Introduction	234
	Serving ordinary belief	234

Dimensions of the task	235
Illustrations from the Church of England	237
Conclusion	241
Bibliography	243
Index	263

Acknowledgements

Many people have helped me to write this book.

I am grateful for a grant from Fordham University's 'Varieties of Understanding Project', under the leadership of Stephen Grimm, which provided funding for one set of conversations that fed my thinking; I am grateful to my colleagues Chris Cook, Karen Kilby, Gerard Loughlin, Walter Moberly and Robert Song for forming the core group in Durham for that project, to Michael Raubach, who assisted me in running it, and to Sarah Coakley, Ash Cocksworth, Hazel Henson, Andrew Moore, Richard Sudworth and Susannah Ticciati, each of whom shared their thinking with us.

I am grateful for a grant from my own institution, Durham University, which allowed me to do some preliminary research on approaches to the doctrine teaching in the Theological Education Institutions that are part of the Common Awards network, to all those from those institutions who replied to my questions, and especially to Marika Rose for helping me carry out the research.

I am grateful to Adam Shaeffer for the assistance he provided for my trawl through the proceedings of General Synod.

I am grateful to Anna Turton and Veerle Van Steenhuyse from Bloomsbury, for helping me along the path towards publication.

I am grateful to the small group of my PhD students who met to discuss, and to give me invaluable feedback on, drafts of the central chapters of the book (especially given that they waded through versions that were even longer and baggier than the ones below): to Ben Coleman, Jenny Leith, Peter Leith and Jameson Ross.

I am grateful to my colleagues on the Faith and Order Commission over the past ten years, and to those on the Living in Love and Faith Project over the past two, especially in the various different small groups of which I have been a part.

I am grateful to all those who, in addition to the people already mentioned, have discussed some of the subject matter of this book with me, given me specific ideas or bits of information and advice, provided feedback on draft chapters, or simply answered queries on Twitter: to Nick Adams, Andrew Atherstone, Paul Avis, Al Barrett, Keith Beech-Gruneberg, Luke Bretherton, Mark Chapman, Frances Clemson, David Clough, Susannah Cornwall, Russell Dewhurst, Beth Dodd, Paul Fiddes, Jim Fodor, David Ford, Ben Fulford, Julie Gittoes, Andrew Goddard, Paula Gooder, Brett Gray, Kat Gregory-Witham, Tom Greggs, Pete Gunstone, Isabelle Hamley, Dan Hardy, Steve Holmes, Julian Hubbard, Cherryl Hunt, Tim Jenkins, Eeva John, Morwenna Ludlow, Judith Maltby, Ian McIntosh, Mark McIntosh, Patrick McKearney, Rachel Muers, Paul Murray, Paul Nimmo, Simon Oliver, Gaël Pardöen, Ian Paul, Sanjee Perera-Child, Ben Quash, Greg Ryan, Mike Snape, Stephen Spencer, John Swinton,

Gabby Thomas, Steve Walton, Frances Ward, Pete Ward, Clare Watkins, Jeremy Worthen and Simeon Zahl.

Scripture quotations are from New Revised Standard Version Bible: Anglicized Edition, copyright © 1989, 1995 National Council of the Churches of Christ in the United States of America. Used by permission. All rights reserved worldwide.

Part One

Doctrine in the life of the church

1

What is doctrine?

Beginning in the middle

In the midst of things – in the midst of people gathering for worship, discovering how to follow Jesus at home and at work, saying their prayers and failing to say them, reading the bible and hearing it read, singing hymns and worship songs, sitting in silence, gathering for baptisms, celebrating weddings, crying at funerals, sinning and repenting, telling and hesitating to tell their friends about their faith, praying for the sick, sitting with the dying, visiting prisoners, helping out at food banks and refuges and credit unions, discovering God's work among their neighbours, praying with icons, attending sung Eucharists, speaking in tongues, praying for healing, arguing about money and about sex and about music and about candles, joining protest marches, struggling with the immigration system, crossing themselves, sitting through sermons quietly or noisily, going on retreats and to big Christian festivals, responding to evangelistic appeals, decorating churches and chapels, leading school assemblies, sneaking into the back pew hoping not to be noticed – in the midst of all this tangled and various life of the church, there are also people pursuing doctrinal theology.

When I say 'doctrinal theology', I have in mind a varied and changing collection of activities. I am thinking of activities of conversation, reflection, confession, teaching, proclamation, deliberation, argument and apology, and all sorts of others. And I have these activities in mind insofar as they provide people with opportunities to express and explore claims about God and God's ways with the world. Christian doctrinal theology takes place wherever Christians express claims about God to which they take themselves and their churches to be committed, and wherever they explore what that commitment demands of them. I am not thinking primarily of the activities of people identified as accredited ministers or professional theologians. I am, instead, thinking of activities that one can encounter among all sorts of people, in all sorts of forms, wherever the life of the church extends – and that are caught up in currents of influence and interaction that stretch far beyond the church.

These activities of doctrinal theology can be found, by an attentive observer, laced through all the activities of Christian life. They are there in the mix, as part of the untidy weave of threads that makes Christian life what it is. They might, at their best, be among the activities that help Christians grow together as followers of Jesus, in worship and witness and discipleship, and in the capacity to share that life with others.

These activities of doctrinal theology are not the whole story, but they are one part of the story of Christian faith. Understanding the forms that these activities take, and the roles that they play – understanding, that is, the 'nature of doctrine' – is the purpose of this book.

Questions and concerns

This book is an attempt to answer two questions. First, there is the question of the relationship between doctrinal theology and ordinary Christian life. The practices of doctrinal theology are laced through the whole of Christian life, and all kinds of people are involved in them – but they are also practices that can be developed and refined to an extraordinary degree. People devote their lives to them; institutions are built to foster them; libraries are filled with writings that emerge from them – and doctrinal theology can appear to become detached from the life of ordinary belief. What is the connection between the community that sings 'Jesus is Lord', and the theological commission that pronounces that 'Following the teaching of our common father Saint Cyril of Alexandria we can confess together that in the one incarnate nature of the Word of God, two different natures, distinguished in thought alone (τῇ θεωρίᾳ μόνῃ), continue to exist without separation, without division, without change, and without confusion'?[1]

I will be arguing that the kinds of articulacy and sophistication displayed in the latter statement – and, more generally, all the forms of articulacy and sophistication of which doctrinal theology is capable – are no more and no less than forms of service undertaken for the sake of the church's life, the life of ordinary belief. Doctrinal theologians who can explain the most *recherché* technicalities of doctrine do not thereby know God better than do ordinary believers. They may know something of the shape that ordinary lives of worship, witness and discipleship should take, if they are to be true to the ways in which God has given Godself to the world. They may help to hold those lives in shape. It is, however, those lives themselves in which God is known, insofar as they respond to and embody the love of God, and such lives will always and endlessly outstrip the diagrams that doctrinal theology draws of them.

The second question emerges from the first. Doctrinal theology, as I have just described it, is involved in the reproduction of the life of the church. Yet the life of the church is always broken, always distorted, always sinful. Whatever true knowledge of God is embodied in the life that any Christian community lives, it is always mixed with ignorance, with misunderstanding and with the deliberate refusal of knowledge. The life of the church is a series of always failing experiments in the knowledge of God. If doctrinal theology helps to reproduce the life of the church, it will be helping to reproduce all of this failure – all of the exclusions and imbalances of power, all of the forms of harm that mar the church's response to God's love. Its work is no freer from

---

[1] Anglican–Oriental Orthodox International Commission, *Christology: Agreed Statement* (2014), §1. Available online at www.anglicancommunion.org/media/103502/anglican-oriental-orthodox-agreed-statement-on-christology-cairo-2014.pdf (accessed 29 November 2019).

these failings than is any other element of Christian life – and it can all too often be what Emilie Townes called 'the doo-wop pom-pom squad for the cultural production of evil'.[2] My second question, therefore, is about the role that doctrinal theology can play in the church's learning – in the processes by which the church is taken deeper into God's love, and taught both to repent of its failings and to discover new ways of inhabiting that love. I will argue that doctrinal theology can, at its best, help equip the church for this journey – a journey deeper into the gift of God's love in Jesus Christ, and at the same time a journey out into the world. These are not two journeys but one: the Spirit of God draws the church further in to the gift it has been given in Christ, by drawing it out into new encounters, engagements and improvisations, and especially by turning it towards the cries of those who suffer, including the cries of those injured, marginalized, erased, ignored or forced into passivity by the existing patterns of the church's life.

As I pursue both of these questions, my discussion will have a dual character. On the one hand, I will try, as far as I can, to remain relentlessly prosaic – to keep in view the people involved in doctrinal theology, their activity, and the contexts in which that activity happens. My focus is on what Nicholas Healy calls 'the living, rather messy, confused and confusing body that the church actually is', and on doctrinal theology as something that particular people in particular contexts say and do, write down, pass on, refer to, think about and discuss.[3] I will be trying to take up Linn Marie Tonstad's challenge to doctrinal theology, to 'recognize its own concreteness and particularity' and 'to make the means by which it means legible'.[4]

On the other hand, my concern is with all this prosaic, creaturely reality insofar as it relates to God. The church owes its life to the word that the God of Israel spoke in the life, death and resurrection of Jesus of Nazareth. In all its prosaic detail, all its diversity, all its failures and disappointments, the life of the church responds to that word, embodies what it has learnt from that word and proclaims that word to the world. The church's life is life lived before God. In the habits of worship that they foster, in the care that they offer to the vulnerable, in the words that their teachers pass on, in the circulations of money around their communities, in the ways they share food together, in their reading of the scriptures, in the attitudes they adopt to the political regimes that surround them, in every aspect of their life together, Christians speak about God – and doctrinal theology concerns itself with that speaking.

---

[2] Emilie Townes used this phrase in 'Thin Human Imagination: Searching for Grace on the Rim Bones of Nothingness', a paper delivered at the Society for the Study of Theology in 2019. Such scholarship, she said, helps to reproduce 'an evil matrix of ableism, racism, sexism, classism, nationalism, militarism, ageism, and more'.

[3] Nicholas M. Healy, *Church, World and the Christian Life: Practical-Prophetic Ecclesiology* (Cambridge: Cambridge University Press, 2000), 3. I will talk from time to time about 'practice', and, like Healy, I mean that in a low-key way. Charles Taylor in *Sources of the Self: The Making of the Modern Identity* (Cambridge: Cambridge University Press, 1989), 204, defines 'practice' as 'more or less any stable configuration of shared activity, whose shape is defined by a certain pattern of dos and don'ts'.

[4] Tonstad used these phrases in 'The Real Problem of Abstraction in Systematic Theology', a paper delivered at the Society for the Study of Theology in 2019.

The path ahead

This book can be read in two main ways. I have, necessarily, asked and tried to answer the questions set out earlier from within my own context – and the Church of England is one important part of that context. Those who, like me, are interested in the work that doctrinal theology can and should do within the Church of England might read the book straight through: the remaining chapters of Part One describe that context, and raise questions about the role of doctrinal theology within it; Part Two develops conceptual resources for answering those questions, and returns to the Church of England very briefly at the end. Readers who are not interested in that Church of England focus may choose to stick to Part Two, which I think will make sense on its own. Such readers should bear in mind, however, that the chapters of Part Two do not set out a view from nowhere: they pursue questions, draw on resources and hazard answers that attracted me as someone shaped by my Church of England context. It may be necessary, while working through Part Two, to glance every now and then at Part One in order to diagnose my eccentricity.

Part One, then, focuses on the Church of England. Chapter 2 looks with a sceptical eye at the idea that this Church has, since the Reformation, displayed a balance and comprehensiveness lacking in other churches, and that an aversion to intellectual system and narrow doctrinal debate is a benign symptom of that comprehensiveness. This is an idea that has roots tangled up with the imposition of royal power under Henry VIII and Elizabeth I; it gains purchase as a self-description after the Restoration, in the midst of a programme of the systematic exclusion and persecution of those who would not conform; it persists alongside the Church's involvement in colonialism; and it gains most prominence in the midst of fierce nineteenth-century controversy. The claim to doctrinal diffidence is part of the Church of England's habitual, polemical mythologizing of its own history and identity. Nevertheless, to be an heir to this history, and to the mythologized ways in which it has been told, is to be an heir to questions about the subordination of doctrinal discourse to other aspects of the Church's life, about the relationship between different doctrinal traditions, and about the exercises of power involved in marking this life's boundaries.

Chapter 3 provides a sketch-map indicating where doctrinal theology can be found in the contemporary Church of England. It begins with 'ordinary belief', and explores the ways in which doctrinal claims and practices are woven into the everyday life of the church. I look at the way in which that life is dynamically reproduced by those who inhabit it, and at the ways in which it is caught up in wide networks of production and consumption, reflection and feedback. The chapter moves on to various other contexts in which doctrinal theology appears around the Church, and argues that they are best seen as nodes in networks that surround, draw upon and influence ordinary believing. I look at formal theological education, and specifically at the role of universities and of the Church's Theological Education Institutions, and I look at some of the church's formal deliberative bodies – General Synod, the Doctrine Commission and its successors, various ecumenical dialogues, and the institutions of the Anglican Communion. I argue that all these together form a complex doctrinal polity, economy or ecology, with ordinary believing at its heart.

Chapters 4–10 form Part Two of the book. In them, I take a step away from the Church of England context, in order to provide a more general theological account of the role of doctrine in Christ's church.

The church begins with the God of Israel raising Jesus from the dead. Chapter 4 explains how the first disciples encountered Jesus alive, in an experience that called forth their worship, confirmed their discipleship and commissioned their witness. In the power of the Spirit, the church lives from this experience and into it, discovering over time more of what it demands and makes possible. Numerous forms of communication emerge within the church's life of worship, discipleship and witness. Some of them – practices of proclamation, teaching, confession and controversy – come to involve the production, transmission and discussion of articulated summaries of Christian belief about God and God's ways with the world. In other words, for quite specific and contingent reasons, doctrinal theology emerges as one facet of the church's life. To ask about the nature of doctrine is to ask about the purpose of this family of practices within the whole life of the people of God.

In Chapter 5, I explore the ways in which the practices of doctrinal theology bring with them a temptation to intellectualism. That is, they bring with them the temptation to think that knowledge of doctrinal theology itself constitutes knowledge of God, and that the articulate claims of doctrinal theologians are the standard against which Christian believing should be measured. I argue instead that, for Christians, knowledge and love are inseparable, and that they are asymmetrically ordered: knowledge serves love. For Christians to grow in knowledge of God is for them to grow together in their imagination of the love of God for them, and in the wisdom that will enable them to live that love out in the midst of their lives. The articulated summaries of doctrinal theology, and all the words with which doctrinal theologians surround them, are nothing more and nothing less than supports for the knowledge of God that consists in love.

In Chapter 6, I ask more positively what it might mean for doctrinal theology to support the knowledge of God that consists in love. I begin with George Lindbeck's account of doctrine as a second-order discourse in relation to the first order of Christian life, but argue that his first-order/second-order distinction is too blunt to be useful. Christian believing involves a complex repertoire of dispositions; it is held in place by all kinds of factors; it is comprehensively social; and it is inextricably tangled in the ways that people make sense of, and make a life together in, the environments in which they find themselves. It is constantly being re-appropriated as Christians improvise responses to new situations and challenges, and in the process discover, or are discovered by, more of the meaning of their beliefs. Doctrinal theologians can, at their best, provide some support for this mobile life of belief. They can warn of certain kinds of danger, and draw attention to certain resources, and more generally they can propose – though only in outline – ways forward for the life of the church. Doctrinal theologians are, however, far too accomplished at ignoring their own particularity, the forms of power that they wield and their complicity in the church's failures; their work is always ambiguous. Nevertheless, their knowledge is in principle oriented towards, and completed in, practical wisdom, and that wisdom is always oriented towards, and completed in, life that shares God's love.

Chapter 7 turns to scripture. The life of Christian believing is a life lived with scripture. It takes the form of multiple different 'settlements' in each of which Christians relate to scripture in some specific way. Within any given settlement, the ongoing reading of scripture can bring readers up against scripture's objectivity: it can inform, challenge and reshape their lives. The possibilities of such learning are, however, relative to the settlement's practices and forms of imagination: inhabitants of different settlements see different things, and learn in different ways, when they turn to the text. With a little help from Hans Frei, and even more from the *regula fidei* tradition, I argue that Christians are called to patterns of reading focused on the identity of Jesus Christ rendered in the gospels, and that doctrinal theology can help to hold that pattern of reading in place. I acknowledge, however, that Christians' patterns of reading are always marked by sin: they encode and transmit exclusion and oppression. Christians always need to be taught to read better. The Spirit teaches them to read better in part by enabling them to hear voices that until now have been excluded or marginalized, but which can prompt the church to hear or see scripture in new ways. By these and other means, the Spirit lures the church deeper into the rich objectivity of the text, which is a gift from God's abundance and an invitation into it. Doctrinal theology can, at its best, help to hold the church to such a process of learning.

In Chapter 8, I explore Christian disagreement, and especially those stubbornly persistent disagreements in which there seems to be no shared language within which to pursue a resolution. I argue that we should be very wary of letting such disagreements turn into separation. We are always called by the Spirit out beyond the confines of our current settlements, into specific journeys of engagement with others who differ from us, and who will challenge, unsettle and enrich us in ways that we can't yet predict, even if we continue to think them badly mistaken. We therefore need to shift from a pattern of imagination in which doctrinal decisions mark out ever more precisely a territory of true theology separated from error, and towards one in which those decisions, even if we continue to think them necessary, mark out divisions across the body of Christ. They always involve complex gains and losses; they always leave misapprehension, disappointment and failure on both sides of the divide. Doctrinal theology is therefore suspended between two forms of the passion for truth. On the one hand, there is the passion to hold fast to what we believe we have already been shown of God's gift in Christ. On the other, there is the hunger for more of that gift – and a willingness to continue engaging across deep divides in pursuit of that 'more'.

In Chapter 9, I ask what it means for the church to be called to forms of repentance that involve a rethinking of its doctrinal heritage. The church is sinful, and that sinfulness affects the whole of the life that the church passes on. Christians are called both to trust what they have received of God's gift in Christ and to accept that their grasp of that gift is partial and distorted, often deeply so. God can call the church out of its current settlements in many ways, including through cries, especially cries of suffering; through encounters with others who think and live differently, especially as those encounters deepen into intimacy; and through the improvisations that arise as its members become involved in new situations. Those calls can trigger the creative re-construal of the church's doctrinal heritage, and processes of reception, by which new patterns of thought and life spread (or fail to spread) around the church. Doctrinal theology can (fallibly and unevenly) help with some of the processes by which the church holds fast to what it has already grasped of God's gift; it can assist with some of the processes by which the church grubs out distortions and restrictions that mar its reception of that gift; it can pursue some of the processes by which the church in deep engagement with the world discovers just how much more it has yet to know, as it journeys deeper into the abundant love God opened for the world in Jesus of Nazareth.

Finally, in Chapter 10, which forms a brief coda to the book, I ask what service doctrinal theology can provide to the church, and specifically to the life of ordinary belief, in the light of the discussion in all the previous chapters. I suggest that, in practice, service will take four overlapping forms – encouraging, amplifying, resourcing and challenging – with all four necessarily animated by an ongoing process of listening and re-construal. I return briefly to the Church of England and to the contexts described in Chapter 3, and ask how this vision of the task of doctrinal theology might play out in three particular locations: the work of bishops, of commissions and of Theological Education Institutions. I argue that doctrinal theology, in these contexts as in every context in which it is found, is only ever one limited and fallible ministry in the life of the church, but that by the grace of God it can provide support for the church's ongoing discovery of the abundant love of God.

Contexts

It will be clear by now that this is, in effect, a book about theological method. Freud said that people who focused on method reminded him 'of people who clean their glasses so thoroughly that they never have time to look through them', and Jeffrey Stout that 'preoccupation with method is like clearing your throat: it can go on for only so long before you lose your audience'.[5] In my defence, I can only say that these methodological questions seem to be live ones in my context – and I have found myself driven to explore these questions as I seek to understand what is possible for doctrinal theology here.

'My context' is (like everyone's) actually a complicated overlapping of multiple contexts. To begin with one of the most obvious: I find myself a member of a Church that is, at the national level, embroiled in high-profile debates about sexuality, sex and gender. These debates have not loomed very large in the local churches in which I have worshipped over the last few years, but they are impossible to avoid at the national level – and, since starting work on this book, I have ended up as a member of the *Living in Love and Faith* process, the Church's latest formal attempt to explore and express its thinking on these matters.

I have been engaged in these debates as someone hoping and working for the Church to change its stance towards people in same-sex relationships, and for it to confirm the unreserved inclusion of trans people in all areas of its life. This book is

---

[5] Freud is quoted in Richard F. Sterba, *Reminiscences of a Viennese Psychoanalyst* (Detroit: Wayne State University Press, 1982), 120. Stout's quote is from *Ethics after Babel: The Languages of Morals and Their Discontents* (Boston: Beacon, 1988), 163.

not directly about those issues, but it does address questions that lie behind them. These debates are, for instance, often framed as taking place between 'traditionalists' and 'revisionists', but I explore in this book an account of the doctrinal tradition in which that distinction doesn't make sense – or at least an account in which it can't be of primary importance. More generally, I ask what work doctrinal theology can contribute in a situation in which there is little agreement about what constitutes a good doctrinal argument – little agreement about the kinds of evidence that should be appealed to, about the weight that those appeals should have or about the forms of argument that might be telling. This book is in part an attempt to understand how to argue well in such a context, and what good – if any – such argument might be capable of doing.

Another context is provided by my participation in my parish church. Many years ago, when (for complicated reasons) my family and I were attending a particular church only infrequently, the vicar worked out during our conversation at the church door at the end of one morning service that I was an academic theologian, and that I taught doctrine to Anglican ordinands. 'Oh,' he said, 'I'm glad you don't come every week.'[6] It was an attempt to make a joke of his own anxiety in the presence of someone he took to be some kind of expert – but it can serve as an awkward pointer to a deeper question. It is not immediately clear how the academic work that I do relates to the believing life of an ordinary congregation (where 'ordinary' simply means 'not inclined, as a matter of course, to read scholarly books about doctrine, or to engage in academic debates about it'). It might be tempting to think of this as a relationship between expert and amateur knowledge, and yet I have a deeply rooted conviction that my ability, say, to discuss the doctrine of the Trinity at greater length than any other member of my congregation does not in any interesting sense mean that I know God better than they do.

Another context is provided by my day-to-day work. My current post, in Durham University, was created as part of the 'Common Awards' scheme. In 2012, Durham won the contract to act as the academic validating institution for most of the Church of England's ordination training, which also means validating programmes taken by students training for a wide variety of other ministries, and training for ministry in various of the Church of England's ecumenical partners. I spend a good deal of my time, therefore, immersed in discussion of theological education syllabuses and standards, and visiting any number of theological colleges and non-residential courses around the country. Given my own academic specialism, I can't help but take a particular interest in the teaching of Christian doctrine that happens in all these institutions, and in the difference that this teaching makes to ministerial students. I have been left with all sorts of questions about the real purpose of this particular strand of ministerial formation, and about the ways in which it might inform and resource the ministry in which students are and will be involved. This book is, in part, an attempt to understand what it might mean for this strand of their education to be handled well.

The institutional context within which I work provides another impetus for my questions. I work in Durham's Department of Theology and Religion – a department whose academic staff work with an unsystematic and happy mix of disciplinary

---

[6] The sequel: we did start going every week; he and I did become friends.

approaches from theology and religious studies.⁷ It is a department with an interesting set of institutional connections with various Christian churches. There is a historic connection with Durham cathedral, now embodied in the shape of two Canon Professors (one an Anglican, one not); there is a Centre for Catholic Studies, and the Michael Ramsey Centre for Anglican Studies, both of which engage with the respective churches in a variety of ways; we have close links with Cranmer Hall, one of the theological colleges training people for ministry in Anglican and other contexts, and with the Wesley Study Centre, a Methodist research institute. But it is also a department that is made up of staff and students with a variety of kinds and levels of religious commitment, or with no such commitments; where staff who are religiously committed make very different kinds and levels of connection between those commitments and their teaching and research; and where very few even of those of our students who are Christians are studying with view to any kind of formal Christian ministry.

Pursuing doctrinal theology in this kind of mixed context generates questions of its own. What can I learn about the nature of doctrine from the experience of teaching it to students 'of all faiths and … none'?⁸ After all, it is obvious to me that my thinking about doctrine has been changed in all sorts of ways by my interactions with these mixed communities of students – by their questions, by their essays and seminar presentations and even by the comments they write on their feedback forms.

Another context is provided by the kind of academic training I have received. Early in my academic career, I ended up, for one reason and another, focusing on the work of Hans Frei and George Lindbeck – the most prominent of a generation of 'postliberal' theologians associated with Yale. One of the features of this postliberalism was a focus on ecclesial practice, and on the idea that doctrinal claims gain their meaning in relation to such practice. Those questions burrowed deep into my brain, and remained there even when I had shifted my focus to other topics and other conversation partners. This book is, in part, an attempt at a reckoning: Where do I now stand in relation to that kind of postliberalism, and to the work of Frei and Lindbeck in particular?

One last context to mention was that provided by my previous job, when I worked for three years as co-director of the Cambridge Inter-faith Programme. That experience confirmed my understanding that 'doctrine' is not itself a neutral category across religions – indeed, that the Christian interest in doctrine is deeply peculiar, and requires explaining. I also had the experience, repeatedly, of being shown my own scriptures again – seeing them with new eyes, or hearing them with new ears – when discussing them with people of other faiths, who approached them with questions and assumptions very different from my own. Even though I will not be focusing on inter-faith questions, much of the argument of this book is animated by that experience of engaging with people of other faiths, and finding myself driven by their questions and suggestions deeper into the sources of my own.

---

[7] This blending of theology and religious studies is found in several UK university departments. For a discussion, see David Ford and Mike Higton, 'Religious Literacy in the Context of Theology and Religious Studies', in *Religious Literacy in Policy and Practice*, ed. Adam Dinham and Matthew Francis (Bristol: Polity Press, 2015), 39–54.

[8] This wording appears on the department website: www.dur.ac.uk/theology.religion/ (accessed 29 November 2019).

Terminology

I have already used the terms 'doctrinal theology' and 'doctrine' a good deal, and before launching into the book proper I should offer some preliminary definitions. We can begin with the fact that there are, in the life of the Christian church, all kinds of activities of discussion, exploration and argument about God and God's ways with the world, and about how we should live in relation to this God. One can imagine all of these conversations as a huge roiling swirl of braided and tangled currents – and one can name the whole lively lot of it *doctrinal theology*.

Within that whole swirl, simply as a result of the fluid dynamics of the church's conversational life, eddies form over time that circle persistently around certain loci. We can use the phrase *the doctrine of x* to name such an eddy. Such a doctrine is a locus, a topic, that deserves attention as one of the emergent organizing foci of the conversation as a whole. The 'doctrine of creation' is, for instance, the name of the eddy of claims about God being the source and sustainer of everything that is, about God being our deepest origin and end, about the material world being more temple to God's praise than prison for our souls – and so on. Claims of that kind keep coming up in the flow of Christian conversation, and they keep on turning out to be important.

It is from within such doctrinal eddies that we sometimes see the emergence of formal *doctrinal statements*. The development of a creed by a Christian council, its slow migration into the liturgy, the roles that it comes to play in various church's self-definitions: those are strands of activity that emerge from the currents that circulate around this eddy, and help shape the life of the church.

Such doctrinal statements emerge in a variety of contexts, and are put to a variety of uses; there is no reason to think that when we focus on formal statements of doctrine the variety and complexity that mark doctrinal theology more widely suddenly fall away.[9] Even with a narrow focus on formal doctrinal pronouncements, it is not clear that there is such a thing as a *nature of doctrine* – a single, unified account of what doctrinal statements are for, of how they work, and of what they achieve. Rather, doctrine has many natures, and there is a complex history of those natures' emergence, development and changing prominence.

Doctrine does not live primarily in the pronouncements of councils or the pages of official documents, and only secondarily appear diffused around the wider life of the church. No: doctrine lives in the thoughts, words and actions of the whole church, and then *also*, and secondarily, in formal statements and authoritative pronouncements – and sometimes even in the pages of books by academic theologians.[10] It is doctrinal

---

[9] Richard Heyduck, *The Recovery of Doctrine in the Contemporary Church: An Essay in Philosophical Ecclesiology* (Waco, TX: Baylor, 2002), 61: 'I would not assume that all doctrines are exactly the same kind of speech act.' Cf. Richard Clutterbuck, *Handing on Christ: Rediscovering the Gift of Christian Doctrine* (London: Epworth, 2009), 10, and Christine Helmer, *Theology and the End of Doctrine* (Louisville, KY: Westminster John Knox, 2014), 1.

[10] Charles Hefling, in 'On "Core" Doctrine: Some Possibly Relevant Soundings', *Anglican Theological Review* 80, no. 2 (1998): 245–6, writes that '"The" doctrine of the Incarnation is not located at any single point: it is "in" the whole movement. ... It does not reside in a single mind, much less in a single text that expresses a single mind. It is the expression of the mind of a community, in many texts and monuments, not all of them doctrinal.' Cf. William Crockett, in 'The Hermeneutics of

theology as it is spread out across the whole surface of the church – and beyond – that I want to talk about in this book.

I do therefore prefer the phrase 'doctrinal theology' to 'dogmatic theology' or 'systematic theology'. To my ear, at least, the emphasis in the phrase 'dogmatic theology' falls too easily on the appearance of doctrinal claims in the pronouncements of ecclesiastical authorities – 'dogma' more clearly than 'doctrine' having about it 'some tinge or taint of administration or government'.[11] 'Systematic theology', on the other hand, places the emphasis on the appearances of doctrinal claims in scholarly discussions; to my ear it sounds more like the name of an academic discipline than like the name of something that happens in the life of the church. I use 'doctrinal theology' in the hope that it can more easily allow a focus on the circulation of doctrinal ideas around the whole church, among ordinary people as well as in clerical and academic circles.[12]

I also prefer to use the phrase 'doctrinal theology' rather than speaking simply about 'theology', because I want to keep the focus on the big theological ideas that do turn up in creeds and confessions – Trinity, incarnation, creation, providence, salvation and the like (the centres of the most stable eddies in the swirls of the church's thinking). I am interested in asking what roles are played in the life of the church by the discussion of these kinds of ideas, and of their meanings, interconnections and implications, without wanting to suggest that such discussion is the sum or centre of all theological endeavour.[13]

I should say one last thing about my terminology. I have repeatedly used the word 'Christian' in my description of this book's content. Ideas about God are taught and discussed in many other religious communities (as well as outside all of them), but the practices involved take different forms and play different roles in each religion. In the history of Christianity, and in many of its manifestations in the present, some kinds of idea about God have played a peculiarly central role – such that, for instance, creeds and confessions have caught more of the limelight in the drama of Christian

---

Doctrine', in *The Future of Anglican Theology*, ed. M. Darrol Bryant (New York: Edwin Mellen, 1984), 60–1: 'The conceptual formulation of a doctrine in a credal or conciliar formula is only the tip of the iceberg. ... Doctrine is not created out of the heads of theologians, but is the product of the lived experience of a community of faith, and reflected at all levels of the life of faith – in liturgy, in patterns of spirituality, in pastoral practice, as well as in credal and conciliar formulations and in theology. It is only when doctrinal formulations are plunged back into the context of lived experience out of which they have arisen that they begin to yield their meaning and power.'

[11] W. R. Matthews, 'The Nature and Basis of Dogma', in Matthews et al., *Dogma in History and Thought: Studies by Various Writers* (London: Nisbet, 1929), 5.

[12] Google's Ngram viewer (books.google.com/ngrams) allows a rough and ready search of the changing popularity of the phrases 'doctrinal theology', 'dogmatic theology' and 'systematic theology' in published English books from 1800 to the present. 'Dogmatic theology' and 'systematic theology' dominate the scene together from 1830 to 1950; systematic theology pulls ahead dramatically from 1950 to the present. 'Doctrinal theology' is a distant third throughout, except for a very brief ascendancy in the late 1820s.

[13] For another attempt to distinguish 'dogma', 'doctrine' and 'theology', see James Orr, *The Progress of Dogma*, 4th edn (London: Hodder and Stoughton, 1901), 12. James Wm. McClendon, Jr., *Systematic Theology vol. 2: Doctrine* (Nashville, TN: Abingdon, 1994), is one of the few examples of someone who prefers, like me, to speak of 'doctrinal theology'; see, for example, p. 24.

life than they have in many other religious contexts.[14] To treat doctrine as a religious universal risks taking a scheme of description peculiarly adapted to this Christian eccentricity and imposing it as if it were a neutral frame within which numerous differing religions could be fairly compared. To pursue deeper conversation between religions, including deeper conversation about God and God's ways with the world, we will need to abandon the notion that we can simply set doctrinal scheme alongside doctrinal scheme. My focus in this book is therefore resolutely on doctrine as a Christian phenomenon.[15]

Since I have assumed that this book will be of interest primarily to a Christian readership, I have allowed myself to say 'we', 'us' and 'our' when talking about the church and about Christian discipleship. When I am not obviously talking some more specific group, I take the 'we' involved to cover anyone who thinks of themselves as trying – however fallibly and fitfully – to follow Jesus.

Final comments

I have two final comments about the contents of this book. First, I should note that this is both a book about doctrinal theology and an exercise in it. I offer an account of how doctrine relates to scripture, of how doctrinal development and disagreement work, of how doctrine supports discipleship and so on – and this account is itself unavoidably shaped by doctrinal assumptions and arguments. I seek to describe the way in which multiple traditions of doctrinal thinking emerge and interact, hoping that my description might prove recognizable to participants in many such traditions – and yet the ways in which I frame my description, and the conclusions that I draw from it, are shaped by the particular theological traditions within which I find myself at home. There is an awkward circularity here, but I don't think there is any way of avoiding it.

My second comment is simply that, despite writing a book of this length on this topic, I don't want to claim too much for the importance of doctrinal theology in the life of the church. John Bowden once said that 'Theologians seldom revive dying churches … nor are they often instrumental in creating belief', and John Webster more recently said of doctrinal theology that 'Its guidance is modest. … It does not rule the church, or require the church to submit to its judgments.'[16] My conviction, cemented by the

---

[14] The opening line of Frances Young's *The Making of the Creeds* (London: SCM, 1991) is 'Christianity is the only major religion to set such store by creeds and doctrines' (p. 1).

[15] Cf. Clutterbuck, *Handing On Christ*, 10. For an approach that treats doctrine as a feature of religions in general, see William A. Christian, *Doctrines of Religious Communities: A Philosophical Study* (New Haven: Yale University Press, 1987). In *The Nature of Doctrine: Religion and Theology in a Postliberal Age* (Philadelphia, PA: Westminster, 1984), George Lindbeck presented his theory of doctrine as an account applicable to multiple religions; I critiqued that element of his account in 'Reconstructing *The Nature of Doctrine*', *Modern Theology* 30, no. 1 (2014): 1–31. See my 'Scriptural Reasoning and the Discipline of Christian Doctrine', *Modern Theology* 29, no. 4 (2013): 120–37, for more on the relationship of doctrine to inter-faith dialogue.

[16] John Bowden, 'The Future Shape of Popular Theology', in *Theology and Change: Essays in Memory of Alan Richardson*, ed. R.H. Preston (London: SCM, 1975), 13; John Webster, *Holy Scripture: A Dogmatic Sketch* (Cambridge: Cambridge University Press, 2003), 128–9.

work that I have done on this book, is that doctrinal theology does have a modest role to play, and that it is worth asking how it can play that role well – but it is only one contribution among many others, and not the most important, to the life and learning of Christ's church.

2

The story of doctrine in the Church of England

Introduction

This is a book about doctrine in the life of the church. That is, it is a book about a family of Christian practices in which doctrinal ideas are developed, discussed and deployed. Those are always the practices of specific people. They happen in particular places, for particular purposes – even if within them people can speak truths that transcend the parochial.

The ingrained habits of my academic discipline, however, tip me towards generalization. They tempt me to speak as if I am describing what doctrine is always and everywhere. They tempt me not to notice that I am responding to doctrinal concerns, or generalizing from doctrinal practices, or reproducing configurations of doctrinal power, that are peculiar to my own locality. It is to strengthen my resistance to that temptation that I have chosen to begin (in this chapter and the next) by speaking about my own context in the Church of England. I want to attend to what I am inheriting, the better to exercise discretion over what I pass on.

A Church of England book

Readers who can't work up any excitement about the Church of England might want to skip this chapter and the next. If they do so, however, they should bear in mind this caveat: those later chapters were written by someone whose theological imagination was shaped by the context that I am about to describe. The questions I have thought worth tackling, the alternatives I have thought worth combatting, the answers that have seemed to me fitting, the depictions I have offered of the life of the church – they have all been shaped by this Church of England context. This is a Church of England book.[1]

That is not to say that any of the questions that I ask, or the ideas that I set out, are somehow Church of England property. I don't mean to plant a Church of England flag on any of the territory that I explore. I say that this is a Church of England book not to claim that it is superior but to acknowledge that it is partial. I am not denying that

---

[1] In earlier drafts of this chapter, I said that this was 'an Anglican book' – but that obscures the fact that it is quite specifically about the Church of England. For the history of the term 'Anglican', see Paul Avis, in *The Identity of Anglicanism: Essentials of Anglican Ecclesiology* (London: T&T Clark, 2007), 19–20, and Kevin Ward, *A History of Global Anglicanism* (Cambridge: Cambridge University Press, 2006), 2–5.

I have been helped to think about the issues in this book by colleagues and students from a wide variety of churches, as well as by colleagues and students from no church, nor that I have borrowed from other theological traditions with happy abandon.

I stress this because I am uncomfortably aware that we Anglicans have sometimes entered theological debates trailing an odour of smugness. I have not been able to track down the person who first proposed that the Church of England should have the strapline 'Loving Jesus with a slight air of superiority since AD 597' – but I can wish it didn't have quite such a sting of truth to it.[2] (At least, it stings when applied to the kinds of White, middle-class English Anglican circles, half conscious of their role in the establishment, in which I tend to move.) I am aware of the need to write from my Church of England perspective without indulging the arrogance that seems to grow well there.[3]

That arrogance is catastrophically misplaced. To write from the Church of England is to write from a church that has engaged in persecution, that has been complicit in slavery and in imperialism, that has harboured abusers and that is marked by deep class divisions and a series of persistent exclusions.[4] Speaking of the English reformation, Alec Ryrie writes, 'Whatever the aspirations of the theologians may have been, the state's grubby fingermarks were all over the process, and shaped the outcome decisively. The sometimes brutal coercion involved remains Anglicanism's original sin, of which it has never yet fully repented and for which it has never yet fully atoned.'[5]

Jeffrey Cox has argued that 'Anglican complicity in the Atlantic system of slavery is with hindsight one of the great moral and spiritual failures in Christian history.'[6] Stephen Sykes, a champion of Anglican identity and one of the founding figures of modern Anglican studies, acknowledged that 'We … helped to destroy Ireland and then forgot about it; persecuted and imprisoned Catholics and Non-Conformists whilst congratulating ourselves on our comprehensive middle way; and in our own day when the government invited vast numbers of Afro-Anglicans from the Caribbean, we failed to make them welcome and to foster their contribution to the Church's life.'[7] That last point is reinforced by Mukti Barton: 'When the newcomers, many of whom

---

[2] The earliest use of this slogan that I can find is given by Diarmaid MacCulloch in '*Our Church* by Roger Scruton – Review', *The Guardian*, 19 June 2013. AD 597 is the date when Augustine, who became the first Archbishop of Canterbury, landed in Kent.

[3] Kit and Fredeerica Konolige, in *The Power of Their Glory: America's Ruling Class: The Episcopalians* (New York, NY: Wyden, 1978), 368, provide one of the finest anecdotal illustrations of this attitude, albeit in a North American rather than an English context. William T. Manning, bishop of New York from 1921 to 1946, was asked whether there was salvation outside the Episcopal Church. '"Perhaps so", the bishop replied after a long, puzzled pause, "but no gentleman would avail himself of it."'

[4] Eddie Izzard's 'Cake or death' sketch (from the 1998 *Dress to Kill* tour) is unfairly kind to the Church of England. Available online at www.youtube.com/watch?v=unkWbEmtYXs (accessed 30 November 2019).

[5] Alec Ryrie, 'The Reformation in Anglicanism', in *The Oxford Handbook of Anglican Studies*, ed. Mark D. Chapman, Sathianathan Clarke and Martyn Percy (Oxford: Oxford University Press, 2016), 43.

[6] Jeffrey Cox, 'The Dialectics of Empire, Race, and Diocese', in *The Oxford History of Anglicanism V: Global Anglicanism, c. 1910–2000*, ed. William L. Sachs (Oxford: Oxford University Press, 2018), 33.

[7] Stephen Sykes, 'The Genius of Anglicanism', in *The English Religious Tradition and the Genius of Anglicanism*, ed. Geoffrey Rowell (Wantage: Ikon / Nashville, TN: Abingdon, 1992), 234.

were Anglicans, arrived they found signs of White supremacy and racism everywhere. But most shocking for them was the experience of rejection in the Anglican churches. They were part of the Anglican Communion, yet they experienced various forms of rejection on account of their skin colour.'[8]

Monica Furlong notes that until very recently the Church of England peddled 'a narrow morality which thought a married couple, however wretched their union, should stay together, which condemned children born out of wedlock (along with their mothers) to a painful stigma, and which refused to countenance the very existence of homosexual feeling'.[9]

I am not interested in claiming a peculiarly awful status for the Church of England; heroic self-flagellation can be just one more way of claiming superiority. The point is not that the Church of England is especially bad, but that it is not especially good. It is not especially moderate, not especially peaceable, not especially innocent. We are one more messed up church among others.[10]

The context from which I write is therefore not *the* church, nor is it the church's secret measure. It is one side stream in the braided delta of church history – even if it is a stream whose fish have tended to believe theirs to be the central current. Most of the life of the church is, and always has been, happening elsewhere.[11]

Looking backward

In Chapter 3, I am going to survey the contemporary Church of England, asking where in it doctrinal discussion can be found. In this chapter, I take a look back at the Church of England's history. Like anyone else involved in doctrinal theology, my work is shaped by the stories I tell myself about what I am up to. Those stories are shaped in turn by the stories I have learnt about my church: the plotlines and anecdotes, the habitual characterizations and polemical asides that circulate in the air I breathe. Those stories perform two contradictory functions. They show me something about the history I have joined – about how we ended up in the state we are in, and about what kind of state it is. But they also hide as much as they show. They are selective; they are romanticized; they are self-serving. They help me ignore the conditions that make

[8] Mukti Barton, *Rejection, Resistance and Resurrection: Speaking Out on Racism in the Church* (London: Darton, Longman and Todd, 2005), 8.
[9] Monica Furlong, *C of E: The State It's In* (London: Hodder and Stoughton, 2000), 3.
[10] I am ambivalent about Michael Ramsey's claim that the Anglican church's 'greater vindication lies in its pointing through its own history to something of which it is a fragment. Its credentials are its incompleteness, with the tension and travail in its soul. It is clumsy and untidy, it baffles neatness and logic. For it is sent not to commend itself as "the best type of Christianity", but by its very brokenness to point to the universal Church wherein all have died.' (*The Gospel and the Catholic Church* (London: Longmans, Green, 1936), 220.) All of this may be true, but I am not convinced that it is especially true of the Anglican church.
[11] This is true both in the sense that most of the life of the Anglican Communion is happening outside the Church of England, and most of the life of the whole church is happening outside the Anglican Communion. This sense of centrality is entangled with the ideology of Whiteness: 'Whiteness operates as an overarching construct, which assumes a central place in all epistemological and cultural forms of production, thereby relegating other positions or perspectives as "other"' (Anthony Reddie, *Theologising Brexit: A Liberationist and Postcolonial Critique* (London: Routledge, 2019), 17).

my work possible, and the interests served by the assumptions I make. It is important, therefore, not simply to relate the stories I have inherited, but to investigate them. It is important to listen to those who have tested these stories against the historical sources. It is even more important to listen to those who have been painted out, or painted into corners, in the stories I have learnt.

In this chapter, then, I attempt a re-telling of the story that I inhabit. I begin with the version that I picked up by osmosis – of the Church of England as a church diffident about doctrine, tolerant in its debates, pragmatic in its policies. I then unpick that story. My re-telling is shaped by one of the deep currents of the intellectual water in which I – and most of the historians whose expertise I borrow – swim. We are surrounded by a long, growing and lively conversation about exclusion. We work in contexts in which it is increasingly natural to ask about uneven distributions of power, about the ways in which those distributions are disguised and about the unacknowledged tidal pull that they exert on all theological work. Those questions were not at the front of the stage in the lecture halls in which I was trained. You won't find them agitating much of what I have written in the past. But even a latecomer like me now finds them impossible to ignore – and finds the Anglican past looking very different when examined in their light.

Doctrinal diffidence?

The Church of England might seem like an odd location from which to write a book about the role of doctrine in the life of the church. I noted in Chapter 1 that creeds and confessions have played a more prominent role in the organization of Christian life than they have in many other religious contexts. The Church of England, with its long reputation for diffidence about doctrine, is an odd choice to make to illustrate this claim.

Rowan Williams, writing when Archbishop of Canterbury, suggested that 'Anglicans have always been cautious about laying too much stress on formulae over and above the classical creeds.'[12] Martyn Percy writes that 'Anglicans occasionally write great theology, but they are better known for poetry, hymnody, liturgy, music, and spirituality.'[13] Judith Maltby and Alison Shell have argued that it is in novels far more than in works of doctrinal analysis that Anglican women have explored theological themes in public.[14]

---

[12] Rowan Williams, *Anglican Identities* (London: DLT, 2004), 1; cf. 81.
[13] Martyn Percy, 'Engagement, Diversity, and Distinctiveness: Anglicanism in Contemporary Culture', in *A Point of Balance: The Weight and Measure of Anglicanism*, ed. Martyn Percy and Robert Boak Slocum (Harrisburg, PA: Morehouse, 2012), 26. Cf. Slocum, 'The Bonds and Limits of Communion: Fidelity, Diversity, and Conscience in Contemporary Anglicanism', in *Point of Balance*, ed. Percy and Slocum, 9–10.
[14] Judith Maltby and Alison Shell, 'Introduction: Why Anglican; Why Women; Why Novelists?' in *Anglican Women Novelists: From Charlotte Brontë to P.D. James*, ed. Judith Maltby and Alison Shell (London: T&T Clark, 2019), 1–14.

It is not hard to find authors suggesting that 'systematic theology' is not really an Anglican pursuit – though that is a claim that has become very much harder to sustain in recent years, given the systematic projects of theologians like Kathryn Tanner, Sarah Coakley and Katherine Sonderegger.[15] Stephen Sykes, writing in 2004, just after stepping down as chair of the Church of England's Doctrine Commission, wrote that 'Anglicans have been notoriously resistant to the idea that there is such a thing as Anglican doctrine, or an Anglican systematic theology.'[16] Elsewhere, he wrote that 'Anglicans are not supposed to know about, or to be interested in, systematic theology.'[17] Mark Chapman has noted that 'While a few Anglicans have written systematic theologies (and it is far fewer than in many other denominations), they have tended to write as theologians who happen to be members of Anglican churches, rather than as *Anglican* theologians.'[18] Luke Bretherton, speaking specifically of Anglican contributions to political theology, writes that the characteristic Anglican thinkers are 'essayists and writers of ad hoc treatises, rather than creators of formal, internally consistent systems of thought'.[19]

The same picture holds when one shifts terminology, and asks about 'dogmatic theology' in the Church of England. Paul Avis, who has served on the Church of England's Doctrine Commission and the Faith and Order Commission, among other bodies, wrote that Anglicans are 'notoriously diffident about theologizing in the dogmatic mode'.[20] Martyn Percy, again, wrote that 'the very idea of an Anglican dogmatics is a contradiction in terms',[21] and the Australian theologian Ben Myers that

---

[15] Kathryn Tanner, *Jesus, Humanity, and the Trinity: A Brief Systematic Theology* (London: T&T Clark, 2001); Sarah Coakley, *God, Sexuality, and the Self: An Essay 'On the Trinity'* (Cambridge: Cambridge University Press, 2013), the first volume of a projected multi-volume systematics; Katherine Sonderegger, *Systematic Theology, Volume 1: The Doctrine of God* (Minneapolis, MN: Fortress, 2015). Graham Ward's *How the Light Gets In: Ethical Life 1* (Oxford: Oxford University Press, 2016) is also presented as the first volume of a systematic project, though Ward says that he is 'not making any claims that I am composing an Anglican systematic theology' (p. 196). John Webster's unexpected death in 2016 cut short what was likely to have been another large-scale Anglican systematics.

[16] Stephen W. Sykes, 'Foreword', in *Contemporary Doctrine Classics from the Church of England* (London: Church House Publishing, 2005), xv.

[17] Stephen W. Sykes, *The Integrity of Anglicanism* (New York: Seabury, 1978), ix.

[18] Mark D. Chapman, *Anglican Theology* (London: Bloomsbury T&T Clark, 2012), 8. Cf. D. R. G. Owen, 'Is There an Anglican Theology?' and W. Taylor Stevenson, 'Is There a Characteristic Anglican Theology', *The Future of Anglican Theology*, ed. M. Darrol Bryant (New York: Edwin Mellen, 1984), 3–13, 15–26.

[19] Luke Bretherton, *Christ and the Common Life: Political Theology and the Case for* Democracy (Grand Rapids, MI: William B. Eerdmans, 2019), 178. Cf. Mark Chapman, in the supporting papers for the Faith and Order Commission report, *Communion and Disagreement* (Church of England, 2016), §4.9: 'In general, in most of the Anglican tradition both historically and in the present day, theology has not been done by "professional" theologians working in universities, but by church leaders and educators who have specific problems to address or who encounter a lack of obedience to what the church has laid down.'

[20] Paul Avis, 'Theology in Dogmatic Mode', in *Companion Encyclopedia of Theology*, ed. Peter Byrne and Leslie Houlden (London: Routledge, 1995), 977.

[21] Martyn Percy, 'The Gift of Authority in the Church of England: Sketching a Contextual Theology', in Faith and Order Group of the Church of England, *Unpacking the Gift: Anglican Resources for Theological Reflection on The Gift of Authority* (London: Church House Publishing, 2002), 87.

'any Anglican dogmatics is already idiosyncratic merely by virtue of being Anglican'.[22] When I searched online recently, I found around twenty-seven unique uses of the phrase 'Anglican Dogmatics'. Compare that with the 78 I found for 'Methodist Dogmatics', 238 for 'Baptist', 873 for 'Evangelical', 3,810 for 'Lutheran', 5,860 for 'Catholic', 11,900 for 'Orthodox', 15,600 for 'Protestant' and 46,400 for 'Reformed'.[23]

This doctrinal diffidence is visible in the dearth of certain genres of publication, when the Church of England is compared to some other Christian communions. Claims about God and God's ways with the world are far from rare, as a glance at almost any Anglican collection of sermons or spiritual writings will demonstrate, but genres devoted to the orderly interpretation, elaboration, defence and criticism of doctrinal claims have been comparatively unusual. That means in turn that there have been few people who made their names by publishing such works. There is no shortage of powerful individuals around whom narrations of Anglican history can be made to revolve. It is nevertheless difficult to generate a list of Church of England theologians whose doctrinal works have led to their surnames becoming isms. Such works, and such 'big-name' doctrinal theologians, have simply not played a very visible role in the intellectual history of the Church, nor in its governance, nor in the resolution (or perpetuation) of its disputes. And because all of this is true, it has been comparatively rare to find academic curricula arranged around such figures and their works, or for such figures and works to become the foci for academic industries, busy with PhD students, symposia and fights over inheritance.

A partial exception might be found in the major ecumenical dialogues of the twentieth and twenty-first centuries, where something like a cumulative tradition of doctrinal works does emerge – not in the systematic works of individual theologians, but in a series of reports, each set out in numbered paragraphs, each anchored by a forest of cross references to earlier examples, and representing together a sustained doctrinal conversation.[24] To an extent, however, this example helps demonstrate the broader point. It is a tradition that has had to be invented for the sake of ecumenical dialogue. The Church of England has had to learn how to show something like the doctrinal face shown by other churches, in order to make sense of its presence at ecumenical tables set for the discussion of doctrine. And the documents generated for this purpose, vital though they have sometimes been in making new forms of

---

[22] Ben Myers, 'Idiosyncratic Dogmatics', *Faith and Theology*, 10 March 2006. Available online at www.faith-theology.com/2006/03/idiosyncratic-dogmatics.html (accessed 30 November 2019).

[23] To get below the Anglican total, you need to go for 'Pentecostal Dogmatics' at 7 references, 'Coptic' at 4, 'Mennonite' at 2 – or, with no references at all, 'Quaker Dogmatics'. Some of the Anglican references are accounted for by the fact that the term 'dogmatic theology' is used in a couple of older Anglican sources: E. A. Litton's, *Introduction to Dogmatic Theology on the Basis of The Thirty-Nine Articles* (London: Elliot Stock, 1882–1892) and Claude Beaufort Moss, *The Christian Faith: An Introduction to Dogmatic Theology* (London: SPCK, 1943).

[24] Some of the most important of these documents are available on the Church of England's Council for Christian Unity web pages: on the 'Working together nationally' page (www.churchofengland.org/about/work-other-christian-churches/working-together-nationally (accessed 30 November 2019)) the 1995 Fetter Lane Agreement, the 2003 Anglican–Methodist Covenant and the 2016 Columba Declaration; and on the 'Working together internationally' page (www.churchofengland.org/about/work-other-christian-churches/working-together-internationally (accessed 30 November 2019)) the 1991 Meissen Agreement, the 1996 Porvoo Agreement and the 2001 Reuilly Declaration.

cooperation and communion possible, have rarely been taken up in theological discussion away from those tables. It is rare to find an Anglican theologian writing in other contexts who makes regular reference to this material, or to any similar body of Anglican doctrinal pronouncements. Even here, the Church of England is diffident about doctrine.

In the next section, I am going to ask how far this characterization of the Church of England holds true, and ask why it has become a commonplace. I don't ask these questions wistfully. I am not hankering after the possibility of teaching a course on the history of Anglican doctrinal theology arranged around the doctrinal works of big-name theologians. That would almost certainly be one more way of narrating the world around the power of dead White men, of downplaying voices less privileged than theirs and of obscuring the structures and the histories that made their work possible.[25] Neither, however, do I ask these questions gleefully. We shall see that Anglican doctrinal diffidence is embroiled in its own patterns of power and privilege, and that these are quite questionable enough by themselves.

Inventing Anglican diffidence

The claim that the Church of England is diffident about doctrine is one expression of an old myth of Anglican identity: the claim that the Church of England is inherently 'Laodicean, tepid – and proud of it', or, more fully, that it is characterized by 'moderation, balance, equipoise, and order, with an instinctive avoidance of dogma and precise doctrinal formulation, a scepticism towards religious enthusiasm, and a tendency to preserve continuity with and a reverence for the past'.[26]

Paul Avis notes that Anglicans have often claimed for their church a peculiar comprehensiveness, 'a unique gift for fostering synthesis between Christian traditions' – a claim that he notes 'will be greeted with amused incredulity by some of our ecumenical partners' and which 'is not generally supported by the internal experience of Anglican churches'.[27]

The reformation

Until quite recently, it was a commonplace of Anglican historiography that this moderation and balance were characteristics of the Church of England from the Elizabethan settlement onwards. The story of Anglican origins was typically told with the help (in Anthony Milton's words) of 'rather woolly and anachronistic assumptions

---

[25] See Rachel Muers's forthcoming article, 'The Personal Is the (Academic-)Political: Why Care About the Love Lives of Theologians?' *Scottish Journal of Theology*, for a fine discussion of this.

[26] Martyn Percy, 'Afterword', in *Point of Balance*, ed. Percy and Slocum, 132, and Anthony Milton, 'Introduction: Reformation, Identity, and "Anglicanism"', c. 1520–1662', in *The Oxford History of Anglicanism I: Reformation and Identity, c.1520–1662*, ed. Anthony Milton (Oxford: Oxford University Press, 2017), 1. Neither author is presenting his own view.

[27] Avis, *Identity*, 23; cf. E. L. Mascall, 'Whither Anglican Theology?' in *When Will Ye Be Wise? The State of the Church of England*, ed. Anthony A. Kilmister (London: Blond and Briggs, 1983), 30.

of inherently English anti-dogmatism and the principled search for a *via media*.[28] More recently, however, that picture has been comprehensively challenged. Alec Ryrie notes that 'the English state and church did, from Henry VIII's time on, relentlessly make rhetorical claims to moderation and to be taking a middle path. Henry did it; Elizabeth did it; Hooker did it with enormous sophistication.' But, he argues, 'The English Reformation's "moderation" was largely a rhetorical smokescreen, to conceal the breathtaking radicalism of what was being done from a conservative and doubtful population.'[29]

What lay behind the smokescreen was, above all, an exercise of extraordinary royal power.[30] The English reformation involved the grasping of the church's rudder by the crown. Any air of moderation in early English doctrinal reform, or any suggestion of hesitancy in the English church's approach to doctrinal definition, flows less from an inherent English anti-dogmatism than from the fact that doctrinal purity was seldom the crown's dominant motive. Under Henry, this exercise of this power looked more like caprice than moderation – though he did, at Smithfield on 30 July 1540, have three Protestants and three Catholics executed simultaneously, which is a *via media* of sorts.[31] Under his successors, the crown's rule of the church's affairs may have been more coherent, but it was still an exercise of often brutal control. 'From the first', A.G. Dickens suggests, 'the coherence of Anglicanism depended on the State';[32] in Hensley Henson's words, it was a matter of 'the personal predilections' of the Tudor monarchs, and 'the cold sagacity of their cynical statecraft'.[33] Rowan Williams cautions against thinking of this as a matter of the state exerting power over the church. Rather it was understood as God's gracious granting of authority to the monarch within the church, just as God had in the past granted authority to the kings of Israel.[34]

Under Henry, Edward and Elizabeth, the English reformation certainly involved a process of doctrinal debate, and saw the emergence of a developing tradition of doctrinal confessions. With the Ten Articles of 1536, the Bishops' Book of 1537, the Six Articles of 1539, the King's Book of 1543, the Forty-two Articles of 1553 and the Thirty-Nine of 1563 and 1571, this is not obviously a history in which doctrinal definition was being downplayed. By the time of Elizabeth, England can plausibly be seen as a 'confessional state',[35] officially committed to a broadly Reformed theology.

---

[28] Anthony Milton, 'Arminians, Laudians, Anglicans, and Revisionists: Back to Which Drawing Board?' *Huntingdon Library Quarterly Review* 78, no. 4 (2015): 724.
[29] Ryrie, 'Reformation in Anglicanism', 40.
[30] Ibid., 35–6, 41.
[31] Thomas Abell, Edward Powell and Richard Fetherstone were executed for refusing to accept royal supremacy; Robert Barnes, William Jerome and Thomas Garrard for professing Protestant doctrines. Edward Hall, *Hall's Chronicle* (London: J. Johnson et al., 1809 (1548)), 840. Henry was 'oddly even-handed in dealing out misery', as Furlong says (*C of E*, 33); Diarmaid MacCulloch calls it Henry's 'murderous ecumenism' (in *All Things Made New: The Reformation and Its Legacy* (Oxford: Oxford University Press, 2016), 123).
[32] A. G. Dickens, *The English Reformation* (London: Batsford, 1964), 180.
[33] Hensley Henson, *The Church of England* (Cambridge: Cambridge University Press, 1939), 59.
[34] Rowan Williams, 'Unity and Universality, Locality and Diversity in Anglicanism' (2009). Available online at aoc2013.brix.fatbeehive.com/articles.php/2287/unity-and-universality-locality-and-diversity-in-anglicanism (accessed 30 November 2019).
[35] Chapman, *Anglican Theology*, 73.

Even if opinion around the church might on some topics have been more unruly and various, 'the bands of confessional discipline in England were steadily tightening ... throughout the sixteenth and early seventeenth centuries'.[36] Archbishops Parker in 1566 and Whitgift in 1584 insisted upon subscription to the articles among the clergy. Subscription was mandated by canon in 1571 and 1604. In 1622 James I insisted that nobody could in their preaching suggest opinions 'which shall not be comprehended and warranted in essence, substance and effect, or naturall inference, within some one of the Articles of Religion ... or in some of the Homelies set forth by authoritie in the Church of England',[37] and in 1628 Charles I, in a Royal Declaration for the Peace of the Church, insisted

> That the Articles of the Church of England (which have been allowed and authorized heretofore, and which Our Clergy generally have subscribed unto) do contain the true Doctrine of the Church of England agreeable to God's Word: which We do therefore ratify and confirm, requiring all Our loving Subjects to continue in the uniform Profession thereof, and prohibiting the least difference from the said Articles.[38]

It is nevertheless true that, under Elizabeth, the English reformation did not take the course of a wholesale remaking of church governance and ceremony in the light of achieved doctrinal clarity. Elizabeth seems to have been doctrinally Protestant, but 'something of a liturgical conservative'. In effect, she imposed a positive answer in the debate among the English reformers as to whether 'remnants of the Catholic past could be redirected to Protestant ends, in order to preserve order, decency, and hierarchy'.[39] She was also a monarch whose political purposes were served by sticking with unexpected rigidity to the pattern of reform achieved in the 1559 Act of Uniformity, and to the pattern of doctrine set out in the Articles of 1563 – making those not, as many reformers may have hoped, staging posts on a journey to greater coherence and clarity, but the framework of an 'Elizabethan settlement' that would stay largely in place well into the 1620s. Theologically, this settlement imposed a form of Protestantism, but mixed with bishops, cathedrals, the parochial system and a sprinkling of Catholic liturgical observances, the whole pinned together by royal authority.[40] Eamon Duffy has therefore said of the Elizabethan settlement that

---

[36] Stephen Hampton, 'Confessional Identity', in *The Oxford History of Anglicanism I*, ed. Milton, 212.
[37] James VI and I, *Directions for Preachers* (1622), in *The Oxford Handbook of the Early Modern Sermon*, ed. Hugh Adlington, Peter McCullough and Emme Rhatigan (Oxford: Oxford University Press, 2011), 558.
[38] His Majesty's Declaration, Book of Common Prayer, www.churchofengland.org/prayer-and-worship/worship-texts-and-resources/book-common-prayer/articles-religion. See Hampton, 'Confessional Identity', 212–14; Jaroslav Pelikan, *Credo: Historical and Theological Guide to Creeds and Confessions of Faith in the Christian Tradition* (New Haven, CT: Yale, 2003), 264.
[39] Diarmaid MacCulloch, 'The Myth of the English Reformation', *Journal of British Studies* 30, no. 1 (1991): 7. Cf. Chapman, *Anglican Theology*, 50; Ryrie, 'Reformation in Anglicanism', 37.
[40] Ryrie, 'Reformation in Anglicanism', 37; Nicholas Tyacke, 'Anglican Attitudes: Some Recent Writings on English Religious History, from the Reformation to the Civil War', in *Aspects of English Protestantism, c. 1530–1700* (Manchester: Manchester University Press, 2001), 179; but see Diarmaid MacCulloch, 'Church of England 1533–1603', in *Anglicanism and the Western Christian*

Embedded like flies in amber in its liturgy, its buildings, its ministerial orders, and in the attitudes and memories of many of its personnel, were vestiges of that [Catholic] past which were to prove astonishingly potent in reshaping the Church of England's future. Like the mosquito blood in the amber of Jurassic Park, from these memories of Catholicism would be extracted new forms of Anglican identity.[41]

The seventeenth century

The complexity of this settlement allowed competing narrations of the Church of England's identity to emerge from the 1620s and on into the 1630s, and it is in that period that we do see the emergence of a new kind of claim to moderation. As early as 1624, a year before Charles came to the throne, Richard Montagu wrote to his friend John Cosin, expressing the need for the Church of England to 'stand in the gapp against Puritanisme and Popery, the Scilla and Charybdis of antient piety'.[42] Members of the Laudian movement of the 1630s, of which both Montagu and Cosin were a part, could see themselves as standing in just this gap. The various elements of the Elizabethan settlement that pulled against a uniform Reformed theology had become resources for a new attempt to narrate the Church's identity. In this new attempt, a purer Calvinism came to stand as a threat equal and opposite to the one posed by the Roman church. A story began to be woven of the Church of England's balanced poise between Geneva and Rome – and, as the Laudians came into positions of ecclesiastical power, that story was deployed with increasing force against those promoting other construals, especially those for whom the story of the Church of England was one of still unfinished Calvinist reform.

This claim to moderation was not the reassertion of a pre-existing and essentially moderate 'Anglican' identity; it was the invention of something new, albeit something confected with materials that lay to hand. It was not yet, however, the invention of doctrinal diffidence. This clash between construals of the Church of England's identity was in part a doctrinal dispute; it involved, for instance, debate between Calvinists and Arminians, or, more accurately, between Calvinists and anti-Calvinists. Even if it is no longer popular to tell the story of this dispute as one in which disagreement about the doctrine of predestination drives the action, it remains a story that has doctrinal claims and doctrinal argument woven deeply into it.[43]

Tradition: Continuity, Change and the Search for Communion, ed. Stephen Platten (Norwich: Canterbury Press, 2003), 37–9.

[41] Eamon Duffy, 'The Shock of Change: Continuity and Discontinuity in the Elizabethan Church of England', in *Anglicanism and the Western Christian Tradition*, ed. Platten, 63–4. Judith Maltby has pointed out to me that the image underplays the extent to which these 'Catholic' elements were being actively maintained and adapted; they were not simply being preserved, awaiting revival.

[42] Richard Montague to John Cosin, 28 June 1624, in *The Correspondence of John Cosin, D.D.*, vol. 1 (Durham: Andrews etc, 1869), 21. Ryrie comments: 'If we want to identify a point at which "Anglicanism" swam into being, though as yet unnamed, we could do worse than this daring attempt at triangulation' ('Reformation in Anglicanism', 40).

[43] See, for an earlier stage of the debate in which doctrine was a focus, Nicholas Tyacke, *Anti-Calvinists: The Rise of English Arminianism c. 1590–1640* (Oxford: Clarendon, 1987), and Peter White, *Predestination, Policy, and Polemic: Conflict and Consensus with the English Church from*

In the 1630s and 1640s argument about the Church of England's identity flared into outright and brutal conflict – one ingredient in the poisonous cocktail that led England into Civil War. Some in this period wanted doctrinal deliberation and pronouncement to play a central role in church government: this is the trajectory that leads towards the Westminster Assembly, the Westminster divine's attempted reform of church government and worship, and their production of the Westminster Confession – and then on to the various styles of Reformed dogmatic deliberation that came to shelter under that Confession.[44]

For some others, those who remained Prayer Book loyalists during the Commonwealth, and afterwards, became supporters of the church of the Restoration, everything about this Westminster endeavour was anathema. It is they who are often seen as the true bearers of Anglican identity in this period, and yet, before the Restoration, they are simply one contending faction in the fight over English ecclesial identity. As Judith Maltby says, 'To single out Prayer Book loyalists as "*the* Anglicans" before the Restoration … implies "ownership" of a Church by particular groups within it and "unchurches" sets of individuals who were as much a part of the *ecclesia anglicana* as those retrospectively canonised as the "true Anglicans".'[45]

The Restoration settlement that followed the War and the Commonwealth was not only one in which different doctrinal claims were made from those that had been insisted upon by the Westminster divines or in the Cromwellian church. It was one in which doctrinal deliberation took different forms, and in which doctrinal definition played a different and somewhat subordinate role in church government. It was the liturgical provisions of the Book of Common Prayer that were now imposed as the defining boundaries of the Church. The Thirty-Nine Articles were also re-imposed as the standard for belief, but that re-imposition did not give rise to the same kind of focus on doctrine, the same kind of vibrant doctrinal debate that grew up around the Westminster Confession. Many in the Church of England began to tell a new story about its identity, in which it was defined primarily by uniformity in prayer and ceremonial practice, and in which that uniformity left room for a certain latitude in doctrinal belief.[46]

Jessica Martin rightly says that 'Only a dangerously heavy reliance on hindsight provides any unambiguous narrative of the beginnings of a distinctive "Anglican" sensibility and pious observation before 1663.'[47] Yet from the 1660s onwards, the story began to be told that this had always been the identity of the Church of England: that the Restoration settlement was the natural successor to the Laudian church, itself

---

the *Reformation to the Civil War* (Cambridge: Cambridge University Press, 1992). Cf. Milton, 'Arminians, Laudians, Anglicans, and Revisionists'.

[44] A fuller telling of this story would need to include the failure of the Westminster Assembly reforms, and the creation of the Cromwellian church, which, despite some attempts to do so, 'never promulgated a Confession of faith' (Jeffrey R. Collins, 'The Church Settlement of Cromwell', *History* 87, no. 285 (2002): 28–9).

[45] Judith Maltby, 'Suffering and Surviving: The Civil Wars, the Commonwealth, and the Formation of "Anglicanism", 1642–1660', in *Religion in Revolutionary England*, ed. Christopher Durston and Judith Maltby (Manchester: Manchester University Press, 2006), 159, emphasis in original.

[46] Chapman, *Anglican Theology*, 160. Rowan Williams, in the 'Foreword to the Series', in *Point of Balance*, ed. Percy and Slocum, xi, speaks of 'the rooted belief that the forms of common worship were the most important clues about what was held to be recognizably orthodox teaching'.

[47] Jessica Martin, 'Early Modern English Piety', in *The Oxford History of Anglicanism I*, ed. Milton, 411.

the natural successor to the Elizabethan settlement. The rhetoric of moderation that had been deployed by Henry and Elizabeth, all those elements of the Elizabethan settlement that had looked least purely Protestant, the remains of the interrupted Laudian reforms – they all became props in a new Anglican self-presentation, and anything that did not fit with that picture was moved to the back of the stage, or unceremoniously kicked off it. Richard Hooker, a somewhat marginal figure in his own day, was retrospectively ushered into the limelight as the Church of England's principal spokesman. His work was re-read as a mandate for the pattern of liturgical uniformity and doctrinal latitude that the Church now claimed for itself.[48] Maltby has said that 'the period from the Restoration to 1689 was Anglicanism's Council of Trent':[49] the period when a distinctive Anglican identity was invented – and it was in this period that the idea of an inherent Anglican doctrinal diffidence arrived.

Yet the establishment of this vision of Anglican latitude and comprehension begins with the 1662 Act of Uniformity – the act that created the Great Ejectment, and ushered in what Claire Cross has called 'the great period of the Puritan persecution'.[50] Just as there had been a mass ejection of ministers under Cromwell,[51] there was now a mass ejection of those who could not in conscience abide the unyielding imposition of liturgical conformity – many of whom, as Ann Hughes says, 'continued to insist to 1689 and beyond that they represented the best of English or Anglican church traditions'.[52] And the Act of Uniformity was part of a wider legislative agenda – the Corporation Act of 1661, the Conventical Act of 1664, the Five Mile Act of 1665 and the Test Acts of 1673 and 1678 – that sought to exclude from public life both Catholics and those on the Protestant side who would not conform, to constrain them from meeting for worship, and to restrict the movement and the habitation of their ministers. Richard Hooker had written that 'there is not any man of the Church of England, but the same man is also a member of the Commonwealth, nor any man a member of the Commonwealth which is not also of the Church of England'.[53] Anglicans learnt to proclaim their breadth at precisely the point that they decisively narrowed this vision.

---

[48] See Ryrie, 'Reformation in Anglicanism', 43. Cf. Peter Lake, *Anglicans and Puritans? Presbyterianism and English Conformist Thought from Whitgift to Hooker* (London: Unwin Hyman, 1988), 229, on the need in the 1660s to discover 'a non-Laudian, prefereably Elizabethan, mildly non-Calvinist and rabidly anti-Puritan ancestry for the restored church'. See also Lake, 'The "Anglican Moment"? Richard Hooker and the Ideological Watershed of the 1590s', in *Anglicanism and the Western Christian Tradtion*, ed. Platten, 120–1.

[49] Judith Maltby, *Prayer Book and People in Elizabethan and Early Stuart England* (Cambridge: Cambridge University Press, 1998), 236.

[50] Claire Cross, *Church and People: England 1450–1660*, 2nd edn (Oxford: Blackwell, 1999), 196.

[51] For the ejections under Cromwell, see Ann Hughes, 'The Cromwellian Church', in *Oxford History of Anglicanism I*, ed. Milton, 447, and Collins, 'The Church Settlement of Cromwell', 29–30. For a broader context, see Alexandra Walsham, *Charitable Hatred: Tolerance and Intolerance in England, 1500–1700* (Manchester: Manchester University Press, 2006).

[52] Hughes, 'The Cromwellian Church', 456. For the Great Ejectment/Great Ejection, see the articles by Paul Avis, David M. Thompson and Paul S. Fiddes in *Ecclesiology* 9, no. 2 (2013). There were attempts, after 1660, to re-establish a more comprehensive identity for the Church of England, including the abandoned 1689 proposal to revise the *Book of Common Prayer*. See Charles Hefling, 'The "Liturgy of Comprehension"', in *The Oxford Guide to the Book of Common Prayer: A Worldwide Survey*, ed. Charles Hefling and Cynthia Shattuck (Oxford: Oxford University Press, 2006), 61–3.

[53] Hooker, *Of the Laws of Ecclesiastical Polity* 8.1.2, in the modern spelling edition of Arthur Stephen McGrade, vol. 3 (Oxford: Oxford University Press, 2003), 190.

A contested inheritance

However complex and compromised, this history did create within the Church of England a space defined more by liturgical conformity than by doctrinal rigour. It was a space in which a certain limited latitude for doctrinal difference was indeed allowed. The Thirty-Nine Articles continued to mark the doctrinal boundaries – with subscription once again demanded of the clergy, and from students at Oxford and Cambridge. Yet the Articles did not, on the whole, become a focus for further elaboration, clarification and definition. The Restoration did not usher the Church of England into a period of Anglican scholasticism.

The character of this space continued to be defined, at least in part, by the Church's subordination to state power (and by the involvement of lay people in its governance that is the corollary of that situation). Parliament became and remained (until the twentieth century) the primary deliberative and legislative body for the Church of England – and though, at times, it has engaged in lively doctrinal debate, it is not a body in which doctrinal theology is a dominant mode of discourse. The character of this space was also reflected in and reinforced by the patterns of elite education that formed those who ruled the Church – whether in parliament or among the bishops. They were more likely to get a grounding in classics and mathematics than in the details of doctrinal theology.[54] The governance of the Church of England was not arranged in such a way as to make it likely that refined doctrinal dispute would become central.

John Henry Newman, writing in 1837, noted that, if looked at with a cynical eye,

> It may be argued that the Church of England, as established by law, and existing in fact, has never represented a doctrine at all or been the development of a principle, has never had an intellectual basis; that it has been but a name, or a department of the state, or a political party, in which religious opinion was an accident, and therefore has been various. In consequence, it has been but the theatre of contending religionists, that is, of Papists and Latitudinarians, softened externally, or modified into inconsistency by their birth and education, or restrained by their interests and their religious engagements.[55]

As this quote suggests, the space defined by liturgical conformity and doctrinal latitude was one that both allowed, and was then reinforced by, the continued existence of differing parties with differing approaches to doctrine: it became a 'theatre of

---

[54] This continued to be true. G. W. H. Lampe, writing about the twentieth century in 'The 1938 Report in Retrospect', in Doctrine Commission of the Church of England, *Doctrine in the Church of England* (London: SPCK, 1982), xxx, notes that 'the traditional approach to theological study by way of an English-style classical education tends to produce a distinctively English (rather than specifically Anglican) method of doing theology: historically oriented, rooted in the study of the biblical and patristic texts, accepting the principles of critical scholarship but applying them cautiously and conservatively, uncomfortable with dogmatics or systematic theology which have never formed a real element of the syllabus of either the Honour School of Theology [Oxford] or the theological Tripos [Cambridge].'

[55] John Henry Newman, *The Via Media of the Anglican Church*, vol. 1 (London: Longmans, Green and Co: 1901 (1837)), 18. This is not his own view, though he recognizes its force.

contending religionists'. The differences between these parties were, of course, not primarily doctrinal. Diarmaid MacCulloch provides one familiar way of mapping the parties in this contest.

> The Church of England has never decisively settled the question of who owns its history. ... Within it remain two worlds: one, the sacramental world of theologians like Lancelot Andrewes, William Laud, the world that still values real presence, bishops and beauty; and the other, the world of the Elizabethan Reformation, which rejects shrines and images, which rejects real presence, which values law and moral regulation based on both Old and New Testament precept. These two worlds contend for mastery within English tradition, and they have created that fascinating dialogue about the sacred which the world calls Anglicanism.[56]

The difference between these two worlds (if, for the moment, we accept this simplified picture of Anglican diversity) involves every aspect of the Church's life. It is a matter of sensibility, style and demeanour; it encompasses differences of liturgical observance, approaches to preaching, architectural preferences and styles of clerical rule; it involves different approaches to missionary work, social engagement and education, as much as disagreements about doctrine.

It also involves different ways of narrating the story of the Church. Mark Chapman speaks of eighteenth- and nineteenth-century controversialists 'trawling through the past in the hope of finding an elusive Anglican identity', 'in a Church that had not developed a universally recognized canon of resources for doing theology' beyond 'Scripture, the writers of the early church and the liturgical and doctrinal resources including the Articles of Religion contained in the Book of Common Prayer'.[57] Inhabitants of the differing worlds described by MacCulloch – and there are, in reality, more than two – have different heroes and martyrs, different canons of hallowed texts,[58] different claims about the deep genius or wisdom of Anglicanism, and they arrange the materials of the Church of England's history into different plots. 'Anglicanism's relationship with the Reformation', for instance, as Alec Ryrie says, 'is that of an adult with his or her own adolescent rebellions. According to taste, the Reformation either shows Anglicanism at its forthright best, or at its chaotic and destructive worst. It is either a period of lost honesty to be rediscovered, or an embarrassing episode to be passed over with discretion and regret.'[59]

Among all these other differences, however, members of these various worlds do tend towards different ways of approaching doctrinal questions, and during the nineteenth century these differences came to push at the doctrinal bonds that held the Restoration settlement together. Two famous controversies illustrate this process.

---

[56] MacCulloch, *All Things Made New*, 216–17; cf. his 'Church of England 1533–1603', 41.
[57] Chapman, *Anglican Theology*, 2–4.
[58] For example, the texts collected and published in the Fathers of the Church series on Newman's side, those published in the Parker Society Library on his opponents'. See Michael Ledger-Lomas, 'Mass Markets: Religion', in *The Cambridge History of the Book in Britain 6: 1830–1914*, ed. David McKitterick (Cambridge: Cambridge University Press, 2009), 344, and Milton, 'Introduction', 4–5.
[59] Ryrie, 'Reformation in Anglicanism', 34.

The first erupted with the publication in 1841 of Newman's Tract 90, *Remarks on Certain Passages in the Thirty-Nine Articles* – and became, in part, a fight about the relationship between the Articles and the Prayer Book.[60] Newman, writing as a champion of MacCulloch's first, sacramental world, states that his intention is 'merely to show that, while our Prayer Book is acknowledged on all hands to be of Catholic origin, our articles also, the offspring of an uncatholic age, are, through God's good providence, to say the least, not uncatholic, and may be subscribed by those who aim at being catholic in heart and doctrine'.[61]

Amid the storm of responses that this Tract provoked, the vice chancellor of Oxford University met with the Heads of House and Proctors. 'Considering that it is enjoined in the Statutes of this University … that every Student shall be instructed and examined in the Thirty-nine Articles, and shall subscribe to them', they resolved 'That the modes of interpretation, such as are suggested in the said Tract, evading rather than explaining the sense of the Thirty-nine articles, and reconciling subscription to them with the adoption of errors which they were designed to counteract, defeat the object, and are inconsistent with the due observance of the above-mentioned Statutes.'[62]

Less than twenty years later, another loud battle took place on an adjacent front, with the publication of *Essays and Reviews*. Here the battle was not over the Articles and the Prayer Book, but over the interpretation of the bible. Just as with the Tract 90 debate, this was an argument about much more than doctrine, even if it was one in which some doctrinal questions were at stake, but it too was an argument in which the function of doctrine in general was in dispute. One of the authors, Benjamin Jowett, wrote that 'It is a received view with many, that the meaning of the Bible is to be defined by that of the Prayer-book; while there are others who interpret "the Bible and the Bible only" with a silent reference to the traditions of the Reformation.'[63] Instead, he argued, what is needed is an unadorned historical approach to the words of Scripture, 'a reasonable criticism', which will 'clear away the remains of dogmas, systems, controversies which are encrusted upon them'.[64]

The polemical literature that poured out in the months and years that followed these two incidents certainly involved many particular doctrinal disagreements. These arguments, however, exposed differences that ran far deeper. To be enlisted on one side rather than another of these disputes was to inhabit a whole different approach to thinking about doctrine. It might involve different densities and styles of biblical exegesis, different attitudes to and levels of appeal to Patristic sources, different uses of precedents from the medieval church, different kinds of appeal to the findings of science and of historical criticism. For participants in these different worlds, there were different intellectual apprenticeships to serve, different conventions to internalize,

---

[60] Cf. Pelikan, *Credo*, 177.
[61] John Henry Newman, *Tract 90* (London: J.G.F and J. Rivington, 1841), 4. Cf. Robert Dudley Middleton, 'Tract Ninety', *Journal of Ecclesiastical History* 2, no. 1 (1951): 81–101.
[62] The text is provided in Robert Hussey, *Reasons for Voting upon the Third Question to Be Proposed in Convocation on the 13th inst.* (Oxford: J. G. F. and J. Rivington, 1845), 2; I have simplified the punctuation.
[63] Benjamin Jowett, 'On the Interpretation of Scripture', in *Essays and Reviews* (London: John W. Parker and Son, 1860), 330.
[64] Ibid., 344, 339.

different styles to imitate. The different parties didn't simply make different doctrinal claims; they spoke different doctrinal languages.

Attempts to secure the legal defeat of one party or another – a definitive ruling by parliament or the courts that its claims and practices were beyond the Anglican pale – largely failed, at least in the long run.[65] The life of the Church of England as it rolled on into the twentieth century involved instead what Chapman calls an 'uneasy coalition', or Aidan Nichols 'an uneasy, and at times aggressive, coexistence of the various strands of thought'.[66] The Church of England is an unresolved mix of at least catholic, evangelical and liberal strands – though a finer-grained accounting would quickly extend this catalogue.[67]

Empire and exclusion

In my presentation so far, I have fallen into a common trap. It turns out to be frighteningly easy to tell the story of doctrinal theology in the Church of England from the sixteenth century onwards as if there were no colonies, no missionaries, no empire and no slave trade. It can be told as if the life of the Church of England were a domestic drama acted out by an entirely monochrome cast.[68] Yet, even in the sixteenth and seventeenth century, members of the Church of England were ruling Wales, reconquering Ireland, forming colonies in North America, engaging in piratical conquests in the Caribbean, establishing trading posts in India, in Java and in the Spice Islands – and taking elements of their Anglican Christianity with them as they went.[69] And these international embroilments only increased. From the beginning of the eighteenth century, as Rowan Strong says, 'Anglicanism, in the form of the institutional Church of England, the Anglican missionary societies, and their supporters, was institutionally, consciously, evangelistically, and organizationally connected and concerned with the English-British empire.'[70] Church of England clergy were first sent out to organize Anglican life in settler communities. They were then sent out, in increasing numbers, as missionaries to bring Christianity to indigenous

---

[65] Mark Chapman, 'Essays and Reviews 150 Years On', in *Point of Balance*, ed. Percy and Slocum, 72: 'Firm and decisive leadership by bishops had proved ineffectual and ultimately pointless.'
[66] Chapman, 'Essays and Reviews', 74; Aidan Nichols, *The Panther and the Hind: A Theological History of Anglicanism* (Edinburgh: T&T Clark, 1993), x.
[67] Ronald Knox suggested that there were nine 'parties': 'Tendencies of Anglicanism', *Dublin Review* 162 (1918): 25–6. John G. Maiden, writing about the late 1920s in *National Religion and the Prayer Book Controversy, 1927-1928* (Woodbridge: Boydell, 2009), 6–9, describes four: conservative evangelical, liberal evangelical, 'Centre-High' (roughly, liberal catholic) and Anglo-Catholic. Cf. Furlong, *C of E*, 324–41.
[68] Famously, Owen Chadwick's magisterial two-volume work on *The Victorian Church* (London: Adam & Charles Black, 1966–1970) barely mentions the missionary societies or their work.
[69] For what follows, see Ward, *History of Global Anglicanism*, 23–37.
[70] Rowan Strong, *Anglicanism and the British Empire, c. 1700-1850* (Oxford: Oxford University Press, 2007), 294. A more detailed telling of this story would need to look at the substantial involvement of Scottish Episcopalians alongside these English Anglicans.

peoples – and, often, to establish and govern for indigenous converts forms of religious life organized along Church of England lines.[71]

This work was, from the start, entangled with the slave trade. Members of the Church of England captured, sold and owned slaves.[72] Anglican clergy provided chaplaincy to slave-trading outposts, established the religious structure for slave-owning communities and governed the religious life of countless slaves. The Church profited from the slave trade in innumerable ways, even after some Anglican laypeople and clergy began to become prominent in the movement for its abolition.

By the end of the nineteenth century, 5 per cent of Anglican clergy were missionaries. There were 1,100 of them, working with some 550 'ordained natives', in numerous missionary societies. At that point, 'Anglicans sent the majority of English missionaries abroad, contributed the bulk of funds supporting missions, and by 1899 accounted for over half of the expanding army of nearly 1,500 unmarried English female missionaries.'[73]

There is a rich story to tell about the ways in which the forms of Anglican life that took root around the world were not simply transplantations from Britain, or impositions by British personnel.[74] Indigenous people exercised their own agency to create distinctive forms of life, sometimes despite and sometimes with the support of the missionaries working among them. The mission field was, in reality if not by design, 'a "contact zone" where Western and non-Western peoples interact[ed] with each other on the basis of mutual respect if not equal power, working to create cultural forms that were neither Western nor indigenous but hybrid, synthetic, creole, transcultural.'[75]

These processes of 'transculturation' were shaped, however, by dramatically unequal distributions of power – military, economic and cultural. Those distributions both fostered and were cemented in place by attitudes of superiority. It was hard for White English settlers and missionaries, and their supporters at home, to take seriously the possibility that indigenous people were conversation partners in deliberation about the faith. Attitudes to the structures and methods of imperial power certainly varied, but many of those engaged in English missionary work were united in a belief that they were instruments of a providentially beneficent influence, bringing Christian light and life to the world.[76] They were lifting native peoples slowly – perhaps very slowly –

---

[71] As 'a territorial, confessional, parochial, geographical Church', the Church of England was 'as ill-adapted for transfer to the British Empire as it was for adaptation to rapid industrial and population growth at home' (Cox, 'The Dialectics of Empire', 30) but the existing structures of parish and diocese were supplemented by the creation of missionary societies – most notably the Society for the Propagation of the Gospel (founded in 1701), and the Church Missionary Society (1799).

[72] Having been left the Barbados estate of Sir Christopher Codrington in 1704, the SPG itself became a slave-owning organization.

[73] Stephen Maughan, *Mighty England Do Good: Culture, Faith, Empire, and World in the Foreign Missions of the Church of England, 1850–1915* (Grand Rapids, MI: William B. Eerdmans, 2014), 12.

[74] The whole of Kevin Ward's *History of Global Anglicanism* focuses on such indigenous agency.

[75] Cox, 'Dialectics of Empire', 29, drawing on Mary Louise Pratt's work on transculturation, in *Imperial Eyes: Travel Writing and Transculturation*, 2nd edn (London: Routledge, 2008).

[76] See Elizabeth Elbourne, *Blood Ground: Colonialism, Missions, and the Contest for Christianity in the Cape Colony and Britain, 1799–1853* (Montreal: McGill University Press, 2002), 48–50.

towards their own level. They had everything to give, and little of real substance to learn.[77]

Indigenous people were certainly engaged as workers in the mission field, and some were ordained. By the nineteenth century, the Church Missionary Society was training 'a succession of Maori, Canadian First Nation, Indian and African students' at the Church Missionary College in Islington.[78] Nevertheless, such clergy and other workers were found subordinate positions in hierarchies still resolutely crowned by White people. With one exception (Bishop Samuel Ajayi Crowther, consecrated bishop of the Niger Territory in 1864, though with responsibility only for territories 'beyond the Queen's dominions'),[79] there was no bishop anywhere in the Anglican Communion who was not English, or a White settler, before 1912.[80]

Doctrinal reflection in the Church of England has inevitably been shaped by this global and imperial context – but it has very largely been shaped by White British involvement in it, and by White British attitudes and responses to it. It has been shaped by 'the power of arguments and ideals brought back to Britain by colonial bishops and returned missionaries';[81] it has been shaped by the work of the missionary societies organizing home support for foreign missions; it has been shaped by the broader colonial imagination that took deep root in Britain from the eighteenth century onwards. It has not, however, been visibly and substantially shaped by the welcoming into its conversations of indigenous people, or of those immigrants from around the empire who came to settle in England. Even when the church of the empire morphed to become an Anglican Communion of independent provinces, the situation changed little. In the words of Anthony Tyrrell Hanson, 'the Church of England on the whole goes its way without paying much attention to the opinions and reactions of the rest of the Anglican Communion'[82] – except, perhaps, when it suits one side or another in some domestic dispute to do so.

Most English Anglicans have been little conscious of their church having been shaped by any other than White voices, and many have been scandalously resistant to being so shaped. Those Anglicans from the Caribbean and elsewhere who came to England after the Second World War, for instance, were all too often met with outright racist hostility, and though the racism is now normally less overt, all too many parts of the Church of England remain unrepresentatively and depressingly White.[83]

---

[77] Maughan, *Mighty England*, 439.
[78] Ward, *History of Global Anglicanism*, 42.
[79] Ibid., 117.
[80] In 1865 the Provincial Synod of the Canadian Church urged the setting up of a general Anglican conference 'by which the members of our Anglican Communion in all quarters of the world should have a share in the deliberations for her welfare'. 'Addresses from the Provincial Synod of the United Church of England and Ireland in Canada, Assembled in Montreal in September 1865', in *The Lambeth Conferences of 1867, 1878, and 1888*, ed. Randall T. Davidson (London: SPCK, 1889), 52. That was in practice, however, a call for the inclusion of White settler voices.
[81] Maughan, *Mighty England*, 40.
[82] Anthony Tyrrell Hanson, *Beyond Anglicanism* (London: Darton, Longman & Todd, 1965), quoted in Ward, *History of Global Anglicanism*, 296.
[83] The Minority Anglican Project, run by Sanjee Perera, has yet to report at the time of writing – but it is likely to be the most significant piece of research to date on the experience of Black, Asian and minority ethnic people in the Church of England.

Two vignettes can serve to illustrate the dynamics that have shaped the Church of England's inattention. The first concerns J. W. Colenso, the first bishop of Natal, who went to Africa in 1832. He worked with the White settlers, but also threw himself into missionary work among the Zulu people. He worked on a Zulu translation of the bible, aided by prolonged and serious conversation with a convert named William Ngidi. During this period of his work, Colenso's theology became increasingly radical, in ways that were driven in part by his historical and scientific questioning of Scripture, and in part by his endeavours to communicate with his Zulu audiences. In 1863, he was tried and declared a heretic by the Church in South Africa, but on appeal the British courts overturned the condemnation, on jurisdictional grounds. His case became a cause célèbre, and anxiety about his teaching was one of the main prompts for the convening of the first Lambeth Conference in 1867.[84] Here we have, it would seem, an example of a colonial theologian shaped by close encounter with indigenous voices, and bringing what he had learnt right into the controversial heart of the Church of England's theological debates.

Colenso's approach to his conversation – with Ngidi, and with Zulu people more generally – is, however, analysed much more critically by Willie James Jennings. Jennings notes that Colenso certainly wanted to understand Zulu language and life, in order better to communicate the gospel – but that the gospel so communicated remained largely unaffected by what Colenso learnt.[85] Colenso believed that the gospel was a universal message, floating above particular cultural identities, whether Zulu or English. He was therefore oblivious to the depth at which his understanding of the gospel was entangled with his own English identity. He was still more oblivious to the dangers inherent in the idea that he had hold of a universal gospel free from cultural particularity. That idea is only possible for someone who can think of his own ideas and assumptions as universal; it is, in other words, itself entangled with the colonial imagination. 'What looks like a radical antiracist, antiethnocentric vision of Christian faith is in fact profoundly imperialist,' Jennings says. 'Colenso's universalism undermines all forms of identity except that of the colonialist'; 'his universalist vision reduces the power and presence of the very things it claims to grasp, the particularities of African peoples.'[86] 'Colenso turned native questions into occasions for theological self-absorption. It was as though he heard their questions, turned away from them, turned toward England, and began to theologize.'[87] In Colenso's work, the work of answering theological questions – the work of real doctrinal deliberation and construction – remained the White man's burden.

A second illustration is provided by a stark juxtaposition from a few decades later, at the 1910 World Missionary Conference in Edinburgh. The conference heard reports from a series of commissions. The first, on 'Carrying the gospel to all the non-Christian world', insisted that 'the missionary enterprise is the projection abroad of the Church at home. It shares in a much larger measure than is usually recognized the ideals and

---

[84] Ward, *History of Global Anglicanism*, 139–41.
[85] Ibid., 145–6.
[86] Willie James Jennings, *The Christian Imagination: Theology and the Origins of Race* (New Haven, CT: Yale University Press, 2010), 145–6.
[87] Ibid., 150.

spirit of the Home Church, and carries their influence into the life of the Church which it creates in the non-Christian world.'[88] The creative agent in this process, the Home Church is the place 'in which are enlisted the pioneers, founders, and leaders of world-evangelisation. ... [It is] the environment or atmosphere in which they form their ideals and habits and receive their training.'[89]

The report that contained this starkly one-way language was presented to the conference, and warmly welcomed, on 15 June. Five days later, in the evening, the conference heard a very different address from Vedanayagam Samuel Azariah, a priest from South India who would, two years later, become bishop of Donakal, and the first Anglican bishop in India who was not a White settler.[90] Azariah challenged the conference delegates, saying, 'the relationship between the European missionaries and the Indian workers [i.e. church workers] is far from what it ought to be, and ... a certain aloofness, a lack of mutual understanding and openness, a great lack of frank intercourse and friendliness, exists throughout the country.'[91] What is needed is friendship, he insisted, and 'Friendship is more than condescending love.'[92] It requires real partnership.

> The exceeding riches of the glory of Christ can be fully realised not by the Englishman, the American, and the Continental alone, nor by the Japanese, the Chinese, and the Indians by themselves – but by all working together, worshipping together, and learning together the Perfect Image of our Lord and Christ. It is only 'with all Saints' that we can 'comprehend the love of Christ which passeth knowledge, that we might be filled with all the fullness of God'. This will be possible only from spiritual friendships between the two races. We ought to be willing to learn from one another and to help one another.[93]

The speech did not go down well.[94] Azariah was confronting what Cox, in a different context, calls 'the overwhelming practice of white privilege and white supremacy in the Church', and against that background a call for cross-cultural friendship was simply inaudible to many.[95] Most of his audience regarded his call as naive. He was, they thought, insufficiently alert to the difficulty and even the inappropriateness of finding a place for native people within the polite structures of English life. He was overestimating the capacity or desire of native people to follow English cultural rules. He was risking giving natives ideas above their social and economic station, in a way that could only lead to social disruption. He was, in other words, disregarding the real

---

[88] World Missionary Conference, 1910, *Report of Commission I: Carrying the Gospel to all the Non-Christian World* (Edinburgh: Oliphant, Anderson & Ferrier, 1910), 344.
[89] Ibid., 345.
[90] Brian Stanley, *The World Missionary Conference, Edinburgh 1910* (Grand Rapids, MI: William B. Eerdmans, 2009), 121–30.
[91] Vedanayagam Samuel Azariah, 'The Problem of Co-operation between Foreign and Native Workers', in World Missionary Conference, 1910, *The History and Records of the Conference: Together with Addresses Delivered at the Evening Meetings* (Edinburgh: Oliphant, Anderson & Ferrier, 1910), 307.
[92] Ibid., 308.
[93] Ibid., 315.
[94] Ibid., 127–8.
[95] Cox, 'The Dialectics of Empire', 31.

distinction between White and Black – a distinction held in place by, and itself helping to keep in place, differences in power, wealth, class, education and culture. A call for equality of regard was meaningless in the light of that distinction.

In one sense, all that is needed for doctrinal deliberation in the Church of England to become more diverse and inclusive is nothing more than the friendship for which Azariah called. All that is needed is a new intimacy between people, who can work together to understand the gospel, and to create forms of Christian life that are genuinely shared. In another sense, however, that call is radical. It questions the whole operating system of power that militates against such intimate co-creation – and it highlights the extent to which the Church of England's doctrinal deliberation, as it exists at present, runs on that operating system.

The integrity of Anglicanism?

Anglicans in the twentieth and twenty-first centuries are heirs of this whole history. We are heirs of the seesawing settlements of the sixteenth and early seventeenth centuries; we are heirs of the Restoration's imposed conformity; we are heirs of the nineteenth century's industrious, creative and incompatible appropriations of earlier Anglican tradition; we are heirs of a whole series of persistent internal and external exclusions.[96] We can't simply go back behind the nineteenth century to the supposed purity of any earlier form of Anglicanism: we are heirs of the whole history; we 'cannot freeze-frame it at any point and say, "This is definitive Anglicanism".'[97]

The 1662 settlement was the product of a messy history. It was a matter of happenstance and the ugly tactics of power, as well as of habits of prayer and patterns of theological imagination. Something similar is true of the settlement that had emerged by the start of the twentieth century, with its braiding of catholic, evangelical and liberal strands. It was the product of contention between parties, and the exhaustion of legal and parliamentary attempts to resolve that contention, more than any positive vision of pluralism.

As always, those of us who inhabitant these settlements tell ourselves stories to disguise how accidental, and how brutal, is the origin of our way of life. We tell stories in which these settlements are the natural unfolding of national character, or the realization of a vision of the Reformers, or the reassertion of the immemorial genius of the English church. Re-reading this history in conversation with others, however – with the heirs of those ejected for nonconformity, perhaps, or those whose lands were colonized by the Church-supported empire – helps reveal just how much those stories disguise.

This history did, nevertheless, create a distinctive kind of ecclesial space, marked by a tendency to subordinate doctrinal to liturgical questions, by the uneasy interaction of multiple theological traditions, and by the possibility of engagement with a worldwide Communion. Seeing that space in the light of its history therefore poses a series of questions. Is the settlement that eventually emerged anything more

[96] Champan, *Anglican Theology*, ch. 1.
[97] Avis, *Identity*, 160.

than a matter of power and accident? Is its uneasy entangling of more catholic and more Protestant strands, for instance, nothing more than a political imposition – a marriage of convenience that makes nothing of interest possible beyond a distinctive flavour of incoherence? Is the supposed Anglican balance of scripture, tradition and reason nothing more than a way of naming a set of characteristic and oft repeated disagreements about method? Is the relative priority given to liturgy over doctrine in the Church anything more than a form of social conservatism? Is it more than a device for placing beyond notice and beyond criticism the forms of hierarchy encoded in that liturgy – the monarchism, the clericalism, the sexism, the rich man in his castle and the poor man at his gate? Is the engagement of the Church of England with the wider Anglican Communion anything more than the continuation of colonialism by other means?

Over the past half-century in particular, a range of Anglican theologians have tried to answer at least some of these questions.[98] Books on Anglican identity or the distinctive ethos of the Church of England have been published by the shelf-load – though, looking at the names appearing on the spines of these books, it has to be said that writing them appears largely to be a pastime for men. Monica Furlong's *C of E: The State It's In* in 2000, and Linda Woodhead's collaboration with Andrew Brown on *That Was the Church That Was* in 2016 are among the very few exceptions.[99]

Some of these authors continue to see the diversity of the Church as reflecting a peculiar Anglican gift for latitude. 'The desire and need to sometimes reach settlements that do not achieve closure', says Martyn Percy, 'is itself part of the deep "habit of wisdom" that has helped to form Anglican polity down the centuries.'[100] Others see, instead, what Paul Avis calls a 'continued lack of mutual understanding and mutual respect' and regard much of the talk about an Anglican genius for comprehension as 'a *post factum* accommodation to the demise of doctrinal accord within the Church'.[101]

Stephen Sykes was one of the earliest and most influential voices in the modern quest to understand Anglican identity. In 1978, in time to catch that year's Lambeth Conference, he wrote *The Integrity of Anglicanism*, bemoaning the fractured nature of the Church. This situation indicated, he claimed, a failure of nerve. 'To put it bluntly, there is something corrupt about an institution which presumes to mould the Christian allegiance of its millions of members and officially states that it bears testimony to the gospel of Christ, but which is unwilling or unable to face the issues of belief which are immediately apparent to any informed Christian.'[102] The idea that the Church

---

[98] This is not new. Rowan Strong, 'Series Introduction', in *Oxford History of Anglicanism I*, ed. Milton, xvii, writes that 'the Church of England, and its later global Anglican expansion, was always a contested identity throughout its history'. Cf. Ralph McMichael, 'What Does Canterbury Have to Do with Jerusalem? The Vocation of Anglican Theology', in *The Vocation of Anglican Theology*, ed. Ralph McMichael (London: SCM, 2014), 17.
[99] Linda Woodhead and Andrew Brown, *That Was the Church That Was: How the Church of England Lost the English People* (London: Bloomsbury, 2016). As far as I can tell, the vast majority of the authors of these books are also White.
[100] Percy, 'Engagement, Diversity, and Distinctiveness', 22; cf. F. A. Peake, 'The Anglican Ethos', in *The Future of Anglican Theology*, ed. Bryant, 33.
[101] Avis, *Identity*, 23, 25.
[102] Sykes, *Integrity*, 5–6.

can hold its various different strands in tension, as if 'all of the contradictory views are true and in some hitherto undiscovered way reconcilable', has 'been disastrous. It must be said bluntly that it has served as an open invitation to intellectual laziness and self-deception.' Instead, Sykes insisted, we ought to acknowledge that 'Anglicanism has a specific content, and that it ought to expose that content to examination and criticism.'[103]

Yet despite the acerbity of his critique, the response that Sykes develops to this situation is one that still tries to make sense of rather than overcome the plurality of the Church. He argues, not for a swift turn to doctrinal coherence, but for a different construal of what the doctrinal incoherence of the Church of England might mean. Instead of accepting a lazy comprehensiveness that refuses to make doctrinal judgements, 'it is the Christian's duty to exercise careful discernment'.[104] The distinctiveness of Anglicanism, according to Sykes, lies in how Anglicans approach such discernment. To put it another way, it does not lie in a distinctive and unified articulation of credal doctrines, but in an ecclesiology.

> [I]t is of the essence of the Anglican view of authority that it should be maintained in principle that the means of judging matters concerning the faith are in the hands of the whole people of God by reasons of their access to the Scriptures, and, further, that it is distinctively Anglican that this means is given to them in the liturgy of the church, backed by canon law.[105]

The judgement of the whole people of God is made possible by the 'liturgical provision that the scriptures should be heard, and ... the scriptures are contextualized in worship which seeks at once to evoke the fundamentals and induct the worshipper into the heart of Christian experience'.[106] Within the space held open by that experience of scripturally focused worship, discernment is approached by means of disagreement. That disagreement should be conducted 'constructively and openly', because 'the reaching of authoritative decisions is a continuous process involving all participants'.[107] The doctrinal diffidence of the Church of England should not at all be a matter of avoiding argument and decision, but of approaching those arguments and decisions slowly and without central imposition. Time should be given for the worship-driven formation of discernment among the whole people.[108]

In *The Identity of Christianity*, a less polemical work written six years later, Sykes developed these claims into an account of Christian identity per se.[109] The discernment to which all Christians are called has a particular shape. First, it is discernment that they undertake as followers of Jesus. As they pursue 'authentic Christian discipleship',

---

[103] Ibid., 19, 68.
[104] Ibid., 94.
[105] Ibid., 93.
[106] Ibid., 99.
[107] Ibid., 99, cf. 94.
[108] 'My suggestion is that we be much less apologetic about being slow and careful, and public too, than we are' (Sykes, 'Genius', 238). Cf. Williams, *Anglican Identities*, 7, on 'theologically informed and spiritually sustained *patience*' (emphasis in original).
[109] Sykes comments on the acerbic tone of *The Integrity of Anglicanism* in 'Genius', 228, 233.

Christians inevitably face questions about how to go on in new situations. They face a 'need both of guidance and of a power of discrimination'. As disciples, their reference point is the complex portrait of Jesus that is passed on to them in scripture. The discernment to which they are called is one in which 'the quality of the attention given to Jesus is the quality of attention given to that which is transcendent'.[110] Or, to put it another way, it is discernment governed by the embodied conviction that Jesus Christ is Lord.

Second, precisely because it is discernment governed by this conviction, it should be approached by way of that worship in which the name of Jesus is invoked.[111] Worship provides the deep context for discernment because 'there has to be somewhere ... where theology is simply not in charge', where 'the tyrannous use of intellectual power' does not hold sway – and where discernment can be formed at a level that goes deeper than argument.[112] Christian worship like this makes possible the preservation of 'the continuous and effective identity of Christianity' – and that is why worship provides the context within which theologians can properly 'participate defensively and aggressively in the contests which nevertheless occur'. Their contests are, ultimately, about the patterns of belief that best do justice to, and best preserve, what the believer knows in worship.[113] Worship 'makes a vital difference to the conditions under which vigorous argument of a radical kind may be regarded as a constructive contribution, not a destructive irrelevance, to the performance of Christian identity in the modern world'.[114] In Sykes's hands, therefore, the differing theological traditions in the Church of England are not simply rivals abiding by an uneasy truce, or exhausted pugilists living in complacent mutual disregard. They are conversation partners locked in contestation for the sake of discernment, sharing patterns of worship that go deeper than their differences.

More recently, an approach similar to Sykes's has been taken by Paul Avis, a keen observer both of the Church of England and of the wider Anglican Communion, and someone with long expertise in the Church's ecumenical dialogues. Like Sykes, Avis bemoans the fact that, among the contending strands of the Church of England, 'compromise may have occurred, but not synthesis'. Like Sykes, he disputes the idea that Anglicanism is peculiarly 'provisional', and he argues that it is possible for Anglicans to have 'confidence in our Anglican ecclesiology, our Anglican tradition and our Anglican Communion'. And, like Sykes, he argues that the distinctiveness of this Anglican way lies 'in the sphere of authority, in the ways that beliefs are defined, legitimated, interpreted and maintained'.[115]

> Anglicanism does aim to conform to the canons of the early, undivided Church. It is orthodox in faith by the standard of the early ecumenical councils. It is catholic

---

[110] Stephen Sykes, *The Identity of Christianity: Theologians and the Essence of Christianity from Schleiermacher to Barth* (London: SPCK, 1984), 26, 20, 255.
[111] Ibid., 265.
[112] Sykes, *Identity*, 7. Cf. Williams, *Anglican Identities*, 30: 'straight ideological instruction is not and cannot be the primary point of worship or the means of growth in holiness.'
[113] Sykes, *Identity*, 268, 275.
[114] Ibid., 265.
[115] Avis, *Identity*, 23, 1, 49; cf. 157.

in its order by the standard of the post-apostolic Church. ... It does not wish to be different in fundamental doctrine or basic practice. The question of Anglican distinctiveness arises, however, precisely when we ask: What is the body that makes these claims and what right has it to make them?[116]

There is, in other words, 'a definite and distinct Anglican ecclesiology', and Avis believes there is no need for the bishops of the Church of England, or of the Anglican Communion more widely, to act simply 'as benevolent pragmatists ... rather than by reference to proven principles of Anglican (reformed catholic) ecclesiology'.[117]

For Sykes, the contestations of Anglican theology were held together as a conversation rather than as a cacophony primarily by the shared experience of worship. For Avis, we need to say more. He holds that it is possible to point to a range of texts in which the 'proven principles of Anglican ecclesiology', and the Anglican commitment to orthodox belief and catholic order, are developed and displayed. There is, he believes, a cumulative textual tradition of Anglican deliberation about these matters, and Anglican theology is properly shaped by ongoing conversation with it. Avis lists the 'historic formularies' (the Thirty-Nine Articles, the Book of Common Prayer and the Ordinal), but then goes on to include various collections of classic sources from the early centuries of the post-Reformation Church, the resolutions of the Lambeth Conferences, the 1938 report *Doctrine in the Church of England*, a range of ecclesiological statements from the Church of England's House of Bishops and a number of key ecumenical statements.[118] There is much to say, he acknowledges, about the varying authority and complex interrelation of these sources, but in engagement with them Anglican theologians and church leaders can learn a language rich enough – and widely enough shared – to pursue their ongoing conversations fruitfully.

A third voice in the debate about Anglican identity suggests a rather different kind of response. Like Sykes and Avis, Timothy Jenkins begins with acknowledgement of the diversity of Anglicanism. In the Anglican church, he says, there 'is an understanding which affirms the rightness of their being a plurality of viewpoints ... embodied in a variety of institutions'.[119] Unlike Sykes and Avis, however, Jenkins is much readier to speak positively about the Anglican 'practice of achieving compromise' in the face of this plurality, noting that Anglicans 'tend to go for solutions that work, and allow a number of viewpoints to be expressed, even if they do not add up in theory'.[120] He recognizes that this might at times represent the kind of laziness that we have heard Sykes decry, but suggests that this is not the whole story: 'the English character oscillates', he says, 'between amoral pragmatism tempered only by indolence at one extreme, and principled plurality held together by conscious toleration at the other.'[121]

---

[116] Ibid., 39–40.
[117] Ibid., 6.
[118] Ibid., 160–2.
[119] Timothy Jenkins, *An Experiment in Providence: How Faith Engages with the World* (London: SPCK, 2006), 25.
[120] Ibid., 25, 27.
[121] Ibid., 27.

Like Sykes, Jenkins believes that the various strands of Anglicanism are held together by rightly ordered worship. In fact, his descriptions of this worship chime in some detail with Sykes's. Anglican liturgy, says Jenkins, 'offers a transforming structure' focused on the reading of scripture. We bring in to worship our attempts to form a common life together with others in the world. All of those attempts are offered up, reflected upon and judged in our worship, and especially as we read scripture together; and we go back out into the world ready to continue our work.[122] Sykes's account similarly focuses on the centrality of public reading of the scriptures in the vernacular, and on the way that this recollection of Christ provides means by which 'the intentions of the recollector are inwardly challenged, reoriented, and offered up'.[123] The liturgy is an engine for the judgement and remaking of lives.

For Jenkins, however, the Christian calling to worship God together, and to live together in ways judged and remade by our worship, 'is something that we *do* better than talk about, for good reason, for pursuing human flourishing and the worship of God are essentially practices, not theories'.[124] We normally work out how to live together in situ, and in practice, rather than by resolving our disagreements by means of argument and intellectual clarity.[125] In fact, Jenkins sees in the Anglican prioritizing of worship a rejection of the idea that we should order the Church's life by principle (or by magisterial authority); it involves the various different parties within the Church recognizing that 'holding together in a common human project is more important than their independent – and sometimes incompatible – claims to truth'.[126] Looking at the Church of England, we won't primarily find either a clear contestation of opposing views or a cumulative tradition of doctrinal deliberation, but a series of pragmatic experiments and settlements – and that, for Jenkins, is just as it should be.

Conclusion

As I said at the start of the chapter, this is a book about doctrine in the life of the church – but it is a book written in a specific context: the Church of England. That fact shapes my approach, in more ways than I will be able to identify or account for. I have thought through the topics of this book in conversation with people from many other contexts, but this Church of England context is my home, and its people are in a peculiar sense my people. I have therefore tried to tell, in very broad outline, the story of doctrinal deliberation in this Church.

---

[122] Ibid., 198, 202, 203.
[123] Sykes, 'Genius', 236; Sykes, *Identity*, 265.
[124] Timothy Jenkins, 'Anglicanism: The Only Answer to Modernity', in *Anglicanism: The Answer to Modernity*, ed. Duncan Dormor, Jack McDonald and Jeremy Caddick (London: Continuum, 2003), 195.
[125] Jenkins, 'Anglicanism', 201. Cf. Robert Boak Slocum, 'Introduction: A Practical and Balanced Faith', in *A Point of Balance*, ed. Percy and Slocum, 1–3, on being 'pragmatic and occasional'.
[126] Jenkins, 'Anglicanism', 191. 'More "principled" Christian Churches tend to regard this pragmatism with suspicion, and sometimes disdain' ('Anglicanism', 194).

I have suggested that there are reasons to be sceptical about the familiar claim that the genius of Anglicanism is shown in its unique 'moderation, balance, equipoise, and order', its capacious inclusion of multiple theological traditions, united by a common worship. That is, at best, a selective story. It leaves out both the exclusions by which this supposedly comprehensive coalition was created and the fractious uneasiness of the relationships within it. Nevertheless, to be heir to this history, and to the mythologized ways in which it has been told, is to be an heir to questions about the subordination of doctrinal discourse to other aspects of the Church's life, about the interrelationship between different doctrinal traditions and about the exercises of power involved in marking this life's boundaries.[127]

Doctrine and disagreement

Doctrinal theology is not one thing. In the history of the Church of England, the phrase 'doctrinal theology' could be used to name a number of different disciplines of thought, marked by complex similarities and differences. There is therefore no one answer to the question, 'What is the nature of doctrine?' It may be possible, in various parts of the church, to identify forms of doctrinal discourse that align with the definitions that I offered in Chapter 1. It may make sense to name them all as forms of 'doctrinal theology' (even if that is not the term used locally). But in each of those differing contexts, the discourse so named will be distinguished from other forms of theological and ecclesial discussion in different ways, with different levels of sharpness. It will be valued to different extents, and will be pursued in different contexts, by different personnel. It will have its own habits, its own styles, its own exemplars, its own libraries, its own syllabuses, its own forms of apprenticeship. All of these forms of doctrinal deliberation will be bound up with different ways of construing the story of the church.

Stephen Sykes suggested that these various traditions need to come to terms with one another – 'to face the issues of belief' that divide the church. His rhetoric suggests that to turn from cacophony to conversation requires little more than an act of will: a resolution to be serious. Yet this assumes that the traditions resemble one another enough for real argument to take place between them. The current state of debate in the Church of England suggests that this might be considerably too optimistic. It is simply not clear that there is enough of an agreement on criteria, on sources or on patterns of reasoning, to allow real argumentative engagement to take place. The problem we face is not indolence; it is our repeated discovery that we are speaking past one another, and don't know how to stop.

Paul Avis argued that there is a tradition of Anglican doctrinal deliberation sufficiently rich, and sufficiently authoritative, to provide the shared language that we need. It is enough, he believes, to ground a robust conversation about the future of the Church. Yet whatever the merits of his proposal as a prescription for how Anglican theology *should* work, it is not particularly helpful as a description of how Anglican

---

[127] Once again, I am not claiming that any of these questions is exclusive to the Church of England, nor that they are posed any more sharply here than elsewhere – simply that they are, in fact, posed here.

theology *does* work. Most of the texts that he cites as the key sources of the tradition are little known around the Church, little used by those who identify as Anglican theologians and little referenced even in the endless reports generated by and for the governing bodies of the Church. They do not, in practice, provide a set of common reference points anchoring the Church's debates – and they do not serve as the primers of a shared language.

In such a context, one set of questions about the nature of doctrinal disagreement rises to the surface. How deep do the differences between traditions of doctrinal theology in the Church go? What are we to do with the recognition that Christians differ not just in their doctrinal conclusions, but in the patterns of activity that they undertake in order to reach those conclusions? What kind of engagement, of argument, remains possible across such intractable differences?

Doctrine and life

As well as painting a picture of doctrinal diversity in the Church of England, this chapter has painted one in which worship has been granted a certain primacy in unifying the church, with doctrinal discourse in some way subordinated to it.[128]

It is far from clear, however, just how unifying the worship of the church is. The descriptions offered by Sykes and Jenkins are compelling, but it is not obvious that they do justice to the sheer variety of worship across the Church of England.[129] Even where authorized liturgies are adhered to (and that is no small qualification) the ways in which they are used and inhabited can diverge quite dramatically. The same liturgy may be used in different churches with very different effects. In one, it might provide a sparse framework surrounding the extended singing of worship songs taken to mediate an affective encounter with God. In another, it may be sung as the heart of an aesthetically gorgeous liturgical celebration. In yet another, it might provide the unadorned pathway for a daily walk of penitence and absolution.

More than that, the ways in which liturgy actually functions for particular communities and particular individuals depend upon the stories and constraints of each locality. It is hard for any generalized description to capture what happens in worship. Confident claims about what common patterns of worship enable, or of how they form people, or of what they mean to those who inhabit them, are often made in the absence of any serious work to discover whether the lives of any real participants match these descriptions.[130] How worship and doctrinal theology are entangled in the different traditions that make up the Church of England is a much more complex question than is sometimes suggested.

That tangled question is only one part of a larger question, however, about the ways in which the practices of doctrinal theology are woven into the wider patterns of

---

[128] I have chosen not to explore this topic by discussing the familiar *lex orandi, lex credendi* tag – on the ground that such discussions seldom deliver clarity. An exception is a recent article by Ashley Cocksworth, 'Theorizing the (Anglican) *lex orandi*: A Theological Account', in *Modern Theology* (forthcoming).

[129] Sykes is aware of this; see *Integrity*, 44–7.

[130] I am grateful to Jenny Leith for helping me think about this.

ordinary faithful life. We heard Sykes wanting to avoid the 'tyrannous use of intellectual power', by keeping doctrinal theology in its place. We heard Jenkins arguing that we are better at discovering how to live faithfully together than we are at talking about it, because 'pursuing human flourishing and the worship of God are essentially practices, not theories'. But where, exactly, does this leave explicit discussion of doctrine? What good can it properly do – and what roles should it be kept from playing – in the midst of ordinary faithful life?

Doctrine and exclusion

A third set of questions has emerged across the whole chapter. It is easy to focus on the broad range of voices that are included in the Church of England's debates. It is easy to think that it is in danger of collapsing into a free fall relativism in which, apparently, anything goes. It can be much harder to ask which voices are still excluded, and how firmly. Yet I have noted just how limited is the range of people whose voices have been audible in the 'identity of Anglicanism' debate in the past forty years. The three voices that I have highlighted earlier – or four, if you include my own – are representative of a debate that has been overwhelmingly White, male and middle class. In fact, the whole of this chapter has not been much better: public discussion of the identity and purpose of the Church of England historically, and academic commentary upon those discussions, has tended to be conducted by a very narrow band of people. If the 'means of judging matters concerning the faith are in the hands of the whole people of God', as Stephen Sykes insisted, what ought that to mean for the future of doctrinal theology in the church? What does it mean for the attitudes and practices of those engaged in doctrinal deliberation – and what does it mean for the structures within which their work takes place?

To begin answering all of these questions, it is important to ask one more cluster – and it is these that will finally tip us into Chapter 3. Where in the life of the Church of England does doctrinal deliberation actually happen? Who is involved in it, and where, and how? How do the different strands of activity interact, and to what extent is there anything like a common conversation, or shared discernment? To answer those questions, I need to shift register, and turn from telling the story of the Church of England's history to surveying its present shape.

3

Locating doctrine in the Church of England

Introduction

Doctrinal theology is threaded through the life of the Church of England. There are all kinds of activities in and around the Church in which people express, explore and inhabit claims about God and God's ways with the world. A rich description of all this activity is far beyond my reach, however, and not only because it would take a book much longer even than this. It is because it would take a battalion of ethnographic researchers, tracing all the ways in which doctrinal theology is woven in to the textures of the Church's life. No survey from a distance can hope to capture this well. In this chapter, therefore, I will content myself with pointing to some of the main locations in which doctrinal theology happens, indicating something of the character of what happens in those locations and of the connections between them, and suggesting some of the kinds of work that might be needed to explore them more fully.

My survey will run all the way from the doctrinal practices of ordinary believers to the formal doctrinal pronouncements of Church synods and commissions. Because that will be a journey that seems to take us from the inarticulate to the articulate, from the local to the national and from the laity to the episcopacy, it might be mistaken for a journey upwards, with the Church's real doctrinal theology sitting at the top. That is not, however, my intention. For reasons that I will explain in later chapters, I take the material with which I begin – the material of ordinary believing – to be the nucleus around which all the rest orbits. I approach all the other forms of doctrinal theology as support structures for (or sometimes hindrances to) ordinary believing. They are not the substantial reality of which ordinary believing is the shadow.[1]

---

[1] In terms of the framework proposed by Helen Cameron, Deborah Bhatti, Catherine Duce, James Sweeney and Clare Watkins in *Talking about God in Practice: Theological Action Research and Practical Theology* (London: SCM, 2010), 49–60, I am interested in both the 'espoused' and 'operant' theologies of ordinary believers (where the former is 'The theology embedded within a group's articulation of its beliefs' and the latter 'The theology embedded within the actual practices of the group') and their interactions with 'formal' and 'normative' theologies (the former being the theologies of the scriptures, creeds, official church teachings and liturgies, the latter the theology of theologians and dialogue with other disciplines – ibid., 54). I am interested in the entanglements and circulations between these voices, and the blurring of the lines between them.

Ordinary belief

Jeff Astley defines 'ordinary theology' as 'the theology and theologizing of Christians who have received little or no theological education of a scholarly, academic or systematic kind'.[2] It has to do with the 'resources of meaning and spiritual strength' that Christians deploy, 'enabling them to cope and even flourish, day to day, as they face and live their lives, and then eventually face and live their deaths. Be it ever so inchoate, unsystematic and even confused, ordinary theology is a theology to live by.'[3] Astley notes the forms in which ordinary theology is most often expressed. It 'is more likely to be aphoristic and anecdotal, autobiographical and unsystematic; and rich in affect-freighted story and metaphor. Its models have not yet been qualified, shaped and clarified to any great extent, so as to create concepts apt for drawing inferences and creating systems, as in more academic forms of theology.'[4] He also notes the locations in which it is found. It 'is learned in the home and the street, and in the workplace, pub and playground. It is, however, articulated somewhat rarely, and often only when conversations in these non-Church, everyday settings take a deeper, more personal and more serious turn.'[5] I will be presenting my own account of the nature of belief in Chapter 6, and will not draw such a sharp line between the ordinary and the academic, or Church and non-Church settings, but Astley's description nevertheless provides a helpful starting point.

The bible and lay people

Precisely because it appears in the forms and locations that Astley names, investigating ordinary belief is challenging. One approach, the quantitative, can be illustrated by the work of Andrew Village. Between 1999 and 2001, Village distributed a questionnaire to eleven different Anglican churches in eight benefices, covering a mixture of anglo-catholic, evangelical and broad traditions. He received 404 responses.[6]

The questionnaire was designed to capture people's beliefs about the bible – about its importance, authority and inerrancy. It also assessed the dogmatism with which those beliefs were held, by assessing people's willingness to sign up to dismissive statements about opposing views. Village constructed a scale that allowed him to arrange people from conservative to liberal in terms of their stated beliefs about the bible. That measure correlated well with the theological tradition of their church (with those attending

---

[2] Jeff Astley, *Ordinary Theology: Looking, Listening and Learning in Theology* (London: Routledge, 2002), 56.
[3] Jeff Astley, 'Ordinary Theology as Lay Theology: Listening to and Learning from Lay Perspectives', *Marriage, Families & Spirituality* 20, no. 2 (2014): 182–90; a pre-published manuscript is available at humanities.exeter.ac.uk/media/universityofexeter/collegeofhumanities/theology/centreforbiblicalstudies/Astley_2014_preprint_INTAMS_2018290.pdf (accessed 30 November 2019) – and my page numbers are for that version. The quote just given is from pp. 3–4.
[4] Ibid., 4.
[5] Ibid., 5.
[6] Andrew Village, *The Bible and Lay People: An Empirical Approach to Ordinary Hermeneutics* (Aldershot: Ashgate, 2007). 'Broad' includes those who called themselves 'traditional Anglican' or 'middle of the road'.

evangelical churches likely to be most conservative, those attending anglo-catholic churches least). It did not correlate with church attendance or frequency of bible reading across the sample as a whole (though it did within evangelical churches). There was some correlation with education: a higher level of formal education was associated with more liberal views. People at both the conservative and the liberal ends of the spectrum tended to be more dogmatic, compared to those in the middle.[7] Village's analysis was able to show that people's views correlated not only with their present church context but with their previous church, that people's views about the bible seem to play some role in their sense of belonging in a particular congregation, and that a typical congregation doesn't function as a 'monolithic interpretative community'.[8]

Village dug deeper into views about 'biblical literalism' – that is, people's beliefs about the historical factuality of events portrayed in the bible. He discovered that the degree of someone's literalism was likely to be influenced by their general educational level as well as by their experience of specifically theological education. 'Decisions about whether or not an event happened appeared to be based on a combination of general doctrinal belief about the Bible, the plausibility of the event and the doctrinal weight associated with it,' he found. 'It seems', he concluded, 'that churchgoers apply a sophisticated reasoning to biblical events, which takes into account ... what is at stake in taking it as fiction rather than as history.'[9]

Ordinary Christology

Quantitative work like this, when handled with the sophistication that Village brings to the task, is good at exposing correlations and trends. It is much more limited in its capacity to show how those beliefs are shaped, how they are expressed and how they function for particular individuals, or in individual communities.[10] A more qualitative

---

[7] Andrew Village, 'Assessing Belief about the Bible: A Study among Anglican Laity', *Review of Religious Research* 46, no. 3 (2005): 243–54.

[8] Village, *The Bible and Lay People*, 137, 142.

[9] Andrew Village, 'Factors Shaping Biblical Literalism: A Study Among Anglican Laity', *Journal of Beliefs & Values* 26, no. 1 (2005): 29, 35.

[10] It is worth comparing Village's work with the ethnographic work undertaken by Andrew Rogers in two non-Anglican contexts. Rogers looks more closely, for instance, at how 'congregational tradition' might shape individuals' approaches to the bible: 'This shaping might be in terms of guiding one's interpretation, of providing interpretive emphases, or through providing boundaries to possible interpretation.' (Andrew P. Rogers, *Congregational Hermeneutics: How Do We Read?* (London: Routledge, 2016), 90.) He looks at the influence of sermons, songs, liturgies and the public display of biblical texts; at house groups and personal bible study; at 'visiting preachers, friends and family outside the congregation, songs, general Christian books, Bible-related books (including study Bibles), Bible study guides, personal Bible reading aids, other churches, parachurch agencies, Christian events, Bible-related courses' (141, capitalization altered). See also the work of Cherryl Hunt, who explored how a range of resources produced by the Bible Society was received and used in a number of congregations. See Cherryl Hunt, 'Be Ye Speakers of, and Listeners to, the Word: The Promotion of Biblical Engagement through Encountering the Scriptures Read Aloud', *The Expository Times* 129, no. 4 (2018): 149–57; 'Seeing the Light: Ordinary Christians Encountering the Bible through Video', *The Expository Times* 129, no. 7 (2018): 307–16; and 'People of the Book? Responses to the Bible as "Big Story" or "Drama"', *The Expository Times* 130, no. 8 (2019): 337–44. See also her PhD, *Promoting Biblical Engagement among Ordinary Christians in English Churches: Reflections on the Pathfinder Project* (University of Exeter, 2016).

approach can be illustrated by the work of Ann Christie. Between 2002 and 2006 she conducted forty-five semi-structured interviews with people from four Anglican churches – all rural congregations in North Yorkshire.[11] She was interested in 'ordinary Christology', and asked her interviewees questions about Jesus's pre-existence, divinity, humanity, virgin birth and miracles.

She met with some reluctance or resistance from her interviewees. Most of them were happy to recite creeds as part of the liturgy, and to declare to her that they believed them – but they had little if anything to say when asked what various phrases from those creeds meant.[12] Quoting a phrase from one of her interviewees, she says that 'The cognitive content of many people's faith is "very vague".'[13] 'Many openly admitted that they were not interested in exploring their beliefs about Jesus or about God, and they did not want to subject their religious beliefs to scrutiny or enquire too closely into the grounds for believing.'[14] They were suspicious of questions and concepts that they heard as being 'academic'.[15] And even that is not the full story: 'It has to be admitted that the story of Jesus may not be that significant a story for every Christian. There are enough hints in the data to suggest that some people do not actually pay that much attention to it.'[16]

When her interviewees did respond more fully, it tended to be by telling stories. 'A few people tell the story of the pre-existent Son becoming incarnate to save us by his atoning death; many more people tell us the story of God creating Jesus, his Son, to show us how to live. It is always a story that is told; ordinary Christology is *story-shaped*.'[17] Her interviewees, she found, hardly think of Jesus 'in abstract or philosophical categories at all, but as a person whose identity and significance is given by the story', and they respond to that story 'primarily in an affective mode'.[18]

Christie's findings are rich and fascinating. They are, however, limited by her method, as she acknowledges and explains. She measured her interviewees' responses against the categories of the articulate Christian tradition and of academic reflection upon it. She divided them, for instance, into those (the majority) who have primarily functional christologies, and those (the minority) whose christologies are ontological.[19] Much of the time, the picture she paints of her respondents highlights their heterodoxy, what they don't believe or what they aren't able to express. She paints the silhouette these ordinary believers cast when the lamp of articulate systematic theology is turned upon them.

---

[11] Ann Christie, *Ordinary Christology: Who Do You Say I Am?* (Aldershot: Ashgate, 2012), 17.
[12] Ibid., 163–5.
[13] Ibid., 175.
[14] Ibid., 153.
[15] Ibid., 155.
[16] Ibid., 183–4. In an essay in *The Modern Churchman* in 1921, Arthur Walker claimed that 'the average Englishman … believes that Jesus Christ once really lived on this earth. He admires and venerates that life; he also believes that the less we say about Jesus Christ the better.' ('The Creed of the Average Englishman', *Modern Churchman*, 11, no. 8 (1921): 409.)
[17] Christie, *Ordinary Christology*, 149, emphasis in original. Cf. Abby Day, *Believing in Belonging: Belief and Social Identity in the Modern World* (Oxford: Oxford University Press, 2011), 158.
[18] Christie, *Ordinary Christology*, 150, 159; cf. 174.
[19] Ibid., 26–31, 33–76, esp. 55–60.

The interview situation is, of necessity, artificial. For thirty of the interviewees, Christie was someone they knew as their vicar's wife. In the interview context, however, she appeared in the guise of an academic researcher. She stepped out of the world that she shared with them, their ordinary modes of interaction and conversation, and asked questions that did not live in that world. Many of her interviewees registered the mismatch, some with a degree of discomfort.[20]

Christie is aware of all this, but it still shapes her account in complex ways. She explores, for instance, the different soteriological imaginations displayed by her subjects.[21] At one point, she asks them to comment on some of the language they regularly encounter in the liturgy – sentences like, 'Lord, by your cross and resurrection you have set us free.' 'When asked to comment on such language, however, most are at a loss and are unable to make any further theological comment, beyond repeating the set phrases given by the tradition or saying, "I just accept that", as if the discourse was self-explanatory.'[22] She says both that 'There is no explicit theology of atonement or salvation here' and that 'This group's theology is hidden and not readily available for inspection. They have great difficulty articulating their soteriological beliefs.'[23] The ability to provide an articulate explanation of liturgical language is here the main measure of belief – and when they lack that ability, it is hard for Christie to say much at all about her subjects' theology.

At one point in his discussion of ordinary theology, Astley says that 'Ordinary theology's voice lies closer to the "earthbound, housebound", "mother tongue" of conversations within relationships, to steal a metaphor form the novelist Ursula Le Guin, than it does to the "father tongue" of one-way communications and apparently disinterested analyses which, Le Guin argues, one has to go to college fully to learn.'[24] The 'mother tongue', in Le Guin's description, is the language of ordinary interactions and conversations, a language used for negotiating the world of relationships and ordinary labour, for 'the art of making order where people live'.[25] In these terms, we could say that in many research interviews (and questionnaires), speech in the mother tongue is measured against the categories employed in the father tongue. That is, it is measured against the language of clearly ordered concepts, of apparently contextless and impersonal distinctions – and it is either validated there or judged lacking. Built into this technique, despite the sensitivity of the interviewer, there seems to be something of what has been called the 'masculine gaze' – 'the masculinity of the "proper" interview', privileging 'such values as objectivity, detachment, hierarchy and "science"', as Ann Oakley put it (and we might in our context substitute 'systematic theology' for 'science').[26] We are caught, here, in a set of mutually reinforcing binaries:

---

[20] Ibid., 27–8.
[21] Ibid., 93–147.
[22] Ibid., 101–2.
[23] Ibid., 102.
[24] Astley, 'Ordinary Theology as Lay Theology', 5, referring to Ursula K. Le Guin, 'Brin Mawr Commencement Address', in *Dancing at the Edge of the World: Thoughts on Words, Women, Place* (New York: Grove, 1989), 147–60.
[25] Le Guin, 'Brin Mawr Commencement Address', 154.
[26] Ann Oakley, 'Interviewing Women: A Contradiction in Terms', in *Doing Feminist Research*, ed. H. Roberts (London: Routledge and Kegan Paul, 1981), 40, 38. See also Oakley, 'Interviewing

intellectual versus emotional, critical versus naive, articulate versus inarticulate, explicit versus hidden, sophisticated versus simple – and those are binaries that, in our culture, are never very far from the further binaries of male versus female, White versus Black, chattering classes versus lumpen proletariat.

What is needed as a supplement to investigations like Christie's and Village's is therefore work that explores the talk about Jesus, the thoughts about Jesus, the affective responses to speech, events and artefacts associated with Jesus, that come naturally to her interviewees, and the patterns of life within which all of these occur. Christie notes that ordinary Christology is story-shaped, because her people regularly gave responses in the interview situation that had a narrative shape. But how and where in ordinary life do they employ this capacity to put narratives together? How varied is the repertoire of narratives they are able to deploy? What role does the consumption and production of these stories play for them? More generally, what role does thought, speech and action related to Jesus play in the forming of their lives, individually and together? That is what we need to know, to get a firmer handle on ordinary Christology.

The religious lives of older laywomen

An example of work that shows how we might try to answer this kind of question is provided by Abby Day, and her study of 'the religious lives of older laywomen'. Day worshipped and worked alongside a community of Anglican laywomen, born in the 1920s and 1930s and so in their eighties and nineties by the time she wrote. She undertook the study over two years, in 'one mainstream Anglican church in southern England' ('more mainstream than evangelical'), with a congregation of 'thirty to forty regulars'.[27] She attended services and mid-week events, went along to socials of various kinds, helped keep the church open and joined the cleaning rota.

The women who are the focus of Day's study are very active in the life of their church. 'They attend the mainstream churches every Sunday, polish the brasses, organize fundraisers, keep the church open on weekdays, bake cakes, and visit vulnerable people in their homes.' They engage in 'Bible study and discussion, praying for people, and participation in specific rituals'. They are also 'teachers, lay preachers, readers, biblical scholars and activists' – even if not always in the most visible of ways.[28]

They worship, and not just because it provides a respite from their labours, a pause in which they can watch 'the men perform work for a change'.[29] Their participation in these services, their recitation of the prayers, and singing of the hymns, even their listening to the sermons, are parts of a form of spirituality that is 'embodied, practised, implicit, and deeply pleasurable', and shaped by sometimes surprising intensities of affective religious experience.

Women Again: Power, Time and the Gift', *Sociology* 50, no. 1 (2016): 195–213. Cf. Pierre Bourdieu, 'The Scholastic Point of View', in *Practical Reason: On the Theory of Action*, trans. Loïc Wacquant (Cambridge: Polity, 1998), 132.

[27] Abby Day, *The Religious Lives of Older Laywomen: The Last Active Anglican Generation* (Oxford: Oxford University Press, 2018), 9, 15.

[28] Ibid., 8, 93, 92.

[29] Ibid., 114.

They pray, and on the whole they pray about ordinary, domestic things, about friends and families, quotidian tragedies and delights. 'Prayer is a form of emotional labour and, like most emotional work, it is usually assigned to women in a society structured through a gendered allocation of responsibility for care, moral integrity, housework, and religious transmission.'[30]

These women also tend God's house, especially by cleaning.[31] As Day joins the cleaning teams, she discovers that their work is a spiritual practice. '[E]fficiency, outputs, and measurements were not their organizing principles … team cleaning was an act of communion, meditation, and belonging … we were one body, a family, joined in our shared beliefs and practices of cleanliness and purity, performed through our physical bodies.'[32] While cleaning, the women are indwelling bodily habits of belonging, they are building and securing relationships, and they are marking out and honouring sacred space. They 'were not only cleaning the church and its sacred objects, but purifying and protecting a certain kind of religion.'[33] They are engaged, precisely, in Le Guin's 'art of making order where people live'.

In the midst of all this, they believe. Their believing is one part of the life that they order together in this way. They recite the creeds, for instance, and they do so seriously; they regard the words 'as non-negotiable instructions from their Lord'.[34] There is no reason to think that they would be more articulate than Christie's interviewees, if asked to explain what these credal words meant. But their reciting of creeds and prayers, their singing of hymns, their discussion of the bible, all the more explicit bits of their Christian believing, are ingredients in a life with a definite shape to it. Those words help structure that life, and are given meaning by it. Within that life, these women know how to go on speaking about and to God in ways that make sense to them; they know how to go on asking and thanking and blessing; they know how to go on being the Lord's followers.

If one asks what sense they make of the credal words that they recite, the answer to that question is not likely to emerge at the level of explicit articulation, but by looking at how these words, and the women's saying of them, fit into the broader pattern of their lives: their reading of gospel stories, their teaching of children, their praying, their taking care of the altar. It is, in other words, in the webs of connections holding this pattern of life together that we will see what they make of the creeds.

It remains possible, of course, to ask about the connections between all this and the sense that academic theologians make of these claims: the articulate knowledge that we generate and disseminate about the origins of these words that the women recite, about the role that they have played in the debates of the church, about why they mattered enough to get into our liturgies. We can ask about those connections, but we don't need to define ordinary belief primarily by its lack of or difference from this articulate knowledge. We can, first, learn to see what sense it makes in its own terms.

---

[30] Ibid., 103.
[31] Ibid., 51–2, 73–8.
[32] Ibid., 74.
[33] Ibid., 78, 89, 91.
[34] Ibid., 91.

I don't want to fall into the trap of taking Day's rich and careful account of these older Anglican laywomen and turning it into an emblem of pre-reflective religious purity. That would, in a wearyingly familiar way, leave all those deadening binaries in place. It would value this precisely as a form of emotional, naive, inarticulate, simple and implicit female spirituality in such a way as to leave me, the male observer, in possession of all the territory that counts as intellectual, critical, articulate, sophisticated and explicit. To erode those binaries, I want to suggest that the life that Day explores is not especially innocent; that the kinds of affective, implicit, inarticulate belief she finds there will resemble the character that belief has everywhere, including among the unusually articulate; and that the processes that mark articulate belief – processes of discussion, teaching and disagreement – are already present here among these women.

So, first, the pattern of life that Day describes is not an especially innocent one. It is not somehow free from conflicts and from patterns of power and exclusion. Day shows that the pattern of life that these women help sustain is one that reinforces male clerical power; she shows how they have gatekeeping practices that are tied to hierarchies of respectability.[35] Theirs is a pattern of life that works for those with settled addresses, living in the same town year after year. It works for people who (however marginalized and patronized they might be) are able to imagine this church to be their own because they have not been made to feel that they do not belong by the church's teaching and habits.[36]

Second, I am not claiming that real believing is happening in this enclave as it is not elsewhere. I am claiming that believing everywhere has something like the lived texture we see here. I don't mean that one can generalize easily from Day's study. It is gender-specific, it is age-specific; it is probably (though Day says less about this) tradition-specific.[37] To broaden this into a fuller picture, one would need not to generalize but to conduct multiple such case studies. My suggestion, however – one to which I will return in Chapters 5 and 6 – is that wherever one looks, even if one looks at the believing in which atypically articulate people like academic theologians are involved, one will find that most of anyone's believing is inarticulate, that it is affectively charged and shaped, and that it is bound up in more ways than we realize with the practical patterns of life that it helps sustain.

My third claim is that it is not possible to draw a neat divide between the spaces in which inarticulate ordinary believing takes place and the spaces in which articulation takes place. We can't, for instance, divide the world of belief up into the space of passive female spirituality and the space of active male rationality. Activities of learning and teaching, explaining and exploring, questioning and challenging happen wherever believing is found. To put it another way: those engaged in ordinary believing are always exercising agency in the reception, arrangement and transmission of their faith. And more than that, their agency in these regards is not isolated, but is part of much wider networks of engagement and conversation around which processes of articulation and exploration circulate – and these circulations stretch all around the church and out into the world.

---

[35] Ibid., 108–13, 152–4, 80–1, 198.
[36] See Day's discussion of race, in ibid., 156–7.
[37] Her women seem to be somewhere on the anglo-catholic side of 'middle of the road', in Anglican party terms.

Circulations

Day does talk about her subjects' worship, spirituality and belief, but she says little about the content of their speech about God and God's ways with the world, or about the ways in which the specifics of this speech helps to hold in place their pattern of life. She says still less about how these habits of speech might be informed by the women's responses to the preaching they encounter in church, or to the liturgies in which they participate, or to the content of the books they read, or to any of the other sources of articulate theology that they encounter.

Yet ordinary believers do think and speak about God, these ways of thinking and speaking do help shape their patterns of life, and this thought and speech and action are learnt from all manner of sources. They are learnt by means of informal conversations, patterns of pastoral care, prayers written and extemporized, hymns ancient and modern, sermons of varying lengths and styles, and the measured words of liturgy. They are learnt in house groups, bible study groups, lent groups, advent groups and confirmation classes, from their participants and their leaders and the resources they use.[38] They are learnt in personal bible study, including from bible study notes. They are learnt from magazines, and websites, and devotional books.[39] They are learnt online, as people share bible verses, ask for prayer, blog their religious experiences and thoughts, express thanks to God, post devotional memes, get into conversations – and get into arguments.[40] They are learnt in Sunday schools and youth groups, from their participants and their leaders, and from the published guides or online resources that they use.[41] They are learnt by means of Godly Play, or the activities of Messy Church.[42] They are learnt from children's books, and from those who by reading them out loud bring them to life. I have a hunch, for instance, that Nick Butterworth and Mick Inkpen's *Stories Jesus Told*, or Leslie Francis and Nicola Slee's Teddy Horsley books, has done more to shape Christian belief in the UK than any book for grown-ups could hope to do.[43]

The sources of ordinary belief go far beyond this, however. Consider the factors that might shape what churchgoers take from their weekly reciting of the words 'Our Father'. They will probably have learnt what to make of this phrase, and how to live with it, from its liturgical surroundings, from other prayers and songs and from the

---

[38] Cf. the Archbishops' First Committee of Inquiry, *The Teaching Office of the Church* (London: SPCK, 1919), 28–9, which describes the many contexts in which teaching takes place from bible classes and summer schools, to diocesan lectures and libraries. The report also bemoaned 'the apparent reluctance of the Church to give even the instructed laity sufficient responsibility in the work of teaching' (ibid., 19).

[39] For a rich study of one genre of magazine, see Jane Platt, *Subscribing to Faith? The Anglican Parish Magazine 1859-1929* (Basingstoke: Palgrave Macmillan, 2015).

[40] See, for instance, Twitter, *passim*.

[41] See, for instance, *Daily Bread*, www.scriptureunion.org.uk/ecards/dailybread/index.html (accessed 30 November 2019).

[42] See www.godlyplay.uk, www.messychurch.org.uk (accessed 30 November 2019).

[43] Nick Butterworth and Mick Inkpen, *Stories Jesus Told* (London: Marshall Pickering, 1994); Nicola M. Slee, Leslie J. Francis and Ferelith Eccles Williams, *The Windy Day: Teddy Horsley Celebrates Pentecost on Whit Sunday* (London: Collins, 1983). There are many other Butterworth and Inkpen bible stories, and many other Teddy Horsley stories.

scriptures. Their imagination is also likely to have been affected, however, and perhaps painfully, by the way that gender is negotiated in the surrounding culture, as well as in the church. It might have been affected, even more disastrously, by their experience of an abusive father or father figure, or by their knowledge of the abuse suffered by others. On the other hand, it might also have been shaped by all the ways in which they have learnt to imagine what it is to be good parents. That in turn is likely to have been shaped by their experience of other people's families, discussions of parenting in school, depictions of parents in Jane Austen adaptations and episodes of *The Simpsons*, discussions in opinion pieces in newspapers and online magazines, and in any number of other ways. It will have been shaped in countless ways by the worshipper's political, economic and cultural context. If we want to understand ordinary believing, we can't restrict attention to what happens in the church, or to what happens in the world of organizations and industries directly engaged with the life of the church. Believing does not happen in isolation.[44]

Ordinary believers are far from being passive recipients of all that comes from these sources, however. Consciously and unconsciously, they adapt what they hear and see, they make their own sense of it, they discover their own ways of inhabiting it and putting it to use. And then, in turn, they pass it on, and the uses they make of what they receive make a difference to the flows of teaching and learning that circulate around and beyond the church. Ordinary believing is caught up in a circulatory system, a complex network of arteries, veins and capillaries by which teaching moves.

A Parochial Church Council meeting

Consider, for instance, my experience in a Parochial Church Council meeting, just a few weeks ago, in which we discussed our church's annual contribution to diocesan funds – the 'parish share'. That discussion illustrates the ways in which ordinary believers speak about God and God's ways with the world, and how that speaking can shape their own lives and the life of their communities.

One member talked about how we are meant to be a generous church; she used familiar language about freely receiving and freely giving, and told an equally familiar story about this particular church's history, and the gifts that we have received. Someone else responded with a comment about being good stewards of the resources we have. A third talked about trust (in the face of budget deficits). Unlike some such financial conversations, this one was amicable, and eventually led to a consensual decision – but even so, all kinds of things were going on in it. To tell the story of that one meeting well, one would need to talk about the key personalities in the room, and the history of their relationships; about rival tellings of this church's history and about who acts as the keeper of those stories; about differing perceptions of the diocese, and the anecdotes and adjectives that crystallize them; about the changing financial fortunes of the parish

---

[44] Cf. Ward, *How the Light Gets In*, 4. Jennifer Leith, in *Between Church and World: Anglican Formation of Christian Political Identity* (PhD thesis, Durham University, 2020), presents a rich account of Christian formation as (necessarily and rightly) taking place simultaneously in the church and in the world. See also Christian Scharen, in *Public Worship and Public Work: Character and Commitment in Local Congregational Life* (Collegeville, MN: Liturgical Press, 2004), 221–2.

– and so on. Woven in with all of that, however, and helping to shape it, are these skilfully deployed theological claims – claims about giving, about stewardship and about trust.

The skill involved in making these interventions in the debate is likely to have been sustained and resourced in part by worship, and by the reading of scripture within worship. The language about 'freely receiving and freely giving', for instance, is scriptural (it echoes Mt. 10:8, in various translations like the Authorized and New International Versions, though not the Revised Standard Version or the Good News Bible); that language has been repeated and reinforced in hymns and songs (such as 'God forgave my sin in Jesus' name'[45]), and driven home in a score of sermons. The person who used it may well have heard others use it in other meetings, and have consciously or unconsciously been imitating, or improvising upon, that usage. And what has been learnt by all these means is not simply a phrase, nor even an idea: it seems to be a shape of thought, imagination and feeling that can be drawn on and put to use in all kinds of situations.

This kind of thing is happening all the time around the church. It is quite ordinary, and yet it is by actions like this that the day-to-day business of the church's life, our negotiations with our context and our resources, even our negotiation of the structures of power within which our communities sit, are woven in with the Christian story, and we make fresh sense of the Christian story in relation to those negotiations.

Inside Alpha

A second example can illustrate the ways in which ordinary believers are far from being passive recipients of the teaching that they receive. It comes from one of the contexts in which huge numbers of people have learnt about Christian faith in recent decades: an evangelistic or discipleship course, like Pilgrim, Simply Christianity or Christianity Explored.[46] The most famous of these is the Alpha Course, developed at Holy Trinity Brompton. The first version ran in 1976, though it went through several revisions before being launched to a wider public in 1993. The course has now been translated into 112 different languages, and has run in 169 countries; thousands of courses run every year in the UK, tens of thousands worldwide.[47]

Alpha is intended for non-Christians, new Christians and those wanting to 'brush up on the basics'.[48] Groups meet for a meal, for worship, for a talk (which may include one of the Alpha videos) and for discussion. After an introductory session, there is a programme of ten sessions running from 'Who is Jesus?' to 'What about the Church'?

---

[45] Carol Owens (1972), Bud John Songs.
[46] For a list and description of several of these courses, see Richard Barrett, *Enquirers' Courses* (Diocese of Lichfield, 2016), cofelichfield.contentfiles.net/media/documents/document/2016/12/Enquirers_Courses_2016.pdf (accessed 30 November 2019). At the time of writing, much of the material on the 'What We Believe' pages of the Church of England's website is based on the Pilgrim Course – www.churchofengland.org/our-faith/what-we-believe (accessed 30 November 2019).
[47] James Heard, *Inside Alpha: Explorations in Evangelism* (Eugene, OR: Wipf and Stock, 2012), 15–17, 21.
[48] Ibid., 35.

There is also, in the middle, a weekend away that focuses on the Holy Spirit.[49] James Heard, who has written a book-length analysis of the Alpha phenomenon, says that 'the ethos and theology of the course is firmly within the Charismatic–Evangelical tradition. … Particular doctrines … within this tradition include a rationalist apologetic, penal substitution, *sola scriptura* and the perspicuity of the Bible, a life changing encounter with the Holy Spirit which brings assurance of faith, and a minimalist ecclesiology.'[50]

It would be easy, particularly given the way in which Alpha is marketed as a package with a predetermined shape, style and content, to analyse it simply as a means by which this doctrinal content is communicated – a flow outwards from an affluent London centre. Heard's analysis, based on participant observation in six courses from 2004 to 2005, shows that the reality is much more interesting.

First of all, Alpha does not simply teach ideas, but ideas that are embedded in a form of life. The course invites people into, and to a certain extent trains them in, that form of life. They are inducted into patterns of embodied relationship and behaviour, as much as taught doctrinal content – and form and content can't easily be separated.

Second, Heard explores the ways in which the doctrinal teaching provided on Alpha is not simply listened to and accepted, but processed and adapted as it is internalized. Heard suggests that this process involves a number of social–psychological factors, such as people's desire to belong to community (and therefore the relationship between the course community and their existing involvements), and their need to deal with loss and trauma or respond to other emotional needs (and therefore the relationship between the narrative offered in the course and their personal histories). It also involves a complex interaction between the materials of the course and the (multiple, overlapping) plausibility structures that people bring with them – an interaction deeply shaped by the social context provided by the course. Information, explanation and argument play a role in all this, but they are not themselves the dominant factors, and the transmission of ideas is not the best model for what is going on. Rather, the participants are engaged in building for themselves emotionally and intellectually habitable shelters from the materials presented to them – and Heard shows that they are both selective and creative in what they take from the course.[51]

Selling worship

A third example can illustrate how this kind of selective and creative agency helps to shape the wider circulations within which ordinary believing sits. One of the most powerful forces shaping how people imagine and inhabit their faith is the singing of hymns and songs. It might be tempting to think that one can simply look at the lyrics in order to determine what doctrine is being taught, learnt and expressed by this singing – and that there is therefore a simple flow from songwriters to singers.

---

[49] Ibid., 36–54.
[50] Ibid., 58–9.
[51] Ibid., 151–75, 179.

The relationship is, however, messier than that, as Pete Ward demonstrates in *Selling Worship* and other works.[52]

In corporate singing, worshippers are invited to inhabit a space defined by the words, the music and the setting, liturgical, social and physical. They are invited to inhabit it bodily (adopting certain postures and demeanours), to take on patterns of emotion, and to take on modes of expression. They are often invited to place themselves into a narrative or into an envisaged relationship. They are invited into particular relationships of power, particular attitudes to leadership and particular ways of imagining the boundary of the worshipping community. All of this can be part of taking on and maintaining a whole form of life.

Just as with the Alpha example, however, there is agency in this 'taking on'. People actively weave together what the song offers them with what they already know and do. People adapt every element of what they are offered: they choose different songs, they sing the same song differently, they skip verses, they alter words, they orchestrate the music differently, they adopt different postures. And although much of that might be directly in the hands of worship leaders, musicians, choral directors and clergy, those people will often (consciously and unconsciously) be responding to feedback from the rest of the worshipping congregation – everything from the enthusiasm with which a particular song is sung or the body language displayed to critical comments made after a service. All of those acts – of leaders and congregations – then play their own small role in patterns of interactive production, consumption and feedback that stretch far beyond the individual congregation. Ultimately, they shape the publishing patterns of the worship music industry, they shape hymnals, they shape the ways in which worship leaders are trained, they shape career paths and patterns of volunteering.

In the midst of all this, people are learning, and working out how to inhabit, ways of imagining God and God's ways with the world, and they are negotiating their relationship to the explicit doctrinal teaching that they have received. In his most recent work, for instance, Pete Ward has described how in evangelical Christianity in recent years there has been an evolving tension between a fairly consistent and clear form of doctrinal teaching – a presentation of Christ's death on the cross for the sins of the world, and of the repentance and faith by which the benefits of that death are appropriated – and a focus on faith as a personal, experiential relationship with Jesus, fostered by and articulated in worship songs.[53] Both sides of this tension are caught up in complex circulations of the kind I have been describing: particular kinds of cultural production (evangelistic tracts and talks on the one hand, for instance; worship songs on the other), particular sites of production and consumption (evangelistic missions; Christian festivals), and multiple interacting forms of agency. The story of ordinary believing is entangled with the story of all these circulations.

---

[52] Pete Ward, *Selling Worship: How What We Sing Has Changed the Church* (Bletchley: Paternoster, 2005); 'Affective Alliance or Circuits of Power: The Production and Consumption of Contemporary Charismatic Worship in Britain', *International Journal of Practical Theology* 9, no. 1 (2005): 25–39; and 'Spiritual Songs as Text: Genre and Interpretation', *Journal of Youth and Theology* 1, no. 1 (2002): 49–64. See also Martyn Percy, *Words, Wonders and Power: Understanding Contemporary Christian Fundamentalism and Revivalism* (London: SPCK, 1996).

[53] Pete Ward, *Liquid Ecclesiology: The Gospel and the Church* (Leiden: Brill, 2017), 101–80.

The life of ordinary believing

In sum, then, we can say that ordinary believing includes doctrinal speech: speech in which claims are made, directly or indirectly, about God and God's ways with the world. We can ask which claims are made, and where they are made, but to understand what people make of those claims, what those claims do for them and to them, we need to look at the whole life in which they are embedded and which they help to sustain. We need to look for the forms of growth and the patterns of relationship that this life involves, and at the exclusions and the gradients of power and privilege that mark it.

We also need to acknowledge that this believing life is not a static fact. It does not form an immobile culture with neat edges, with clear criteria defining what is inside and what out. It is always a life being dynamically reproduced by those who live it. They receive it, adjust it, inhabit it, subvert it and pass it on in ways that always involve a complex mix of passivity and agency. It will be marked by differential, perhaps very unequal, distributions of power, and by all kinds of exclusions and marginalization, but not by any simple division into active and passive.

Finally, we need to look at the ways in which this life is caught up in wide networks of production and consumption, of bricolage and feedback. We need to look at the networks of conversation and transmission that shape it. Here, too, we will find distributions of power; we will find flows of money and other forms of capital; we will find that belief is inescapably entangled with politics. If we want to understand what believers' doctrinal speech does to shape their own lives and the life of their churches, it is never enough to read off the content of that speech as though it were an isolated theological text. We need to understand its place in the making of a world.

Formal theological education

Ordinary believing, in all its complexity and dynamism, lies at the centre of my account of the life of doctrine. In the remainder of this chapter, I turn to some of the other contexts around the church in which we find doctrinal theology taking place, and I try to understand both what happens in each of those contexts and how it connects to the world of ordinary belief. I am interested in the ways in which these more formal and more visible forms of doctrinal theology reflect on or are otherwise shaped by ordinary belief, and how they in turn feed back into it – how they, too, might be ingredients in the circulations that surround and shape ordinary believing.

Some of the people involved in ordinary believing, and in the networks that shape it, acquire a formal theological education. That might simply mean that they read theological books; it might mean that they attend events like training days, clergy conferences and retreats. I am, however, thinking more particularly of those who undertake a lengthy programme of theological study, leading to an academic award or some other kind of certification. A wide range of people acquire this kind of formal theological education, and it can shape their participation in the life of ordinary believing in all kinds of ways, but it is most common among those who have some kind of recognized public ministry in the church. In particular, most clergy and accredited lay ministers gain this kind of formal theological education.

Formal theological education can therefore be understood as one of the networks of conversation and transmission that shape ordinary belief, alongside (and entangled with) the ones discussed in the previous section. Such education inducts people into a set of peculiarly intense conversations about the life of faith. It introduces them to a set of voices engaged in argument with one another – voices captured in the pages of books and articles, the voices of their own teachers and the voices of fellow students working to make sense of all this. It helps them learn something of the language that they need to participate in these conversations. It normally requires them to make their own contributions to these conversations, in written and spoken assignments. And it often asks them to think about what difference to the life of ordinary believing might be made by taking these voices seriously.

Such formal theological education tends to happen in specialized institutional settings, and in what follows I am going to focus on the two settings that I know best: the Church's Theological Education Institutions (TEIs) and those universities that offer courses in Christian theology.

Theological Education Institutions

The bulk of the Church of England's ordination training, and some of the training of its licensed lay ministers, is provided by a varied community of educational institutions. They range from traditional residential colleges to regional courses teaching at evening classes and weekends away. Some have hundreds of students, some only a handful. Some students are full-time, some part-time, some blend study and active ministry. In some, the Anglican ordinands are only one cohort alongside students from other churches, or students studying for other forms of ministry, or students studying for general interest and development. In some, all the programmes on offer are university-validated, leading to an academic award; on others, the validated programmes are only one part of a wider menu.[54]

There is no centralized curriculum for the programmes that the TEIs provide, but there is a framework of basic expectations. For instance, the Church of England expects those it ordains to 'understand Christian beliefs and practices: how they have developed in historical and cultural contexts and are interpreted today', to understand how they 'shape the moral life of individuals and communities', and 'to reflect critically on how Christian doctrine and ethics relate to discipleship, church and society'.[55] Most students, therefore, take some modules that focus, in one way or another, on doctrinal theology, but the precise content, the pedagogical approaches and the forms of assessment can all be very different from institution to institution.

---

[54] Most of the TEIs that train the Church of England's ordinands are validated by Durham University, and I need to declare an interest: together with my colleague Frances Clemson, I provide academic leadership for this validation partnership from the university side.

[55] *Formation Criteria with Mapped Selection Criteria for Ordained Ministry in the Church of England* (Church of England, 2014). Available online at www.churchofengland.org/sites/ default/files/ 2017-10/formation_criteria_for_ordained_ministry.pdf (accessed 30 November 2019).

Their teachers also understand the purpose of this aspect of their students' training in a variety of ways. In 2014, I sent out an informal questionnaire to these teachers as a discussion starter. The most common responses to a question about the purpose of studying doctrine was that it was important for shaping or informing Christian practice, or enabling theological reflection upon that practice. Some talked about the study of doctrine helping students to root themselves deeply in the faith they had inherited, or helping them to see how all that they were learning hung together. Some said that its core purpose was to deepen student's praise, and help them wonder at the glory of God. Others focused on the help it could provide students in communicating their faith to others. Some focused on enabling students to critique or question the faith they inhabited, and others on helping students understand how that faith had developed over time, and was still developing.[56] However different these expressions of purpose might be, the teaching of doctrinal theology in the TEIs is clearly intended to be a support structure for ordinary belief, and it is intended, one way or another, to induct students into a network of conversations, especially conversations with the wider church and with the church's past, that can inform and enrich ordinary belief.

In discussions of this work with students, teaching staff, sponsoring bishops and others, it is very common to run into questions about the relationship between the 'academic' and the 'formational' (or the 'academic' and the 'practical'). This is a rather mobile tension, and people can mean different things when they bring it up, but most often the word 'academic' is used to name an approach that values informational content or theory, the writing of lengthy essays, and explicit engagement with the articulate tradition (the forms of Christian reflection and discussion that have been written down, reproduced, and preserved in libraries). 'Formational' is used to name learning that is directly engaged with the demands of ministry and mission, that provides resources and habits and skills that students will need day by day, and that connects to the spirituality, the know-how and the patterns of understanding that they brought with them.[57]

---

[56] I am grateful to Marika Rose for helping with this questionnaire project, which was supported by a small grant from my university.

[57] For a small sample of pieces in which these debates are audible, see David Heywood, 'Educating Ministers of Character: Building Character Into the Learning Process in Ministerial Formation', *Journal of Adult Theological Education* 10, no. 1 (2013): 4–24, and my response in the same issue, 'Theological Education between the University and the Church: Durham University and the Common Awards in Theology, Ministry and Mission': 25–37; see two documents that were produced for the Common Awards partnership: *Preface to the Common Awards in Theology, Ministry and Mission* (2012), available online at www.churchofengland.org/sites/default/files/2018-07/Preface%20to%20the%20Common%20Awards%20in%20Theology%2C%20Ministry%20and%20Mission.pdf; and *A Vision for Theological Education in the Common Awards* (2016), available online at www.dur.ac.uk/theology.religion/common.awards/projects/theological.agenda/ (both accessed 30 November 2019), and see also Ian McIntosh, 'Formation in the Margins: The Holy Spirit and Living with Transitions in Part-Residential Theological Education', *Journal of Adult Theological Education* 11, no. 2 (2015): 139–49; Susannah Cornwall, 'Identity and Formation in Theological Education: The Occasion of Intersex', *Journal of Adult Theological Education* 12, no. 1 (2015): 4–15; Eeva John, Naomi Nixon and Nick Shepherd, 'Life-Changing Learning for Christian Discipleship and Ministry: A Practical Exploration', *Practical Theology* 11, no. 4 (2018): 300–14; Andrew Village, 'Does Higher Education Change the Faith of Anglicans and Methodists Preparing for Church Ministries through a Course Validated by a UK University?' *Practical Theology* 12,

Many different concerns and caricatures are in play when people speak about this tension, but at their heart is a persistent worry about the connection between the life of ordinary believing and the conversations into which formal theological education draws people. Students come into the TEI world as people already involved in belief, in all the senses discussed in the previous section: they participate in certain patterns of life, partly held in place by a variety of claims about God; they receive this life, adjust it, inhabit it, subvert it and pass it on; they are involved in various of the networks of conversation and transmission that surround it. Are the languages that they are made to learn in their TEIs, and the questions that they are made to ask, ones that enable them to speak about, to understand and to value their and their communities' believing lives – or are they in some sense turned away from ordinary belief? And does their induction into these conversations equip them with questions, ideas, patterns of imagination, and habits of attention and ongoing conversation that will, once they leave, plunge them more fully into the life of ordinary belief?

In my experience, TEI staff in general, including those who teach doctrinal theology, care deeply about these questions and work hard to answer them well. Many of the students who come through their classes are excited and inspired by what they learn, and find it deeply relevant to their ministry. Yet this question about the disconnect between the 'academic' and the 'formational' refuses to go away. In Chapter 5, I will try to explain why it might be so tenacious – and why it goes deeper than is reached by questions about how exciting or how relevant students find the teaching of doctrine to be. I will suggest that the possibility of a disconnect from the life of ordinary believing is built in to the very processes by which doctrinal theology works.

Theology in the universities

There are many connections between the world of TEIs and the world of university theology, but the latter is a distinct institutional space. That wasn't always the case. Theological teaching in the university sector used, in England, to be dominated by institutions with close ties to the Church of England, by teaching staff who were ordained and who moved jobs with ease between Church and university settings, and by students who were studying the subject with a view to ordained ministry or other church roles.

Over the past several decades, that landscape has changed. As a recent report from the British Academy says, 'While religious bodies still use universities for the validation of professional training, our universities are not seminaries and are no longer inextricably linked to the Church or reliant upon its financial or political support.'[58] Christian theology is now at most one strand among the multiple subdisciplines taught in departments of Theology and Religious Studies (TRS), or in

---

no. 4 (2019): 389–401, and Kirsten Birkett, 'The Theological Curriculum for Twenty-First Century Ministry: A UK Perspective', *Practical Theology* 12, no. 4 (2019): 402–14.

[58] The British Academy, *Theology and Religious Studies Provision in UK Higher Education* (London: 2019). Available online at www.thebritishacademy.ac.uk/sites/default/files/theology-religious-studies.pdf (accessed 30 November 2019). This quote is from the foreword by Roger Kain and Gillian Clark (p. 2).

other kinds of department or school where TRS is itself only one strand of activity among others.[59] Academic staff involved in TRS come from a wide range of religious backgrounds or none – though among the subdisciplines Christian theology and, to a lesser extent, biblical studies still attract high proportions of staff with some kind of Christian commitment. The denominational diversity of those staff members who do have a church involvement has increased substantially. It is rare to find members of academic staff who are ordained, though there are some, and there do remain a very few positions that are joint church/university appointments reserved for ordained applicants. Staff diversity – in relation to religious background, ethnicity, gender, class and disability – is increasing. TRS nevertheless in general remains one of the less diverse spaces in university life, and there are increasingly serious debates about the forms of exclusion that shape the discipline, and about how deep they go into our curricula, our pedagogies, our forms of organization and our institutional cultures.[60]

The students studying TRS at university have also become more diverse (though again, not in general as diverse as other student cohorts across the university). There is no requirement for students to have any kind of Christian or other religious commitment, though many still do in those departments that focus on Christian theology and history and on biblical studies. Very few students take a university TRS programme as part of a programme of training for ordained ministry, or any other kind of recognized ministry. On the whole TRS students go into similar careers after graduation to those chosen by graduates from any other humanities subject.[61]

Christian doctrinal theology – the exploration, critique, defence and elaboration of Christian claims about God and God's ways with the world – is one strand in the tapestry of TRS. Or, rather, it is one set of strands. It is taught in diverse ways, with

---

[59] TRS UK, a body that provides a forum for discussion between academic staff involved in TRS teaching and research, and (as its constitution says) 'To advocate for the academic study of religion with government, universities, and other relevant institutions and persons', defines 'academic study of religion' as follows: 'For the purposes of this constitution, "academic study of religion" shall include all academic disciplines concerned with the significance and meaning of religion and religions, incorporating fields of study such as theology, divinity and religious studies, in addition to sub-fields applying different theories and methods to the study of religions, such as the sociology or psychology of religion.' (TRS UK Constitution, no date. Available at trs.ac.uk/about-trs/ (accessed 30 November 2019).)

[60] 'Theology and Religious Studies has an ageing staff profile in universities which is predominantly white and male,' according to the BA report; the staff profile is older and much more male than other humanities subjects; 'Staff are also predominantly white, but the proportions of black and minority ethnic staff are more in line with all humanities and languages disciplines than they are for gender' (The British Academy, *Theology and Religious Studies Provision in UK Higher Education*, 4). Cf. Mathew Guest, Sonya Sharma and Robert Song, *Gender and Career Progression in Theology and Religious Studies* (Durham: Durham University, 2013). Available online at trs.ac.uk/wp-content/uploads/2013/11/Gender-in-TRS-Project-Report-Final.pdf (accessed 30 November 2019).

[61] Not everyone welcomed these shifts. E. L. Mascall, an ordained Anglican theologian whose career moved between ecclesiastical and university spaces from 1933 to 1973, spoke with horror in 1984 of it being 'often the boast of a theological faculty that it neither required not expected any religious profession for its members and that its courses could be followed as successfully by a student who believed that Christianity was the most degrading superstition that had ever enslaved mankind as by one for whom it was the sole means of salvation and the source of eternal felicity'. He found this intolerable in part because the work done in these faculties 'still appeared to be accepted by the authorities of the Church as providing the basis of the doctrinal formation of their ordinands'. (*Theology and the Gospel of Christ: An Essay in Reorientation* (London: SCM, 1984), xii.)

different subject matters, different kinds of disciplinary emphasis, different intellectual styles and different understandings of the relationship of the discipline to the life and discourses of the churches.[62] You could think of university-based doctrinal theology as consisting of a set of overlapping networks of intensive conversation. These networks often spread internationally (though they are mostly dominated by the North Atlantic world), and they often spread into other disciplines (with uneven levels of seriousness and reciprocity). In each of them, a different set of question will tend to be pushed with eccentric determination; a different library of resources will be the habitual recourse when people are caught up in argument; a different range of voices will be taken seriously (and a different range dismissed or patronized).

All of this activity sits alongside – often fairly cheerfully, and with complex overlaps and exchanges – other subdisciplinary clusters: biblical studies, philosophy of religion, the historical and the social scientific or anthropological study of religion and so on. Hence the most common single designation for the field as a whole is precisely TRS: theology *and* religious studies.[63] There are, nevertheless, some serious debates within doctrinal theology between approaches that depend upon explicit and disciplined attention to the patterns and politics of ordinary practice, and those for whom such explicit attention appears to be more peripheral.

As I have already said, the world of university-based doctrinal theology is no longer primarily a church space – one which the Church of England, and to an extent other churches, employed to conduct a portion of its intellectual business. There are, however, still numerous flows connecting the doctrinal work that goes on in the universities, the TEIs and the church. There is a flow of attention, as it becomes more common for those involved in doctrinal theology in the university and the TEIs to pay disciplined attention to ordinary believing and to the wider life of the churches. In the past, most university-based doctrinal theologians could think of themselves as writing from the church and for the church; those connections were givens. The growing visibility in doctrinal theological work of explicit and disciplined attention to the life of the church – of, say, reliance upon or engagement with ethnographic and other descriptive work – is perhaps an index of the separation that has taken place.[64]

Alongside this flow of attention, there is a flow of publications and other forms of academic dissemination. Thanks to the expectations now placed upon those holding research-active university posts, an incontinent flood of articles and books appears

---

[62] One way to map the complex range of possibilities here would be to examine the various annual conferences at which one might find doctrinal theology taking place (if one defines that term as widely as I have tried to do). One would need to attend (at least) the Society for the Study of Theology, the British and Irish Association of Practical Theology, the British Society for the Philosophy of Religion, the Ecclesiology and Ethnography conference, the Catholic Theological Association, the Society for the Study of Christian Ethics, the Societies for Old Testament and New Testament Studies and the British Association for the Study of Religions.

[63] See Ford and Higton, 'Religious Literacy in the Context of Theology and Religious Studies', 39–54.

[64] The work of the 'Ecclesiology and Ethnography' network illustrates this turn. See, for instance, Pete Ward (ed.), *Perspectives on Ecclesiology and Ethnography* (Grand Rapids, MI: Wm. B. Eerdmans, 2011), and Christian B. Scharen (ed.), *Explorations in Ecclesiology and Ethnography* (Grand Rapids, MI: Wm. B. Eerdmans, 2012).

every year, and some of them (a very few) find their way into the conversations that shape the life of the church.

More importantly, however, there is a flow of people. Some of that is simply a matter of Christian students whose involvement in the life of belief is somehow shaped by what they learn (though we don't know much about the impact of their studies upon their believing).[65] Some of it is a matter of individual members of the clergy who have acquired a very extensive formal theological education, and remain plugged in to academic discussions. Some of it, however, has to do with institutional connections. It is far less common than it once was for people to move from a university post to a church post or vice versa, or even to move between a university and a TEI, though it does happen. But doctrinal theologians working in university, TEI and church contexts often know each other, they meet at conferences and they are parts of the same intellectual networks. There is a web of informal engagement and exchange. More formally, some doctrinal theologians from the university sector get invited to speak from their academic expertise on a variety of church consultations and commissions. In the Church of England, there has been a noticeable long-term shift from a situation in which the bulk of the academic input in such contexts would come from priests and bishops who were also scholars, to one in which much of it is provided by lay academics. Questions about who gets invited, and on what grounds – about the messy intersections between academic and ecclesial power, and the problematic nature of both – are not often asked.

The world of university TRS can be thought of as a conversational space – a space in which a variety of diverse but overlapping intensive conversations are sustained. Various of the strands in the circulations of conversation and transmission that surround and shape the Church's life of belief flow through this space.

Ecclesiastical deliberation

In the last part of this chapter, I am going to turn to the more formal and visible contexts in and around the Church of England in which doctrinal deliberation and debate happens. Here, however, my attempt to sketch the patterns of circulation uniting the church's various practices of doctrinal theology to ordinary belief will falter. That is in part simply because there is a lack of research in this area: I have not, for instance, been able to find much to help me understand how the deliberations and decisions of General Synod are received around the church, and what difference they make to the life of ordinary belief. In part, however, it is because it is not clear how much circulation there actually is between these contexts and ordinary believing – how much what happens in the Church's various doctrinal commissions, for instance, either responds to or has an impact upon the life of ordinary belief. In the remainder of this

---

[65] Mathew Guest, Kristin Aune, Sonya Sharma and Rob Warner's *Christianity and the University Experience: Understanding Student Faith* (London: Bloomsbury, 2013) is about students studying any subject at university, but it does include some discussion of students studying TRS, and the impact it has on their faith; see, for example, p. 128.

chapter, therefore, I can only offer a series of vignettes, and indicate some of the ways in which the activity that I describe might be part of wider patterns of circulation that stretch into ordinary belief – and some of the ways in which that circulation might be constricted or missing. I will begin, however, simply by describing the main contexts that I have in mind.

The Church of England is sometimes said to be 'episcopally led and synodically governed'.[66] The first thing to mention is therefore the role of bishops, who have a formally defined role as guardians of the Church's doctrinal teaching. That role of doctrinal oversight can be exercised in all kinds of ways: in their own preaching and speaking; in their involvement in the various bodies discussed later in this section;[67] in the joint production of theological statements on particular issues; in commissioning the work of TEIs; in decisions about who to ordain and in the oversight of the teaching of clergy within their dioceses.[68] Any account of the life of doctrine in the Church of England is going to need to explore the role that bishops play in practice in sustaining and directing that life. I will be returning to these questions in Chapter 10.

To say that the church is synodically governed as well as episcopally led refers to fairly recent developments in the Church's life. The twentieth century saw major changes in the location and process of formal doctrinal deliberation in the Church. The power of the ancient Convocations of Canterbury and York – synods bringing together bishops and clergy within each province – had been limited since the Reformation. They had effectively ceased to meet as deliberative bodies in the eighteenth century, and it was parliament that was the church's primary deliberative and legislative body. From the middle of the nineteenth century, however, that situation began slowly to change. First, the Convocations began to meet again, and to hold substantial discussions. Next, lay people began to be involved. Then, in 1919, the National Church Assembly was created, with the power to develop legislation and propose it directly to Parliament.[69] Finally, in 1969, the Synodical Government Measure was passed, leading to the creation in 1971 of the Church of England's General Synod. The Synod has three houses: the House of

---

[66] See, for instance, The Archbishops' Commission on the Organisation of the Church of England, *Working as One Body* (London: Church House Publishing, 1995), §1.19. For a critique of the phrase, see Colin Podmore, 'The Governance of the Church of England and the Anglican Communion' (2009), §§3.21–22. Available online at www.speakcdn.com/assets/1145/governance_of_the_coe _and_ac.pdf (accessed 30 November 2019).

[67] For example, The House of Bishops of the General Synod, *Eucharistic Presidency: A Theological Statement* (London: Church House, 2014).

[68] The Church of England's formal processes for clergy discipline don't really address doctrinal matters. Since 1963, the Court of Ecclesiastical Causes Reserved has had jurisdiction over matters of doctrine. Since its creation, however, the court has only met twice, and in both cases it was to hear appeals from other courts about issues where no doctrinal questions were at stake. No prosecution for doctrinal offences has ever been brought to the court. A revision of the processes for clergy discipline was initiated by General Synod in 1996, but by the time a new measure was passed by Synod in 2003, matters of doctrine and ritual had been excluded from it. A separate measure was prepared that did cover matters of doctrine and ritual, but it was rejected in 2004. See Neil Patterson, *Ecclesiastical Law, Clergy, and Laity: A History of Legal Discipline and the Anglican Church* (London: Routledge, 2018).

[69] John D. Zimmerman, 'A Chapter in English Church Reform: The Enabling Act of 1919', *Historical Magazine of the Protestant Episcopal Church* 46, no. 2 (1977): 217; see also Maiden, *National Religion and the Prayer Book Controversy, 1927–1928*, 10.

Bishops (with all diocesan bishops and a number of suffragans), the House of Clergy (with elected and appointed representatives from across the dioceses) and the House of Laity (with representatives elected by deanery synods).[70] In legislative matters, it still proposes legislation to Parliament, but the weight of deliberation and scrutiny has shifted decisively to Synod. Synod's debates are also widely reported in the church press, though these days they seldom make a splash in the secular press. It is possible to watch the proceedings of Synod live-streamed online, and there are often flurries of discussion on social media, at least among certain loose networks of clergy and theologians.

Alongside General Synod, there are a variety of commissions and committees either set up for some specific and temporary purpose or playing a longer-term role in the Church's deliberations. A Doctrine Commission existed on and off from 1922 until 2010, when it was superseded by the Faith and Order Commission (on which I currently sit). A Liturgical Commission was set up in 1955 to pursue revisions to the Church's authorized liturgies, and continues to meet. A number of formal ecumenical dialogues exist, variously staffed and sustained. And there are any number of other short- and long-term committees, commissions, councils, working groups, panels and consultations. Between them, they produce a fairly constant stream of reports, some of which attract wide attention.

And then there is the Anglican Communion – the worldwide community of autonomous Anglican provinces. There is no centralized legislative structure for the Communion; each of the provinces has authority over its own affairs. There are, however, various institutions that allow for deliberation and coordination between provinces: the Lambeth Conference, which has been gathering many of the bishops of the Communion roughly once every ten years since 1867; the Primates' Meeting, which gathers irregularly but more frequently than the Lambeth Conference; and the Anglican Consultative Council, which gathers bishops, clergy and laity roughly every three years. The Communion has set up its own range of commissions and committees for specific purposes, including (until 2008) the Inter-Anglican Theological and Doctrinal Commission and (since 2008) the Inter-Anglican Standing Committee on Unity Faith and Order.[71] Among these, the Lambeth Conference is a highly visible affair, widely reported and discussed around the church, the other fora rather less so.

Simply listing all these spaces in which doctrinal deliberation takes place is not enough, however. These spaces are connected, issues flow from one to another – and there are strands of communication and influence that tie at least some of these spaces to the world of ordinary believing, though they are difficult to trace. The following

---

[70] There have often been questions about how representative the General Synod's House of Laity is. See, for instance, Ed Thornton, 'Campaigners Seek to Change the System', *Church Times*, 30 November 2012. Available online at www.churchtimes.co.uk/articles/2012/ 30-november/news/uk/campaigners-seek-to-change-the-system (accessed 30 November 2019).

[71] For discussion of the instruments of unity, see IASCUFO, *Towards a Symphony of Instruments: A Historical and Theological Consideration of the Instruments of Communion of the Anglican Communion* (2012). Available online at www.anglicancommunion.org/media/209979/Towards-a-Symphony-of-Instruments-Web-Version.pdf (accessed 30 November 2019).

vignettes are a rather fragmentary attempt to illustrate some of these flows and connections.

Responding to abuse

Sometimes, fairly clear flows link ordinary belief to the work of formal Anglican deliberative bodies. In 2016, for instance, the Church of England's Faith and Order Commission released a report called *The Gospel, Sexual Abuse and The Church: A Theological Resource for the Local Church*, and in 2017 it followed up with *Forgiveness and Reconciliation in the Aftermath of Abuse*.[72] This work was commissioned in the context of the growing recognition across the Church of England, long overdue and still incomplete, of just how badly and how often it had failed victims of sexual abuse. It was work that, in other words, was rooted deeply in urgent practical and pastoral questions facing the whole Church, and potentially affecting everybody's participation in that life. The Faith and Order Commission was not asked to draw up new safeguarding policies or practices – that work was already going on elsewhere. Instead, it was asked to accompany that work with theological reflection.

> In order for safeguarding work at all levels to enter fully into the life of the church, it is vital that every member of the Church of England is enabled to affirm the relationship between compliance with policy and faithfulness to the gospel – bishops, clergy and laity alike: good safeguarding is integral to the mission of the Church of England.
>
> This is a theological task. That is not to say that it is a task reserved for the academically minded, although it will benefit from careful engagement with academic studies. It is a theological task because it concerns how we speak about the God of Jesus Christ in relation to the practical challenges the church faces here.[73]

These reports emerged from a lengthy process of consultation. Members of the commission (themselves academically trained theologians from church and university contexts) talked with individual survivors and survivors' groups, with people involved in the development and delivery of safeguarding policy in the church and in other contexts, and with academics who worked on sexual abuse. The intention was that the results of their work, shaped by all these conversations, would then flow back into the life of the church: 'It is not', the report said, 'intended to be a treatise for academic discussion, but a text to be used by Christian communities who want to think through how the church speaks about the gospel when facing the reality of sexual abuse.' It

---

[72] Faith and Order Commission, *The Gospel, Sexual Abuse and the Church: A Theological Resource for the Local Church* (London: Church House Publishing, 2016). Available online at www.churchofengland.org/sites/default/files/2017-10/theologicalresourcefaocweb.pdf; *Forgiveness and Reconciliation in the Aftermath of Abuse* (London: Church House Publishing, 2017). Available online at www.churchofengland.org/sites/default/files/2017-10/forgivenessandreconciliation_0.pdf (both accessed 30 November 2019).
[73] From Christopher Cocksworth's Preface to the first report, ibid., 6–7.

was intended to be read by 'all who hold the bishop's license to preach and teach' and to be a resource for 'formal and informal teaching – training sessions, church groups, sermons, for example – with clergy, laity, staff and volunteers'.[74] The Commission's work served as a space within which a set of deep concerns from the midst of the life of ordinary belief were brought into a particular set of intensive conversations, with the results of those conversations intended to flow back into the ordinary deliberations and discussions of the church. What impact that work is actually having on thinking and practice around the Church is, however, difficult to judge.

Imagining salvation

A second vignette illustrates a different kind of flow. In the 1980s and 1990s, a number of formal church reports included discussion of the richness and variety of scriptural and traditional images of salvation. In 1986 the Anglican–Roman Catholic International Commission, for instance, published a statement on *Salvation and the Church*.[75] Digging behind the specific terms of the soteriological debates that have divided the churches, the statement notes that

> In order to describe salvation in all its fullness, the New Testament employs a wide variety of language … there is no controlling term or concept; they complement one another. The concept of salvation has the all-embracing meaning of the deliverance of human beings from evil and their establishment in that fullness of life which is God's will for them … of reconciliation and forgiveness … of expiation or propitiation … of redemption or liberation … of adoption … [of] regeneration, rebirth and new creation … of sanctification … of justification … [76]

This approach is echoed in the Doctrine Commission's 1996 report on *The Mystery of Salvation*. Speaking about the New Testament depictions of Christ's saving work, the report's authors said that

> we have emphasised above all the primacy of the event of the passion with the cross as its central symbol. Story and symbol come first. They are worked out in images and metaphors, sometimes striking often paradoxical. Eventually doctrines of the atonement emerge, which are attempts to devise as coherent answers as possible to the questions raised by the narrative; and these doctrines have been many and varied in the history of Christian thought. To try to reduce this variety to a single agreed statement on the doctrine of the atonement would be untrue both to the New Testament and to our Anglican heritage. Far better, and consistent with our

---

[74] Ibid., 8–9.
[75] ARCIC II, *Salvation and the Church: An Agreed Statement* (1986). Available online at www.anglicancommunion.org/media/105239/ARCIC_II_Salvation_and_the_Church.pdf (accessed 30 November 2019). The document was not itself an authoritative statement: it was published by the Commission, but not proposed for formal adoption by General Synod.
[76] Ibid., §13.

rich Christian tradition, to provide a series of angles of vision, to sketch the great mystery of the atonement.[77]

The third space in which we can find a similar move towards a multifaceted soteriological imagination is, however, not in a report, but in liturgy. The story of liturgical revision in the Church in the twentieth century runs from the 1928 revision of the Book of Common Prayer that was approved by the Church Assembly but rejected by Parliament, through the temporary authorization of a range of alternative liturgies (Series 1, 2 and 3) in the 1960s, to the 1980 *Alternative Service Book* and finally *Common Worship* in 2000. This whole process has led to a variety of texts being made available in *Common Worship* – most notably, several different Eucharistic prayers. And when it is compared to the *Book of Common Prayer*, this material allows for a much wider range of understandings of the nature of salvation, which mirror the understandings mentioned earlier.[78]

The work of the Liturgical Commission emerged within the same broad theological context as the work of ARCIC II and the work of the Doctrine Commission, and it draws on similar intellectual currents. The whole discussion has long roots in popular debate about salvation in and around the churches, in shifting social imaginaries which have shaped the church's reception of traditional soteriological language, and in academic work on biblical and traditional texts. There is no one obvious prompt for this discussion; it is not a response to a particular crisis or easily identifiable pastoral need; it is, rather, a symptom of a centuries-long shift in sensibilities and theological imagination. The various formal bodies I have mentioned can be thought of as spaces within which the thinking prompted by these long shifts is gathered, explored and crystallized – spaces within which an attempt is made to take stock of the developing mind of the church. Their work – the reports they issue, and still more the liturgies they produce – can then be thought of as an invitation to ordinary believers to inhabit the forms of theological imagination that the commissions have explored.

Once again, however, it is difficult to trace the difference this work may have made to ordinary believing around the church. It has certainly changed the words that people hear and say in services, and that presumably makes a significant difference – but how, say, do the changes that I have just outlined interact with those I mentioned earlier: the development and spread of new kinds of worship song, and the tendency of those songs to focus people's soteriological imaginations on a personal relationship with Jesus? The story of changing patterns of soteriological imagination that I have just

---

[77] Sykes (ed.), *Contemporary Doctrine Classics*, 356. The report was also trying to reflect the rich variety of 'Anglican piety in practice' through history, a variety richer than the historic formularies might lead one to expect (439).

[78] I am indebted here to Pete Gunstone, whose MA dissertation, 'Penal Substitution in the Worship of the Church of England: Historic Texts and Contemporary Practice' (Durham University, 2019), explores this change well (including with reference to *The Mystery of Salvation*). Cf. Douglas J. Davies, 'Anglican Soteriology: Incarnation, Worship, and the Property of Mercy', in *Salvation in Christ: Comparative Christian Views*, ed. Roger R. Keller and Robert L. Millet (Provo, UT: Religious Studies Center, Brigham Young University, 2005), 53–67, and Eric Woods, 'Innumerable Benefits: The Soteriology of the Book of Common Prayer', *Faith and Worship* 65–66 (2010): 23–38.

told, and Pete Ward's story, mentioned earlier, of the patterns imagination fostered by recent generations of worship song, don't easily cohere.

Debating the incarnation

A third vignette illustrates the more fractious connections that sometimes exist between ordinary belief and the church's formal deliberations. In 1977 a collection of essays was published under the title *The Myth of God Incarnate*.[79] The opening essay was provided by Maurice Wiles, Regius Professor of Divinity at Oxford University. Wiles's chapter, 'Christianity without Incarnation?', argued that Christianity can and should do without the claim that God uniquely became incarnate in Jesus, in such a way that Jesus was at once fully human and fully divine. The book, and Wiles's chapter in particular, triggered an explosive response. It made front page news in national newspapers. Multiple reviews and comment pieces appeared across the secular and religious press, which also published a large number of letters; a far greater number of letters were sent to the authors and to church leaders. Reactive articles and books were rushed into publication.[80] In General Synod that July, there were calls for an emergency debate. The Archbishop of Canterbury, Donald Coggan, denied the request, noting that there had not been enough time for members of Synod to read the book and form careful judgements, but when in the course of another debate Graham Leonard, the bishop of Truro, loudly proclaimed his belief in the incarnation, he was greeted with cheers.[81]

The public furore that met the publication of this book had everything to do with the connections between different spaces in which doctrinal discussion takes place. Perhaps the most important trigger was the fact that Maurice Wiles had until the previous year been the chair of the Church of England's Doctrine Commission: his was the voice of someone who had a key role in shaping the church's formal deliberations about doctrine. More generally, the book presented arguments familiar among academics to a more popular audience. It was not by any means written as an introductory guide, but it was launched at a press conference in St Paul's Cathedral, with a clear expectation that it would make a splash. The religious correspondent of *The Times* wrote that it 'sets out views that have been in circulation for some time, but they are now presented as a challenge to beliefs that most Christians hold precious',[82] and that it 'seems to indicate a deliberate, almost show-business desire to shock the general public'.[83] The shock was, in part, the product of a clash between the different languages spoken in the academic, ecclesiastical and popular spaces that the book crossed. A great deal

---

[79] John Hick (ed.), *The Myth of God Incarnate* (London: SCM, 1977).
[80] See, for example, Michael Green (ed.), *The Truth of God Incarnate* (London: Hodder and Stoughton, 1977); Michael Goulder (ed.), *Incarnation and Myth* (London: SCM, 1979), and A. E. Harvey (ed.), *God Incarnate* (London: SPCK, 1981). Herbert McCabe's responses are printed in *God Matters* (London: Continuum, 2005), 54–74.
[81] See the account in 'Old Tactics from New Vinedressers', *Third Way* 1, no. 14 (14 July 1977): 12.
[82] Clifford Longley, 'Theological War Opens over Divinity of Christ', *The Times*, 29 June 1977, 1.
[83] Clifford Longley, 'Are the Gospels a "Myth?"' *The Times*, 1 July 1977, 18. Furlong, in *C of E: The State It's In*, 124, detects a 'slightly smug academic enjoyment in knowing better than most ordinary Christians'.

of public discussion focused on questions about translation between these contexts, and especially on the different connotations that the word 'myth' has among ordinary people from those that it has among readers of Strauss and Bultmann.

The circulations that tie the Doctrine Commission, General Synod and the press to ordinary believing do not simply consist of flows of influence and reception; they are marked by fractiousness, disputes and misunderstanding, too. Mapping those circulations will therefore need to involve attending to the conflicts that they generate.[84]

Agreeing technical Christology

A different set of questions about the connection between doctrinal spaces can be suggested by a fourth and final vignette. In 2014, an agreed statement on Christology was produced by the Anglican–Oriental Orthodox International Commission. The statement begins:

> We confess that our Lord, God and Saviour Jesus Christ is the Only-Begotten Son of God who became incarnate and was made human in the fullness of time for us and for our salvation. We believe in God the Son incarnate, perfect in His divinity and perfect in His humanity, consubstantial with the Father according to His divinity and consubstantial with us according to His humanity, for a union has been made of two natures. For this cause we confess one Christ, one Son and one Lord.[85]

The statement goes on to clarify that the two natures 'distinguished in thought alone, continue to exist without separation, without division, without change, and without confusion'.[86] This is a restatement of Chalcedonian orthodoxy, but clarified in subtle ways for the sake of this specific ecumenical dialogue: it is a carefully worded work of technical theology.

It is not immediately clear, however, how the work done in this particular deliberative space relates to the wider doctrinal life of the Church. It would be hard to find the technical clarifications made in this document reflected in the Christological language used in General Synod or in reports of the Doctrine Commission – and still harder to establish the connections between this discourse and the patterns of ordinary believing (though I happen to think that those connections can be made). The work that the report does in its own space is clear; its place in the networks and flows of the Church's doctrinal life is not.

---

[84] Public theological scandals could, at a stretch, be added to the list of institutions within which conversations take place that shape the life of belief. These scandals take a familiar form: a controversial statement or event, a flare of angry publicity, urgent questions asked in the Church's formal deliberative bodies, the mobilization of popular opinion for and against, and the slow fading of attention and interest, before the next scandal strikes. These scandals are one of the enduring social forms of the Church's life. See Keith W. Clements, *Lovers of Discord: Twentieth Century Theological Controversies in England* (London: SPCK, 1988).
[85] Anglican–Oriental Orthodox International Commission, *Christology: Agreed Statement*. §1.
[86] Ibid., §2.

Conclusion

Doctrinal deliberation happens in many spaces around the Church of England, and there are some complex flows between those spaces, binding them into a tangled network of communication (and miscommunication). It is often, however, difficult to trace those flows – or difficult to know how much of a flow there is. It is not always obvious what difference the work of bishops, synods, doctrinal commissions and the like makes, or how it is plugged in to the believing life of the church. It is, nevertheless, clear that ordinary believing, itself varied, mobile, and interconnected, is caught up in multiple forms of wider circulation. It is surrounded by these circulations, sometimes disturbed or challenged by what flows through them, and sometimes enriched.

You could think of this tangled network as a doctrinal economy, a doctrinal polity or a doctrinal ecology. To call it an economy might highlight the way in which resources are unevenly distributed around it. Access to books, to the relevant patterns of education, to the spaces in which deliberation takes place – all of this is a matter of financial resources, and of other kinds of capital (institutional, cultural and educational). To call this network a polity might highlight the way in which power of various kinds is unevenly distributed about it. The ability to have one's voice heard, to be taken seriously, to make a difference (or think it plausible that one might make a difference), is certainly not spread uniformly. This is a network marked by multiple forms of exclusion and marginalization. To call it an ecology might highlight the complex interaction of multiple forms of agency that are involved in this network, and the unmanageable richness of the life that it sustains. It might emphasize the flows and interactions, the collaborations and dependencies, that hold this network together.

I have said that this is a book about doctrine in the life of the church – a book about a family of Christian practices in which doctrinal ideas are developed, discussed and deployed. It is about the doctrinal ideas which circulate around the Church's doctrinal economy, polity or ecology, and the contribution that they make to forming the Church's life in the world. To understand why such ideas circulate here, however, and to understand what work they might do, we need to turn back to the beginning of the story, and to understand how doctrinal ideas and practices first emerged within the life of the Church.

Part Two

The nature of doctrine

4

The emergence of doctrine

Introduction

Doctrine is not natural. There is no law dictating that religious communities have to sprout doctrinal practices – and yet most Christian communities, including my own Church of England, are rife with them. In this chapter, I ask why.

Christian life is a series of experiments in following Jesus, who was, and is, and is to come. Each experiment discovers possibilities of worship, witness and discipleship in some specific location; each unfolds something new of the gift given by God in the resurrection; each is a re-reading of the scriptures. Each also demonstrates the human propensity for misunderstanding and betrayal. Practices of summarizing, articulating and arguing about the faith emerge within this shared life, in contexts of proclamation, confession, teaching and controversy. These doctrinal practices help shape both Christian explorations and Christian betrayals. They do not float above Christian life, but are ingredients within it: they are among the things that specific Christians do; they are tangled in Christianity's webs of power, privilege and property; they exist in different forms in different Christian locations, each with its own contingent history. To understand the nature of doctrine, and the roles that it can play in the life of the church, we need to understand something of these histories.

The life of the church

Resurrection

To understand the life of the church, we first have to understand the ground on which it is built. That ground is the action of God: the God of Israel called the church into being by raising Jesus of Nazareth from the dead. The church measures its life from the resurrection of the crucified Messiah, and doctrine condenses out of the church's life as it lives in relation to its crucified and resurrected Lord.[1]

---

[1] Gerard Loughlin hopes that 'the church ... may again understand its doctrine as the grammar and the rule, the stage-direction, of a traditioned performance of the story that alone calls it into being: the life, death and resurrection of Jesus Christ'. ('The Basis and Authority of Doctrine', in *The Cambridge Companion to Christian Doctrine*, ed. Colin E. Gunton (Cambridge: Cambridge University Press, 1997), 43.) For the more general point that doctrine is grounded in the story of

In Luke's stories of the resurrection, our attention is repeatedly drawn to the fact that it is specifically Jesus of Nazareth who has been raised. The resurrected one is the same Jesus whose words and deeds the gathered disciples remember, the one in whose story they have been sharing. 'Remember how he told you, while he was still in Galilee …', say the angels to the women at the tomb (Lk. 24.6); 'Then they remembered his words' (24.8). 'These are my words', says the risen Jesus to the disciples gathered in Jerusalem, 'that I spoke to you while I was still with you' (24.44), and 'Look at my hands and my feet; see that it is I myself. Touch me and see' (24.39). The disciples on the road to Emmaus tell the stranger that they are thinking 'about Jesus of Nazareth … mighty in deed and word' (24.19), about the 'things that had happened', 'the things that have taken place in these days. … The things about Jesus of Nazareth' (24.18-19; cf. 14). They tell him especially about how their Jesus has been 'handed over' and 'crucified' (24.20; cf. 24.7). And it is when this stranger 'took bread, blessed and broke it, and gave it to them' (24.30), echoing what he had done on the night that he was betrayed, that 'they recognized him' (24.31). The gift of the resurrection is a re-presentation of the one they know.[2]

Yet this recognition is complicated in three ways. First, they discover in encountering this Jesus risen that they do not yet know him. The women at the tomb are asked, 'Why do you look for the living among the dead?' (24.5), by angels surprised that they do not know what to expect of the one they seek. The disciples on the road to Emmaus not only walk beside Jesus unawares throughout a long conversation, they are upbraided by him: 'Oh, how foolish you are, and how slow of heart to believe all that the prophets have declared! Was it not necessary that the Messiah should suffer these things and then enter into his glory?' (24.24-25). All the disciples, women and men, are still walking a road towards understanding.

Second, this encounter with the risen Jesus is an encounter with one who is still living, acting and teaching. One should not look for the living among the dead, and

---

Jesus, see Charles Gore, 'Dogma in the Early Church', in W. R. Matthew et al., *Dogma in History and Thought: Studies by Various Writers* (London: Nisbet, 1929), 69–70; Colin E. Gunton, 'Dogma, the Church and the Task of Theology', in *The Task of Theology Today*, ed. Victor Pfitzner and Hilary Regan (Adelaide: Australian Theological Forum, 1998), 21–2; Alister E. McGrath, *The Genesis of Doctrine: A Study in the Foundation of Doctrinal Criticism* (Grand Rapids, MI: Eerdmans, 1990), 12, 32, 53–7, 172, 179; McMichael, 'What Does Canterbury Have to Do with Jerusalem? The Vocation of Anglican Theology', 20–1, and Rowan Williams, 'Doctrinal Criticism: Some Questions', in *Wrestling with Angels: Conversations in Modern Theology*, ed. Mike Higton (London: SCM, 2007), 292. I am not denying Katherine Sonderegger's insistence that not all doctrine is Christology (*Systematic Theology 1: The Doctrine of God* (Minneapolis, MN: Fortress Press, 2015), xvii). Her insistence is still that 'Jesus Christ, and His Lordship, can be properly honoured' by focusing on other doctrines (ibid., xvii, xviii). To say the doctrine is made necessary for the church by the resurrection is not to dictate the form that such doctrine must take.

[2] A lot of what follows is drawn from Luke–Acts. I am not reading it as simple reportage, but as a theological narration, shaped by various convictions about how God was at work. My re-telling is similarly theological, though it seeks to be responsible, if not reducible, to historical-critical work. If I claim, for instance, that there was diversity in Christianity as far back as we can judge, that claim is responsive to what I know of critical historical reconstructions of Christianity's early years. If I claim that the Spirit guided the formation of the church, that claim is not independent of critical reconstructions – I can imagine reconstructions that would make it very hard indeed to say this – but neither is it a conclusion that one would expect critical historical work to come to, as that work is currently configured.

Jesus is a living teacher, one who will accompany the church in its history, and who will go on speaking. There are more references in Acts, for instance, to the risen Jesus teaching his followers in visions and ecstatic encounters than there are to his teaching before the ascension.[3] By the Spirit, the risen Jesus leads the church on into his truth.

Third, the resurrected Jesus is one who will return. 'This Jesus', says the angel at the ascension, 'will come in the same way as you saw him go into heaven' (Acts 1.11). Paul in front of the Areopagus tells the assembled Athenians that God 'has fixed a day on which he will have the world judged in righteousness by a man whom he has appointed, and of this he has given assurance to all by raising him from the dead' (Acts 17.31). There is a future horizon towards which the church's journey is heading.

The church lives from the resurrection of Jesus. It is called into being by the news of the resurrection. Its life is a journey of exploration, discovering the identity of the resurrected one; it is accompanied on its journey by him, living and active; it travels towards him, awaiting the full revelation of his glory. The church exists in relation to Jesus, who was, who is and who is to come.[4]

Worship, discipleship, witness

The one who raises Jesus from the dead is the God of Israel.[5] The one who raises is the same one whose mighty word created the world, formed a people, established covenants, inspired prophets, demanded obedience, provided for sacrifices, proclaimed forgiveness, poured out blessings and ministered healing. In the life, death and resurrection of Jesus, the disciples recognized this same word spoken to them again. They found a new creation being made, a people being drawn together, a covenant renewed, sinners being convicted, forgiveness being proclaimed and the sick being healed. Jesus's life, death and resurrection were spoken to them by the voice they knew as the voice of God.

The Christian church is nothing more – and should be nothing less – than the community of those who hear this word spoken to them in the risen one, and who pass it on. The church therefore begins with Mary Magdalene, Joanna and Mary the mother of James, and the other women with them (Lk. 24.10). They are the first to hear the news of the resurrection (24.5) and the first to pass it on (24.9). They are the first apostles, and the church is the community of those who have been joined to their hearing and their speech.

On the Day of Pentecost, Peter stands up, filled with the Spirit, and is compelled to give voice to the word that first reached him from these women. 'Jesus of Nazareth', he says, was 'a man attested to you by God with deeds of power, wonders, and signs that God did through him among you'; he was 'handed over to you according to the definite plan and foreknowledge of God' and then 'God raised him up, having freed him from death' (Acts 2.22-24). 'God has made him both Lord and Messiah' (2.36). This is Peter's

---

[3] See p. 80.
[4] Cf. McGrath, *Genesis*, 73–4.
[5] Jacob Jervell, *The Theology of the Acts of the Apostles* (Cambridge: Cambridge University Press, 1996), 18.

telling of the word that forms the church, and the whole book of Acts could be read as a drama which has this word as its protagonist. It is the story of the word's advance. 'The word of God continued to spread' (6.7); 'the word of God continued to advance and gain adherents' (12.24); 'thus the word of the Lord spread throughout the region' (13.49); 'the word of the Lord grew mightily and prevailed' (19.20).[6]

As this word is spoken, people encounter God. The crucifixion and resurrection are surrounded by the trappings that in the history of Israel had accompanied theophanies – those moments of incursion when God's presence with God's people is made terrifyingly apparent. Darkness falls (Lk. 23.45) and angels stand in attendance (24.4). The sounding of this word tips people into wonder: they are by turns 'terrified' (Lk. 24.5), 'amazed' (24.12), 'astounded' (24.22), 'startled' (24.37), filled 'with great joy' (24.52); 'bewildered', '[a]mazed and astonished', 'perplexed' (Acts 2.6-7, 12), and 'cut to the heart' (2.37). They are thunderstruck by the resurrection, the return to them of the crucified one, and they respond in the only way they can. '[T]hey worshipped him' (Lk. 24.52); they were to be found 'continually in the temple blessing God' (24.53); they devoted themselves to prayer (Acts 2.42). The church is the community of this astonishment, and of the worship to which it gives rise.[7]

As those thunderstruck by the resurrection, and tipped into worship, the followers of Jesus also become witnesses – members of the community of Joanna and the two Marys. The story of Acts is the story of a story: an account of the repeated telling of the story of the resurrection. It is always the same story, and it is always being told in new forms. The Spirit poured out on this community empowers it above all things to speak, whether in tongues, or in speeches before councils and magistrates, crowds and households, in word-accompanied deeds and deed-accompanied words. The final verse of the book tells us again what the whole book has been about, as it leaves Paul in Rome, 'proclaiming the kingdom of God and teaching about the Lord Jesus Christ with all boldness and without hindrance' (28.30).[8]

The experience of the resurrection, the hearing of the word of God spoken in the life of Jesus, calls his followers to the reordering of every area of their lives. They enter into new patterns of relationship, new distributions of property and new arrangements of power. They devote themselves to fellowship (Acts 2:42), hold all things in common (2.44, 4.32) and find new ways of serving one another (6.3). They experience healings and exorcisms together (3.1-10; 9.32-42; 14.8-10; 16.16-18). They are brought into conflict with political and religious authorities; they are imprisoned. The relationship between Jews and Greeks is altered (15.1-17). The ways in which they handle food, blood and purity are changed (15.19-29). In being given the risen Jesus, these people are drawn into the negotiation of a new life together in the world. They are called to

---

[6] Cf. Ernst Haenchen, *The Acts of the Apostles: A Commentary* (Oxford: Basil Blackwell, 1971), 49.
[7] Cf. Larry Hurtado, *Lord Jesus Christ: Devotion to Jesus in Earliest Christianity* (Grand Rapids, MI: Eerdmans, 2003), 2.
[8] In Acts, the followers of Jesus are always proclaiming. They proclaim the resurrection of Jesus from the dead (2.24, 32; 3.15; 4.10, 33; 10.40-41; 13.30-31; 17.18, 31; 26.23); they proclaim that he is the Messiah (2.31; 3.18; 5.42; 8.5; 9.22; 17.3; 18.5, 28; 26.23); they proclaim the kingdom of God (8.12; 20.25; 28.31); they proclaim repentance from sins (2.37; 3.19; 26.20); they proclaim the good news of God's grace (20.24); they proclaim good news (8.12, 25, 35, 40; 13.32; 14.7, 15, 21; 15.7; 16.10; 17.18; 20.24).

die and to rise with him, to turn away from old and towards new patterns of life; they become the 'saints' (9.13, 32, 41; 26.10). They are given this risen Jesus as their Lord, and called to a life of discipleship: they are followers of the way of the Lord (9.2; 18.25-26). They are 'Christians' (11.26).[9]

This, then, is the shape of the church called into being by the resurrection: it is a church of worship, witness and discipleship. These define it, or are meant to define it: the church is a community discovering how to worship, how to witness to and how to follow Jesus of Nazareth.

The unfolding gift

The experience of the resurrection yields its content over time. On the road to Emmaus, two disciples meet the risen Jesus. He sets out for them the meaning of the scripture-wrapped gift that they have been given, yet they do not realize what is happening until he is gone. His conversation with them happens over a defined stretch of time, but the disciples do not possess the experience in that moment. It takes more time for it to register.

When they say, 'Were not our hearts burning within us while he was talking to us on the road?' (Lk. 24.32), they draw one another's attention to what had happened, and confirm the experience with one another. Their conversation brings it into focus. It is not that the experience had taken place and was complete for them, and that they then began to interpret it. Rather, it is as they interpreted it – as they spoke to one another about it – that it unfolded for them. Before they named to one another what had happened on the road, seeing it in the light of what happened next around the table, they did not register it. The registering of the experience is part of the having of it, not something subsequent to the having. The experience unfolds for them as they find words for it together.

The whole story of the early church replays this logic on a larger scale. It is not that the experience of resurrection was first safely received and acknowledged, and that a process of response then began. The followers of Jesus discovered what that experience was as they entered into it. It was unfolded for them as they learnt to respond to it in worship, witness and discipleship. In improvised speeches, in arguments about money, in deliberations about the inclusion of the gentiles, in the selection and interpretation of scripture, in missionary journeys, in their whole life together, the followers of the way discovered what way they were on.

The life of the church is the unfolding of the gift that founds it. That process of unfolding is not simply the ever-richer recall of a past event; it is not simply a matter of memory. The gift of the resurrected Jesus is the gift of one who was, who is and who is to come, and the process of unfolding is also a process of continuing reception.

One sign of this can be seen in the references that the book of Acts makes to Jesus's teaching. There are a few references to the teaching Jesus gave before the crucifixion,

---

[9] 'What unites [Christians] is a concern for true discipleship, proper reflection in human words and deeds of an object of worship that always exceeds by its greatness human efforts to do so.' (Kathryn Tanner, *Theories of Culture: A New Agenda for Theology* (Minneapolis, MN: Fortress, 1997), 152; cf. 156.)

and between the resurrection and the ascension (1.2-3; 10.36; 20.35), but, as I have already mentioned, they are outnumbered by the moments in which his followers hear fresh teaching, instruction and encouragement from Jesus risen and ascended (9.4-5; 9.10; 10.3-6, 13, 15, 19-20; 22.7, 10, 18, 21; 23.11; 26.15-18 – and, if one includes teaching mediated by angels, 1.10-11; 5.20; 8.26; 12.7-8; 26.21-26). It is, of course, the same Jesus (and the author of Acts is also the author of the Gospel that precedes it) so the point here is not to make a contrast between what had already been given and what carried on arriving. Nevertheless, the church has been given an ongoing relationship with its Lord, and it goes on receiving his instruction.

The fresh teaching that the church in Acts receives is sometimes attributed simply to the Spirit (8.29; 16.6-9). Jesus promises his followers that the Spirit will make them his witnesses: 'I am sending upon you what my Father promised; so stay here in the city until you have been clothed with power from on high' (Lk. 24.48; cf. Acts 1.5), because 'you will receive power when the Holy Spirit has come upon you; and you will be my witnesses' (Acts 1.8). They wait; Jesus teaches them 'through the Holy Spirit' (1.2), and then after his ascension the Spirit propels them into testimony. From then on, it is the Spirit who enables and directs the proclamation of Jesus's disciples (4.8; 4.19-20; 4.31; 5.29-32; 7.55-56), and we should probably hear the characteristic accent of the Spirit's compulsion every time – and there are many – that Acts insists that those disciples proclaimed Jesus 'boldly' (4.13, 29, 31; 9.27; 13.46; 14.3; 18.26; 19.8; 28.31). Just as Acts can be read as the story of the word, it can be read as the story of the Spirit. The Spirit is the power of God animating the whole story of the word's spread, and of its unfolding.

The polycentric church

The work of witness begins at Pentecost with a miraculous proliferation of voices testifying to God's deeds of power (2.11). The miracle is not that everyone in the crowd is enabled miraculously to hear and understand the one tongue of the gospel, but that the Spirit translates that gospel into the tongues of all those present (2.6). The Spirit translates God's word into the nuances, the possibilities and constraints, the embedded history and culture of each person's native language.[10] From Pentecost onwards, the story of the church does not take the form of a single developmental history. It is no *Bildungsroman*, telling the tale of a single community's growth from childhood to maturity. Instead, it is polycentric. After the death of Stephen, the community scatters and takes root in multiple different locations. We find it in Judaea and Samaria (Acts 8.1), in Galilee (9.31), in Damascus (9.10), in Phoenicia, Cyprus and Antioch (11.19) – and then in all those cities visited by Paul, from Antioch to Rome.

Watered by the Spirit, the faith takes root differently in these different locations (11.19-20). As Lamin Sanneh puts it, 'There were as many birthplaces of the religion as there had come to be new communities of faithful people, and as many visitations of

---

[10] Willie James Jennings, writing about this material in Acts, asks what it means to learn another's native language. It involves coming 'to love the people – the food, the faces, the plans, the practices, the songs, the poetry, the happiness, the sadness, the ambiguity, the truth' and 'their land, their landscapes, their home' (*Acts* (Louisville, KY: Westminster John Knox, 2017), 30).

Pentecost as there had been hearts and minds set aflame and occasions of bold witness.' The faith is translated in each of these locations (into new languages, and into new cultures) and we have no access to the original, but only to its multiple translations.[11] Pentecost is not the reversal of Babel but its redemption.

Although all are united in following the same Lord by the same Spirit, their understanding of what following demands, and of how their Lord is to be proclaimed, develops differently. The first witnesses to this unfolding gift invite others to share in its unfolding, and in the process they lose possession; they lose the ability to dictate what it will mean. The unfolding does not take place primarily by their agency, but by another agency that works no less through others than through them.[12]

To put it another way, the recipients of this word become converts, not proselytes. That is, they are not asked by those who witness to them to take on an already formed way of life, but to be converted by the same word that is converting the witnesses. They are asked what this word will make of their lives – how it will convert their histories, their cultures, their hearts. And, as Andrew Walls puts it, compared to proselytes, 'Converts face a much riskier life. Converts have to be constantly, relentlessly turning their ways of thinking, their education and training, their ways of working and doing things, toward Christ. They must think Christ into the patterns of thought they have inherited, into their networks of relationship and their processes for making decisions.'[13] That is why the story of Acts is not simply a story of new converts being added to the number of Jesus's followers. It is also a story of the ongoing conversion of existing followers by the inclusion of those new members. When the Spirit adds the gentile Cornelius and his household to the community of the faith, the first sign of the Spirit's work is their speaking in tongues (Acts 10.46); the second is the earthquake that is triggered in the Jerusalem church (11.1-18).[14]

This joining of the gentiles as gentiles into the people of God is the most surprising work of the Spirit in Acts. They are included as people who can follow Jesus without circumcision, and without the forms of purity that had been taught to Israel (11.3; 15.1-29) and which Jesus and his disciples had until now diligently observed (10.14). In the house of Cornelius, Peter witnesses the Spirit falling on those he knows to be unclean, turning them into God's witnesses. But the Spirit falls on them without

---

[11] Lamin O. Sanneh, *Disciples of All Nations: Pillars of World Christianity* (Oxford: Oxford University Press, 2008), 14. See also his *Translating the Message: The Missionary Impact on Culture*, 2nd edn (Maryknoll, NY: Orbis, 2009), 1, 251.

[12] Cf. Ephraim Radner, *Church* (Eugene, OR: Cascade, 2017), 160–1; cf. Craig S. Keener, *Acts: An Exegetical Commentary 1: Introduction and 1:1–2:47* (Grand Rapids, MI: Baker Academic, 2012), 521.

[13] Andrew F. Walls, 'Converts or Proselytes: The Crisis over Conversion in the Early Church', *International Bulletin of Missionary Research* 28, no. 1 (2004): 6; cf. Sanneh, *Disciples*, 56.

[14] Nathan Kerr speaks of 'an apocalyptic hope according to which alone our missionary encounter with the other is an *embodiment* of ... our ongoing conversion to the coming reign of God' (*Christ, History and Apocalyptic: The Politics of Christian Mission* (London: SCM, 2008), 188, emphasis in original). 'We might thus speak of the "space of encounter" opened up by the inaugural rupture ... of Jesus as the space of a praxis by which we are delivered over to the believing testimony of another; one is "Christian" only in being continually *converted* by and to the other's witness to Jesus' (ibid., 178). He speaks of the 'praxis of missionary encounter with the other by which we are together given over – converted – to the "more" of Jesus' life, the shape of whose pneumatological excess we cannot possibly control' (ibid.).

bringing them across the line that Peter could have sworn marked the boundary of God's sanctifying work. 'If then God gave them the same gift that he gave us when we believed in the Lord Jesus Christ', he says, 'who was I that I could hinder God?' (11.17). The Spirit makes these gentiles into witnesses differently, unexpectedly, in their own unprecedented way.

The Spirit does not, of course, replace the Jews with gentiles. As Willie James Jennings says, the Cornelius story is not about a God who 'has always been poised to render Israel inconsequential and now was moving on past covenant with Israel and finally overcoming their religious ethnocentrism'. God's life with Israel was not 'simply a dress rehearsal for the real play'.[15] Yet neither does the Spirit simply set these new gentile believers alongside the existing Jewish believers, making available two discrete versions of the same project. Rather, the Spirit gives these two communities to each other as members of the one household of God, and as questions and challenges to one another. How are they to live the faith together, when they receive and embody it differently? 'Acts renders the Gentiles as a profound question to the Jews of diaspora: What will you do if I join you at the body of Jesus and fall in love with your God and with you?'[16] Jesus draws Jew and gentile together 'not moving past the one to get to the other, not choosing one and rejecting the other, but precisely bringing together, drawing close what was far apart'.[17]

More generally, Jennings notes that

> The deepest reality of life in the Spirit depicted in Acts is that the disciples of Jesus rarely, if ever, go where they want to go or to whom they would want to go. Indeed the Spirit seems to always be pressing the disciples to go to those [with] whom they would in fact strongly prefer never to share space, or a meal, and definitely not life together. Yet it is precisely this prodding to be boundary-crossing and border-transgressing that marks the presence of the Spirit of God.[18]

By drawing the disciples out to encounter these different peoples – drawing them out into shared life with the gentiles, 'the rich multiplicity of peoples who each and every one are beloved creatures of the Creator God' – the Spirit invites them to become 'like quilters joining beautiful fragments of cloth'. 'The Spirit creates joining.'[19] The Spirit creates neither empire nor diaspora but a woven catholicity, polycentric but intimately joined.

As they travel, Jesus's disciples testify to his resurrection, and proclaim the fact that they were witnesses of it. No less fervently, however, they testify to this ongoing work of the Spirit. They testify to the Spirit's work in empowering their proclamation, in adding others to their number and in weaving them into the unexpected tapestry into which the gift of resurrection is unfolding (Acts 2.33; 4.23; 10.30-33; 11.4-17; 14.27; 15.3, 4,

[15] Jennings, *Acts*, 88.
[16] Ibid., 8. For Jennings, 'diaspora' is life focused on the preservation of cultural identity in context of scattered minority, over against all the (very real) threats of assimilation and imperialism.
[17] Ibid., 111.
[18] Ibid., 11.
[19] Ibid., 22, 28.

7-11, 12; 20.18-35; 22.1-21). The Spirit animates the whole polycentric, woven story of the church. The Spirit leads people into the memory of Jesus, in ongoing discovery of what they have been given; the Spirit leads people into the presence of Jesus, speaking in their midst as soon as two or three are gathered together; the Spirit leads towards the future of Jesus, into ongoing discovery of God's surprising abundance. In all this, the Spirit enables the church to tell the story of Jesus, and to re-tell around him the story of their lives, their world and their God.

Reading

The gift that founds the church – the gift of the resurrected Jesus, and the new life that he awakens – comes wrapped in scripture. It came, first of all, to readers of the Jewish scriptures, and the story of its unfolding is in part the story of their learning to re-read those scriptures around this new life. The whole story of the Spirit's polycentric and woven work, seeding the church in new places and uniting all its parts into one, is a story of reading and re-reading.[20]

On the road to Emmaus, Jesus, 'beginning with Moses and all the prophets, … interpreted to them the things about himself in all the scriptures' (Lk. 24.27; cf. 25). Back in Jerusalem he reminds the disciples that he had already said to them that '"everything written about me in the law of Moses, the prophets, and the psalms must be fulfilled." Then he opened their minds to understand the scriptures' (Lk. 24.44-45). When Peter preaches to the crowds at Pentecost, his whole sermon is larded with scripture; he quotes Joel and David (Acts 2.17-21, 25-28, 31, 34), and claims that scripture has been fulfilled in Jesus and is being fulfilled among his disciples (cf. Acts 2.16, 25, 31; cf 1.16). Larry Hurtado describes the process well.

> According to the earliest traditions, very soon in the 'post-Easter' setting Jewish followers of Jesus had experiences of 'seeing' Jesus as uniquely resurrected to eschatological existence and heavenly glory. … In a dynamic interaction between devout, prayerful searching for, and pondering over, scriptural texts and continuing powerful religious experiences, they came to understand certain biblical passages in an innovative way as prefiguring and portraying God's vindication of Jesus. These 'charismatic' insights into biblical passages in turn shaped their understanding of their experiences, reinforced their confidence in the validity of these experiences, stimulated their openness to further experience of Jesus' exalted status, and helped shape these subsequent experiences.[21]

The experience of Jesus happened to people whose minds were soaked in scripture. From its sounding in scripture, they recognized God's living word as it spoke to them in Jesus; they knew its character and force. From scripture, they knew that this word

---

[20] Cf. Graham H. Twelftree, *People of the Spirit: Exploring Luke's View of the Church* (Grand Rapids, MI: Baker Academic, 2009), 212. For a good guide to the nature of this re-reading, see Richard B. Hays, *Echoes of Scripture in the Letters of Paul* (New Haven: Yale University Press, 1989); and *Echoes of Scripture in the Gospels* (Waco, TX: Baylor University Press, 2008).
[21] Hurtado, *Lord Jesus Christ*, 184–5.

was the organizing principle of the world, its foundation and the source of the wisdom needed to navigate it. From scripture, they knew that this word demanded their lives in worship and obedience.

The same scriptures, however, were remade around the disciples' experience of the resurrected Lord. As he 'interpreted to them the things about himself in all the scriptures', and as the Spirit continued that work, the Jewish scriptures became Old Testament: words pointing forward to Jesus the Messiah. The text became a field of prophecy, a garden of figures pointing forward to the story of Jesus. Parts of their familiar scriptures became luminous in the light shining back from the resurrection – though the disciples did not know at first, and would only slowly discover, how to read the rest around those pools of light. It was as if the resurrection had burst the text into fragments, and those slips of parchment were only slowly settling into a new shape. And that transformation was not simply metaphorical: in place of scrolls, Christians turned to codices, notebook texts in which the reader could flip from figure to figure, prophecy to prophecy, the separated pages given in Jesus a new organizing principle external to themselves.[22] And as they read them around that new axis, those texts were woven into a story and became backstory to the events that the disciples had experienced and were experiencing. Their scriptures became the prequel to the story that they now lived. The process by which the members of the young church learnt to re-tell around Jesus the story of their lives, of their world and of their God, was a process by which their scriptures were remade.

While they re-read the Jewish scriptures, Christians also began to write. Luke 'wrote about all that Jesus did and taught from the beginning' (Acts 1.1). He wrote about the process by which the word of Jesus spread – the story of the church. Others wrote about the questions that arose as Christians in the different birthplaces of the faith, facing different pressures, asked what it meant to be converted by the word of the Lord in their situation. They wrote about their arguments and agreements, their discoveries and perplexities. In all this they witnessed to Jesus and to the life that he made possible.

The life of the church is a life of reading, of Old Testament and New, each focused upon Christ. The lives that Christians lead together and apart are lives of reading. In a sense, therefore, all Christian life is exegesis – a discovery of how to read the words of scripture around Jesus, and at the same time a discovery of how to read life, the world and God in Jesus's light.

Sin

The life of the church was, and is, also a sinful life. Of course, Luke tells us that 'the whole group of those who believed were of one heart and soul, and no one claimed private ownership of any possessions, but everything they owned was held in common. With great power the apostles gave their testimony to the resurrection of the Lord Jesus, and great grace was upon them all' (Acts 4.32-33). The next moment, however, Ananias and Sapphira are lying to the church and to God, and being struck down (5.1-

---

[22] See Frances M. Young, *Biblical Exegesis and the Formation of Christian Culture* (Cambridge: Cambridge University Press, 1997), 15–16.

11). Hellenist widows are neglected, and the Hellenists complain (6.1); the Jerusalem church is reluctant to accept what God has done in Saul (9.26); Peter is criticized for eating with gentiles (11.2-3); wider dissension erupts (15.2); Paul and Barnabas fall out and split up (15.39). Even in Acts, before we have turned to the epistles, or to the letters to the seven churches in Revelation, we find the life of the church marked by failures and fractiousness. The church's worship falters, its witness is divided and discipleship is disputed.

There are also, in these early stages of the church's story, signs of some of the deep distortions that will become more starkly obvious in later chapters. We could look, for instance, at the way that the community of those joined to the witness of the two Marys and Joanna becomes nervous of women's power. We could look at the ways in which the same missionary expansion that can be read as polycentric can also be read (and was soon read) in more imperialist ways, the triumph of the word a reverse march upon Rome, one empire giving way to another. Or we could look at the ways in which the church was already beginning already to forget God's promises to Israel, and to twist those promises into curses.

The calling into being of the church was not, after all, an absolute beginning. God's speaking in the resurrection was addressed to a people already gathered by God's word. This new speaking called the church into being in the midst of Israel, but Israel was and remained God's people. Israel is not replaced in God's purposes by the church; God's promises are not revoked. The temptation for Christians to treat them quite differently was, however, growing. When Christians began to re-read the scriptures around Jesus, for instance, the same scriptures continued to be read by many Jewish readers who did not recognize Jesus in them. Christian reading emerged alongside, and in contest with, these other patterns of Jewish reading – and the most audible form taken in Acts by the interaction between these forms of reading is argument:

> Paul and Silas ... came to Thessalonica, where there was a synagogue of the Jews. And Paul went in, as was his custom, and on three sabbath days argued with them from the scriptures, explaining and proving that it was necessary for the Messiah to suffer and to rise from the dead, and saying, 'This is the Messiah, Jesus whom I am proclaiming to you.' (17.1-3)

Again and again, we find Paul pursuing this argument (17.17; 18.4, 19, 28; 19.8, 9), and with hindsight it is hard not to read here the early chapters of a disastrous story. These arguments begin as a contest over meaning; they become a contest over ownership. Christians begin by reading alongside and against other Jewish readers; before long, they are reading without them, and then in their place. The scriptures are, they come to think, theirs and theirs alone; they mistake God's promises for a possession.[23]

---

[23] For a discussion of Christians reading the scriptures with and without Jewish readers, see my 'Whose Psalm Is It Anyway? Why Christians Cannot Read Alone', in *The Text in Play: Experiments in Reading Scripture*, ed. Mike Higton and Rachel Muers (Eugene, OR: Wipf and Stock, 2012), 71–92.

The life of the church is a life not just of worship, witness and discipleship; not just of the Spirit's work and of polycentric catholicity. It is a life of long hatreds, doggedly pursued; it is a life of harsh exclusions, enthusiastically upheld; it is a life of cruel subordinations, justified from the scriptures and upheld as God's will. It is a life of sin.

The emergence of doctrine

The church lives its life from the resurrection of Jesus, who was, and is, and is to come. It is a life of worship, witness and discipleship. It is a life lived in exploration and discovery of the abundant meaning of the word spoken in the resurrection. It is a life lived in the Spirit, expansive, polycentric and woven into catholicity. It is life lived in relation to scripture: a life of embodied, creative reading. It is also, always and everywhere, a life twisted and broken by sin. To understand the role that doctrine plays in the life of the church, we need to understand how it relates to all of this.

The life of the church is a life full of communication. It is a life of conversations and gestures, hints and reminders, suggestions and discussions, pauses and exclamations. It is a life of praying, singing, chanting and preaching. Scripture lets us hear the early church's proclamations, prophecies, teachings, hymns, letters, apologias, legal defences, apocalypses and liturgies – but before they were caught on the page, all of them swam in a broad sea of more informal, now inaudible speech. Doctrinal theology – both formulaic doctrinal statements and the discussions that surround them – comes into being at the confluence of pressures exerted within four particular areas of this Christian speech: proclamation, confession, teaching and controversy.[24]

Proclamation

The growth of the church is powered by proclamation. The women at the empty tomb are commissioned to pass on the news to the other disciples; the disciples collectively tell all those around them what God has done in Jesus of Nazareth.

They do so as people who have been taught by Jesus new meanings for old words. They have learnt what it means for him to be Messiah, for him to usher in the kingdom, for God to enact salvation through him, only by following through his story – by learning to hear his words in the context of his life, death and resurrection. To proclaim the truth he taught, it seems that they have to proclaim the proclaimer. In their proclamation, therefore, they tell his story.

---

[24] My telling of this story has been influenced by J. N. D. Kelly, *Early Christian Creeds*, 3rd edn (Harlow: Longmans, 1972); Young, *The Making of the Creeds*; Pelikan, *Credo: Historical and Theological Guide to Creeds and Confessions of Faith in the Christian Tradition*; Christoph Markschies, *Christian Theology and Its Institutions in the Early Roman Empire: Prolegomena to a History of Early Christian Theology* (Waco, TX: Baylor University Press, 2015); Ward, *How the Light Gets In: Ethical Life 1*, 8–15, and Wolfram Kinzig (ed.), *Faith in Formulae: A Collection of Early Christian Creeds and Creed-related Texts* (Oxford: Oxford University Press, 2017). I have covered some of the material from the following few pages in my paper 'Doctrine and Prayer' in Ashley Cocksworth and John C. McDowell, *The T&T Clark Companion to Christian Prayer* (London: Bloomsbury, forthcoming); and in *Why Doctrine Matters* (Cambridge: Grove, forthcoming).

Things could have been otherwise. This community could have been gathered by some other form of discourse. The dominant form could, say, have been a pattern of legal reasoning, in which the story of Jesus's life would play a strictly subordinate role. It could have been a depiction of the cosmic backdrop against which the events of Jesus's life played out, in relation to which those events, and his teachings, became cryptic and dispensable signs. There is no necessity built in to the way that religious communities work, or in to the storytelling propensities of human beings, that makes it inevitable that Christianity should come to be shaped by proclamation of a story, still less this kind of story. Yet as the earliest Christians sought to make sense of what had happened on the cross and in the resurrection, as they asked how to make sense of the resurrection as a mighty act of the God of Israel, they did in fact fall into this habit of storytelling: weaving together the story of Jesus, the story of God's dealings with Israel, the story of God's making and remaking of the world, the story of their community and the stories of their own lives.[25]

They did not pursue this storytelling in one way only. There is not a single Christian story. Rather, we see in the early church a habit, a developing practice of storytelling. No two presentations of the gospel in Acts are the same. Similar stories are told, but always with particular emphases, particular elaborations. People improvise in the light of their circumstances with the material they have inherited. As the Spirit gives them words to speak, they tell distinctive versions of the story of Jesus to ever-changing audiences.

The very fact that this is a skill learnt, practised and passed on, however, means that a common stock of elements does begin to emerge, a repertoire of motifs and tropes in which some elements prove to be more central, and some less. The storytelling turns out, much of the time, to swirl around common nodes (regularly repeated plot points, key distinctions, common ways of identifying the characters). Once this has begun to happen, it becomes possible to notice these nodes, talk about them, insist upon them and explore how they are connected.[26] It becomes possible to engage in summarizing and articulating Christian proclamation. As soon as one person instructs others on how they might themselves become proclaimers, summarizing and articulating begin to become necessary. We begin to see something like doctrine and something like doctrinal theology emerging in the family resemblances, the rhythms, the formulaic

---

[25] Not everything in their proclamation was storytelling. As they told the story, Christians depicted, at various scales, the scene within which the action takes place; they elaborated distinctions necessary to it; they portrayed the characters involved in it. Their proclamation shaded off into other forms of discourse: prophecy, law, ethical teaching, wisdom. When I speak about 'storytelling', I mean the term loosely and generously; it included all these elements. Heyduck, *The Recovery of Doctrine in the Contemporary Church*, 55, 204, speaks of doctrine in relation to the Christian story's characters, plot and setting. Kevin J. Vanhoozer, in *The Drama of Doctrine: A Canonical-Linguistic Approach to Christian Doctrine* (Louisville, KY: Westminster John Knox, 2005), 110, speaks of doctrine as 'program notes for identifying the *dramatis personae*', and Frances Young (*Making of the Creeds*, 12) of early creeds as '"confessions" summarising the Christian story, or affirmations of the three "characters" in the story'. Cf. Pelikan, *Credo*, 80, and Lewis Ayres, 'On the Practice and Teaching of Christian Doctrine', *Gregorianum* 80, no. 1 (1999): 53.

[26] Gerard Loughlin ('Basis and Authority', 54) says that 'All later developments, from the creeds of the ecumenical councils to the great *summae* of the medieval period and on to the conciliar and other doctrinal statements of the twentieth century, are finally no different in intent: to rule the proper and faithful telling of Christ's story in the life of the church.'

turns of phrase that mark proclamation – and in the patterned statements in which Christian teachers summarize the gospel.[27]

Articulated summaries are never, however, the whole story. Those who summarize follow after the performances of Christian storytellers, stepping back from surface detail to grasp the broader structure holding it together. They work by leaving things out. They are like doctors in a culture in which no one has ever seen the human skeleton uncovered, asked to determine by observation, without scalpels or saws, where the bones run. They offer construals, inherently creative and questionable, attempting to diagram the bones and joints, explaining how the body holds together and what freedom of movement it has.

There are other things missing, too. These summaries are offered by specific people, and not by others. Increasingly, for instance, they became the province of men, not women. Amy-Jill Levine sees in Acts 'a systematic dismantling of any authority women in the early church may have had: the prophesying daughters are silenced, widows become victims in need of rescue by the male leaders of the church … the chain of command is restricted to men'.[28] The history of the emergence of doctrinal practices is part of the broader history of power in the Christian community: a history of anxiety about who gets to tell and to control the telling of the Christian story – a history of anxiety about succession. And, by shaping proclamation, doctrinal practices wield significant power to shape people's imagination, their sense of what makes Christian sense, or what is natural. They can therefore help rationalize or undermine the privilege of those in leadership; they can help write others into or out of the margins. Doctrinal practices emerge amid the communicative habits of Christian life, as supports for that life, and they are every bit as ambiguous as the life they serve.

Confession

In the early church, Christian identity was not simply a reflex of geography; it was not a natural concomitant of being one of the people belonging to a particular place.[29] Christians marked themselves out from their surroundings. It came to be the case that one of the central forms that such marking took was a declaration of allegiance to the central claims of the faith, the claims passed on in proclamation. By such declarations, Christians acknowledged that the story they had heard was their own story.

I said earlier that the church is founded by the resurrection and by the witness of the women at the tomb. It is also built upon Peter's confession of faith.

> Now when Jesus came into the district of Caesarea Philippi, he asked his disciples … 'who do you say that I am?' Simon Peter answered, 'You are the Messiah, the

---

[27] The whole enjoyable but unwinnable game of identifying early credal, liturgical and hymnic forms in the New Testament takes flight here.

[28] Amy-Jill Levine, 'Introduction', in *A Feminist Companion to the Acts of the Apostles*, ed. Amy-Jill Levine with Marianne Blickenstaff (London: T&T Clark, 2004), 1.

[29] See Rowan Williams, 'Does It Make Sense to Speak of Pre-Nicene Orthodoxy?' in *The Making of Orthodoxy: Essays in Honour of Henry Chadwick*, ed. Rowan Williams (Cambridge: Cambridge University Press, 1989), 5–6.

Son of the living God.' And Jesus answered him, 'Blessed are you, Simon son of Jonah! For flesh and blood has not revealed this to you, but my Father in heaven. And I tell you, you are Peter, and on this rock I will build my church, and the gates of Hades will not prevail against it. (Mt. 16.13-18)

Peter is not, in this act of confession, simply voicing an opinion, nor is he by an act of will throwing in his lot with Jesus. He is voicing his recognition of what is taking place in Jesus, and so his recognition of the movement of God in which he is being caught up – a recognition to which he has been brought by the work of the Father. It is both an act of worship and a declaration of allegiance.[30]

Both as worship and as declaration, confession leans towards a certain terseness and repeatability; it leans towards the formulaic. As a declaration of allegiance, it involves naming what is central in one's faith in a form that will be recognizable to others – a banner around which others can rally. As an act of worship, it shares that common tug present in all worship towards the liturgical – towards the repeatable, towards a distinction from ordinary speech, towards patterns of words that get bound in place by the affective power that gathers around them.[31] Confession of faith is therefore one of the places where, from very early on, we see the development of summary articulations of the faith that begin to look like rules of faith, and like creeds.

The simplest such formula, and perhaps the most basic confession of Christian faith, is the declaration that Jesus is Lord. '[I]f you confess with your lips that Jesus is Lord and believe in your heart that God raised him from the dead, you will be saved' (Rom. 10.9); 'at the name of Jesus every knee should bend, in heaven and on earth and under the earth, and every tongue should confess that Jesus Christ is Lord, to the glory of God the Father' (Phil. 2.10-11).[32] All other Christian confessions can be thought of as an elaboration of this basic confession; it is the most concentrated form of all the articulated summaries of the Christian faith.[33]

---

[30] On Peter's confession, see Helmer, *Theology and the End of Doctrine*, 133–5, and Pelikan, *Credo*, 133. For confession as both worship and declaration of allegiance, see Edmund Schlink, 'The Structure of Dogmatic Statements as an Ecumenical Problem', in *The Coming Christ and the Coming Church*, trans. I.H. Neilson et al. (Edinburgh: Oliver and Boyd, 1967), 17, 19, 23. Cf. Francis A. Sullivan, *Creative Fidelity: Weighing and Interpreting Documents of the Magisterium* (New York: Paulist, 1996), 31; Richard S. Briggs, *Words in Action: Speech Act Theory and Biblical Interpretation* (Edinburgh: T&T Clark, 2001), 186; John Webster, 'Confession and Confessions', in *Nicene Christianity: The Future for a New Ecumenism*, ed. Christopher R. Seitz (Grand Rapids, MI: Brazos, 2001), 119–31.

[31] Young, *The Making of the Creeds*, 6–7, discusses the threefold shape of baptismal confession, and the way in which that shape could be filled out with a repertoire of stock phrases that could be deployed as occasion demanded – 'because they "ring bells" with people, they are part of the traditional "in-language" of Christian teaching and worship' (ibid., 7–8).

[32] See Pelikan, *Credo*, 59–60 on 'Jesus is Lord' as the primary form of confession; cf. Hurtado, *Lord Jesus Christ*, 108–17, 179–82.

[33] Liuwe H. Westra, in *The Apostles' Creed: Origin, History, and Some Early Commentaries* (Turnhout: Brepols, 2002), 68–9, summarizes the role of the 'Christological sequence' in the development of second-century confessional formulae. Simon J. Gathercole, in 'The Christ of the Canonical Gospels and the Christs of the Apocryphal Gospels', in *The Oxford Handbook of Christology*, ed. Francesca Murphy (Oxford: Oxford University Press, 2015), 534–5, describes the way that the Gospels themselves already display an implicit Christological rule, affirming '(i) the identity of Jesus as the "Christ"' (i.e. 'anointed by the Creator God of Israel') '(ii) the work of Christ as fulfilling Scripture; (iii) the atoning death of Christ; and (iv) the resurrection.'

The other form of confession that can claim to be the basic confession of Christian faith is confession of the triune God – a form associated with baptism. Baptismal confession was both a pedagogical form (an epitome of the catechesis that the new Christian had undergone, now summarized, articulated and made memorable) and a confessional form (formulaic precisely in order to indicate that new Christians were declaring the same faith as their teachers, declaring their membership of the community of this shared confession).[34] That dual nature is visible in the dual location of these confessions: on the one hand, in the engagement between catechist and catechumen prior to baptism, offered from teacher to pupil and then pupil to teacher as a marker of the passing on of the faith; on the other, in the emerging liturgy of baptism itself, offered as an element of the catechumens' prayers, the beginning of a lifelong journey deeper into the knowledge of God.[35]

The history of the development of the 'rule of faith' in the second and third century, and of the creeds on into the fourth century and beyond, is shaped by the elaboration of both the Christological confession and the triune, and by their combination.[36] These formulae are often seen primarily through the lens of controversy – as bulwarks erected against theological error – but if we consider them first as forms of confession, emerging from a history of such confession, we might understand F. D. Maurice's insistence that, in the creeds, 'That which is believed is not a certain scheme of divinity, but a name'.[37] 'Trust', Maurice says, 'must be in a Person', and the one who says the creeds declares trust in God, insisting that 'I cannot see Him, but I know his *Name*'; they declare that 'the greatest privilege they possessed was to know this Name fully, to be stamped and sealed with it'.[38]

Here too, however, it is worth attending to the ambiguities. Declarations of allegiance are not offered in lofty isolation, but in the midst of people's complicated lives. In the church, any such declaration is unavoidably a declaration of allegiance to a particular community, and to its leaders, as well as of allegiance to God. By the time we reach the fourth century, confession has become 'a public declaration of theo-political allegiance' – a response to the imperial power by which the creeds are backed, as well as to the one the creeds name.[39] Doctrine and power are never very far apart.

Teaching

Alongside the proclamation of the good news to those who had not yet heard it, and the confessions of those who took this good news as their own, practices of teaching

---

[34] Young, *Making of the Creeds*, 3.
[35] Everett Fergusson, *The Rule of Faith: A Guide* (Eugene, OR: Cascade, 2015), 69–70.
[36] See Pelikan, *Credo*, 178–9; Kelly, *Creeds*, 1–5, 100–30, and Westra, *The Apostles' Creed*.
[37] Frederick Denison Maurice, *The Kingdom of Christ: Or, Hints on the Principles, Ordinances and Constitution of the Catholic Church. In Letters to a Member of the Society of Friends*, 2nd edn (London: J. G. F. and J. Rivington / Darton and Clark, 1842), 7.
[38] Frederick Denison Maurice, *The Prayer Book: Considered Especially in Reference to the Romish System: Nineteen Sermons Preached in the Chapel of Lincoln's Inn* (London: John W. Parker, 1849), 154–5, emphasis in original. See Mark Chapman, 'F.D. Maurice and Reciting the Creeds', in *Bishops, Saints and Politics: Anglican Studies* (London: T&T Clark, 2007), 133–48. Cf. Clutterbuck, *Handing on Christ*, 112: 'Christian doctrine has as its aim the appropriate naming by the Church of the triune God whom it worships and serves.'
[39] Ward, *How the Light*, 24. Cf. Virginia Burrus, 'History, Theology, Orthodoxy, Polydoxy', *Modern Theology* 30, no. 3 (2014): 9.

also shaped the church from the beginning. That is, the church was shaped by all that communication in which one follower of Jesus sought to instruct others in their discipleship. Such teaching could take many forms, and occur in many settings, from Lois teaching her grandson Timothy to Paul speaking late into the night to the Christians in Troas. We could think of there being an ecology of teaching, in which all God's people are involved in teaching one another, but in which some are called to pursue that task more deliberately and visibly, so earning themselves the name of 'teachers'.[40]

Some of this teaching sets out the backdrop against which the life of Christian discipleship takes place. That is, teachers articulate claims about God and God's ways with the world, telling the story of how God has acted, and calling for forms of worship, witness and discipleship that will respond to and fit with that story. Think, for instance, of the form of many of the epistles, in which a rehearsal of God's acts precedes a body of ethical instruction – the two parts joined together by some kind of 'therefore'.[41]

Once again, there was no antecedent necessity that Christian teaching should take this form. It could, instead, have become and remained a matter of learning at the feet of the apostles and their successors, imitating their lives, joining in their prayers, listening to their wisdom sayings and parables. There need not have been any intensive investment in the development of a canopy of truth claims, a metanarrative that really was an articulated narrative.

One of the factors that pushed Christian teaching in the direction of doctrinal theology, however, was Christianity's polycentricity. Those who responded to Christian proclamation were, as I have explained, asked not so much to take on an already formed way of life as to be converted by the same word that had converted those witnessing to them. The invention or discovery of this polycentric form of life involved the invention or discovery of a distinction between the converting word and the converted life. That is, it required the deployment of a distinction between the proclamation of truth about God and the working out of the implications of that truth for ordinary life. It is hard to think polycentricity without thinking some such distinction, even if the place where the distinction is drawn is far from stable.

The invention or discovery of that distinction was bound up with one of the characteristic forms of early Christian teaching: the ministry of itinerant apostles. If your teachers are no longer present, so that learning the ways of the faith cannot any longer be a matter of sitting day by day at their feet, then continuing in their teaching must take some other form. One response is for the teacher to insist (more or less convincingly) that members of the community already know all they need to know in order to respond to whatever new situations or controversies they are facing. The deposit of received teaching becomes the apostle's proxy, and the answers to the community's pressing questions can be made to flow from that deposit. They know

---

[40] For the diversity of forms of teaching in the church, see Claire S. Smith, *Pauline Communities as 'Scholastic Communities': A Study of the Vocabulary of 'Teaching' in 1 Corinthians, 1 and 2 Timothy and Titus* (Tübingen: Mohr Siebeck, 2010), James Wm. McClendon, Jr., *Systematic Theology 2: Doctrine* (Nashville, TN: Abingdon, 1994), 23; Pelikan, *Credo*, 67; Schlink, 'The Structure of Dogmatic Statements', 24–7, and Briggs, *Words in Action*, 257–90.

[41] See my discussion of Ephesians in Chapter 5.

the storyline of the faith, and that should be enough to enable them to know how to go on in the present.

The development of Christian polycentricity involved, then, the emergence of the idea that all these diverse experiments in Christian life were rooted in common teaching about the one gift that enabled all of them: the story of God and God's ways with the world. And as this story now had to be something to reason with, to argue from, because it was serving as the foundation on which the decisions of everyday faithfulness could be built, there was a constant pressure towards something like propositional form. Christian teaching, like Christian proclamation, gives rise to doctrine and to doctrinal theology.[42]

Once again, however, the development is ambiguous. The kind of theological discussion that we see in the epistles does not emerge simply as the natural accompaniment of religious teaching; it emerges from the demands of a complex social situation. It is bound up with the attempts of distant teachers to exert authority. It is bound up with the processes by which these scattered communities are persuaded that they are a single fellowship, around which money can flow. It is bound up with the emergence of disciplinary regimes, and practices of exclusion.[43] These doctrinal practices can't be disentangled from the mixed motives, the complex forms of power, the messy rivalries and contests of the people among whom they appear.

Controversy

As the Christian faith spread, and communities sprang up living it differently, the question was bound to arise as to whether all these communities were following the same Lord. Christianity had developed in such a way that it was held together – or was supposed to be held together – by allegiance to the same claims about God and God's ways with the world, but the diverse forms that lives of worship, witness and discipleship took, and the diverse ways in which Christians articulated what they knew, made the question of unity unavoidable.

The same articulated summaries that emerged from and shaped proclamation, confession and teaching became fodder for controversy. The question of the unity between scattered Christian communities became, in part, a question of the mutual recognizability of their doctrine, and scrutiny of each other's summary articulations of the faith became one of the means by which Christians held one another to account, or called one another's faith into question.[44] In the midst of such holding to account, the assertion of one's position in the various controversies of the faith often became a matter of brandishing the articulated summary of the faith that one had received and learnt to inhabit.

---

[42] Ellen T. Charry, in 'The Moral Function of Doctrine', *Theology Today* 49, no. 1 (1992): 33, insists that doctrinal texts are 'constructed to influence the reader', seeing dogmatic explication as 'an instrument of individual and societal formation and transformation, as an instrument of moral pedagogy'. Cf. Charry, *By the Renewing of Your Minds: The Pastoral Function of Christian Doctrine* (New York: Oxford University Press, 1997).

[43] For example, 2 Cor. 10–12; 8–9; 1.23–2.11 and 6.14-18.

[44] See pp. 183–4.

The story of the emergence of Christian doctrine is not a story driven wholly by controversy. Yet, alongside the pressures generated by proclamation, confession and teaching, the pressures of controversy did play a particular role, driving the community towards a more technical language for the summarizing and articulation of its beliefs.[45] In controversy, a cloud of possible ways of talking about some particular topic condenses into rival options; particular terms become the characteristic ways of expressing those options, and those terms become shibboleths: to use them is to declare one's allegiance to one side or the other. By dint of persuasive exposition, repetition or loud assertion, claims about where the use of these terms leads – what features of the Christian story they are supposed to protect or betray – become ingrained, and technical vocabulary and rules for its deployment begin to coalesce from the rich soup of informal Christian speech.

It is important not to think of this as a history happening entirely at the level of the concepts in dispute. The history of Christian controversy is a history of disputes about power, of alliances and compromises. It is a political history that cannot be told without attention to Christians' shifting relationship to empire – and, increasingly of the empire's interest in a unified and quiescent Christianity. It is a history of developing institutional forms: of episcopacy and the diocese, councils and their pronouncements, catechetical schools and their curricula. Doctrinal forms of speech were squeezed into shape by all of these histories. The practices of doctrinal theology emerge under multiple pressures within the life of the church, entangled with all the ambiguous forces that shape that life.

Conclusion

The life of the church is the continuous and uneven unfolding of the word that God spoke to the world in the life, death and resurrection of Jesus – the one who was, who is and who is to come. This unfolding takes place in the lives of worship, witness and discipleship that Christians negotiate together in the midst of the world. It takes shape in the care they offer to the vulnerable, in the circulations of money around their communities, in the ways they share food together, in the attitudes they adopt to the political regimes that surround them, in the habits of worship that they foster, in the words that their teachers pass on and in their readings of the scriptures. It always takes shape in the life that particular people are building and tending together in some specific place. The unfolding of God's abundant gift takes the form of a polycentric collection of lived experiments in faithfulness.

The life of the church is not glorious. Every one of these experiments in faithfulness is a failure. Some of the experiments are luminous, some ignominious – but all of them are experiments conducted by people caught up in the circulations of harm that we call sin. All of these experiments both acknowledge and betray Christ's lordship; all of them both help and harm the world.[46]

---

[45] See Fergusson, *Rule of Faith*, 72–4; cf. Kelly, *Creeds*, 98.
[46] For a strong account of the theology of failure, and the failure of theology, see Marika Rose, *A Theology of Failure: Žižek against Christian Innocence* (New York: Fordham University Press, 2019).

As Christianity spread across the ancient world, its life was shaped for good and ill by the telling and retelling of God's ways with the world. Christians pursued this telling and retelling in proclamation, confession, teaching and controversy. For contingent reasons – reasons of habit, memory, effectiveness and power – this telling and retelling coalesced into recognizable shapes, arranged around familiar loci. Practices arose in which those loci could be named and the flow of Christian storytelling around them discussed. The articulated statements of the faith became building blocks for argument, the means by which the faithfulness of Christian forms of living could be debated. Doctrinal theology emerged in the midst of Christian life, as one of the ingredients by which the church became what it was.

Doctrinal theology is no freer from ambiguity than any other ingredient in the life of the church. From the start, it has been entangled with the processes by which the story of Jesus is passed on, explored and embodied. From the start, it has been no less entangled with the power plays of Christian leaders, the forms of inattentiveness and exclusion that have marred the church's life and the fractiousness that has split churches apart. Those engaged in its practices don't stand at any safe distance from the church's broken life.[47]

The question I will be exploring over the remainder of this book is whether, and in what forms, doctrinal theology might be of service to the church in the midst of all this ambiguity. How, precisely, might it help Christians negotiate lives of worship, witness and discipleship together? How might it help them acknowledge the failures that in every situation mar their negotiations? How might it help the church explore and inhabit in the midst of the world the abundant word spoken to that world by God in the resurrection of Jesus of Nazareth?

---

[47] Cf. Natalie Wigg-Stevenson, *Ethnographic Theology: An Enquiry into the Production of Theological Knowledge* (London: Palgrave, 2014), 2–3.

5

Doctrine and intellectualism

Introduction

From the resurrected body of Jesus, new life spread. Worship, witness and discipleship travelled contagiously outwards, changing as they went. More and more communities received the faith passed on to them, and in their turn remade it. They discovered together in their various locations patterns of life that embodied this faith – and patterns that betrayed it. As they did so, they both inherited and invented ways of telling the story of God and God's ways with the world, and ways of defending, discussing and passing on this storytelling.

In among all this speaking, in proclamation, confession, teaching and controversy, Christians developed ways of summarizing the content of their faith, and arguing with and about those summaries; they began to pursue doctrinal theology. It was an ingredient in the webbing of mutual accountability that wove the church together; it was weaponized in the disagreements that divided it. It played roles both in encouraging and resisting change, in the enforcement of conformity and the justification of innovation. Doctrinal theology is one fallible and ambiguous ministry among many that together shape the body of Christ. It might be a ministry that can help build up that body, but only in among every other ministry in the body's life. It is a ministry that makes no sense on its own.

In this chapter, I am going to focus on intellectualism, one of the characteristic deformations of doctrinal theology. For many of those intensively engaged in the practices of doctrinal theology – people I will call 'doctrinal theologians' – there is a constant temptation to think they know best. They can end up thinking themselves the arbiters of Christian knowledge, and Christian life the application of the knowledge they arbitrate. Closer attention to the nature of Christian knowing can, however, weaken this temptation. Christian knowing involves an imaginative indwelling of the love of God, and the ongoing discovery of how to live that love out in the world. It involves Christians learning to love in the communities and contexts in which they find themselves; it involves learning to love against the powers that corrupt the world.

Doctrinal theology both emerges from and serves such learning, or it is nothing.

The lure of intellectualism

However fresh and variegated their own language might be, doctrinal theologians work with summaries squeezed into reproducible forms by the pressures of proclamation, confession, teaching and controversy. Specific meanings and connections are drawn into the foreground, and the language of doctrinal theology begins to become technical: a language with a circumscribed vocabulary and explicitly stated rules. Once these counters and rules of play are on the table, the game can take off; no more is needed to make possible extraordinary elaboration.

The partial technicality of doctrinal theological language inevitably awakens in some the desire to achieve a still purer technicality. They disambiguate and clarify, trying to make the terms of the game more fully explicit. Because it is generated out of the unruly materials of living speech, there is always more to this language than has yet been made explicit, or something in it that runs counter to the rules so far identified – but that simply means that there is always more work to be done to refine the system.[1] The repeated emergence of scholastic forms of Christian theology (in Byzantium, in the medieval West, among the Protestant orthodox, in the academic wake of almost every major modern theologian) should be no surprise. The impetus towards such refinement is baked in to the procedures of the discipline.

This drive to technicality can generate intellectual tools of tremendous power. It can uncover deep connections shaping Christian life, and enable the recognition of responsibilities and possibilities that might otherwise have been missed.[2] It can be a kind of spiritual discipline, by means of which something of the order of God's ways with the world is uncovered, and minds and lives are attuned to that order.[3] There can be a sharp joy in the ability to handle the terms of such a system. It can have something of the character of a physical skill, a facility, a way with words. But precisely this intellectual power and the joy of wielding it prime the temptation. Doctrinal theology can become a game running in isolation from the life that it is supposed to serve. The vocabulary and the grammar, the counters and the rules, are enough, and the game can sustain itself by feeding solely on its own productions. Refinements are eventually generated that are necessary only for the ongoing playing of the game, and that make no ripples in the wider wash of life that the game is meant to serve.

Criticisms like this can themselves be levelled too easily. Technical refinement, subtle distinctions and highly explicit argumentation are not inherently trivial.

---

[1] Linn Marie Tonstad, *God and Difference: The Trinity, Sexuality, and the Transformation of Finitude* (New York, NY: Routledge, 2016), 3, examines theologians' efforts to stipulate the proper meaning of their terms, but finds the connotations they have excluded doing far more work in their arguments than they acknowledge. See also p. 106.

[2] See Mike Higton and Steve Holmes, 'Meeting Scotus: On Scholasticism and Its Ghosts', *International Journal of Systematic Theology* 4, no. 1 (2002): 81. We were younger then.

[3] Anna Williams, *The Architecture of Theology: Structure, System, and Ratio* (Oxford: Oxford University Press, 2011), 17, argues that 'The rational quality of theology is ... not what the attackers of reason claim for it, a human "engine 'gainst the Almighty", but ... the Almighty's invitation to humanity to view the world as the exposition of *ratio*, the array of wisdom and love.' Cf. my discussion of Anselm in *A Theology of Higher Education* (Oxford: Oxford University Press, 2012), ch. 1.

Scholasticisms of all sorts come in for lazy caricature by those too impatient to trace the threads that run back from their refinements into the life of worship, witness and discipleship. There never was any medieval debate about the number of angels that could dance on the head of a pin. Yet the possibility remains, and is sometimes realized, that the ropes holding a theological system to earth can fray and snap, and the whole beautiful construction float off into the blue.[4]

Becoming intellectualist

Such intellectualism is visible in a strange backlit way in the literature surrounding the 'nature of doctrine', despite the insistence in all of it that doctrine is deeply connected to the life of the church. Its echo can be heard in the repeated claim that doctrinal seriousness is in sorry decline in the church, that it is in need of defence, and that doctrinal theologians are the ones to ride to its rescue.[5]

Kevin Vanhoozer, for instance, opens his discussion of doctrine with the complaint that

> For many in our postmodern age, 'feeling is believing'; to formulate one's beliefs in doctrine is thought to be unnecessary, impossible, or divisive. Members of mainline churches find it increasingly difficult to articulate the doctrinal distinctiveness of their respective denominations.[6]

It is not hard to find older examples. W. R. Matthews wrote in 1929 about 'a falling away from "organized religion," and with it a revolt from "dogmatic theology"'. James Orr in 1897 bemoaned the rising conviction that 'the development of dogma ... is a gigantic monument of human folly, a momentous aberration of the human spirit, an incubus on the intellectual and moral progress of the race'. John Henry Newman complained in 1838 that increasing numbers of his contemporaries now believed that 'every man's view of revealed religion is acceptable to God, if he acts up to it; ... no one view is itself better than another.' Doctrine, it seems, is always at death's door.[7]

These laments may have a basis in fact. There may be a story to tell of a widespread decline in doctrinal literacy, or of diminishing enthusiasm for doctrinal debate across

---

[4] '[T]echnical distinctions are important only because of the effects they make possible on the way the world is seen, experienced, and discerned.' Ward, *How the Light Gets In*, 118.
[5] A nice illustration is provided by Richard Heyduck. He wrote a book called *The Recovery of Doctrine in the Contemporary Church*, but it turns out not to be about a recovery that has happened or is happening, but about one that should happen. The thesis on which the book was based was called *The Marginalization of Doctrine in the Modern Church* (Fuller Theological Seminary, 1998).
[6] Kevin J. Vanhoozer, *The Drama of Doctrine: A Canonical-Linguistic Approach to Christian Doctrine* (Louisville, KY: Westminster John Knox, 2005), xi.
[7] W. R. Matthew et al., *Dogma in History and Thought: Studies by Various Writers* (London: Nisbet, 1929), v; Orr, *The Progress of Dogma*, 5; John Henry Newman, *Discussions and Arguments on Various Subjects* (London: Longmans, Green, and Co., 1907), 129. For an example that has acquired the status of formal church policy, see Standing Order 524 of *The Constitutional Practice and Discipline of the Methodist Church*, vol. 2 (London: Methodist Publishing, 2017). Some lay the blame at the feet of theologians: see Helmer, *Theology and the End of Doctrine*, 7, and Mascall, *Theology and the Gospel of Christ*, 1.

swathes of popular Christianity – though I suspect the reality is complex and uneven. The sheer persistence of these claims, however, the regularity with which accounts of doctrine are framed as attempts to recover a doctrinal seriousness recently lost, and the fact that this decline can be dated to so many different periods, are hints that something else might also be going on.[8] I suggest instead that the deeper picture is of an abiding tension between doctrinal articulation and ordinary belief, and of a process by which doctrinal theologians are trained to misrecognize that tension.

An individual Christian, a member of the uneven ordinary, for some reason gains a training in doctrinal articulacy. The patterns of thought that such a training makes possible come as a discovery and a delight – or at least they do to most of those who find the energy to pursue the training for long. There are previously undreamt-of ways of expressing and articulating the faith, of seeing how its parts connect and of peering into its recondite depths. This delight becomes ingrained: the theologian learns to love the smell of new books, the look of a well-produced bibliography, the click of precisely deployed terminology.[9]

New theologians are introduced to these patterns of thought by being inducted into a community of articulacy. They learn a tradition of explicit statement and argument that stretches far back into the Christian past. It is a tradition that stretches back in a chain of texts, of words put on paper by others who delighted in doctrinal articulacy. In effect, theologians are introduced to a paper church that sits within the fleshy church they know. The tradition to which they now have access is by definition articulate, and few of them can help but compare the present church in all its unimpressive inarticulacy to the purity of this paper past. It is hard for the newly articulate theologian not to frame this perception temporally: the church of the present has fallen into doctrinal inarticulacy, and the theologian is one of the few in whom the intellectual seriousness of the past is being kept alive.

The typical product of this process is a particular kind of knowing subject. Stereotypically, it is in our own era the White, male, middle-class theologian, who now knows better than the church what the church should believe.[10] He is the champion of the articulate whole from which the fragmentary ordinary has declined. He has lost sight of the ways in which the articulations in which he trades are themselves,

---

[8] 'One loses count of the number of predictions of imminent collapse through internal incoherence' (Sykes, 'The Genius of Anglicanism', 228). For a brief history of exasperation with doctrine, see Clutterbuck, *Handing on Christ*, 52–69; Pelikan, *Credo*, 490, and Geoffrey Wainwright, 'Does Doctrine Still Divide?' *Ecclesiology* 2, no. 1 (2005): 11.

[9] Natalie Wigg-Stephenson describes the production of the researcher's academic habitus in *Ethnographic Theology*, 47–82. Cf. Sarah Burton, 'The Monstrous "White Theory Boy": Symbolic Capital, Pedagogy and the Politics of Knowledge', *Sociological Research Online* 20, no. 3 (2015): 1–11.

[10] See Linn Marie Tonstad, *Queer Theology: Beyond Apologetics* (Eugene, OR: Cascade, 2018), 63, on the 'liberal subject', 'white, male, propertied and rational'; cf. John Webster, 'Theological Theology', in *Confessing God: Essays in Christian Dogmatics II* (London: T&T Clark, 2005), 14–15 on 'the assumed subject of university theology'. Reddie, *Theologsing Brexit*, 62, argues that 'One of the most common conceits bequeathed to us by White predominantly male theologians is the belief that there is little [connection] to discern between the knowing person who undertakes the theological task of talking about God and the theology that results from that process.' This subject has also typically lost site of the ways in which his own practice is made possible by economic privilege and the labour of others, especially women.

and always have been, no more than fragments of the life of the church; he mistakes them for the real substance of the church's faith.[11] He reads the inarticulate present in the unforgiving light of the articulate past, and takes ordinary Christian practice to be the inconsistent application of intellectual principles inadequately grasped, not the skilful deployment of a repertoire of practical habits.[12] He might even suppose that, as a doctrinal theologian, and by means of his articulacy, he knows God more fully and more clearly than do others.

The articulate and the ordinary

The idea of an abiding tension between doctrinal articulacy and ordinary belief has played a significant role in recent discussions of Anglican identity. In the course of a discussion of Richard Hooker, for instance, Rowan Williams contrasts the 'mythical, traditional and (normally) very material modes of making sense ... associated commonly with "the people" at large, and the analytic styles of a class that has "escaped" from myth and tradition'.[13] Williams draws on the work of Debora Shuger, who argues that Hooker was defending the 'sensuous and ceremonial worship of Christian populism', a 'visible mystical body of persons united by common agreement on the objects of their love: a community realized in antiphonal chant, sacramental participation, and pastoral care', in which 'the love and longing that these acts embody constitute the common bond linking vulgar and learned, rich and poor'.[14] In Shuger's words, Hooker was defending this life from 'the exclusionary rigor of Puritan ecclesiology'; in Williams's, Hooker was fighting against 'contemptuous rationalists struggling to impose something upon "lower orders" who habitually communicate and make sense in other terms'.[15]

According to Williams, Hooker 'makes a powerful bid for imagining a sacred community in which the effective furthering of the community's goals does not depend upon the successful manipulation of the community's express beliefs by the work of an elite'.[16] He does not deny that ordinary Christian life should be 'subject to severe criticism and pruning when it ... colludes with our unreconstructed passions'. There remains a role for the articulate theologian in guarding ordinary

---

[11] See Shannon Craigo-Snell, 'Tradition on Fire: Polydoxy, Orthodoxy, and Theological Epistemology', *Modern Theology* 39, no. 3 (2014): 31.
[12] For this account of ordinary practice, see Timothy Jenkins, 'Fieldwork and the Perception of Everyday Life', *Man* 29, no. 2 (1994): 433–55. Cf. Bourdieu, 'The Scholastic Point of View', 127–40, and Tanner, *Theories of Culture*, 82. See also Chapter 3, pp. 49–50. For a different account of the relationship between articulate and inarticulate Christian knowledge, see Mascall, 'Whither Anglican Theology?' 43.
[13] Williams, *Anglican Identities*, 32–3.
[14] Debora Shuger, '"Societie Supernaturall": The Imagined Community of Hooker's Laws', in *Richard Hooker and the Construction of Christian Community*, ed. A. C. McGrade (Tempe, AZ: Medieval & Renaissance Texts & Studies, 1997), 316, 324. 'Christian populism' is Peter Brown's term for Augustine's focus on the faith of the ordinary Christian community; see Peter Brown, *Power and Persuasion in Late Antiquity: Towards a Christian Empire* (Madison, WI: University of Wisconsin Press, 1992), 74.
[15] Shuger, 'Societie Supernaturall', 316; Williams, *Identities*, 33. This is Williams's attempt to capture Hooker's attitude to the Puritans, rather than being a direct expression of his own attitude.
[16] Williams, *Identities*, 32.

belief against certain kinds of failure.[17] Yet the very theological vision on which Hooker draws as he plays that critical role also places limits upon it. Williams argues that Hooker's defence of the 'present complexity and variety of the believing community' rests upon his understanding of 'the priority of divine action'.[18] As Williams says in a related study of George Herbert, too strong a focus on 'a "perfect", fully conscious faith might delude us into thinking that faith as a human virtue saved us. Our faith can be no more perfect than our righteousness.'[19] Or as Herbert himself puts it, 'Thus dost thou make proud knowledge bend and crouch / While grace fills up uneven Nature.'[20]

There are two caveats that I need to place beside this argument. First, it is not simply an account of Hooker; it is part of Williams's account of Anglican identity. As my discussion in Chapter 2 will have suggested, I see such claims less as descriptions of Anglicanism's abiding essence than as polemical moves in the present. This is one more proposal of a way forward for the Church of England, buttressed by the construction of a contestable genealogy in that Church's past.[21] The polemical nature of Williams's approach is clear: he suggests that Hooker 'might be worth listening to if we want to preserve the Church from new forms of elitist conceptualism (right or left)'.[22] This latter point is echoed by Ben Quash, who says that

> Both those 'conservatives' concerned with a sub-Calvinist 'purity' of doctrine delivered by a cadre of sound knowers to an audience of obedient recipients, and those 'liberals' confident that they know better than the tradition because of their superior intellectual and analytical resources are thereby challenged ... to beware of selling short the principle of the free, prevenient grace of God; the priority of the divine initiative, and our dependence on it at every point, whether in our growth in sanctity or in our growth in knowledge.[23]

Williams and Quash are channelling a prominent strand of Anglican self-description. Hensley Henson, for instance, writing in 1939, wrote that

> The doctrinal incoherence of the Church of England, though it is unquestionably perplexing, practically embarrassing, and not infrequently actually scandalous, has its roots in something far more respectable than an indolent acquiescence in undiscipline or a respectable indifference to truth. It reflects the reluctance

---

[17] Ibid., 35.
[18] Ibid., 27.
[19] Ibid., 62, emphasis removed.
[20] George Herbert, 'Faith', lines 31–2, from *The Temple: Sacred Poems and Private Ejaculations* (London: Pickering, 1838), 43; discussed by Shuger, 'Societie Supernaturall', 322.
[21] Cf. Anthony Milton, 'Introduction: Reformation, Identity, and "Anglicanism", c. 1520–1662', in *The Oxford History of Anglicanism I: Reformation and Identity, c.1520–1662*, ed. Anthony Milton (Oxford: Oxford University Press, 2017), 7.
[22] Williams, *Identities*, 39.
[23] Ben Quash, *Found Theology: History, Imagination and the Holy Spirit* (London: Bloomsbury, 2013), xiv–xv.

of considering and responsible English churchmen to thrust the rough hand of authority into the sphere of religious opinion.[24]

There are deep Anglican roots to this account of doctrinal theology's limited role. But it is not the only Anglican account, and it has always existed in tension with other possible Anglicanisms – including those championed by Hooker's opponents and by their more recent heirs.

My second caveat – one to which I will be returning in Chapter 6 – is that this tension should not be seen as a stand-off between sharply separated sides, but as a set of stresses existing between differing regions of a complex continuum. We are not faced, in the church, simply with articulacy and inarticulacy, but with a complex map of differing kinds and levels of articulation, shading off into one another without sharp boundaries. There is no hard border where ordinary belief meets doctrinal theology.

The knowledge and love of God

Learning Christ

Intellectualism, then, is the tendency to look down upon the knowledge of ordinary believers from the vantage point of achieved articulacy. It is the temptation to think that the doctrinal theologian who can play like a virtuoso on the resources of the articulate tradition thereby knows God better than do those believers who can barely explain a word of the creeds that they recite in worship. My claim in this chapter, and in the book as a whole, is that such intellectualism involves a deep misunderstanding of belief, of the knowledge of God and of the point of doctrinal theology.

The Epistle to the Ephesians paints a very different picture of the knowledge of God, and of the role of Christian teaching, from the one that underpins such intellectualism. We can begin to explore that picture by attending to the contrast that the epistle draws between those crafty speakers whose windy doctrines blow people off course, and those good teachers whose words build up Christ's body (4.11-12; 4.14). That contrast makes sense within the epistle's broader picture of God's sanctifying work. God, says Paul, chose the members of the body 'to be holy and blameless before him in love' so that they might 'live for the praise of his glory' (1.4, 12). In Christ Jesus, they have been made anew, 'created according to the likeness of God in true righteousness and holiness', created 'to be imitators of God, as beloved children' and to pursue 'good works, which God prepared beforehand to be [their] way of life' (4.24; 5.1; 2.10). They are being reshaped so that their lives might display the glory of God.

This involves the 'renewal in the Spirit' of minds that would otherwise be futile, darkened and insensitive (4.23; 4.17-19). That is, it involves a reordering of minds shaped by distorted desire, so 'corrupt and deluded by [their] lusts' that they can

---

[24] Henson, *The Church of England*, 108; discussed in Avis, *The Identity of Anglicanism*, 34–5. Cf. Ephraim Radner, *Hope among the Fragments: The Broken Church and Its Engagement of Scripture* (Grand Rapids, MI: Brazos Press, 2004), 45–7, on the 'adjustable churchman'.

produce only the 'unfruitful works of darkness' (5.11). The Spirit works upon such minds so that they might instead be filled with desire for God, and desire for the growth of the whole body into unity with Christ (4.22).

This transformation takes the form of a journey into the unfathomable riches of the God who can 'accomplish abundantly far more than all we can ask or imagine' (3.20). The members of the body are being drawn into knowledge of 'the riches of [the Father's] glorious inheritance among the saints, and what is the immeasurable greatness of his power for us who believe', 'far above all rule and authority and power and dominion' (1.19, 21). They are being drawn into knowledge that will not be complete until all of them 'come to the unity of the faith and of the knowledge of the Son of God, to maturity, to the measure of the full stature of Christ' (4.13). They are being drawn 'to comprehend, with all the saints, what is the breadth and length and height and depth, and to know the love of Christ that surpasses knowledge, so that [they] may be filled with all the fullness of God' (3.18). They are, that is, being drawn into knowledge of a reality that surpasses knowledge, to grasp something that can never exhaustively be grasped; the measure of their knowledge is the immeasurable love of Christ.

Paul's audience are urged to learn what it means to 'lead a life worthy of the calling to which [they] have been called'. They have already 'heard the word of truth' which told them the gospel of their salvation (1.13); they have already received the Spirit as a pledge of their growth into 'the praise of his glory' (1.14). But Paul prays that God will give these people 'a spirit of wisdom and revelation as [they] *come* to know him' (1.17). They already have 'faith in the Lord Jesus'; he prays that they might come to 'know what is the hope to which he has called [them]' (1.15, 18). Paul is, in other words, praying that the Ephesian Christians will come to know what they already know, growing into what they have already been given.[25]

That journey deeper into what has already been received is a journey that can involve real discovery.[26] Paul is clear that his readers have 'learned Christ' (4.20). He is equally clear that they have more of Christ to learn, and that what they have to learn is not simply a matter of clarification around the edges. At the heart of the epistle is Paul's communication of the surprising mystery of God's love in Christ – a facet previously hidden but now revealed to Paul and to the other apostles by the Spirit. They have been led to the discovery that 'the Gentiles have become fellow-heirs, members of the same body' with the Jewish followers of Jesus (3:6). The whole of Paul's preaching of the gospel is shaped by this discovery, this new appreciation of the breadth and power of God's love. When he asks his audience to pray for him, 'so that when I speak, a message may be given to me to make known with boldness the mystery of the gospel', he is speaking about this mystery. God's sanctifying work in Christ reaches unexpectedly across the boundary between Jew and Gentile (6.19; 2.11ff).

---

[25] The whole epistle conveys this call deeper into the knowledge that the audience have already received. Ben Witherington III (*The Letters to Philemon, the Colossians, and the Ephesians: A Socio-Rhetorical Commentary on the Captivity Epistles* (Grand Rapids, MI: Eerdmans, 2007), 220, 227–8) suggests that it is, rhetorically, *epideictic*: that is, it assumes knowledge on the part of its audience, and seeks to enhance the knowledge that it assumes – or at least it tries to persuade its audience that what they are receiving is an enhancement of knowledge they already possess.

[26] Ibid., 265.

The epistle envisages, therefore, an ongoing and sometimes surprising deepening of knowledge, but it consistently envisages knowledge of a particular kind. Summarizing its message, Ester Petrenko argues that it envisages for each believer 'a transformation of the centre of decision and motivation ... through the knowledge of God's plan of salvation ... and through an intimate relationship with God and Christ mediated by the Holy Spirit'. It envisages a 'refashioning of the mind through the knowledge and internalisation of the gospel of reconciliation'.[27]

First, believers are given knowledge of the love of God who has lavished grace upon them and blessed them in Christ 'with every spiritual blessing' (1.8, 3). In the words of Ben Witherington III, Paul expects his addressees to be 'rooted in that love, experiencing it, indeed ... grounded in it'.[28] They know this love already, but they are called to imagine it ever more richly and fully.

Second, they are drawn into knowledge of what this love of God makes possible for them and demands of them. The letter as a whole turns from setting out the grand vision of the 'love of Christ that surpasses all knowledge' to a plea that the Ephesians might 'lead a life worthy of the calling to which [they] have been called' (3.19; 4.1). This will involve the community discovering in prosaic detail how this love might work itself out in the pattern of their life together. 'Try to find out', Paul says, 'what is pleasing to the Lord' (4.1; 5.10). Clothing themselves with God's love is going to involve, for instance, thieves learning to 'work honestly with their own hands, so as to have something to share with the needy' (4.24, 28). It will involve the believers learning about 'bearing with one another in love' so as to exhibit 'the unity of the Spirit in the bond of peace' (4.2-3). This is knowledge in the form of wisdom – practical wisdom, on which the Ephesians will draw as they take care over how they live (5.15). It is a wisdom that is worked out and displayed in the building up of the body of Christ in each specific place, but it is also a political, even a cosmic wisdom. It involves recognition that 'the rulers and authorities in the heavenly places' are invested in our divisions, a realization that 'every family in heaven and on earth' takes its name from the same Father, and a commitment to the discovery of how this realization might be lived out in opposition to the power of evil within and around the body (3.10, 15; 4.1-6).

Growth in the knowledge of God, then, is inseparable from this growth in imagination and in practical wisdom – in the Ephesians knowing themselves to be loved and knowing how to love. And it is in relation to this whole picture of growth in love that we can understand the role of good and bad teaching within the body of Christ. All within the body are called to speak the truth in love to one another, in ways that will promote growth into Christ, and into love. All are called to the overcoming of division, in defiance of the powers of evil (4.15).[29] Some are given a specific calling as teachers (4.11), but that is only in order that they might support this wider communicative life. Their role is 'to equip the saints for the work of ministry, for

---

[27] Ester Petrenko, *Created in Christ Jesus for Good Works: The Integration of Soteriology and Ethics in Ephesians* (Milton Keynes: Paternoster, 2011), 31.
[28] Witherington, *Letters*, 274–5.
[29] Ibid., 292: 'Paul sees all in one sense called to some sort of educational ministry, not just the leaders.'

building up the body of Christ' (4.12).³⁰ The role of a teacher is to aid the people of God as they draw one another deeper into God's love.

It is in that context that we can make sense of Paul's insistence that the Ephesians 'must no longer be children, tossed to and fro and blown about by every wind of doctrine' (4.14). False doctrine is any teaching that does not lead people deeper together into the abundant love of Christ, and into the practical and political wisdom that expresses that love. True teaching, by contrast, is teaching that enables them to 'grow up in every way into him who is the head', into the one who 'promotes the body's growth in building itself up in love' (4.15,16). It is that teaching that enables the church's learning of love.

Knowledge and love are, then, inseparable, and they are asymmetrically ordered: knowledge serves love. For Christians to grow in knowledge is for them to grow together in their imagination of the love of God for them – their grasp of its breadth and length and height and depth. It is for them to grow in knowledge of the God-imaging love to which they are called, discovering the wisdom that will enable them to live that love out in the midst of all the relationships – local, political and cosmic – in which they find themselves. Knowledge of God consists in this deepening knowledge of love, and any supposed knowledge of God that does not take this form is simply fatuous.³¹ In the words of Henry Scott Holland, 'We know by loving and we love because we have experienced the fact that God loves us. ... The Word, then, can only be fully intelligible to those who love. Only from within can you know.'³²

Doctrine and spirituality

Doctrinal theology develops and explores summary articulations of Christian speech about God. That speech is meant to serve growth in love of God and love of neighbour; doctrinal theology is meant to enable this service.

Such claims are not unfamiliar in recent discussions of the nature of doctrine. Ellen Charry, for instance, insists that dogmatic explication is 'an instrument of individual and societal formation and transformation, ... an instrument of moral pedagogy', and Medi Ann Volpe describes how, for Gregory of Nyssa, doctrinal theology is 'inseparable from the purification of the soul.'³³

---

[30] Most modern translations make the second clause depend on the first like this. See Sydney H. T. Page, 'Whose Ministry? An Appraisal of Ephesians 4:12', *Novum Testamentum* 47, no. 1 (2005): 26–46, for an argument that the clauses are parallel: teachers are to equip the saints *and* to do the work of ministry.

[31] Writing about a different Pauline letter, Chris Tilling writes that Christians are called to 'a way of knowing that isn't prior to but indeed *is* discipleship'. 'For Paul, the knowledge of God is not possessed, mastered, and treated as formula external to the graced knower, but is part of that subject's life and interpersonal relations.' When 'expressed in sentences', the words 'gain their meaning in terms of that muddy network of ground-level relationships in which disciples live'. ('"Knowledge Puffs Up, But Love Builds Up": The Apostle Paul and the Task of Dogmatics', in *The Task of Dogmatics: Explorations in Theological Method*, ed. Oliver Crisp and Fred Sanders (Grand Rapids, MI: Zondervan, 2017), 95–6.)

[32] 'The Ministry of the Word (i)', Appendix 2 in *The Teaching Office of the Church: Being the Report of the Archbishops' First Committee of Inquiry* (London: SPCK, 1919), 74. Cf. Ward, *Light*, 32, 116, 183.

[33] Charry, 'The Moral Function of Doctrine', 33; Medi Ann Volpe, *Rethinking Christian Identity: Doctrine and Discipleship* (Oxford: Blackwell, 2013), 196. Cf. Frances M. Young, 'Paideia and the

Mark McIntosh, in his book *Mystical Theology*, insists that Christian life is a response to the 'mysterious beckoning of divine love'. That beckoning leads one out 'towards the other, both the divine other and the human other, and especially the divine by way of responsibility for the human other'. It is a beckoning incarnate in Jesus, and one is led by it into 'the struggle to love the human other in all his or her angularity and difference from oneself'. This struggle 'becomes the process by which one is drawn into the knowledge and love of God'.[34]

This is a process worked out in the body. That is true in the literal sense: this process is worked out in materiality, in public space; it is quotidian and prosaic. And it is true in an extended sense: this process is worked out in the body of Christ. We 'live into the knowledge and love of God through the hard work of being members one with another of the Body of Christ'. It takes place in 'the hard communal praxis of spiritual growth, in mutual openness to the hidden presence of the divine in the ordinary struggles and rituals of ecclesial life'. It involves 'a new pattern of personal growth taking place in the community of those who have been sought out, converted and cherished by the risen Christ'.[35]

This struggle is, however, intellectual at precisely the same time that it is practical and communal. It is a matter of 'heightened wakefulness', of 'discovery', of 'new perceptions' and 'new understandings'. It involves 'the transformation of consciousness', 'a new kind of knowing ... brought to life as believers are drawn ecstatically beyond their usual habits of mind and heart'. This consciousness 'emerges in people as they seek to discover, by sharing in the pattern of Christ's self-giving love, the true meaning of their own lives' and thereby 'come to see reality more and more through the eyes of the risen Christ'.[36]

For McIntosh, this deepening of knowledge involves learning to hear Christ as God's beckoning word, calling one to repentance and to new life. It involves learning to see all things in relation to the God who beckons, and God as the one to whom all things relate. God leads people into this new vision by the Spirit, through scripture, through the tradition, through each other and through their experience in the world, in a process anchored in worship and the life of prayer. McIntosh insists, however, that this deepening of knowledge happens primarily in and through 'the hard work of talking and working together', and cautions against pursuing 'individualistic quests for something "inner"' that allow an 'avoidance of the reality of the other'. This growth does, nevertheless, yield a 'discovery of the true "self"' made possible by 'encountering the divine and human other'.[37]

Doctrinal theology should serve this discovery. It should 'guide one into participative encounter' with God, not 'offer an impossible series of descriptive propositions about it'. In this sense, 'the lives and spirituality of people are the meaning of doctrine'.[38]

Myth of Static Dogma', in *The Making and Remaking of Christian Doctrine: Essays in Honour of Maurice Wiles*, ed. Sarah Coakley and David A. Pailin (Oxford: Clarendon Press, 1993), 273.

[34] Mark A. McIntosh, *Mystical Theology* (Oxford: Blackwell, 1998), 3–4, 9–10.
[35] Ibid., 79–82, 6, 62.
[36] Ibid., 6, 62, 103.
[37] Ibid., 5, emphasis removed. Cf. Aristotle Papanikolaou, *The Mystical as Political: Democracy and Non-Radical Orthodoxy* (Notre Dame, IN: University of Notre Dame Press, 2012), 197; I am grateful to Jenny Leith for drawing my attention to this passage.
[38] McIntosh, *Mystical Theology*, 27, 26.

Another recent writer, Sarah Coakley, insists that 'the questions of right contemplation of God, right speech about God, and right ordering of desire all hang together. They emerge in primary interaction with Scripture, become intensified and contested in early Christian tradition, and are purified in the crucible of prayer.'[39] She emphasizes the tangled relationships between doctrinal theology, desires, and the patterns of our ecclesial, social and political life in which those desires are expressed and sustained. Learning to know God more truly is inseparable from a deep and sometimes painful reordering of these desires, and from a broader reordering of our lives, as 'God the "Father", in and through the Spirit, both stirs up, and progressively chastens and purges, the frailer and often misdirected desires of humans, and so forges them, by stages of sometimes painful growth, into the likeness of his Son.'[40]

Doctrinal theologians often try to deploy terms as if they were counters in an intellectual game played at arm's length from the quagmire of our desires and their social and institutional entanglements. They behave as if their words could be cleaned for this purpose by simple acts of stipulation, moments of definition that allow the game to be played with a clear conscience. But, says Coakley, 'Let anyone who claims that he has passed well beyond the need for "male" or "female" images of God, or that (more ingeniously) "Father" to him means nothing whatever to do with ordinary human fathering, examine his actual relations with women in church and society. Things are not always what they seem.'[41]

Part of the work involved in deepening knowledge is an uncovering of the sometimes invisibly fine tendrils linking our words, our desires and the patterns of our lives, across 'the whole realm of the personal and the political'. Learning how to deploy these words truthfully will require not an instant purification by stipulation, but an ongoing and painful moral and spiritual purgation.[42] '[O]ur perception of God, and thus too our grasp of doctrinal verities … is appropriately open to its object only to the extent that the faculties have been progressively purified' in a process that 'will often … involve long years of moral and spiritual preparation, prolonged practice in "sensing" the presence of Christ' – 'practice in seeing the world differently', 'a progressive unfolding of insights based in patient moral transformation.'[43] It is within such a process, and only within such a process, that we learn to use our words for God well; it is only within such a process that we learn what those words mean.[44]

Ordinary knowing

These descriptions could be taken to give talk about God a rarefied air, as if it lived only high up on the slopes, some way above the cheerful or disappointing mediocrity

---

[39] Coakley, *God, Sexuality, and the Self*, 2. Cf. John Webster, 'What Makes Theology Theological?' *Journal of Analytic Theology* 3 (2015): 18; Austin Farrer, *Lord I Believe: Suggestions for Turning the Creed into Prayer*, 2nd edn (London: SPCK, 1962), 9–23.
[40] Coakley, *God*, 6.
[41] Sarah Coakley, *Powers and Submissions: Spirituality, Philosophy and Gender* (Oxford: Blackwell, 2002), 64.
[42] Coakley, *God*, 5.
[43] Coakley, *Powers*, 136, 139, 140, 146.
[44] Coakley's focus on painful purgation has been critiqued by Tonstad, in *God and Difference*, ch. 3.

of ordinary life. We can, however, draw into the foreground McIntosh's discussion of 'the hard work of talking and working together', or Coakley's of 'patient moral transformation', and look to the quite ordinary processes by which people learn how to love one another, discovering together patterns of life in which they can live out the love of Christ. If we do that, the primary place in which we situate knowledge of God will be in the midst of ordinary life. It takes place as people learn, with God's help, to live loving lives together in their particular locales, and discover how to negotiate the wider social and political realities that constrain and enable them. Such attempts, fallible and various, are shaped by people's ways of imagining God, their ways of telling the story of God's love in Jesus Christ. They are shaped by the contingencies of their landscape, their community, their history. They are shaped by what is discovered by these specific people, in this specific place, of how to go on – how to deal with the forms of disorder by which they are threatened, and what possibilities there are of living well-ordered lives together. The working out of love in the ordinary is where knowledge of God lives – and the work of doctrinal theology, of summary, articulation and debate serves that knowing.

In the words of William Temple,

> the life of faith is not the acceptance of doctrine any more than the life of the natural man is the acceptance of mathematical equations, or the life of the artist is the acceptance of aesthetic canons. The canons and the equations assist the effective adjustment and intercourse of organism and environment, but the life of art, or of mere organic continuance, has its being in that adjustment and intercourse. ... [F]aith is not the holding of correct doctrines, but personal fellowship with the living God. Correct doctrine will both express this, assist it and issue from it; incorrect doctrine will misrepresent this and hinder or prevent it. Doctrine is of an importance too great to be exaggerated, but its place is secondary, not primary.[45]

I can put a sharper edge on this claim by making it more specific. I am writing these words five minutes' walk away from our parish church – the church that I attend with my family, and in which I occasionally preach. In a few weeks' time, I am slated to preach on Trinity Sunday. I will do so confident in the knowledge that I know the doctrine of the Trinity better than anybody else in the building. I can speak about its history, I can deploy and explain its concepts, I can discuss its biblical roots, well enough to get through at least a couple of hours of undergraduate lecturing, and I am close to certain that the same could not be said of any who will be hearing my sermon. Yet it is obvious to me that I cannot thereby claim to know the triune God better than all those people. They know the triune God to the extent that they have learnt to recognize themselves as loved by God, and have learnt to love their neighbours with the same love. To put it another way, they know the triune God to the extent that they have learnt to live as faithful followers of Jesus, with the guidance of the Spirit, in adoration of the Father. There is not some higher kind of knowledge of God, separate from the kind of knowing involved in ordinary faith, open only to doctrinal theologians. There is only this.

---

[45] William Temple, *Nature, Man and God* (London: Macmillan, 1956), 321–2.

As a doctrinal theologian, I know how to deploy certain kinds of talk about this path that my fellow parishioners are on. I know, for instance, how to use phrases like 'faithful followers of Jesus', 'the guidance of the Spirit' and 'adoration of the Father'. More than that, I know that the doctrine of the Trinity insists that this path *is* the path into knowledge of God, and that it leads all the way into the depths of God's life. There is no reserve in God's life, off the beaten track of Father, Son and Spirit. My doctrinal theological knowing is a kind of knowing, and it is a kind of knowing about God – but on its own it is thin and abstracted. It is certainly not a kind of knowing that by itself can take me above or beyond the knowledge of God enjoyed by my fellow parishioners.[46]

I might, nevertheless, hope to offer something useful or salutary when I preach. I might – on an optimistic day – hope to help my hearers' developing imagination of God's love for them, and of the kind of love to which they are called. I might alert them to forms of misunderstanding that could be constricting their imagination or distorting their action. I might help them grasp the shape of their pursuit of knowledge and love in a way that encourages them. I might help them see some of the forces arrayed against love in the world that we inhabit. But even if all that does, by the grace of God, happen, I might still walk home after the service secure in the conviction that many of my hearers know the triune God with a depth and richness that puts my meagre knowledge to shame. I might also walk home knowing that I am no less embroiled than any of them in the misrecognition of God, the failure to know in love.[47]

Failing to know

The knowledge of God consists in an ever deeper imaginative indwelling of the love of God, and the ongoing discovery of how we might live that love out wisely together in the world. That knowledge is worked out in all the processes by which people learn to recognize themselves as loved by God, and learn to love their neighbours with the same love; it is discovered by means of 'the hard work of talking and working together'.[48]

This is, I think, both true and important – but there is a danger in my presentation so far of romanticizing the everyday and of silently shrinking the circle of those who count as 'neighbour'. By focusing on my local church, I might suggest that love is

---

[46] In *A New Apophaticism: Augustine and the Redemption of Signs* (Leiden: Brill, 2013), 4, Susannah Ticciati says that 'there can be no "aboutness" with respect to God'. I am, however, only investing in a quite minimal sense of 'aboutness'. There is a difference between life that follows this threefold way and life that does not; it *makes a difference* to live as faithful followers of Jesus, with the guidance of the Spirit, in adoration of the Father; and it is *because of who God is* that life on this threefold way is life on a journey into knowledge of God in a sense that life differently shaped is not. This does not, I think, fall foul of Ticciati's stricture, as she later clarifies it: 'doctrine does not point away from itself to God as something separate'. Doctrine does, however, render God present, and in so doing it 'does make present a genuine other'. It, therefore, 'transcends the difference between referential and non-referential, descriptive and non-descriptive language' (ibid., 228).

[47] Cf. Nicholas Lash, *Newman on Development: The Search for an Explanation in History* (London: Sheed and Ward, 1975), 63. The text of the sermon I preached after writing these words is available under the title 'One-Bit Word Game' (27 May 2018). Available online at www.stbrandon.org.uk/wp-content/uploads/2018/05/2018-05-Trinity-Sermon.pdf (accessed 2 December 2019).

[48] McIntosh, *Mystical Theology*, 5.

worked out only in the local and the personal. And yet, as Vincent Lloyd insists, I and all the members of my church inhabit a culture

> that perpetuates anti-black and anti-indigenous racism resulting in the ongoing suffering and premature death of millions, that steals the labor and wealth of billions in the global South for the comfort of wealthy North Americans and Europeans, that degrades and violates women and queer folks, and that is committing such violence to the earth every day that the planet's fever will soon become irreparable devastation of the land and death to millions of plants, animals, and people.[49]

We live, in other words, 'in a world composed of interlocking layer upon layer of systems of domination'. Learning to love in such a world cannot mean bracketing out this broken backdrop to our lives. It has to mean learning to 'interrupt domination' and 'to join with others in seeing the world otherwise, and acting otherwise'.[50] If, in such a world, I think that my local neighbours and I, focused inwards on the dynamics of our little life together, can discover what it means to love well, I will miss the depth of love's challenge. I will miss the fact that, because we do not yet know how to recognize our involvement in and support of these systems of domination, because we do not yet know how to join in with those who are seeing and acting otherwise, because we do not yet know how to live well with all the wider circles of neighbours given to us by Christ, we do not yet know how to love.

If doctrinal theology is to assist the people of God in knowing God, by assisting their imagination and embodiment of the love of God, it will be because it connects not just to the lives of its immediate audiences, but because it also connects to 'those at the margins, those who feel domination on their bodies the most brutally'.[51] Without that, it cannot serve the knowledge of God.

Conclusion

The articulated summaries of doctrinal theology, and all the words with which doctrinal theologians surround them, are nothing more than supports for the knowledge of God that consists in love. They either promote the discovery of that love or they are useless – and worse than useless.

In this chapter I have done no more than gesture towards the kind of help that doctrinal articulation might hope to give to those seeking to grow in the knowledge of God. I have done little to explore how doctrinal claims and the life of ordinary belief might connect. I have done even less to explore how the work of doctrinal

---

[49] Vincent Lloyd, 'Virtue against Domination', *Syndicate*, 23 September 2019; syndicate.network/symposia/theology/the-character-of-virtue/ (accessed 3 December 2019).
[50] Ibid. Cf. Lloyd, 'What Love Is Not: Lessons from Martin Luther King, Jr.', forthcoming in *Modern Theology*.
[51] Ibid.

theology might respond to the lives most directly battered by the powers that corrupt our world. This chapter has done no more than gesture towards the horizon in the general direction that I will be pursuing over the remaining chapters of the book. Whether there is anything out there – whether and in what form doctrinal theology might hope to be a genuine contribution to Christian learning – remains to be seen.

6

Doctrine and belief

Introduction

God is at work beckoning people deeper into love, luring them beyond their divisions and the disorder of their lives and their world. Christians are called to acknowledge and explore God's love. They are called to recognize their failures, their exclusions and their hatreds – all the ways in which they resist and reject this love – and to repent of them. They are called to see themselves and their world in the light of this love, and to discover how to live it out in all the contexts in which they find themselves. Their discovery and inhabitation of this love is their knowledge of God. It is a knowledge that they have already received but that can go on being unfolded for them, as they are drawn out of their sin, and as they are drawn further up and further in, into God's inexhaustible abundance. If doctrinal theology has any role to play, it will be because it can support Christians on this journey.

Even if it can play such a role, however, doctrinal theology remains secondary. It supports Christians in their discovery of the knowledge of God; it is not itself that knowledge. In this chapter, I try to give more precision to this picture of doctrinal theology's secondariness. I begin by exploring one influential recent account – George Lindbeck's insistence that doctrinal statements are 'second order' in relation to the 'first order' of ordinary Christian believing. I then move beyond it to something messier. I explore the complex reality of ordinary believing, attending to its dispositional nature and its conceptual and social structures. I explore the processes of improvisation by which Christians learn to live out their beliefs in new situations and in so doing discover more of what those beliefs mean. Finally, I turn back to doctrinal theology, acknowledging its limits and its capacity to do harm, but also suggesting roles that it can play, pursuing certain kinds of conversation in the midst of the negotiations that shape Christian life and so inform Christian knowledge of God.

Doctrine as second order

Lindbeck's regulative account

In his most famous work, *The Nature of Doctrine*, Lindbeck's main purpose was to make sense of, and to provide a toolkit for, ecumenical discussions of doctrine.[1] His account

---

[1] See my 'Reconstructing *The Nature of Doctrine*', 1–31. Some of the material for this section was previously published in my 'George Lindbeck and the Christological Nature of Doctrine', *Criswell Theological Review* 13, no. 1 (2015): 47–62.

was driven by a basic theological conviction. He believed that we can trust *that* our words apply to God but cannot know *how* they apply.[2] If we say, for instance, that God is creation's good source we are speaking truly about God, but we do not and cannot know what the word 'source' means in this case. In God, there can be none of the material or temporal processes that we assume when we use the word 'source' of creatures. The word cannot provide us with an intelligible description of what is going on in God's life; it cannot give us a graspable account of *how* anything comes from God. Doctrinal claims cannot, says Lindbeck, bear information in the ways that ordinary propositions can.

Doctrines can, however, shape people's lives as, together, they respond to God. Being taught by God to say that God is creation's good source might teach people to live in delighted gratitude towards God. It might teach them to treat good things as gifts rather than as possessions. It might lead them to recognize one another as gifts. It can shape people's imaginations; it can draw them into worship; it can fire their generosity.[3]

Lindbeck insists that this kind of lived response to God, nurtured by God's own revealing and sanctifying work, can bring people into correspondence with God's being and will. It is meet and right to give thanks unto the Lord our God – and it is meet and right precisely because of who God is. The bare doctrinal statement that God is creation's source does not provide an informative description of God's life, and neither do human lives that display gratitude. Yet while we might be tempted to think empty a proposition that refers only in a way that is impossible for the mind to grasp, it is clearly far from empty to live a whole life that, by the grace of God, responds and conforms to God's ineffable generosity.[4] Such a way of life has a definite content; it has it from God, and by it people's lives are truly oriented to God. There is a real correspondence between such lives and God, a conformity to God of people's attitudes, imaginations and actions. The correspondence in question is the kind asked for in the opening clauses of the Lord's prayer: that God's name be hallowed, God's will be done, God's kingdom come, 'on earth as it is in heaven'. Lindbeck could therefore say that 'Those who learn to speak of God rightly may not know what they are saying in any cognitively significant sense, but yet their very beings may be transformed into conformity with him who alone is the high and mighty One.'[5]

---

[2] Lindbeck, *The Nature of Doctrine*, 66. The creation example is not Lindbeck's but my own.

[3] Susannah Ticciati provides a compelling account along these lines, in which doctrinal language can't itself represent God, but contributes to the redemptive transformation of human beings who in their transformation become signs of God. 'To say that God is wise, that God is good, and above all that God is love, is to tell you where to look in order to find God: God is there where creaturely wisdom, goodness and love are to be found.' *A New Apophaticism*, 242. See also Mike Higton, 'Apophaticism Transformed', *Modern Theology* 31, no. 3 (2015): 511–16, and Susannah Ticciati, 'Response to Mike Higton', *Modern Theology* 31, no. 3 (2015): 517–22.

[4] I trust that, as I am led deeper into the knowledge and love of God, I will be led deeper into thanksgiving in such a way that I will recognize my current thanksgiving as a tentative beginning on the right pathway. My current practice gestures towards a truth that I am as yet incapable of grasping. Cf. Lindbeck, 'Discovering Thomas (1): The Classical Statement of Christian Theism', *Una Sancta* 24, no. 1 (1967): 49.

[5] Lindbeck, 'Discovering Thomas', 51. See also Gilles Emery, 'Thomas Aquinas, Postliberal? George Lindbeck's Reading of St. Thomas', trans. Matthew Levering, in Emery, *Trinity, Church, and the Human Person: Thomistic Essays* (Naples, FL: Sapientia Press, 2007), 287.

Lindbeck's central claim about doctrine is that, when they deploy doctrinal claims, theologians are not passing on information about God; they are saying how the church's life, its embodied speech about God, should be ordered so as to be true to God.[6] They are offering rules for the shaping of this living speech. The doctrinal theologian's work is, therefore, 'second order': it seeks to work upon or to regulate the 'first order' of Christian life and speech.[7]

A Christological example

Lindbeck offers, as an example, a regulative reading of incarnational Christology. He takes that Christology to involve three rules:

> First, there is the monotheistic principle: there is only one God, the God of Abraham, Isaac, Jacob, and Jesus. Second, there is the principle of historical specificity: the stories of Jesus refer to a genuine human being who was born, lived and died in a particular place. Third, there is the principle of what may be infelicitously called Christological maximalism: every possible importance is to be ascribed to Jesus that is not inconsistent with the first [two] rules.[8]

Lindbeck's discussion at this point is too brief to be wholly convincing. The first two rules still look like informative propositions, and the third (at least as formulated here) seems to stop short of insisting that Jesus must be of decisive significance in every area of life. Nevertheless, elsewhere in *The Nature of Doctrine* and in other writings, Lindbeck shows how this material might be reformulated more convincingly, not so much as three separate rules but as one rule elaborated in three steps.

The first step specifies that Christians should take the deepest story about their world to be the story of 'a being who created the cosmos without any humanly fathomable reason, but – simply for his own good pleasure and the pleasure of his goodness – appointed Homo Sapiens steward of one minuscule part of this cosmos, permitted appalling evils, chose Israel and the church as witnessing peoples, and sent Jesus as Messiah and Immanuel, God with us'.[9] To believe in God is, for Lindbeck, to be committed to living within this story, and to proclaiming in one's living that there is no more fundamental story than this to be told about the world.

---

[6] Ticciati says that doctrinal language is 'both the engine and the product of the church's development over time – a deep sign, as it were, of the mind of the church as the locus of divinely redemptive transformation' (*New Apophaticism*, 223).

[7] Kevin Vanhoozer asks of Lindbeck's approach, 'Does doctrine refer to God, or does it merely describe how members of the Christian community talk about God?' (*The Drama of Doctrine*, 7). From a Lindbeckian point of view this question is simply confused: doctrine is about God by being about the ways in which the Christian community can truly correspond to God.

[8] Lindbeck, *Nature*, 94.

[9] Ibid., 121.

The second step is a hermeneutical rule. Christians should read the gospels as a narrative identification of Jesus of Nazareth – the depiction of someone 'as entirely and concretely human as you or I'.[10] This is what Christians are to take the name 'Jesus' to mean, and they are to read the gospels in particular, and the scriptures in general, as a truthful witness to him.

The third step puts the first two together. Christians should live in such a way as to acknowledge that this Jesus is 'the unsurpassable and irreplaceable clue to who and what the God of Israel and the universe is'.[11] The first step turned the question 'How then should we live?' into the question 'How should we live as creatures of God, in the world that God creates and sustains?' This third step rewords this question again, as 'How should we follow Jesus?' Christians should so live as to display their conviction that there is no deeper form that this question can take.[12] To the extent that they do, their lives will proclaim in the clearest and most direct way available the truth encoded in the doctrinal claim that 'the incarnation is the fullest possible eruption into our history of the infinite mystery that surrounds all our beginnings and ends'.[13]

Whatever its merits and omissions, this regulative interpretation of incarnational doctrine does not give up on the idea that doctrine is concerned with the objective truth of who God is, or the truth of how the human being Jesus of Nazareth relates to God. In Lindbeck's reading, however, the truth to which the doctrinal statements point – truth about God, about Jesus and about the world – is expressed most directly not by the doctrinal words themselves, but by doctrine-regulated lives.[14]

Lindbeck's crusader

Lindbeck's account, then, involves a distinction between a first and a second order. The ordinary life of the church is the first order. Doctrines as doctrines – that is, doctrinal statements when they are deployed in the work of doctrinal theology, as opposed to the same words put to any other use – are second-order commentaries upon that first order. These second-order statements tell us the shape that first-order life should have, the rules that it should follow, in order to be obedient to what God has shown of Godself to the world. Doctrines are like grammatical rules, setting out the patterns that

---

[10] George A. Lindbeck, 'Justification and Atonement: An Ecumenical Trajectory', in *By Faith Alone: Essays on Justification in Honor of Gerhard O. Forde*, ed. Joseph A. Burgess and Marc Kolden (Grand Rapids, MI: Eerdmans, 2004), 213.

[11] George A. Lindbeck, 'The Story-shaped Church: Critical Exegesis and Theological Interpretation', in *Scriptural Authority and Narrative Interpretation*, ed. Garrett Green (Philadelphia, PA: Fortress Press, 1987), 164.

[12] George A. Lindbeck, 'Unbelievers and the "*Sola Christi*"', in *The Church in a Postliberal Age*, ed. James J. Buckley (Grand Rapids, MI: Eerdmans, 2002), 85.

[13] George A. Lindbeck, 'Atonement and the Hermeneutics of Intertextual Social Embodiment', in *The Nature of Confession: Evangelicals and Postliberals in Conversation*, ed. Timothy Phillips and Dennis Okholm (Downers Grove, IL: IVP, 1996), 238.

[14] For an attempt to develop a more detailed Chalcedonian Christology along similar lines, see David Yeago, 'Jesus of Nazareth and Cosmic Redemption: The Relevance of Maximus the Confessor', *Modern Theology* 12, no. 2 (1996): 163–93.

ordinary speech should follow.[15] Doctrine is a commentary upon the life of the church, setting out rules intended to keep it faithful.[16]

Lindbeck explores this in a famous passage in *The Nature of Doctrine*:

> for a Christian, 'God is Three and One', or 'Christ is Lord' are true only as parts of a total pattern of speaking, thinking, feeling, and acting. They are false when their use in any given instance is inconsistent with what the pattern as a whole affirms of God's being and will. The crusader's battle cry '*Christus est Dominus*', for example, is false when used to authorize cleaving the skull of the infidel (even though the same words in other contexts may be a true utterance). When thus employed, it contradicts the Christian understanding of Lordship as embodying, for example, suffering servanthood.[17]

It is worth distinguishing two elements that Lindbeck runs together here. The simplest is the idea that the words spoken by the crusader are given a definite meaning only in the immediate surroundings in which he speaks. If you want to know what the crusader takes his own words to mean, or what meaning he is conveying to those around him, you have to look at how he is using his words in that particular time and place. In that context, it is pretty clear what the word 'dominus' means. It is a word that could be used of a feudal lord, perhaps, someone for whom one might properly fight in battle, and whose glory can be enhanced by the violent death of his enemies. The circumstances in which the crusader speaks, and the actions he takes as he speaks, show us what he meant. If we are to make a judgement about whether the crusader was speaking truly or falsely, it is this meaning that we will need to judge. Is it true that Christ is *that* kind of lord?

Lindbeck is also making a second point, however. For him, as I have said, it is properly the whole life that the crusader is living that refers, and that might speak truly or falsely about God. The truth about Jesus's lordship is such that 'the only way to assert this truth is to do something about it, i.e., to commit oneself to a way of life'.[18] The crusader is asserting something about Jesus by the way of life that he has chosen. Uttering this sentence on this occasion is simply one element of this path. By speaking these words, the crusader is expressing and so reinforcing his commitment

---

[15] Lindbeck did not invent the metaphor. Harold Fielding, *The Hearts of Men* (New York: Macmillan, 1901), 313, for instance, used it much earlier – to describe theologians as pettifogging grammarians who squeezed the life out of religious speech.

[16] Alister McGrath, 'An Evangelical Evaluation of Postliberalism', in *The Nature of Confession*, ed. Phillips and Okholm, 36, wrongly claims that Lindbeck's approach 'entails the abandonment of any talk about God as independent reality, and any suggestion that it is possible to make truth claims ... about him'. A better reading of Lindbeck's approach is provided by Bruce Marshall, in 'Aquinas as Postliberal Theologian', *The Thomist* 53, no. 3 (1989): 353–402, and endorsed by Lindbeck in his 'Response to Bruce Marshall', *The Thomist* 53, no. 3 (1989): 403–6; see also Lindbeck's 'Reply to Avery Cardinal Dulles', *First Things* 139 (2004): 13–15.

[17] Lindbeck, *Nature*, 64. The story this passage tells, of a Christian crusader killing an 'infidel', is in our context an uncomfortably raw image to use as a casual example, however much it may have seemed more safely distanced to an American Christian writing in 1984.

[18] Ibid., 66.

to following Jesus in this way; he is insisting that he does what he does as a follower of Jesus. 'Look!' he is saying; 'This is who my Jesus is!' – and then he swings his sword.

Lindbeck – acting, in this instance, as a doctrinal theologian – insists that the crusader's cry is false. And it is clear (or, at least, it is made clear by Lindbeck's later explanation of what he intended to say here) that he believes the crusader to be wrong in the most straightforward of ways.[19] By proclaiming Christ to be some kind of battle lord the crusader is in Lindbeck's judgement saying something that fails to correspond to Christ's true lordship. Lindbeck's response is to say, 'No, that is really not who Jesus is.'

Beyond that simple, realist point, however, things get murkier, because it is difficult to pinpoint the basis on which Lindbeck thinks he is making this judgement. It is clear that he thinks the crusader's cry has broken the rules for Christian speech, but what does that mean? Much of Lindbeck's language suggests that he is simply talking about a mismatch between what this crusader says about Jesus (in life and word) and what the wider church says. The crusader's words are false, Lindbeck says, 'when their use in any given instance is inconsistent with what the pattern as a whole affirms of God's being and will'. It sounds as though the theologian is meant to look, empirically, at the 'total pattern of speaking, thinking, feeling, and acting' found in the wider Christian community, and use that pattern as the standard by which to judge the crusader's claim. Given Lindbeck's underlying realism, this would require him to assume that the church's wider life, as a whole, can be relied upon to speak truly about Jesus.[20]

Looking at Lindbeck's work more widely, however, it becomes clear that this is simply not the approach that he takes – not least because he has a well-developed sense of the sinfulness of the church.[21] The second-order rules that he thinks define authentic Christian life are not themselves derived by looking at the church, at least not in any direct way. They are not simply read off from the surface of the church's present or past behaviour. They are, instead, derived from a Christ-focused reading of scripture, in which the scriptures are allowed to stand over against the life of the church and so to call it to account. Lindbeck does assume that, however unevenly and inadequately observed in practice, the wider life of the church displays an implicit commitment to this kind of reading. He also believes that this kind of reading can't be justified in any more neutral or abstract way: we only know this to be the right way of reading because God has drawn the church into reading in this way. There is, therefore, a descriptive starter motor involved in the generation of doctrinal rules. The engine itself, however, is powered by the ongoing reading of scripture.[22]

To summarize: Lindbeck argues that it is only when embedded in practice that claims about God gain enough meaning for us to ask whether they are true or false. When we do ask that question, we are asking about the truth of the claim-in-the-

---

[19] See the works cited in n. 16.
[20] Cf. Reinhard Hütter, *Suffering Divine Things: Theology as Church Practice* (Grand Rapids, MI: Eerdmans, 2000), 51–6. Hütter is in part responding to the analysis provided by George Hunsinger in 'Truth as Self-Involving: Barth and Lindbeck on the Cognitive and Performative Aspects of Truth in Theological Discourse', *Journal of the American Academy of Religion* 61, no. 1 (1993): 41–56.
[21] See pp. 206–9.
[22] See p. 151.

practice, or, better, of the practice-that-contains-the-claim. Only if that practice has been drawn by God into correspondence with God's own being will it in fact be true. Doctrinal theologians are tasked with helping to tend this correspondence, by deploying doctrinal claims as rules to regulate Christian life and speech. The rules expressed in doctrinal claims are not derived by describing the shape that Christian life happens to have taken; they are derived from – and need to go on being chastened by – the church's practice of reading scripture as a witness to Christ. That is the means that God has provided to enable correspondence. Doctrinal claims are second order; its scripturally formed life is the church's first-order speech about God.

Entangling the orders

Lindbeck tends to speak as if there is a sharp distinction between the first and the second order.[23] It is as though there is first-order Christian life on the one hand, and then on the other, and quite distinct from it, a whole other practice of second-order regulative speech. It can at times seem as though the doctrinal theologian will relate to the Christian community primarily as an observer, as someone distanced from its life.[24] Yet every word that doctrinal theologians use, every action they take, every pose they strike, gets caught up in the processes by which life is shaped in the world around them. Even their attempts at objectivity or neutrality are moves made within a social context, that help shape the life taking place in that context. Second-order critics are unavoidably and pervasively entangled in first-order life.

Separating the orders too neatly also misses all the ways in which second-order elements are already embedded in the first order. That is, there are always already possibilities and processes of critique and regulation, discipline and disruption, built in to ordinary life. Lindbeck's crusader, for instance, would have been involved in practices of confession, and in patterns of obedience to a religious hierarchy; he might have been encouraged to pursue forms of self-scrutinizing prayer; he might have attended liturgies, heard preaching, consumed texts and images. He would not simply have indwelt a set of habits: he would have been involved in processes by which those habits were questioned, undermined, reinforced and redirected. He would have been caught up in the circulation of all kinds of pressures to conform, all kinds of visions of propriety and excellence, all kinds of practices of attention and deliberation.

Imagine, for instance, that on the long road to the battlefield he encountered some of his enemies in a context that allowed him to recognize their humanity. Some complex alchemy of influences, and some chance encounter like this, might combine to make him question his military mission.[25] We might imagine the crusader then

---

[23] For example, Lindbeck, *Nature*, 69, 80, 94. For other criticisms of this split between the orders, see Tanner, *Theories of Culture*, 71–2, and Ward, *How the Light Gets In*, 120–3.

[24] Robert L. Fossett critiques any 'theory' that 'supposedly stands outside of a particular practice in order to govern it' (*Upon This Rock: The Nature of Doctrine from Antifoundationalist Perspective* (Eugene, OR: Pickwick, 2013), 43). Fossett provides his own rehabilitation of first-order/second-order distinction on pp. 142–3. For an account from the anthropological side that complicates this distinction, see Jenkins, 'Fieldwork and the Perception of Everyday Life', 433–55.

[25] Cf. the story of Gomes Eanes de Zurara in Jennings, *The Christian Imagination*, ch. 1; see also Chapter 9, pp. 219–20.

attending a solemn mass before heading into battle, and, prompted by what he has seen on the road, hearing in the chanted Magnificat, just past the edges of his familiar understanding, the possibility of identifying differently the proud and the humble, the mighty and the meek. We might then imagine these doubts being quelled by his confessor, or by his hearing again a friar preaching the cross and calling him to be another Joshua. Or we might – though this seems more like historical fantasy – imagine instead his doubts amplified by other encounters and conversations; we might imagine them finding anchors in his faith and growing into conviction, into a moment of real resistance and change.

In other words: there are always already possibilities in Christian life of learning to think and act differently, and of being pulled back into conformity. There are always already multiple processes of assessment and reassessment, of questioning and acquiescing. These are woven pervasively into first-order Christian life, for good and ill. There is no sharp line between first order and second. There is one tangled life, in which all are involved – which all are making, all are reflecting upon and all are negotiating. And doctrinal theologians do not stand apart, looking on; they are involved, as dirty handed as any.[26]

Belief

To understand better the relationship between doctrinal theology and ordinary belief, we need to understand the nature of belief.[27] In this section, I am going to suggest that belief is dispositional, that it has both a conceptual and a social structure and that it is decisively shaped by the unavoidable improvisations of Christian life. Doctrinal theology will fall out of view for a while, before we return to it in the final section of the chapter.

Belief and dispositions

Gilbert Ryle suggests that belief is dispositional.

> Certainly to believe that the ice is dangerously thin is to be unhesitant in telling oneself and others that it is thin, in acquiescing in other people's assertions to that effect, in objecting to statements to the contrary, in drawing consequences from the original proposition, and so forth. But it is also to be prone to skate warily, to shudder, to dwell in imagination on possible disasters and to warn other skaters. It is a propensity not only to make certain theoretical moves but also to make certain executive and imaginative moves as well as to have certain feelings.[28]

---

[26] Cf. Wigg-Stevenson, *Ethnographic Theology*, 62.

[27] 'I am not nearly as puzzled by people who say, "I believe in God" as I am by people who think they can give a straightforward and satisfactory account of what they mean when they say that they believe in God.' Nicholas Lash, *Theology on Dover Beach* (London: Darton, Longman and Todd, 1979), 46.

[28] Gilbert Ryle, *The Concept of Mind* (London: Hutchinson, 1949), 134–5. This text is discussed by Eric Schwitzgebel in 'A Phenomenal, Dispositional Account of Belief', *Noûs* 36, no. 2 (2002): 249–75. I

In this vein, believing that Jesus is Lord would be a matter of having acquired a set of relevant dispositions, or at least it would be something that shows itself in such dispositions.[29] I might be disposed to say (or to sing) 'Jesus is Lord', or something like it, in appropriate circumstances. I might be disposed to reject denials of it. I might find myself calling the idea of Jesus's lordship to mind, and mentally affirming it. I might have habitual patterns of imagination, desire and feeling focused upon him, and those might play a role in how I imagine and experience my life more broadly. I might be disposed to act in various ways that show that I take Jesus to be Lord, regardless of whether I ever state the claim explicitly. I might habitually join in with corporate activities of worship or evangelism that depend for their intelligibility upon his lordship. All of this, and more, might be what we mean when we say that I believe Jesus to be Lord.[30]

I might display some of these dispositions more fully than others, perhaps even to the exclusion of others. My patterns of speech, thought, feeling and action might be uneven or inconsistent. My speech might be belied by my action.[31] Alternatively, I might display many of the dispositions that constitute belief, but little tendency to express it, still less to elaborate upon it.[32] The actions that flow from my dispositions might in some cases be quite deliberate, in others more purely habitual. They might be more determined or more tentative. My believing that 'Jesus is Lord' is not an on/off matter; it admits of degrees, of complexities, of tensions. A complete answer to the question of whether I do indeed believe, or of how strong my belief is, would require an impossibly complex mapping.[33]

I might believe all sorts of things in this kind of way, but among those beliefs might be some – like this belief that Jesus is Lord – that involve an imaginative backdrop to all my speech and action: beliefs about God and about God's ways with the world. It is not likely that my believing will project a seamless, static and complete canvas. Only people in theology books and bad sermons inhabit anything quite so orderly as a coherent world view or metanarrative. It is much more likely that I will project bits and pieces of backdrop, with all kinds of omissions and inconsistencies, and that I will have an evolving repertoire of such fragments on which I will find myself drawing in various ways, according to circumstance.

---

am broadly following Schwitzgebel, but have no particular need here to settle the dispute between his approach and the kind of representational riposte made by J. Quilty-Dunn and E. Mandelbaum in 'Against Dispositionalism: Belief in Cognitive Science', *Philosophical Studies* 175, no. 9 (2018): 2353–72. A dispositional approach is taken by Anthony C. Thiselton in *The Hermeneutics of Doctrine* (Grand Rapids, MI: Eerdmans, 2007), 19–42, drawing on H.H. Price, *Belief: The Gifford Lectures Delivered at the University of Aberdeen in 1960* (London: Allen and Unwin, 1969).

[29] See Anthony Thiselton, 'Knowledge, Myth and Corporate Memory', in *Believing in the Church: The Corporate Nature of Faith*, ed. The Doctrine Commission of the Church of England (London: SPCK, 1981), 76.

[30] Compare the range of meanings associated with πίστις in the New Testament: intellectual assent, trust, faithfulness, a disposition to certain kinds of action. For a different multidimension account of belief, see Day, *Believing in Belonging*, ch. 8.

[31] Cf. Mt. 25.11-12.

[32] Cf. Mk 8.34 and parallels. See also Anthony Harvey, 'Attending to Scripture', in *Believing in the Church*, ed. Doctrine Commission, 32.

[33] This is another reason to be sceptical about research that relies too heavily upon questionnaires and interviews. See Chapter 3, pp. 49–50.

The conceptual shape of belief

The various elements of my believing – the many dispositions involved, the convictions and imaginings that they express – are held in place in all sorts of ways. They may simply be habits that have become ingrained. They may be duties I feel I owe to those around me. They may be supported by stories I tell myself about my own motivations, or my identity. They may be channelled by the topography of my affective life.

In among all this supportive webbing, there are likely to be all kinds of strands that bind together the content of my beliefs. The ideas that I am disposed to affirm, the images that I habitually call to mind, the stories that I tell, may be linked to one another in such a way that I can be said to affirm one idea *because* I affirm another. I need not be very aware of these connections, but I might register them in certain circumstances. I might, for instance, habitually avoid expressing anger in sharp words, or think I ought to avoid it – and it may be that one of the things holding this habit in place is its fit with my understanding of the story of gentle Jesus.[34] That connection may not be something I could describe clearly to myself or to others, but it might be revealed were I, say, to hear a sermon describing Jesus's actions among the money changers as expressions of anger. I might find myself experiencing some dissonance, some anxiety not simply about the content of the sermon but about the way I value my own placidity, and casting about for reassurance that I can carry on as before. That anxiety might be the most obvious sign that there is, in the pattern of my believing, a connection there, and that the connection has been disturbed.

I might be more explicitly aware of some of these connections, and have the capacity to speak about them – in effect saying, 'I believe that x is true because I believe that y is true.'[35] Of course, my ability to voice these connections may not be very insightful. It might do less justice than I think to the ways in which these beliefs are actually held in place for me. I might think that I believe x because I believe y, but then find that my commitment to x survives the death of my belief about y with suspicious ease. And even where I do have some insight into why I believe something, it will not be complete. The factors that hold my belief in place are likely to be as rich, as varied and as subtle as life itself. They may turn out to be different in different circumstances; they may depend upon my mood, upon the relationship I have to the person I'm talking to, upon the last sermon I heard or upon all sorts of other contextual and psychological factors. To the extent, however, that my beliefs are held together in part by *becauses* and *therefores* we can say that my belief has a conceptual shape. That is hardly likely to mean that my beliefs hang together in a shape that is persistent, coherent and comprehensive; it may be partial, inconsistent and changeable – but it will mean that my belief is more than a collection of isolated fragments, a soup of intellectual atoms. It is a web; it has structure.

Some of the kinds of persuasion that might influence my beliefs – whether it is others trying to persuade me, or me trying to persuade myself – might work with this

---

[34] This is not an autobiographical example.
[35] I am not suggesting that beliefs are discrete and countable. For some purposes, I might analyse my believing by stating a number of propositions, but that will always be a skeletal model of my believing, and will do it only partial justice.

conceptual structure. I might be persuaded that what I already believe requires me to believe some new thing too; I might be persuaded that it requires me to stop acting in some way. Of course, thinking that I have been persuaded in these ways might be a post hoc rationalization. My coming to these conclusions may have had much more to do with my desire to be respected by the person I'm talking to, or with embarrassment, or with other factors that I am neither ready to acknowledge nor capable of articulating. Nevertheless, the reasons explicitly deployed in persuasion may from time to time genuinely be among the factors that bring me to a belief and hold me there.

Such persuasion can at times involve me in construing the relative depth of different beliefs. I might, for instance, slowly realize that there is a contradiction between what I tell myself I believe about God's forgiveness and the way in which I harbour a bitter shame about a sin long past. I might realize that I am too invested in preserving an image of myself as decent, and too little invested in recognizing myself as forgiven – and so I might try to learn in prayer both more frankly to admit my failings and more fully to imagine God's forgiving love. The habit that I am trying to change might be one that has roots holding it very tightly in the soil of my life – but I might think that my belief in God's forgiveness is deeper in another sense: I might judge that it gets at a more important truth than does my belief in my own innocence, and that the latter ought to give way to the former.[36]

Finally, among the various forms of connectedness displayed by my belief, I might turn out to have some beliefs about my beliefs: beliefs about where they come from, about what authorizes them and so on. These beliefs about belief might be just as complex and messy as any others. I might, for instance, say that my beliefs are based on the bible, but that need not mean that in practice I actually derive my beliefs from biblical reading. It might mean that I have acquired through my membership of a particular Christian community a pattern of belief that includes beliefs about the bible, and all sorts of other beliefs that I am assured have a good biblical pedigree. I might find that this whole pattern of belief is reinforced by most of the ways in which I encounter the bible – in sermons, in personal bible study or however else – but my reading may in practice serve only to confirm beliefs already held. My belief that my beliefs derive from the bible may survive quite well even when I am aware of all sorts of passages that fit very ill with what I believe. I may be happy to assume that these uncomfortable passages fit in somehow – perhaps trusting that others in my community will know better than do I how to read them.

The social shape of belief

That brings me to another fundamental aspect of belief. Believing is pervasively social. It is not simply that, in an ungovernable tangle of direct and indirect ways, I learn my believing from others. Nor is it simply that many of the factors holding the elements of my believing in place will involve my encounters with and relationships to other people. It may also be that I have a very limited grasp on what I believe – a limited

---

[36] This kind of construal of the relative depth of different beliefs will turn out to be important when I discuss processes of doctrinal change in Chapter 9.

ability to elaborate upon it, to see or show how it connects to other beliefs, to show how it derives from the authoritative sources of my faith or to draw out its implications. I may regularly have to fall back upon others to supply what I lack.

There is a division of labour in believing, and I am continually deferring to others – to other people (past and present), to institutions, to texts – as the bearers of the understanding that I lack. I rely upon the memories they retain; I rely upon the work that they have done or that is embodied in them.[37] When I said earlier, for instance, that I may trust that others in my community will know better how to read difficult passages than do I, we could say – to borrow language that makes me wince – that I have outsourced at least some of the work of attending to the authoritative sources of my faith.[38] Or consider what it means for me to join in with the saying of the Nicene Creed in my parish church, and to be serious about affirming that Jesus Christ is 'eternally begotten of the Father' – or perhaps simply serious about affirming that this is the proper belief for my community. If our account of belief is focused entirely upon what each individual is independently capable of elaborating, we are likely to get no further than the dispiriting discovery that most of us don't know what we're talking about.[39] Either we have no idea at all what we are saying when we recite those words, or the images and ideas that these words bring to our minds sit very awkwardly with the meanings that historians and theologians attribute to them. The picture will be significantly different, however, and much richer (though not necessarily easier), if we are able to take into account the ways in which many people take such words on trust – affirming them, perhaps, in the confidence that those who coined them and handed them on knew what they were doing. People often trust that knowledge of what they mean is held, somehow, in the wider community.[40]

As another example, think about my belief that 'Jesus is Lord'. I have talked about it enough that you might fairly expect me to be able to tell you something about this Jesus. If you sat me down on my own, however, and asked me who he was, you might find that I could give you only a rather paltry sketch – squeezed out of the messy heap of impressions, feelings, images and stories that I associate with the name. But I might say, instead, explicitly or implicitly, 'Come to my church, and listen; there you'll find out who he is.' It may be important to me that Jesus is Lord, but I may well regard the

---

[37] See Maurice Bloch, 'Deference', in *Theorizing Ritual: Issues, Topics, Approaches, Concepts*, ed. Jess Kreinath, Jan Snock and Michael Stausberg (Leiden: Brill, 2006), 495–506, and Gloria Origgi, 'Croyance, Déférence et Témoignage', in *Philosophie Cognitive*, ed. J. Proust and E. Pacherie (Paris: Éditions Ophrys / Éditions de la Maison des Sciences de l'Homme, 2004), 167–83. There are other aspects to the social structure of belief that are distinct from deferral: the ways in which our belief is unconsciously influenced by others (Basil Mitchell, 'I Believe, We Believe', in *Believing in the Church*, ed. Doctrine Commission, 11; cf. A. E. Harvey, *Believing and Belonging: The Practice of Believing in the Church* (London: SPCK, 1984), 4, 10); the way members of some group can agree to behave and speak in conformity to some belief when acting on the group's behalf (Margaret Gilbert, 'Collective Epistemology', *Episteme* 1, no. 2 (2004): 95–107); and the way people outside the church can rely on church leader and churchgoers to believe, in some sense, on their behalf (Grace Davie, *Religion in Britain: A Persistent Paradox*, 2nd edn (Chichester: Wiley, 2015), 81–2).
[38] There's a route here towards consider all Christian believing as a deferral to Christ's believing – but I'm not heading that way today.
[39] See Chapter 3, pp. 49–50.
[40] I don't mean to suggest that such docile deferral will be the norm. Many, perhaps most of the people involved in the web will turn out to hold tenaciously to idiosyncratic positions or make unusual connections. To say that believing is social does not stop it being awkward and contested.

community around me as holding – on my behalf – a fuller picture of who Jesus is than I possess on my own. The one I follow is the one we know together, or that others know on my behalf, as much as the one I know for myself. My independent ability to elaborate upon who Jesus is, and on what following him demands, may be very limited; but my believing happens in a community that together can do much to supply my lack.

Belief, then, is social. I believe more than I know alone; I believe more than I understand alone – because I believe as part of a wider community. I trust my community to hold that knowledge and understanding on my behalf. 'My' believing is caught up in a complex social web of deferral, stretched out in time and space.[41] If we want to identify and understand people's beliefs, our focus can't exclusively be on what is going on inside individual heads. Rather, our focus will need to be on the middle distance: the scale at which people interact, relate, communicate and form patterns of life together – the scale at which they rely upon and defer to one another. The middle distance is the level suspended between the broader patterns of culture and power in which people are embedded, and the depths of their personal histories and psychologies. We might focus on the small-scale local environment, or we might broaden our gaze to take in wider national and trans-national canvases, but belief is inextricably tangled in the ways that people make sense of, and make a life together in, the environments in which they find themselves.

Belief and profound intellectual disability

These reflections on the nature of belief can be pushed further if we take seriously the presence in and contribution to the church of people with profound intellectual disabilities. These are people who, often alongside other complex needs, may have a very limited capacity to communicate verbally, or to process others' verbal communications. In societies – and churches – that use the 'criteria of independence, productivity, intellectual prowess and social position to judge the value of human beings', people with profound intellectual disabilities face multiple forms of exclusion.[42] They may 'find themselves unable to narrate their own stories without the assistance of groups of people all of whom may misunderstand their stories', and they may have very limited ability to resist and reorder the narrations that others give.[43]

John Swinton, Harriet Mowat and Susannah Baines tell the story of 'Mary', a young woman with cerebral palsy.

> Mary ... has no speech but makes sounds. She has muscle spasms continuously. She has limited vision but her hearing is excellent. She cannot feed herself and

---

[41] We are 'always partly, but very significantly, living in a sea of deference' (Bloch, 'Deference', 505). 'Deference' is another of those words, like 'conformity', that should make us rightly suspicious: we are not far from questions of power, here (and my decision to say 'deferral' rather than 'deference' should not have fooled anybody).

[42] John Swinton, 'The Body of Christ has Down's Syndrome: Theological Reflections on Vulnerability, Disability, and Graceful Communities', *Journal of Pastoral Theology* 13, no. 2 (2003): 67.

[43] John Swinton, Harriet Mowat and Susannah Baines, 'Whose Story Am I? Redescribing Profound Intellectual Disability in the Kingdom of God', *Journal of Religion, Disability and Health* 15, no. 1 (2011): 6.

she is entirely dependent on her caretakers for all her physical needs. Mary is a Quaker. She was made a member of that community when she was a baby. Quakers understand the significance of silence. In the service, Mary shouts noisily. She shouts and sometimes lets out long rather winsome wails. However, as the community moves into times of silence, Mary becomes silent. As the silence of the community engulfs the room, so Mary shares in the silence … her response is regular … patterned … engaged.[44]

Trying to interpret what Mary's silences mean to her personally – what she has understood of the situation and what her response signals – may well be futile. But Swinton, Mowat and Baines approach the story differently. 'Mary's spirituality', they say, 'is not simply something she alone has. It is not a feeling or an emotion that is simply within her. It is something she shares in; it is an experience that rises beyond her; an experience that happens in the space between the members of the community: the space of meeting.'[45]

They also suggest, tentatively, that Mary is involved in the community's knowledge of God. In the relationship she has with this community, in her participation in the rhythms of its practice, she is a part of the life that they are weaving together before God. By her 'smiles, her touch, her sensitivity, her love' she contributes to that weaving.[46] Yet that life *is* this community's knowledge of God, and the community together knows more than any one of its participants knows alone.

Swinton takes stories like Mary's, and weaves them into an account in which friendship plays a central role. The church's knowledge of God is held together by friendship, and friendship is the means by which each of us participates in what we know together. 'Friendship', he says, 'is a deeply intimate and committed relationship that encompasses people in all their fulness.'[47] Radical friendship overcomes the barriers of otherness that mark out outcasts and strangers; it 'takes its shape from the relationships of Jesus the Messiah, and seeks to embody and act out something of his life and purpose'.[48] In response to God's gift of friendship in Christ, and constantly animated by attention to that friendship, Christians are called to learn friendship with one another. They are called to discover 'what it means to encounter the God who is love and to live within that relational space of belonging that is opened up and offered to us in Jesus'.[49] 'Friendship towards others is the place where we meet God. The full revelation of love requires bodies and not just words.'[50]

---

[44] Ibid., 13.
[45] Ibid., 14.
[46] Ibid., 16.
[47] John Swinton, *Resurrecting the Person: Friendship and the Care of People with Mental Health Problems* (Nashville, TN: Abingdon, 2000), 37.
[48] Ibid.
[49] John Swinton, 'From Inclusion to Belonging: A Practical Theology of Community, Disability and Humanness', *Journal of Religion, Disability and Health* 16, no. 2 (2012): 188.
[50] John Swinton, 'Who Is the God We Worship? Theologies of Disability; Challenges and New Possibilities', *International Journal of Practical Theology* 14 (2011): 306; cf. 'Restoring the Image: Spirituality, Faith, and Cognitive Disability', *Journal of Religion and Health* 36, no. 1 (1997): 24.

The knowledge of God is received by a community as it discovers such friendship, negotiating it in the midst of the world. To be involved in knowing God means being involved in this friendship, being caught up in it, contributing to it in whatever ways one's capacities, one's history, one's body makes possible. It is the community together that names this friendship's source; it is the community together that seeks to be receptive to the gift and challenge of God's friendship in Christ; it is the community together that responds to threats to its friendship, and discovers how that friendship might deepen and extend.

The community together believes, and because Mary is involved in the community's life, she is involved in that believing. She is, admittedly, dependent upon the other members of the community for this believing – but then so is every other member; not one of them believes alone. And Mary is not simply 'included' in a believing that would be complete without her. By her presence, by her responses, by her cries and smiles, she helps to shape the community's life, and so helps shape its belief. She would be missed if she were not there. And, as Swinton says, 'To be included you just need to be there, [whereas] to belong you need to be missed; to miss one another we need to lean what it means to love with the passion of Jesus.'[51]

Practical wisdom and improvisation

Belief, then, has a dispositional, a conceptual and a social shape. It is a life in which we are involved together. And lest the word 'shape' be taken to imply coherence and stability, you might after reading the previous sections of this chapter imagine belief having the shape of a bramble patch on a windy day: our belief is an unruly sprawl of connections, constantly shifting, and traceable only with elaborate care. There is no layer of primitive, simple believing that does not already have some such complexity to it. Believing is always embodied in the knotted patterns of life that people weave together in particular locales.

This is the material on which God's sanctifying purposes are being worked out, and it is the material in which those purposes are resisted, rejected and betrayed. The drama of sin and sanctification is played out in this tangled ecology of our dispositions and relationships, the interconnected metabolic flows of our imagination and action, our speech and thought. To put it another way, referring back to language that I used in Chapter 5: the renewal of the mind is a process worked out in the body, just as is resistance to that renewal; they take place in the sheer prosaic materiality of ordinary life, and in the interwoven shapes of our lives together in the world. God's Spirit is at work in and through all of this material; all those other spirits that fight for our allegiance are at work here too.[52]

One of the sites in which this conflict is played out is in the creativity inherent in the life of belief. Life outstrips thought. Life does not consistently yield to our recipes and

---

[51] Swinton, 'Inclusion to Belonging', 188.
[52] See Eugene F. Rogers Jr., *After the Spirit: A Constructive Pneumatology from Resources Outside the Modern West* (London: SCM Press, 2006), for the insistence that the Spirit characteristically works on bodies.

our plans, even though recipes and plans can function well enough much of the time. Life is simply too complex, too rich. In the words of Joseph Dunne, we are faced with 'the uncircumscribable range of potentially noticeable features and the consequently unlimited possibilities of action that inhere in each situation'.[53] As our lives bring us into new situations, new contexts, new relationships, following Jesus cannot simply be a matter of applying what we already know.[54] What is demanded is not *technē*, which is the kind of rationality involved when we can specify the end result in advance, and can work out the processes needed to achieve that result. What is needed is *phronēsis*, or practical wisdom. Such wisdom is needed to discover a good that 'cannot be determined in advance of the actual situations in which it is to be realised'.[55] It is 'the characteristic mode of knowledge of a being who has no escape from contingency and is forever deprived of an absolute standpoint'.[56]

Dunne, drawing on the work of R. G. Collingwood, likens this to the kind of process that a painter might undergo. In the *Principles of Art*, Collingwood had written that

> One paints a thing in order to see it. ... You see something in this subject, of course, before you begin to paint it ... but only a person with experience of painting, and of painting well, can realize how little that is, compared with what you come to see in it as your painting progresses. ... [A] good painter ... paints things because until he has painted them he doesn't know what they are like.[57]

Dunne comments: 'The watching of his own work with a vigilant and discriminating eye, which decides at every moment of the process whether it is being successful or not, is not a critical activity subsequent to, and reflective upon, the artistic work, it is an integral part of that work itself.'[58]

In many situations, we can't determine precisely what we *must* do, so we balance the different things we know, the constraints we are aware of, the hunches of what might work, and we hazard something that we *can* do. As we take that step, the situation unfolds, just a little: we see more of what might be possible, more of what might go wrong, more of what might fit well. We adjust. We take another step. A picture emerges.

---

[53] Joseph Dunne, *Back to the Rough Ground: Practical Judgment and the Lure of Technique* (Notre Dame, IN: Notre Dame University Press, 1993), 312. Cf. Tanner, *Theories of Culture*, 78, 158; Frances M. Young, *The Art of Performance: Towards a Theology of Holy Scripture* (London: Darton, Longman and Todd, 1990), 160–86, and Martha C. Nussbaum, *Love's Knowledge: Essays on Philosophy and Literature* (New York, NY: Oxford University Press, 1990), 94–5. Vanhoozer refers to 'creative fidelity' and 'ruled spontaneity' (*Drama*, 129), 'constancy and creativity' (132), and 'Faithful improvisation' (335). For him this is framed as a matter of creative continuation of the story so far – a question of finding a way forward that has a 'dramatic fit' (59) with that story. This is a 'sapiential task' (254); it requires *phronēsis* (329).

[54] See Stephen Sykes, *The Identity of Christianity: Theologians and the Essence of Christianity from Schleiermacher to Barth* (London: SPCK, 1984), 232.

[55] Dunne, *Rough Ground*, 273.

[56] Dunne, *Rough Ground*, 81. Charles Taylor, 'To Follow a Rule', in *Philosophical Arguments* (Cambridge, MA: Harvard University Press, 1997), 179, says that 'reason giving has a limit, and in the end must repose in another kind of understanding'. 'Express rules can only function in our lives along with an inarticulate sense encoded in the body' (ibid., 180).

[57] R. G. Collingwood, *Principles of Art* (Oxford: Clarendon, 1938), 303–4.

[58] Dunne, *Rough Ground*, 281.

Just so, Christians seeking to live faithfully in some new situation are, to an extent, forced to step out into the unknown. Unlike the situations we face in our fantasies and our theology books, any real situation will be inherently beyond our prediction and control. We won't necessarily be able to see in advance what faithfulness should look like just here. We might think of ourselves as seeking to paint a Christlike portrait with the materials we find to hand, and discovering only as we work what his face can look like in this context. In pursuing this task, we draw upon all our accumulated understanding, but it is only as we act, and scrutinize our action, and see what is becoming visible in it, that we become aware of the precise contours of the faithfulness that we sought. *Phronēsis* is, as Dunne puts it, 'a habit of attentiveness that ... allows the present situation to "unconceal" its own particular significance'.[59] In the pithier words of Hannah Arendt, *phronēsis* 'reveals itself fully only ... to the backward glance'.[60] It might be a matter of hesitation and agonized deliberation; it is no less likely to be a matter of barely recognized skill, even of flair, but we often discover how to be faithful only by stepping out in improvisatory faith.[61]

This process of improvisation is, however, always and inherently fallible. The pictures that we paint can be distortions, and the faithfulness we think we have found can be a betrayal. What we understand to be the work of God's Holy Spirit, luring us into some new configuration of life in the world, can be the work of quite other spirits. Every improvisation is fraught with the possibility of distortion as well as the possibility of discovery. Yet the distinction between betrayal and faithfulness cannot be mapped on to the distinction between innovation and stability. Our action in the world unavoidably demands innovation; we are always, whether we like it or not, involved in the dynamics of improvisation. The question we face is not whether to improvise, but whether our improvisations will take us away from or more deeply into the gift that we have been given in Christ.

That question is made more difficult to answer by the fact that any attempt to apply what one already knows to a new situation changes one's grasp of that knowledge; it makes new features of it visible, or enables one to see in new ways how it connects. Improvisation in Christian life unavoidably involves not just the application but the re-appropriation of the whole tangle of belief that we bring with us. It obviously involves developing beliefs about how, specifically, we are to live out our faith just here. It can also, however, change our sense of the backdrop against which this improvisation is happening, changing our sense of what is meant by our beliefs about God and God's ways with the world. Precisely because we are learning to think differently about what that background implies just here, we learn to see the background itself in a new light. As we improvise, our beliefs about God turn out to contain more than we knew, or even to mean something different from what we had previously thought, as the existing patterns of our belief are disturbed and settle into new configurations. This is happening all the time, even when we barely notice it: we find that, over time, through

---

[59] Ibid., 306–7, emphasis removed.
[60] Hannah Arendt, *The Human Condition* (Chicago: University of Chicago Press, 1958), 192; discussed in Dunne, *Rough Ground*, 91–3.
[61] Ibid., 292.

a thousand small chances and decisions, our minds have changed; we have ended up believing differently.

In the church, such improvisation involves a re-appropriation of the Christian tradition. The process involved is analogous to the process of 'rational integration' described by Robert Brandom in his discussion of common law.

> Common law differs from statutory law in that all there is to settle the boundaries of applicability of the concepts it employs is the record of actually decided cases that can serve as precedents. There is no explicit statement of principle governing the application of legal universals to particular sets of facts – only a practice of applying them in always novel circumstances. So whatever content those concepts have, they get from the history of their actual applications. A judge justifies her decision in a particular case by rationalizing it in the light of a reading of that tradition, by so selecting and emphasizing particular prior decisions as precedential that a norm emerges as an implicit lesson. And it is that norm that is then appealed to in deciding the present case, and is implicitly taken to be binding in future ones. In order to find such a norm, the judge must make the tradition cohere, must exhibit the decisions that have actually been made as rational and correct, given that the norm she finds is what has implicitly governed the process all along. Thus each of the prior decisions selected as precedential emerges as making explicit some aspect of the implicit norm, as revealing a bit of the boundary of the concept.[62]

This is, he says elsewhere, a process in which we do not simply apply concepts already to hand, but determine what concepts are expressed by our words – and the ambiguity of the word 'determine', which hovers between 'discover' and 'decide', is apt.[63] The processes of improvisation and re-appropriation that take place in ordinary believing are normally far less explicit than those involved in common law – and they are normally focused rather less on isolated moments of decision. They nevertheless bear something of the same logic.[64]

Lewis Ayres gives a scriptural example of this logic, referring to the Jerusalem 'council' – the meeting of 'the apostles and elders' portrayed in Acts 15, called to

---

[62] Robert B. Brandom, *Tales of the Mighty Dead: Historical Essays in the Metaphysics of Intentionality* (Cambridge, MA: Harvard University Press, 2002), 13–14.

[63] Robert B. Brandom, *Reason in Philosophy: Animating Ideas* (Cambridge, MA: Harvard University Press, 2009), 83. Cf. ibid., 89: 'prior use does *not* close off future possibilities of development by setting in advance a unique correct answer to the question of whether a particular concept applies in a new set of circumstances. The new circumstances will always resemble any prior, settled case in an infinite number of respects, and differ from it in an infinite number of respects. There is genuine room for choice on the part of the current judge or judger, depending on which prior commitments are taken as precedential and what respects of similarity and difference are emphasised.'

[64] John E. Thiel, *Senses of Tradition: Continuity and Development in Catholic Faith* (Oxford: Oxford University Press, 2000), 85: 'Tradition is recognised, and in the community of recognition affirmed, from the perspective of regional acts of faith as these acts of faith look back to the past to find occasions for continuity in the beliefs and practices of the previous generation[s]. ... Since continuity is a relationship that can be postulated only through a judgment made in the present moment, the continuity in which tradition is established can be affirmed only retrospectively from a present standpoint.'

consider the question of whether the gentiles should be circumcised and required to keep the law of Moses. The assembled company is reminded by Peter of the work of the Spirit among the gentiles, and told by Paul and Barnabas of the signs and wonders that they have seen God do there. They then hear James re-reading scripture – re-appropriating scripture – in the light of this testimony, and they receive his judgement that they 'should not make it difficult for the Gentiles who are turning to God'. 'The interpretation that occurs here is radical and unpredictable', Ayres says, 'and yet in drawing it out of the community God shapes also a harmony and continuity with Israel's history of prophecy about the role of non Jews.'[65]

This re-appropriation involves a judgement of 'harmony and continuity', of fittingness. It is no straightforward matter to specify what this fittingness involves, however. It is, in part, a matter of aesthetics as much as of argument: Peter, Paul and Barnabas paint a compelling picture for the other apostles and elders; they shape a frame through which to look again at all that they already know together. The judgement that they make together in the contested present involves a creatively rearranged perception of the inheritance of faith: the discovery or invention of a new way of telling the story, within which the decision they make can appear as the obvious next step to take. That kind of re-telling is what I mean by a 're-appropriation of the Christian tradition' – it is the kind of move that Ormond Rush calls a 'reconstructive and reinterpretative imagining', and that in Chapter 9 I will call the process of 're-construal'.[66]

We should not think of fittingness in purely individual and intellectual terms, however. It is, more fully, a matter of a community discovering or inventing a habitable pattern of life together, worked out on a middle-distance scale of practical arrangements and promises, habits and adjustments. A community builds such a life with what lies to hand, responding to the gifts of their neighbours and the demands of their social situation, as well as their engagement with the sources and inheritance of their faith. For good or ill, they find a way to live together with each other and with their past, with their scriptures and with the demands that they face. They find a workable settlement.

At any given moment, then, Christians do not yet know what they mean. They do not yet know all that the concepts they deploy will demand of them in the situations they face, and so they do not yet know what these concepts mean as fully as they will. The meaning of their beliefs is something that they are (fallibly, unevenly, fitfully) discovering, or being discovered by. Their existing commitments in all their bodily complexity meet the uncircumscribable reality of the present situation, and they

---

[65] Lewis Ayres, 'What Is Catholic Theology?' in *The Oxford Handbook of Catholic Theology*, ed. Lewis Ayres and Medi Ann Volpe with Thomas L. Humphries (Oxford: Oxford University Press, 2019), 8. Cf. Luke Timothy Johnson, *The Acts of the Apostles* (Collegeville, MN: Liturgical Press, 1992), 279–80. In Chapter 7, I discuss how this process transformed the early church's reading of scripture; see pp. 160–1.

[66] Ormond Rush argues that 'there is a creativity at the core of a believer's on-going act of faith'. *The Reception of Doctrine: An Appropriation of Hans Robert Jauss' Reception Aesthetics and Literary Hermeneutics* (Rome: Gregorian University Press, 1997), 218. Cf. Rowan Williams, who in 'Newman's *Arians* and the Question of Method in Doctrinal History', in *Newman after a Hundred Years*, ed. Ian Ker and Alan Hill (Oxford: Oxford University Press, 1990), 266, reads Newman as saying that 'There is a "sacramental" dimension to theological vocabulary, an element of anticipation of further understanding and fruition.'

somehow grasp (or are grasped by) a way forward that allows them to do bearable justice to both.

Our believing, in all its bodily complexity, is among the material on which God's sanctifying purposes are being worked out, and God's Spirit is at work in and through all this material, beckoning it into truthful response to God. We might understand the pervasive improvisatory dynamic of believing as a tool that the Spirit can employ – a creaturely reality that the Spirit can guide and turn to its purposes. The Spirit certainly cannot be identified with the improvisatory dynamic of belief, as if that dynamic had any inbuilt tendency to lead us deeper into truth. It can, and regularly does, take us in quite the opposite direction. And yet, if we see the Spirit as the source of whatever gifts of discernment, of wisdom, of good judgement there are present in the body, we will recognize this dynamic as one that the Spirit can use to draw people deeper into the truth that they have already been given.[67] Believers have received the faith passed on to them, but they do not yet possess it – and they press on in the hope of taking hold of it. The Spirit forms belief, working with the messy material of believers' corporate and individual life, beckoning people forward into knowledge of God together in part by beckoning them out into the world, into creative improvisations in the face of situations and encounters and relationships that they have not yet imagined.

Doctrinal theology and ordinary belief

Christians are involved in the ongoing discovery of what it means to follow Jesus.[68] Our understanding of what 'Jesus is Lord' means is taken deeper the more we understand what it means to live as Jesus's disciples, in context after context. As Gerard Loughlin says, the story of Jesus is presented to us in the four gospels, in the entire canon and in the church's multiple re-tellings – but it is a story that we go on to discover most fully

> in the prayerful reading and performing of the narratives in the church's liturgies and common life. The story is known to piety, in and through the faithful practice of ecclesial life; learned through its telling in the sacramental and virtuous life of the community. It is above all a practical knowledge, *phronesis* rather than *theoria*, and doctrine is simply the rule and discipline of the practice.[69]

Jesus is, he says, 'known as he is received in the community to which the Spirit is given, so that only in telling the story of all its members can his story be fully told'.[70] G. B.

---

[67] 'The expectation of wisdom is that we should be able to find how to live in our complex situation from the dynamism of God.' Daniel W. Hardy, *Finding the Church: The Dynamic Truth of Anglicanism* (London: SCM, 2001), 59.
[68] '[T]he church can be understood ... as the *locus* and embodiment of a set of ongoing arguments about how best to witness to Jesus Christ and to follow him in true discipleship.' Nicholas M. Healy, *Church, World and the Christian Life: Practical-prophetic Ecclesiology* (Cambridge: Cambridge University Press, 2000), 70.
[69] Loughlin, 'The Basis and Authority of Doctrine', 54.
[70] Ibid., 53.

Caird said something similar: 'Love can be known only where it is practised', he said, and so 'it takes the combined experience of all Christians to comprehend' the love of Christ.[71]

After my long detour into the nature of belief, I am now in a position to examine the role played by doctrinal theology in Christian life.[72] How does doctrine, how does the work of doctrinal theologians, relate to ordinary believing?

We can say that someone is pursuing doctrinal theology to the extent that

(i) they concern themselves with the content and conceptual structure of Christian believing – with what Christians believe and why, and how their beliefs connect;
(ii) they pay attention to those ideas about God and God's ways with the world that have proven to be persistent foci of Christian proclamation, confession, teaching and controversy over the centuries; and
(iii) they work on this belief so that the Christian life of which it is a part might respond more fully to God's grace and be drawn more deeply into God's love.

On this definition, all sorts of people are engaged in doctrinal theological work, in all sorts of contexts and by all sorts of means. Some of them end up producing discussions of belief that, characteristically in textual form, gain a significant audience beyond their original context. Their work joins (at least for a time) the loose and varied collection of accounts that remain in wide circulation around the churches. This is what I called in Chapter 5 the 'articulate tradition': the raucous parliament of theological texts proclaiming their articulations of Christian belief, and the strange company of those who read and discuss them. I use the term 'doctrinal theologian' for anyone who is fairly intensively engaged in the practices of doctrinal theology, but especially for those who engage in conversation with voices from this articulate tradition.

To understand the various contributions that doctrinal theology can make to Christian believing, consider again the process of improvisation. Faced with some situation in which they don't quite know how to go on, a Christian community draws upon all its accumulated understanding, it acts in faith, and it scrutinizes what is becoming visible in its action. In relation to processes like this, doctrinal theology can warn, it can resource and it can propose.

First, doctrinal theology can warn. It can be understood as regulative in something like the Lindbeckian sense discussed earlier. In order to improvise well, doctrinal theologians say, Christians should avoid certain pitfalls. They should speak and act in ways that fall within certain boundaries. Consider, for instance, Sarah Coakley's

---

[71] G. B. Caird, *Paul's Letters from Prison* (Oxford: Oxford University Press, 1976), 68, 70; emphasis removed; the passage is discussed in Vanhoozer, *Drama*, 30.
[72] On the connection of doctrine and life, see Ellen T. Charry, *By the Renewing of Your Minds: The Pastoral Function of Christian Doctrine* (New York: Oxford University Press, 1997), 5; Thiselton, *Hermeneutics of Doctrine*, xvi–xvii; Helmer, *Theology and the End of Doctrine*, 21; and Stanley Hauerwas, 'On Doctrine and Ethics', in *The Cambridge Companion to Christian Doctrine*, ed. Gunton, 22.

reading of the Christological definition produced at the Council of Chalcedon. This definition, she says,

> sets a 'boundary' on what can, and cannot, be said, by first ruling out three aberrant interpretations of Christ (Apollinarianism, Eutychianism, and extreme Nestorianism), second, providing an abstract rule of language (*physis* and *hypostasis*) for distinguishing duality and unity in Christ, and, third, presenting a 'riddle' of negatives by means of which a greater (though undefined) reality may be intimated. ... [I]t leaves us at that 'boundary' ... without any supposition that this linguistic regulation thereby *explains* or *grasps* the reality towards which it points.[73]

The rules set out in this doctrinal text are intended to keep Christians from idolatry, and to keep them oriented towards the God who is beyond all speech and imagination. They are intended to set out something of the shape that any of our improvisations should take if we are not to be untrue to the way in which God has shown Godself to us.[74]

Knowledge of doctrine, on this negative view, does count as a kind of knowledge of God. Doctrinal theologians do know something of the shape that Christian life and speech must take on the journey into knowledge of God. They know something definite, and what they know is, in a sense, about God. It is only, however, knowledge at a remove. The doctrinal theologian does not know what the community should do next. The doctrinal theologian has not gone on ahead into the knowledge that the community will discover as it moves. She or he is simply someone who warns.

Second, doctrinal theology can resource; it can be a work of *ressourcement*.[75] Improvisation requires the Christian community to draw upon its accumulated understanding, but that accumulation is not immediately present in each individual mind. It is held by the wider church, and in its archives. The doctrinal theologian can be someone who draws from this treasury for the sake of the improvising community, helping thereby to shape a 'Christian imaginary'.[76] A Christian community faced with decisions about how to use its money, for instance, might need reminding of the story of God's generosity, or of what has been discovered of that generosity by other communities in different times and places. A doctrinal theologian might draw from the community's treasury a picture of God as giver, and pictures of Christian action as caught up in the divine gift economy.[77]

---

[73] Sarah Coakley, 'What Does Chalcedon Solve and What Does It Not? Some Reflections on the Status and Meaning of the Chalcedonian "Definition"', in *The Incarnation: An Interdisciplinary Symposium on the Incarnation of the Son of God*, ed. Stephen T. Davis, Daniel Kendall and Gerald O'Collins (Oxford: Oxford University Press, 2002), 161, emphasis in original.

[74] The double negative is important. It is not the case that everything that might be done in accordance with this rule will thereby be guaranteed to correspond to God's life.

[75] I am not thinking simply of the Catholic movement of this name, though that is one example of this aspect of theology. See Gabriel Flynn and Paul Murray (eds), *Ressourcement: A Movement for Renewal in Twentieth-Century Catholic Theology* (Oxford: Oxford University Press, 2011).

[76] Ward, *Light*, 125.

[77] See, for instance, Simon Oliver, *Creation: A Guide for the Perplexed* (London: Bloomsbury, 2017), ch. 5.

The doctrinal theologian can offer a picture – a carefully articulated picture – but God is beyond all picturing. As I said earlier, in my discussion of Lindbeck, we can picture God as giver, but nothing in that picture enables us to grasp how giving works in God; we do not and cannot know what our words mean. Yet belief is always more than picturing, and in being grasped by that picture we are being turned by God's gracious guidance towards thankfulness. By the grace of God, we might learn the wisdom to pursue this path, and in that pursuit learn more of what it means to live in response to the God who gives. By the Spirit's work employing these words as instruments, we can be brought into a truer relation to God. As Katherine Sonderegger puts it, God is 'raising in us created words for that which is ineffable', 'quickening our appetite for divine things, our search into the Mystery of God, the pilgrimage of the Christian life'.[78]

The doctrinal theologian's knowledge of God as giver is oriented towards, and completed in, wisdom. That wisdom is oriented towards, and completed in, a life that shares God's life. It is that life that deserves to be called knowledge of God – but this allows us to say, in a secondary sense, that the picture that shapes it does convey something of that knowledge. There is an anticipation of the knowledge of God in the theologian's desiccated words, and those same words may well be taken up and used in praise and prayer, and become ingredients in the knowledge that the community inhabits. On their own these words are lifeless, but they can nourish life.

Third, doctrinal theology can *propose*. That is, the doctrinal theologian can be among those who suggest what the next step for the community should be, and who advocate that step by showing the Christian sense that it would make. What the theologian proposes is both a construal of the story so far and an outline for the next episode – and these two aspects of the proposal are inseparable.

This third function of doctrinal theology is the most basic. Even when it sounds like they are simply warning or resourcing, doctrinal theologians are nearly always also proposing. They have an eye on some future for the church, or are taking sides in fights over its direction. The logic of proposal is, however, more difficult to disentangle than the logic of either warning or of resourcing – and it won't be until Chapter 9 that I am able to give it proper scrutiny. For now, I will simply note that doctrinal theologians don't make their proposals from some privileged position that grants them an overview, but from ground level. If they make any contribution – good or bad – to the community's discernment, it is always only from the thick of the conversation of partial insights and contestable suggestions that shape that community's whole life.

The dangers of doctrinal theology

It would be possible, but deeply misleading, to see doctrinal theologians simply as facilitators. Ordinary belief is a tangle already marked by forms of articulation and deferral – that is, by conceptual and social structure. Doctrinal theologians work, implicitly at least, with both of these. They might begin, perhaps, with what

---

[78] Katherine Sonderegger, *Systematic Theology I: The Doctrine of God* (Minneapolis, MN: Fortress, 2015), 23. Cf. Ephraim Radner, *Time and the Word: Figural Reading of the Christian Scriptures* (Grand Rapids, MI: William B. Eerdmans, 2016), 173, 190.

their addressees already take to be their deepest beliefs: 'You say you believe these foundational truths of the gospel? Well, let me show you what follows from that.'[79] They might work with people's acknowledgements of authority – their deferral to scripture, say, or to voices from the tradition. 'You acknowledge these authorities? Well, let me help you see some of the demands that they make on your belief.' In other words, we might see them as working with the grain of believers' existing structures of belief, not imposing something of their own. They assist in the forms of self-regulation that are already built into believing. Or so we might think.

We might further think that, if doctrinal theologians can provide such assistance, it is simply because they draw from what they know of the wider tradition. They draw on language about God that has been honed and deployed in the wider conversations of the Christian faith. They don't speak on their own behalf; they speak on behalf of the church that has already explored the authoritative sources and the foundational beliefs acknowledged by their addressees. They draw attention to what the church has discovered about those beliefs and sources, the warnings or resources that can be found in them, or that can be derived from them by the exercise of reason. We might be tempted to think of them (or they might be tempted to think of themselves) simply as messengers bringing gifts from the wider church to the local, or from the past to the present.

I don't want to erase this picture completely, but it is as it stands deeply misleading, even dangerous. First, the doctrinal theologian's subjectivity – their materiality, their history, their location – has been all but erased from this picture. Any queries about their own authority have been forwarded to the authorities on whose behalf they claim to speak – the scriptures, the tradition, the wider church – and the theologians themselves haven't been asked to take any responsibility.[80] Doctrinal theologians are, however, always people who stand in some particular position. Their eyes are open to some things in the sources on which they draw, and closed to others. Their sense of what is fitting and what jars is personal. Their construals of the connections and content of belief are peculiar. And they have all sorts of reasons for their own beliefs, far beyond the rational. They are shaped by their histories, their involvements, their privilege, their inattentiveness, the happenstances and biases of their education, the institutions and systems of which they are a part, the strange gradients of their emotional lives, and the cluttered furniture of their imaginations.[81] They are able to set out their positions in clean diagrams only by hiding, deliberately or accidentally, from others and perhaps also from themselves, the nature of their believing. They hide the ways in which their belief is itself uneven, incomplete, tangled, inconsistent and changeable, much more like ordinary belief than like the simulacrum presented in their lectures or the pages of their books. They hide the ways in which their belief is fallible, broken and harmful, the ways in which it is complicit in, reproduces and

---

[79] Cf. my analysis of Ephesians in the Chapter 5.
[80] Cf. Tanner, *Theories of Culture*, 72. See also Chapter 5, p. 98.
[81] Cf. Simeon Zahl, 'Tradition and its "Use": The Ethics of Theological Retrieval', *Scottish Journal of Theology* 71, no. 3 (2018): 310 on 'the effects of personal, communal, material and even biological locatedness'.

sometimes intensifies the sinful patterns of the church's life. Doctrinal theologians are not a breed apart from ordinary believers.[82]

Second, this picture misrepresents the ways in which doctrinal theologians are heard. When they are granted any kind of hearing by others, there is always far more going on than an acknowledgement of the cogency of their reasons or the authoritative nature of their sources. They are heard, in part, because of the voices with which they speak. Those voices, the access they have to audiences, the reception they elicit – all of these are shaped by class, race, gender and sexuality. They are often enabled by unearned privilege, by the expenditure of educational capital itself generated from cultural and economic capital. In the contexts with which I am most familiar, a doctrinal theologian may be (knowingly or unknowingly) drawing on the cachet that comes with a university post, or with the title 'Professor', or with the fact of having published fat books; they may be bolstered by the signals sent by accent, by clothing, by posture – by all manner of factors that orbit some distance from the sun of intellectual cogency.

Third, this picture overestimates doctrinal theologians' insight into the belief of those to whom they speak. Doctrinal theologians may not be a breed apart from ordinary believers, but their work is unusual. It displays a deeply eccentric level of explicitness – and it gains that explicitness only by being thinner than ordinary belief. However poetic or multifaceted their approach might be, doctrinal theologians inevitably offer something more precise and more formal than ordinary belief. They tend to work with only some of the kinds of connections, involvements and forms of deferral built in to that belief. Believing is as rich as life, and there is simply no way of tracing all the connections that animate it, and of bringing them all to the surface. When they are not heard, doctrinal theologians might be tempted to blame their hearers' obtuseness or ignorance. They might think that believers should and would have been moved if only they had been properly capable of grasping the theologians' arguments. But even if that is sometimes partly true, it is also the case that the theologians themselves will often have failed to grasp the full bodily complexity of ordinary believing. They may have argued against some belief without understanding the emotional and aesthetic patterns than hold it in place, and that make it a buttress for a habitable pattern of discipleship. They might have advocated for a particular belief without recognizing its connections to patterns of privilege that oppress those to whom they are speaking. Doctrinal theology is all too often dangerously obtuse.

Fourth, this picture ignores the nature of the resources on which doctrinal theologians draw. They draw from an articulate tradition that is itself moulded by a dense tangle of forces, visible and invisible, salubrious and deadly. That tradition is a cacophony of arguments conducted between people all of whom were and are as complex, all of whom were and are as mired in the unchartable marshes of ordinary believing, as anyone else. No text from the tradition fully displays the reasons for its

---

[82] 'Theology's investment in racism, sexism, and homophobia does not necessarily become evident via baldly racist, sexist, and homophobic statements on the page, though of course that happens too. Theology's investment here may also lie elsewhere, in intellectual genealogies, habits of thought, and, especially, in the denials and evasions theologians permit themselves.' Linn Marie Tonstad, 'The Real Problem of Abstraction in Systematic Theology', paper presented to the Society for the Study of Theology in 2019, 5.

author's positions; they are all shaped by far more than will ever appear even in their voluminous footnotes. And the articulate tradition as a whole is an unrepresentative selection from the churches' past and present life. It is overwhelmingly skewed towards contexts in which enough financial, political, cultural and educational resources have concentrated to allow writing and publication to be a priority. It is skewed towards the topics that interest those who have access to such resources, and who are not preoccupied with the practicalities of survival. It is predominantly written by the hands of men elevated into positions of cultural, political and ecclesiastical authority, and held there by the unseen labour of countless others. Most Christian knowledge of God is simply missing from the pages of the articulate tradition.

In all these ways and other, doctrinal theologians have not simply failed to live up to the standard of love that we acknowledge. We have all too often energetically and doggedly pursued its opposite. We have sustained and reinforced the church's anti-Semitism and woven that hatred into the pictures we have painted of salvation and the work of Christ; we have promoted White supremacy and anti-Black racism and claimed them as features of God's providential plan; we have insisted that women be subordinated and seen that as a law written into the fabric of creation. We have, all too often, worked with all our might against God's sanctifying purposes, and brought all our learning, all our knowledge, all our skill and authority to the task.

Learning from ordinary belief

Doctrinal theologians and all their works suffer from the same distortions of vision, the same deep corruptions and inadequacies that shape the life of the church and all human life. They stand in as much need of the Spirit's sanctifying work as anyone else if they are to be of service. As with everyone else involved in belief, they need their twisted grasp of what is good to be exposed and corrected, their half-closed minds opened, their selfishness overthrown. And the instruments that the Spirit uses to interrupt their flow, to call them to account and to lead them deeper into truth are the same instruments that the Spirit uses on anyone.[83] The Spirit calls them to account by means of the scriptures, by means of voices from the tradition, and by means of the critiques and questions of their fellow theologians – but also, and animating their understanding of all these, by means of the lives of their fellow believers, and by drawing them with their fellow believers out into the world, into new situations, new encounters and new relationships, to discover possibilities of life together. Their work may be one form of ministry that the body of Christ needs, but doctrinal theologians themselves need the life of that whole body, a life that will always outrun their thinking, to enable them to do their work well.

I have repeatedly said that doctrinal theologians do not, simply by means of their expertise in doctrine, know God better than do ordinary believers. Their knowledge – when it is knowledge at all – is of something like a set of guidelines for the life of belief,

---

[83] I have borrowed the phrase 'interrupting the flow' from Al Barrett, *Interrupting the Church's Flow: Engaging Graham Ward and Romand Coles in a Radically Receptive Political Theology in the Urban Margins* (PhD thesis, Vrije Universiteit, Amsterdam, 2017).

or of some resources that such life could include, of some limits that it should observe, if it is to be true to the ways in which God has given Godself to the world. This is a kind of knowledge of God. It is, however, a secondary form of that knowledge. It is in lives of worship, witness and discipleship – lives lived in love together, lives in which any contributions made by doctrinal theology are brought to life – that knowledge of God is properly found.

Doctrinal theologians can therefore learn from ordinary belief as much as they contribute to it. The Spirit works on and in the whole body, in all its density and angularity, drawing people into lives together that explore and embody something of the truth of the gospel. That life is shaped by the Spirit in all manner of ways, including much that flies below doctrinal theology's radar. By it, the Spirit can teach doctrinal theologians to see their subject matter differently. This might occasionally take the form of a head-on challenge at the level of abstract conceptualization, when voices emerge which directly question doctrinal theologians' ideas and arguments. Explicit work on doctrinal theology happens, after all, in all sorts of unexpected places, and involves far more and far more varied people than typically appear in doctrinal theologians' footnotes. This schooling of the theologians is perhaps even more likely to happen, however, at the level of ordinary Christian practice. The ideas deployed in doctrinal theology are grasped only when we understand the ways in which the life of ordinary belief is or could be shaped by them, only when we see how the life of ordinary belief could embody them. When we attend to that life, however, and to the ways in which it embodies the ideas about which we talk, doctrinal theologians can discover that things are not quite as we expect. We can discover questions we had not thought to ask, alternative ways in which our ideas might hang together, connections that we had thought absolute shown to be relative, problematic implications emerging at which we had not guessed, language that we thought dead come alive in unexpected ways, language that we thought vivifying turning to dust. We might see the Spirit at work in places we had thought unclean. Openness to being schooled by ordinary belief does not stand opposed to commitment to the gift that God has given to the church. It is a means by which the Spirit can draw doctrinal theologians deeper into that gift.[84]

Conclusion

Belief is social, and improvisatory. Christians discover together habitable settlements. They find ways of living together with each other and with their collective past, with their scriptures and with all the demands that they face. Every such settlement is an

---

[84] I am not imagining that doctrinal theology should adopt, as a matter of course, the surveying of ordinary believers as to their opinions on technical theological matters, as if the results of a questionnaire asking, 'How many persons of the Trinity do *you* think there might be?' would be especially illuminating. If, however, we recognize that the technical language of theologians provides (at whatever remove) instruction for how ordinary Christian life, speech and thought should be shaped and filled so as to refer to God, then the life of ordinary Christians will often rub against those rules in interesting ways.

experiment in faithfulness, an essay in quest of the truth of the gospel in this particular place. Every such experiment is in part a failure, a betrayal of the love of God.

The Spirit can work in and through the processes of improvisation that form these experiments, leading people deeper into God's truth. The Spirit's characteristic work is to hold people fast to what they have already been given: the gift of God in Jesus Christ, in whom all the fullness of God was pleased to dwell. The Spirit's characteristic work is also to draw people forward, enabling them to uncover or receive more of the abundance of what they have been given, and challenging them to think again about what they thought they had received. The holding fast and the drawing forward are not two works, still less dynamics that stand in tension with one another. They are one work: the Spirit continually beckons people further up and further in to the gift already given to them, by beckoning them further out into the world.[85]

It is because of this shape to the Spirit's work – luring the church deeper into what it has already received by leading it out into the world – that the church cannot avoid asking: How does what we are discovering fit with what we have already been given? How does this work of the Spirit in the present relate to the work of the Spirit in Christ? How do the new possibilities we think we have seen relate to scripture, or to the apostolic tradition? These questions are asked in all sorts of ways, explicitly and implicitly. They are asked and answered by the whole church. There is no reason to think that it falls particularly to doctrinal theologians to provide answers to them. They are answered primarily by a practical wisdom that discovers, or is discovered by, fittingness. People find a way to live together with what they already know, and with what they are finding.

Nevertheless, doctrinal theologians can, by the grace of God, play a role in this. Theirs is only one ministry among others, but they can bring certain kinds of resources to the process (though one should be wary of their selectivity); they can warn of some of the ways in which it might go wrong (though one should be wary of their hastiness in judging, and of their misplaced certainties); and they can propose ways forward (though they have no special vantage point from which to do so). Their resources, warnings and proposals need to be tested, challenged and interrupted in conversation with the whole body of Christ. There must not be a one-way process here, with doctrinal theologians engaged simply in delivery; that is a recipe for the reproduction of the church's existing failures, and for the amplification of the theologians' own sins.

Their work is better thought of as a venue in which certain kinds of conversation can be staged – conversation between the life of ordinary belief in the present and

---

[85] Sergius Bulgakov, 'Dogma and Dogmatic Theology' (1937), trans. Peter Bouteneff, in *Tradition Alive: On the Church and the Christian Life in Our Time: Readings from the Eastern Church*, ed. Michael Plekon (Lanham, MD: Rowman and Littlefield, 2003), 79, writes that 'The life of the Church is a continuous revelation of the full truth that the Church bears in itself. This revelation ... is understood not through a passive-mechanical action, but through the creative unfolding of the truth, in response to the calls of life and the quests of thought.' Cf. *Doctrine in the Church of England: The Report of the Commission on Christian Doctrine Appointed by the Archbishops of Canterbury and York in 1922* (London: SPCK, 1938), 40: 'This revelation [in Jesus] is final, but its content is being ever more fully apprehended in the life of the mystical body of Christ'; and see also Anthony Harvey, 'Attending to Scripture', 28: 'The Church, like the individual, discovers what it believes only by interpreting the faith which it has received in the light of its present experience.'

the articulate tradition, conversation between local belief and the belief of the wider church, conversation between the scriptures and the whole history of the church's believing. There are no guarantees of insight, no guarantees of progress or growth in such conversations, but in them a church may learn to see its present life differently in the light of its inheritance, and its inheritance differently in the light of its present life. And through such conversation and discovery, by the grace of God, the Spirit might at times work upon our life together.

There is much more to say. We need to look at what is going on when Christians improvise differently, making incompatible claims about what it means to follow Jesus. We need to explore the processes by which doctrinal change happens, and by which the churches and their theologians recognize and respond to distortions in their doctrinal inheritances. We need to understand more fully the logic of 'proposing', by which doctrinal theologians offer constructive construals to their churches, and have those construals tested and received. First, however, we need to look more closely at the church's engagement with scripture, and especially at the dynamic by which the church can be drawn deeper into those scriptures by being drawn out together by the Spirit, in creative improvisations in the world.

7

Doctrine and scripture

Introduction

The Spirit of God is at work, beckoning the church further up and further in to the gift of life that we have been given in Christ, by beckoning us further out into the world, into new situations and relationships. The Spirit of God is at work luring us deeper into the love of God, by luring us into ways of working out that love together in the world, continually discovering and being discovered by it. The Spirit of God is at work, opening up for us the abundance of God.

The Spirit works in and through all the experiments – the always failed experiments – of Christian life, the settlements in which we embody both our knowledge of God and our ignorance. Each of these experiments is also a way of living with scripture, of reading and responding to it. Each is a pattern of life built and found by people who have been shaped by all the ways in which they hear, pray, sing, read, ponder and discuss scripture. Scripture has shaped their understanding of the love that God has for them, and of the love that they are to have for God and their neighbours. Each of their lived experiments is a way of coming to terms with scripture, of knowing how to go on with it.

There is something missing, though, from this way of talking. It can make scripture sound like nothing more than an old friend, dog-eared and familiar, incapable of surprising. And yet scripture is supposed to be an instrument in the hands of the Spirit as the Spirit works upon us. In the words of Katherine Sonderegger, 'we are brought into the fiery Presence of the Lord through this earthen vessel'; 'we meet God there, the very One who chose and formed and taught the People Israel, and the very One who came among us in the Son, mighty to save.' Scripture is 'a mighty sword, an unchained word'.[1]

This is the territory that I will be exploring in this chapter. The church lives with scripture; I ask what it means for it to read scripture listening for a word that stands over against its life, as a gift and a challenge. It cannot mean that the church should simply be passive: hearing only happens through some form of reading, some active engagement with the text. It cannot mean that Christians should simply be urged to read diligently: there is no one neutral and obvious practice called 'reading'. It has to mean that the church is called into specific kinds of reading, specific kinds of life

---

[1] Katherine Sonderegger, *Systematic Theology, vol. 1: The Doctrine of God* (Minneapolis, MN: Fortress, 2015), 509; and 'Holy Scripture as Sacred Ground', in *The Task of Dogmatics: Explorations in Theological Method*, ed. Oliver Crisp and Fred Sanders (Grand Rapids, MI: Zondervan, 2017), 143.

with scripture, within which and by means of which the objectivity of the text can be registered. And this, perhaps, is where doctrinal theology comes in. It can – with all the caveats expressed at the end of Chapter 6 – help to keep the church to a specific scriptural discipline. It can indicate boundaries beyond which reading should not go. It can help to shape the church's imagination of what scripture is, of what reading involves and of where life with scripture is supposed to lead.

The church is called to a form of reading in which a certain priority adheres to the literal sense of the gospels, because they render Jesus's identity to us. It is called to reading as a spiritual discipline, a means by which the Spirit can draw readers on a journey of purification and ascent. It is called to reading that has as its goal the ongoing discovery and embodiment of the abundant love of God. The journey on which the Spirit leads the reading church is not, however, simply a journey deeper into what the church already knows. It is not simply a journey into the more diligent pursuit of its existing disciplines of reading. The church's existing knowledge and disciplines are broken; they are marred by the church's sin, and help to perpetuate that sin. The journey on which the Spirit invites the church is a journey on which readers are continually drawn out into new contexts, new encounters and new relationships in the world, including with those who have been excluded from the church's life or marginalized within it. On this journey, the Spirit repeatedly unsettles the ways in which readers have settled with one another and with scripture, and teaches them to read and to live differently. The Spirit opens the scriptural word to the church in new ways precisely by leading the church out beyond the circle of its present life, calling it to repentance and to amendment of its ways.

Scripture is a gift unwrapped in all the experiments in faithfulness that Christians live in the world. Each experiment is a failure and each urgently needs correcting, but each can in principle enable Christians to see in a new light something of scripture's textured surface. Scripture is a gift but not a possession. It is something that we have received but that we need to go on receiving, a text that we know and do not yet know. The abundance of the text, its endless openness for this kind of rediscovery, its rich objectivity, is a gift from God's abundance, and an invitation into it.

The unchained word

In his second letter to Timothy, Paul urges his 'beloved child' to 'hold to the standard of sound teaching' and to 'Guard the good treasure' entrusted to him, in order that he might inhabit 'the faith and love that are in Christ Jesus' (1.13) and learn how to 'pursue righteousness, faith, love, and peace, along with those who call on the Lord from a pure heart' (2.22). Being fitted in this way to live and reign with Christ demands discipline (2.11-12): Timothy should behave like an athlete who competes 'according to the rules', or like a soldier obeying orders (2.4-5). And he should lead his community in the same discipline. His work will involve 'correcting opponents' (2.25), and he can expect opposition, 'For the time is coming when people will not put up with sound doctrine' (4.3) (i.e. with healthy teaching that leads people into the life of Christ). He should 'be persistent' in the face of such obtuseness, working to 'convince, rebuke, and encourage' (4.2).

In all this work, Timothy can rely upon the scriptures, because 'All scripture is inspired by God and is useful for teaching, for reproof, for correction, and for training in righteousness, so that everyone who belongs to God may be proficient, equipped for every good work' (3.16-17). Timothy's teaching can therefore take the form of 'rightly explaining the word of God' (2.15). Scripture's role is clear: it is a God-given tool for interrupting and directing the community's life, calling it back to the demanding path that leads into the faith and love of Christ. The community can be kept true to God, and true to God's gift in Christ, by remaining true to scripture.

There is, however, a second strand to Paul's exhortation woven around the first. The sound teaching to which Timothy is to hold is the teaching that he has heard from Paul (1.13). That teaching guides Timothy's approach to scripture, setting out for him scripture's nature and the purpose of reading, and setting out in summary form the faith that he can expect to find proclaimed there: the good news 'of our Saviour Christ Jesus, who abolished death and brought life and immortality to light' (1.10). Timothy is to read scripture as one who has heard this teaching from Paul – and not just heard his teaching, but observed his conduct, his faith, patience, love, steadfastness and persecutions (3.10). Paul is both a teacher who expounds scripture and a disciple who inhabits it. Timothy is also to remember that he received his faith from his mother Eunice and his grandmother Lois; their household was his first school in the faith (1.5).[2] The knowledge of scripture to which he is to hold fast is the knowledge that he learnt from them – knowledge he has had since his childhood (3.14-15). Thanks to them, scripture is familiar to him, and he is at home in it.

Timothy, then, is to hold fast to scripture, with its God-given capacity to discipline and direct the church's life, to challenge and correct the habits and teachings of the Christians among whom Timothy lives. He is also, however, to hold fast to the explicit and implicit teaching that he has received from the women in his family, and from Paul himself – people with whom he lived, whose habits and teaching have deeply shaped his reading of scripture. And Paul shows not the slightest interest in the possibility of a tension between the two sides of this exhortation.

Scripture over against the church

John Webster, on the other hand, does raise the possibility of a tension.[3] He raises it, not in relation to Timothy, but in relation to George Lindbeck. Lindbeck, he says, focuses on the way in which the church is a community that has learnt to live with scripture – such that to attend to scripture and to become socialized into this community are all but the same thing. In such an approach, Webster says, the text of scripture becomes 'a durable linguistic artefact which organises the Christian religious and cultural system, and so shapes Christian thought, speech, and action'. It becomes a text effectively possessed by the church, a norm with which the church has settled

---

[2] He should remember 'the texture of their faithful lives'. (Thomas G. Long, *1 & 2 Timothy and Titus* (Louisville, KY: Westminster John Knox, 2016), 232.)

[3] I am drawing here and elsewhere in this chapter on material I have covered in more detail in 'Hans Frei, George Lindbeck, and the Objectivity of Scripture', a chapter written for an as yet untitled book of essays edited by George Hunsinger and forthcoming from Rowman and Littlefield.

and made its peace. Lindbeck therefore has (in Webster's eyes) no serious account of how the text of scripture can serve 'the *viva vox Dei*' as it breaks out against the life of the church.[4]

For Webster, by contrast, 'Attending to Scripture ... is not a matter of being socialised, but of being caught up in the dissolution of all society – including and especially church culture – through the word of the one who smites the earth with the rod of his mouth.' 'Scripture is not', he says, 'the domestic talk of the Christian faith, or simply its familiar semiotic system. It is the sword of God, issuing from the mouth of the risen one.'[5]

For Webster, Scripture is a creaturely reality sanctified by God. The Spirit has been and is active in 'all the processes of the text's production [and] preservation', 'annexing and ordering' creaturely reality to yield a text that is fitted for the work that God has for it. Its textual features, its qualities as an object in the world, are shaped by God to be the means of God's activity. And, by this divine activity, the church is also shaped to be a hearing church: 'Scripture works by forcing the church into an external, "ecstatic" orientation in all its undertakings; it builds the church up by breaking the church open, and therefore in large measure by breaking the church down.' Therefore, 'Scripture is as much a destabilising feature of the life of the church as it is a factor in its cohesion and continuity.' 'Holy Scripture serves the ... church as the instrument through which the Spirit breaks out and reforms the community.'[6]

Timothy learnt scripture from Eunice and Lois; he was socialized in their household into their ways with scripture. Webster, however, worries that the 'domestic' and 'familiar' represent the captivity of scripture. Or perhaps, given the language of force, annexation, breaking, smiting and 'the sword' that Webster favours, we should say that he worries that the domestic and the familiar represent scripture's emasculation.

A similar worry, though expressed in less troubling language, animates Kevin Vanhoozer's criticism of Lindbeck. In *The Drama of Doctrine*, for instance, Vanhoozer writes of both Hans Frei and George Lindbeck that 'There is a palpable tension between their professed intertextuality, on the one hand' – that is, their professed determination to allow their understanding of Christian faith to be shaped by the words of scripture – and 'their focus on the church's use of Scripture, on the other. The urgent question for cultural-linguistic theology is whether genuine Christian identity is received through the apostolic witness – mediated by the biblical text – or whether it is produced in and by the community's performance, a social construction.'[7] 'Theologians', says

---

[4] Webster, *Holy Scripture*, 48–9. At the 1958 Lambeth Conference, the report on 'The Holy Bible: Its Authority and Message' argued that 'The Church is the witness and keeper of Holy Writ, charged to interpret it and expound it by the aid of the Spirit of truth which is in the Church. But on the other hand the Church is not "over" the Holy Scriptures, but "under" them.' (*The Lambeth Conference 1958: The Encyclical Letter from the Bishops together with the Resolutions and Reports* (London: SPCK / Greenwich, CT: Seabury, 1958), §2.5.) As a later Anglican report put it, the question is whether 'it really is scripture that is being heard, not simply the echo of our own voices ... or the memory of earlier Christian interpretations.' (The Lambeth Commission on Communion, *The Windsor Report* (London: The Anglican Communion Office, 2004), §59.)

[5] Webster, *Holy Scripture*, 50, 52.

[6] Ibid., 24, 26, 46, 52.

[7] Vanhoozer, *The Drama of Doctrine*, 170, emphasis removed. Vanhoozer is criticized by Fossett, in *Upon This Rock*, 69, for assuming that 'either the text is authoritative or the reading community is'.

Vanhoozer, 'should pay less attention to how this or that Christian community uses the Bible ... and greater attention to the Bible as itself a communicative act of the triune God.' 'The supreme norm for church practice is Scripture itself: not Scripture as used by the church but Scripture as used by God, even, or perhaps especially, when such use is over against the church.'[8]

All the experiments that constitute the church's life are failures; all are distorted by sin, all do harm, all are complicit in – and more than complicit in – horrors. All stand in need of interruption and reordering, and we should not underestimate how urgent and how deep that need is. There is much about the church that is deadly, and that betrays the love of God. Both Webster and Vanhoozer are rightly concerned that scripture should be allowed to stand over against this life, so that God can use the text to interrupt, to challenge, to judge and to call to repentance. Both express this concern, however, by criticizing a focus on the church's durable habits of reading, its familiarity with scripture – and yet each acknowledges that attending to scripture's objective content itself demands a certain kind of practice. Vanhoozer, for instance, says that '*sola scriptura* stands for a certain church practice, a certain way of using Scripture in the church'.[9] He insists that the primary use of scripture we have to reckon with is the 'dominical and spiritual' use – that is, the use that God makes of scripture by Word and Spirit. But this dominical and spiritual use is acknowledged in 'an ecclesial practice', an 'embodied social practice of biblical interpretation', something that the church 'performs'.[10]

Similarly, for Webster, 'the "hearing" church is not simply a passive reality but also – under the rule of God – a community which engages in visible acts.' These will be acts of a distinctive character, because 'reading can only occur as a kind of brokenness, a relinquishment of willed mastery of the text, and through exegetical reason's guidance toward that encounter with God of which the text is an instrument'. They will, fundamentally, be acts 'of those who are being made holy, that is, transfigured by the Holy Spirit into conformity with the dying and rising of the Son of God'. Nevertheless, they remain genuinely 'the acts of creatures'.[11]

We are in a tangle here. How are we to understand the relationship between the church's practices of reading, familiar and durable, by means of which it hears the divine word spoken in scripture, and that word's capacity to challenge, overthrow and remake all the broken practices of the church? To begin the process of untangling, we need to look much more closely at what we mean by 'the church's practices of reading'.

Reading settlements

I said in Chapter 6 that Christians discover together habitable settlements. They find ways of living together with each other and with their collective past, with all

---

[8] Vanhoozer, *The Drama of Doctrine*, 63 (cf. 149–50), 16–17, emphasis removed.
[9] Ibid., 114, 153.
[10] Ibid., 114, 152, 176.
[11] Webster, *Holy Scripture*, 71, 88, 92.

the demands that they face and with their scriptures. Every such settlement is an experiment in faithfulness, an essay in quest of the truth of the gospel in some particular place. Every such experiment is in part a failure, a betrayal of the gospel and of the love for which it calls.

The word 'settlement' here is meant to evoke a certain rough-edged pragmatism. It is meant to suggest a pattern of life that results, not from the application of an abstract plan, but from the attempts of some collection of people to rub along coherently enough in some place to make a habitable life together. It is any pattern of life that Christians have found, or been found by, in which they know roughly how to relate to one another, to their neighbours and to all that they have inherited, including the scriptures. It is a pattern of life in which they know how to go on.

Think of a group of people who sustain a particular pattern of Christian life together: a community, a network, a movement; it doesn't matter on what scale, how widely scattered or how fuzzy-edged.[12] Imagine a group that sustains some fairly consistent way of living with the bible. This might be visible in sermons, in bible study groups, in quiet time notes, in the references to scripture that are made in some arguments and avoided in others, in the presence of posters with biblical texts on them, in Sunday school teaching, in ordinary conversation and in verses appended to people's email signatures.[13] It might be surrounded by, and might draw upon, uses of scripture in popular culture: in films, in plays, in school Religious Education lessons and in internet memes. It might be carried and passed on in practices, in artefacts, in habits, in patterns of affect, in rituals, in architecture and in deliberate teaching – just as it was passed on to Timothy on Eunice's knee.

You might by now be imagining some community with well-formed scriptural apprenticeships, agreed paradigms of maturity, and clearly policed boundaries. I also have in mind, however, very much messier examples. I am thinking of tendencies that one might trace across a wide landscape, mapping different intensities as one goes, hardly registering where they finally become undetectable. I am thinking of the kind of reality that would be a gift to ethnographers interested in fractures, misrecognitions and absences. I am thinking of the kind of reality that might be marked by widely differing levels and kinds of participation, and in which the boundaries of the group might look very different to different participants. At one level of precision, we might be looking at a pattern of scriptural practice spreading across wide tracts of history. We might then turn the focus ring and look at the eccentric usage of a little local community. I don't mean to privilege any particular scale.

Some of the time, if it is to count as a settlement at all, the people involved must be able to talk to each other about scripture, at least in certain contexts and about certain topics. They will be able to feel, even if they are disagreeing, that they are having a real conversation rather than talking past one another. They might be able to talk about what in scripture they are familiar with and what not, about what speaks to them and

---

[12] See my 'Patterns of Interfaith Reading I: Scriptural Settlements', in Mike Higton and Rachel Muers, *The Text in Play: Experiments in Reading Scripture* (Eugene, OR: Cascade, 2012), 115–18; and 'Reason', in *The Routledge Companion to the Practice of Christian Theology*, ed. Mike Higton and Jim Fodor (London: Routledge, 2015), 9–22.

[13] Cf. Chapter 3, n. 10.

what does not, about what puzzles them, about what in scripture clarifies what, about what they find they can do little with, about how certain scriptures make them feel and about what it is okay to joke about.

Each settlement will also sustain, and be sustained by, different ways of imagining scripture, and different ways of understanding what reading involves. It makes a difference to imagine scripture as a series of vignettes from the history of progressive revelation, or as a field of figures and types, or as evidence for the reconstruction of the early church, or as an inerrant compendium of doctrine, or as a love letter, or as a collection of voices each with its own theology and so on, and on. Different patterns of imagination cohere with different expectations, different attitudes, different tapestries of feeling and different habits of reading.[14]

It might seem that the text of scripture is simply there for all such groups: the same text is open in front of any one of them that is open in front of every other.[15] In another sense, however, the scriptures read in any one settlement will differ from those read in every other. Within any one settlement, various features of the text will be recognized and talked about; there will be particular kinds of thing that get noticed and discussed, or that can easily be referred to. One member of the group might say to another, 'Have you ever noticed that …', and even if her conversation partner has to answer 'No', he might still recognize that she is pointing to the kind of feature of the text that it makes sense to notice and discuss.[16] For participants in any scriptural settlement, the text they see or hear is the ensemble of features that they are in a position to take into account.

In one sense, this is not really a matter of interpretation. A capable sighted reader does not first see a set of black marks and then, in a subsequent and deliberate process, interpret these marks as letters and the letters as words – making something of what is 'really' only marks. Rather, they see letters, words and groups of words. Just so, a community that has a habitual way with scripture will see or hear it as a field of noteworthy features. They will simply see or hear stories, questions, challenges, promises, commands; they will see or hear themes, contrasts, cross references and arguments; they will see or hear familiar landmarks and unfamiliar territories. That is simply what is there for them, open in front of them when they turn to the text. It will take effort, undertaken for some unusual purpose, to decompose these features into supposedly more basic components.[17]

---

[14] Zoë Bennett, 'Finding a Critical Space: Scripture and Experience in Practical Theology', in *Theologians on Scripture*, ed. Angus Paddison (London: Bloomsbury, 2016), 34, advocates attending to 'where we are' with scripture, always already 'reading and interpreting Scripture with a whole history of prior encounters, feelings, commitments, and intellectual development'.

[15] This is only partly true, of course. Different translations are in use, of somewhat different canons of texts – and different groups may have very different experiences of how much the text is actually open in front of them, if by that we mean that they are given access to it and authorized to read it for themselves.

[16] Michael Drosnin, in *The Bible Code* (London: Weidenfeld & Nicolson, 1997) and other works, searches the Hebrew text of the Torah for regular patterns of letters spelling out secret messages. The patterns that he finds are from my point of view not 'the kind of feature of the text that it makes sense to notice and discuss'.

[17] I don't mean to suggest that there is one real baseline of evidence to which all others eventually reduce, as if (say) the only true features of the text are varying patterns of chemicals soaked into the fibres of a number of fragments of parchment. Patterns of argument that seek to identify the true

The features that are visible or audible to participants in a settlement will characteristically be those that are registered in their various practices. Members of the group will register these features by learning to do things with them, learning to work with them in different ways. The features will stand out for them because they are salient in the course of their lives. A participant can certainly notice something simply as a curious fact about the text, one that sets off no wider ripples in her life, but on the whole the ways in which she uses and lives with the text will shape what she notices. Like a climber facing a rockface she will see the text largely as a field of graspable features. This does not mean that she will register only those things that are 'relevant' in some banal and modish sense. She might be involved in reading scripture aloud, and find rhythms and repetitions salient; she might be involved in a practice of *lectio* that leads her to hear the variety of ways in which God is named in the Psalms; she might be involved in an academic project that has her noticing subtle patterns in the use of Greek tenses in the Gospel of Mark. What counts as a feature of the text, and what features she registers, will be contingent. It will be relative to the settlement that she inhabits, and therefore inextricable from the life that she leads with others around the text. This would have been as true for Timothy as for anyone: formed in his mother's and his grandmother's faith, inducted into their familiar ways of reading, he would have been enabled to grasp in scripture much the same kinds of feature that they grasped, the kinds of feature that mattered for the life they lived together.

Registering objectivity

I do not mean this description of settlements to be cosy. The patterns of life that any given group lives with scripture may be ones that allow it to justify harmful practices; they may encode racist or misogynist assumptions; they may help sustain this group's marginalization of queer voices; they may enable it to obfuscate and so sustain various kinds of unearned privilege. Any given settlement might be poisonous – and all settlements are poisonous to some degree. They all stand in need of being unsettled, and that need is often urgent and deep.

Webster's and Vanhoozer's arguments suggest that the first recourse when thinking about this need for the disruption of settlements is to think about the objectivity or over-againstness of the text – its capacity to interrupt and contradict the uses that are made of it within a given settlement. I will argue, as this chapter proceeds, that a simple focus on the objectivity of the text is not enough, and that we need to think about the means by which the Spirit can draw us to encounter that objectivity differently. Nevertheless, thinking about scripture's objectivity is a reasonable place to start.

To focus on the patterns of use of scripture within settlements does not mean giving up on the idea of scripture's objectivity. After all, objectivity can only be registered

baseline never in fact bottom out. We quite properly begin our arguments in the midst of things, in contexts where it makes sense to take certain things for granted, and dig deeper only in response to specific problems and questions.

within some practice, within some pattern of use. Imagine a community that relies, in word or deed, upon the claim that 'the Bible says x'. At its simplest, we might say that the members of this community can acknowledge scripture's objectivity if they meet the following conditions. They must, in practice, treat the question of whether the bible does in fact say x as one that should be settled by attention to the text. They must be involved in practices of attention that could in principle yield a negative answer. Those practices of attention must in principle be capable of securing agreement about that answer among the group, so that the group as a whole could end up affirming that the bible does not say x. And this must in principle be true, however deeply the claim that the bible does say x is ingrained in this group's life. If all this is true, we might accept that this group is capable of acknowledging in scripture something that stands over against their life, something that can resist and unsettle their habits, something to which they can be held accountable.

In order to register the objectivity of scripture, then, we must do something with it. We must, trivially, open it or have it opened for us. We must have learnt the language in which we read or hear it. We must be able to parse sentences, follow plots and arguments, make connections and put those skills to use as we read. We must be able, to a degree, actively to make sense of what we find. Scripture's objectivity only appears to us if, between us, we have these capacities and draw upon them in specific bouts of activity. Scripture's objectivity appears within these activities, and these activities are necessary if we are to register it.

The form of objectivity that scripture has for any group, however, will be relative to that group's specific practices of reading – relative, that is, to its settlement. We can only acknowledge the resistance of features that we are capable of registering in the text, and yet what features we can register depends upon how we read. This does not make the features that we register any less objective, any less capable of challenging and reordering our community's conclusions, but it does mean that there is a contingency to the objectivity that we are able to grasp.

To register subtle patterns in the Greek text we must have access to that text, and must be able to marshal the grammatical and lexical skills needed to read it. To register resonances between the gospels and narratives in the Old Testament, we must be in the habit of reading Old and New Testament together, and of allowing our minds to settle on rather than flit past the echoes between them. These are practices within which particular kinds of feature can be registered and grappled with, and those kinds will differ from the ranges that could be registered and grappled within different practices. The rock face has different objective features for the climber, the miner and the geologist.

To put this point another way: there is an ethnography and a history of the objectivity of scripture – an ethnography and a history of the practices within which the objectivity of scripture is registered, and so of the kinds of feature that constitute that objectivity within any given settlement. The ensemble of features that properly constitute the objective content of scripture has been identified in different ways at different times in the history of scriptural interpretation, and any particular account of the disciplines involved in reading for scripture's objectivity is likely to be datable by a good historian of hermeneutics. There is no one practice, no one way of seeing or hearing the text, that counts as the one, obvious way of taking it seriously. There is no one obvious way of attending to scripture's objectivity.[18]

The call to listen to scripture, to remain true to it, to hold fast to it must then be more than a generic call to read diligently, or to take seriously what the text says. It must be – and it has been, in the history of the church – a call into specific patterns of reading, specific ways of living with the text.

The call to Christian reading

Hans Frei on the sensus literalis

The work of Hans Frei provides just such a call into a specific practice of Christian reading, within which the objective word spoken to the church in scripture can be registered in certain ways. In his early work, Frei focused on portions of the gospel narratives, above all the passion and resurrection narratives, which are 'realistic' or 'history-like' in the sense that they depict the interactions of characters and circumstances in a public world.[19] He sought to demonstrate that the meaning of those narratives is simply the story that they tell. More specifically, those narratives can render their central character's identity to us in such a way that the depiction has a certain objectivity over against us. Frei considered that rendering of the identity of Jesus Christ to be the proper foundation for theology.[20]

Frei later came to believe, however, that this argument did not stand up – or at least, that it did not stand up on its own. He did not abandon his central claims about the objective sense of the gospels, but he raised a question that he had so far left unaddressed: Why should one attend when reading to this narrative sense of the text? Scripture has, after all, been read in all sorts of ways, and in some of those ways this form of objectivity is downplayed or overlooked.[21] What could one say to readers who adopt those other ways of reading, if one wished to persuade them instead to attend to and learn from this narrative sense? In his earlier work, Frei's implicit answer had simply been to insist that this text is a realistic narrative, and that this is how

---

[18] For a beautiful exploration of the changing form of objectivity in a different disciplinary context, see Lorraine Daston and Peter Galison, *Objectivity* (New York: Zone Books, 2007).

[19] Hans W. Frei, *The Eclipse of Biblical Narrative: A Study in Eighteenth and Nineteenth Century Hermeneutics* (New Haven: Yale University Press, 1974); *The Identity of Jesus Christ: The Hermeneutical Bases of Dogmatic Theology* (Philadelphia: Fortress Press, 1975). For a detailed discussion of Frei's core argument in his early work, see my *Christ, Providence and History: Hans W. Frei's Public Theology* (London: T&T Clark, 2004), especially ch. 3–6. For a quicker and clearer summary, see my 'Foreword', in Hans W. Frei, *The Identity of Jesus Christ: The Hermeneutical Bases of Dogmatic Theology*, revised and updated edn (Eugene, OR: Cascade, 2013), xi–xix.

[20] For Frei, this interest in the text's rendering of Jesus's identity is not in competition with an interest in history. He argued that the gospels press us to recognize that the resurrection truly happened in our world. See my 'Foreword', xv.

[21] For a reading of the gospels that does not take them to be a story about Jesus, see John M. Allegro, *The Sacred Mushroom and the Cross* (London: Hodder and Stoughton, 1970).

such narratives demand to be read.[22] In his later work, he became convinced both that such a response provided no convincing answer to the question and that the answer it tried to give was in any case undesirable. It made his claim about scripture's objectivity subject to the limitations, and to the changing fortunes, of a general theory of narrative meaning. It did not allow it to be a sui generis claim about what God communicates by means of scripture.[23]

Frei remained convinced, nevertheless, that the realistic narrative reading championed in his early work *is* the appropriate way for Christians to read these portions of scripture. He remained convinced that, so read, these texts do indeed render objectively the identity of Jesus Christ. He now, however, took two steps to explain where that reading comes from. The first step is descriptive. Frei describes what he takes to be a very broad settlement uniting most Christian reading down the centuries. He argues that there is indeed a form of reading of certain portions of scripture that has become for very wide swathes of Christianity the 'plain sense', the communal sense, the sense that comes naturally to them. Despite all the many variations that one can find in Christian patterns of reading, there are some deep regularities – a set of regularities that Frei calls the '*sensus literalis*', uniting nearly all the many settlements of the church.

This *sensus literalis* is precisely the form of reading that attends to the gospels' rendering of the identity of Jesus Christ.[24] This reading is gathered around 'a very simple consensus: that the story of Jesus is about him, not about somebody else or about nobody in particular or about all of us; that it is not two stories … or no story and so on and on'.[25] And it acknowledges that telling us the story of Jesus in this way is the text's true purpose (rather than a misleading surface feature beneath which reading should seek to penetrate). To put it more briefly: at least when it comes to the gospels, Christians have on the whole assumed that the texts tell the story of Jesus, and that they mean what they say. For Frei, participation in this low-key agreement about the task of reading is enough, in principle, to enable readers to register the kind of scriptural objectivity that he cared about.[26]

Frei's second step is to ask why the church catholic should have come to read in this specific way. He does not say that it is simply a sociological fact, and that full

---

[22] Hans W. Frei, 'The "Literal Reading" of Biblical Narrative in the Christian Tradition: Does It Stretch of Will It Break?' in *Theology and Narrative*, ed. George Hunsinger and William C. Placher (New York and Oxford: Oxford University Press, 1993), 142.

[23] Ben Fulford, *Divine Eloquence and Human Transformation: Rethinking Scripture and History through Gregory of Nazianzus and Hans Frei* (Minneapolis, MN: Fortress, 2013), 237, notes that 'Frei's concern is clearly to avoid any kind of move that would impose an alien explanatory theory onto the specific practices of Christian faith and the specific meanings they have.' Cf. Robert Jenson, 'Hermeneutics and the Life of the Church', in *Reclaiming the Bible for the Church*, ed. Carl E. Braaten and Robert W. Jenson (Edinburgh: T&T Clark, 1995), 98: 'There can be no churchly reading of Scripture that is not anchored and guided by the church's teaching. We will either read the Bible under the guidance of the church's established doctrine, or we will not read the Bible at all.'

[24] See Hans W. Frei, *Types of Christian Theology*, ed. George Hunsinger and William C. Placher (New Haven: Yale University Press, 1992), 3, 16, 141–2; and 'The "Literal Reading" of Biblical Narrative', 122.

[25] Frei, *Types of Christian Theology*, 140.

[26] 'Literal reading actually fosters a binding of the reading community to features of Scripture that exert a counterpressure to their categories, ideologies, and habits, the features that make possible its normative function' (Fulford, *Divine Eloquence*, 261).

membership of this community depends by definition upon compliance with the community's rules. Rather, he says – albeit rather diffidently – that the church has learnt to read this way as the Spirit has guided it to attend to the scriptures, and that the church has learnt in that process that the text is God's witness to Godself, God's textual re-presentation of God's self-presentation in Jesus. This is not just the way that the church happens to have ended up reading; it is the way that the church should read. Frei says that there is no more neutral way of specifying the kind of reading to which the church is called than by using the language learnt in the course of this reading. Only by using terms like 'God' and 'witness', and thinking of 'God's self-presentation in Jesus', can Christians express why it is that they should read in this way, whatever analogies they might be able to find in other ways of reading.[27]

From one angle of view, then, this pattern of reading is entirely contingent. It so happens that this particular religious community valorizes reading that works in this way, though it could in principle have ended up reading in some quite different way. Within this way of reading, a certain kind of objectivity to the text can appear, but attention to this specific form of objectivity is a contingent feature of the church's practice. Other practices of reading are also available, focused upon different kinds of objectivity, or avoiding them all.

From another angle of view, however, the fact that the church registers just this objectivity is the work of the Spirit. The Spirit is the one who brings the church up against scripture's witness to the word of God spoken in Jesus Christ. The Spirit is the one who has so ordered the text and so ordered the church's engagement with the text as to make the church's hearing of this word possible. The reading to which Christians are called is a form of reading that one can only learn within the life of the church, but it is a form that allows the church to hear the voice of one who stands over against its life.

The rule of faith

Frei was a doctrinal theologian, speaking into the life of the church. He had arrived at a creative construal of the church's inheritance: the identification of the *sensus literalis* as the stable heart of the church's reading. He offered that construal back to the church as a proposal. He believed that the church (or at least its theologians) needed reminding of the centrality and power of such reading. When he died, he was at work on a history of modern Christology that he hoped would involve an account of the reading practices of ordinary Christians – a delve into the details of what I have been calling their reading settlements.[28] His *sensus literalis* proposal, however, operates at a different level. It is not an attempt to specify the precise pattern of life that Christians

---

[27] Frei, *Types of Christian Theology*, 141–2; 'Theology and the Interpretation of Narrative: Some Hermeneutical Considerations', in *Theology and Narrative*, 109; and 'Conflicts in Interpretation', in *Theology and Narrative*, 164. Cf. John Webster, *Holy Scripture*, 72: the church's act of reading is 'not an instance of something else, but an act which, though it is analogous to other acts, is in its deepest reaches *sui generis*'. See also Katherine Sonderegger's account of scripture's uniqueness in 'Holy Scripture as Sacred Ground'. Fulford, *Divine Eloquence*, 246, says that 'We might best sum up his position by saying Frei sees the text as the (only) true verbal icon of the Word', and this is 'a specific claim about Holy Scripture seen in Christian terms'.

[28] See my *Christ, Providence and History*, ch. 8.

should lead with scripture, but to set out a broad shape within which such lives should be negotiated and lived. He both stated a rule (read the gospels as the story of Jesus!) and invited readers into a certain way of imagining their relation to the text.

In all this, Frei was echoing (however distantly) the theologians of the early church who advocated the 'rule of faith'. Statements of the 'rule of faith' – flexible and various, but marked by strong family resemblances – emerged from the pens of various theologians from the second century onwards. They drew on a history of Christian reading of scripture, and they sought to provide a summary articulation of what is found by that reading. The rule of faith is therefore, by design, ruled by scripture. It seeks to reflect faithfully what has been read there, and to be capable of surviving testing against ongoing reading. At the same time, however, the rule serves to hold in place the pattern of reading that produced it. And since any testing of the rule against scripture must be a testing against scripture read in some specific way, we might say that one of the functions of the rule is to set the terms of its own testing.[29]

There is much that could be said about this rule of faith tradition, but I want simply to highlight three facets: its prioritizing of a certain kind of literal sense, its invitation of readers into a certain kind of spiritual discipline and its inculcation of a certain kind of doctrinal imagination.

The recent work of Lewis Ayres helps to specify the first of these facets: the priority of a particular pattern of literal reading. In effect, Ayres puts historical flesh on the bones of Frei's terse description of the *sensus literalis*. He attends to the development and deployment of the rule by Irenaeus in his contest with the Valentinians, and demonstrates that it involved Irenaeus advocating for a contingent form of literal reading. In the light of this history, Ayres can say that 'Christians became the scriptural community they did not merely by choosing books and making distinctions between those books and others, but also by choosing to use and read those books in a certain way, by means of certain reading practices.'[30] And these choices 'were not self-evident, nor were they fundamental for the earliest Christian writers' in the generations before Irenaeus.[31]

---

[29] Some theologians, like Vanhoozer (*Drama of Doctrine*, 206), focus primarily on the rule's summarizing of the content of scripture: 'The church fathers never intended the Rule to control what Scripture must mean but rather to confess what Scripture *does* mean.' Cf. Webster, 'Confession and Confessions', 125. Others take a less linear, more circular approach. Lewis Ayres, in 'Augustine on the Rule of Faith: Rhetoric, Christology, and the Foundation of Christian Thinking', *Augustinian Studies* 36, no. 1 (2005): 36, says that 'The *regula* ... both comes from Scripture and guides the interpretation of Scripture'; cf. Fergusson, *The Rule of Faith: A Guide*, 19, Wiesław Davidowski, 'Regula Fidei in Augustine: Its Use and Function', *Augustinian Studies* 35 (2004): 296. John Behr, in *The Formation of Christian Theology 1: The Way to Nicaea* (Crestwood, NY: St Vladimir's Seminary Press, 2001), 12, insists that 'we must avoid reading [this history] in the manner set by the polemics of the Reformation and Counter-Reformation, in which Scripture is opposed to tradition, as two distinct sources of authority'; cf. Tomas Bokedal, 'The Early Rule-of-Faith Pattern as Emergent Biblical Theology', *Theofilos Supplement* 7, no. 1 (2015): 58.
[30] Lewis Ayres, '"There's Fire in that Rain": On Reading the Letter and Reading Allegorically', *Modern Theology* 28, no. 4 (2012): 618, emphasis removed.
[31] Ayres, 'Fire in that Rain', 618. Irenaeus's choices also differ from those made after him. The 'literal sense' for which he reads is, for instance, not quite the same as that read by Aquinas, Calvin or Charles Hodge.

The specific reading practices that Irenaeus employs involved such things as 'careful attention to whose voice a given section of a text should be understood to represent', 'close comparison of phrases and titles taken to be parallel and mutually illuminating', 'etymological analysis of names' and so on – and these forms of attention do not come from nowhere: Irenaeus borrowed them from 'Hellenistic literary-critical techniques' – and did so to an unprecedented degree.[32]

Other forms of reading were certainly available; indeed, that is why Irenaeus deployed his rule. The Valentinians against whom he was writing could themselves produce commentaries that involved 'a detailed and dense analysis of grammar and styles of expression', but they did so 'in order to argue that the texts … must be read as fundamentally enigmatic and parabolic discourse'.[33] They sought to demonstrate that the texts were ciphers, that the narrative which provided their true content was not there to view on the surface of the text.

Irenaeus's deployment of the rule is therefore at once a display of what his way of reading can yield, and a form of advocacy for that way of reading itself. Of course, if we adopt his form of literal, literary reading and use that form of reading to judge between him and the Valentinians, there is little doubt as to who will win – but the logic of that position is inherently circular. If one does follow Irenaeus, however, one is led into a form of literal reading capable of setting the story of Jesus before the church, and focusing the church's attention upon it.

The second facet of the rule that I want to consider is its calling of Christians to understand their engagement with scripture as a certain kind of spiritual discipline.[34] Ayres highlights this in his writings on the rule of faith not in Irenaeus but in Augustine.

> For Augustine, the fullness of the rule of faith includes not only the narrative of God's action in Christ, and the doctrinal propositions embedded in the telling of that story, but also the movement and ascent that Christ accomplishes in Christians, the transference of attention from things of this world to the divine mystery. This movement, the very logic of Christian existence, is sometimes treated as simply part of the rule, and sometimes treated as that which results from grasping the rule in any spiritual depth.[35]

To read within the rule of faith involves a 'journey of the affections', 'faith-formed growth in contemplation of the divine mysteries revealed and yet still hidden'. It

---

[32] Ayres, 'Fire in that Rain', 618; 'Irenaeus versus the Valentinians: Toward a Rethinking of Patristic Exegetical Origins', *Journal of Early Christian Studies* 23, no. 2 (2015): 153. Cf. Young, *The Art of Performance*, 115–29; McGrath, *The Genesis of Doctrine*, 5.

[33] Ayres, 'Fire in that Rain', 619. Cf. Frances M. Young, *Biblical Exegesis and the Formation of Christian Culture* (Cambridge: Cambridge University Press, 2007), 16, noting how a direct line could be drawn from the earliest practices of Christian reading to a Marcion or to a Valentinus.

[34] Paul Hartog, 'The "Rule of Faith" and Patristic Biblical Exegesis', *Trinity Journal* 28, no. 1 (2007): 81, says that 'the endeavour of scriptural study builds various virtues in the faithful reader, and in turn the virtuous reader more clearly understands Scripture'. Cf. Darren Sarisky, *Scriptural Interpretation: A Theological Exploration* (Oxford: Wiley-Blackwell, 2013), 232: 'Reading requires and effects purification.'

[35] Ayres, 'Augustine on the Rule of Faith', 36–7.

involves what Ayres calls elsewhere 'the action of the Spirit and Christ within the soul, forming human lives into lives that exhibit the charity which is God's essence'.[36]

James Andrews spells out this aspect of Augustine's approach to scripture in slightly different terms. Augustine teaches his readers to approach scripture bearing in mind what Andrews calls 'the "*caritas* criterion", the principle that states if something cannot be connected to the realm of love, then it must be interpreted figuratively'. This rule for reading, which sets limits on the literal sense, derives from a grasp of 'the overall communicative intent' of scripture. Scripture is given to us to enable the ascent of the mind to God, the redirection of all our loves by the love of God. Drawing us into the love of God is scripture's 'intrinsic telos'; 'scripture stands outside the community because it stands between the community and God as a means of transport to move it closer to him.' To read within the rule of faith is to read on a journey into the love of God.[37]

The third facet of the rule that I want to highlight is its inculcation of a certain kind of doctrinal imagination. It is not just that the rule holds in place a certain kind of literal reading, within a certain vision of reading as a spiritual discipline. It also shapes readers' perception of scripture's content. Irenaeus's crafting of the summary that he offers, for instance, does more than simply transmit what his literary reading techniques find on the surface of scripture: it construes all of that material in a particular way, abstracting from it a laconically expressed plot, a deep shape to the action.[38] Irenaeus speaks of

> faith in one God the Father Almighty, who has made the heaven, the earth, the seas, and all things in them, and in one Christ Jesus the Son of God, who was made flesh for our salvation; and in the Holy Spirit, who has proclaimed through the prophets the plans of God and the comings of Christ, both the birth from the virgin, the passion, the rising from the dead, and the bodily ascension into heaven … and his coming from heaven in the glory of the father for the summing up of all things and the raising of all humanity.[39]

This is a creative act of summarizing, and summaries like this have tremendous power to shape the imagination of readers. They can mediate and shape scripture's influence on the whole of a reader's life, and they can influence what readers are capable of finding in scripture, even by means of their most diligent and humble efforts. They

---

[36] Ayres, 'Augustine on the Rule of Faith', 38, 49; 'The Soul and the Reading of Scripture: A Note on Henri De Lubac', *Scottish Journal of Theology* 61, no. 2 (2008): 176. Cf. Brian E. Daley, '"In Many and Various Ways": Towards a Theology of Theological Exegesis', *Modern Theology* 28, no. 4 (2012): 601–3.

[37] James A. Andrews, *Hermeneutics and the Church: In Dialogue with Augustine* (Notre Dame, IN: University of Notre Dame Press, 2012), 4, 101, 105, 161, 198.

[38] John Behr speaks of the rule as 'a crystallization of the hypothesis of Scripture itself' (*The Way to Nicaea*, 15). 'The point of the canon of truth is not so much to give fixed and abstract statements of Christian doctrine. Nor does it provide a narrative description of Christian belief, the literary hypothesis of Scripture. Rather, the canon of truth expresses the correct hypothesis of Scripture itself, that by which one can see in Scripture the picture of a king, Christ' (35–6); after all 'it is Christ who is being explained through the medium of Scripture, not Scripture itself that is being exegeted; the object is not to understand the "original meaning" of an ancient text, … but to understand Christ' (27).

[39] Irenaeus, *Against Heresies*, 1.10.1, translated in Fergusson, *Rule of Faith*, 4.

influence, in ways deeper than explicit reflection can reach, what features of the text readers will most readily grasp, and the sense they will have of how the text as a whole hangs together.[40]

Specifically, the Irenaean rule of faith, and the doctrinal tradition that grows around it, is an invitation to inhabit a trinitarian imagination, which can shape reading in quite specific ways. For those engaged in detailed exegesis, for instance, reading from within this tradition might mean having one's attention attuned to certain features, certain patterns and resemblances, across the surface of scripture. One might notice, and give prominence to, passages with a trinitarian structure; one's attention might fall on other hints – the plural pronoun in the creation account, the shifting identification of the visitors at Mamre – that would otherwise have passed one by. One's ears might snag on a passage that awkwardly declares that 'the Lord is the Spirit' – a passage that to other ears might have remained unremarkable. One might be inclined to pay particular attention to indications that the Spirit is being treated as one of the dramatis personae in the story. And so on, and on: Scripture is a landscape which reveals distinctive peaks and troughs when seen from the vantage point of a trinitarian imagination.

More generally, a trinitarian imagination can provide a basic plot or shape that organizes people's whole engagement with scripture, and their perception of the life that Christians are called to live in relation to scripture. As Brooke Foss Westcott said,

> Such a summary as the Apostle's Creed serves as a clue in reading the Bible. It presents to us the salient features in the revelation which earlier experience has proved to be turning-points of spiritual knowledge. It offers centres, so to speak, round which we may group our thoughts, and to which we may refer the lessons laid open to us. It keeps us from wandering in by-paths aimlessly or at our will, not by fixing arbitrary limits to inquiry but by marking the great lines along which believers have moved from the first.[41]

This pattern of imagination need not be restricted to those who reflect explicitly upon trinitarian doctrine. It might be shaped and held in place by the recitation of the creeds, by the patterns of liturgy, by prayers, hymns and sermons, by art and architecture. To be invited into this tradition is to be invited to build and discover a whole way of living and reading that will embody the trinitarian pattern. This is not an invitation for doctrinal theologians alone.

This doctrinal imagination is not a superfluous aspect of the broad settlement that I have been describing. It provides the basic terms in which we can make sense of

---

[40] Cf. Young, *Art of Performance*, 60–1. See also W. H. Mallock, *Doctrine and Doctrinal Disruption: Being an Examination of the Intellectual Position of the Church of England* (London: Adam and Charles Black, 1900), 42: 'whatever may have been the attitude towards tradition which the Reformers assumed consciously, they practically accepted without question a very large proportion of it. It constituted a mental atmosphere from which they could but partially escape, and the Bible, which they believed themselves to regard as their sole authority, was seen by them invested with the colour which this atmosphere of tradition shed on it, and surrounded with forms and presences with which the atmosphere of tradition was peopled.'

[41] Brooke Foss Westcott, *The Historic Faith: Short Lectures on the Apostles' Creed* (London: Macmillan, 1883), 22–3.

the whole – including the call to the literal sense, and the call to reading as a spiritual discipline. According to this doctrinal construal, Christian reading is, at its heart, an ongoing encounter with the Jesus whose identity is re-presented to us by the literal sense, in the power of the Spirit who draws us to this Jesus in a journey of purification and ascent, on the way further up and further in to the abundant love of God. This is the trinitarian form of reading to which Christians are called by the rule of faith.

The rule of faith is not a detailed description of any particular Christian community's reading settlement. It is not even an attempt to specify in detail what such settlements ought to involve. It is, rather, an attempt to set out a broad shape to which such settlements should conform. It is a construal of the inherited shape of the church's reading, offered as a proposal for the church's future. It involves both rule-like elements and the opening up of a certain pattern of imagination. It is both deeply shaped by the reading of scripture, and an attempt in turn to shape that reading. It is, in other words, a classic example of the work of doctrinal theology, offered in service to the ordinary life of faith. And, like all works of doctrinal theology, it is open to question.[42]

Reading differently

The church interprets scripture by living in relation to it, discovering ways of inhabiting the text in the world. In the words of Musa Dube, 'the biblical story is an unfinished story; it invites its own continuation in history; it resists the covers of our Bibles and writes itself on the pages of the earth.'[43] The church's interpretations of scripture show themselves in the diverse patterns of life that Christians build in the world. They are embodied in Christians' liturgies, their songs, their art and the forms of ecclesial and social life that they invent together. They are sustained by the rules that Christians develop to guide their reading, and by the ways in which they imagine what reading involves. All of this is shaped by scripture, and in turn shapes how scripture is read.

Growing up in Botswana, Dube encountered the bible in the midst of the world of White colonialism that European Christians had built. The bible was a text that was enacted and inhabited by people caught up in that world, and it was read to support and perpetuate it. It was a text about a White Jesus and his White disciples, with whom the colonizers habitually identified; it was a text about Pharisees, pagans and those 'foolish Galatians', with whom there always seemed to be reason to identify the colonized populations. 'To read the Bible as an African', Dube says, 'is to relive the painful equation of Christianity with civilization, paganism with savagery.' It is to read

---

[42] The questioning of this tradition might be triggered when we recall that it has been held in place by ecclesiastical and eventually by imperial power, by the weight of synods and councils, by the insistence of bishops and then emperors. It has been held in place by legal proceedings and by threats of punishment, by exclusions, and by violence. It is not an innocent tradition, and if it is possible to see it as a settlement within which the voice of God can be heard, it is no less possible to see it as one against which the voice of God might break out.

[43] Musa W. Dube, 'Toward a Post-Colonial Feminist Interpretation of the Bible', in *Postcolonial Feminist Interpretation of the Bible*, ed. Musa W. Dube (St Louis, MO: Chalice, 2000), 12.

'a colonizing text' that 'has repeatedly authorized the subjugation of foreign nations and lands'.[44]

Dube became a biblical scholar. In other words, she was trained in some of a Western Christian settlement's key practices of critique and correction – tools that might be thought sufficient to undo the colonial appropriation of scripture. She was trained to turn away from the readings of modern colonial Christians, and focus instead on the original contexts in which these texts were produced and received. Yet precisely because this involved turning away from the text's use in the present, these tools did not allow her to face, or to begin dismantling, the colonial reading settlement. 'This imperialist history has constructed all of us', Dube says, 'and its reality cannot be bracketed from our critical practice without perpetuating the history of unequal inclusion.' The bracketing of attention to imperialist history also bracketed her voice; it had the effect of divorcing her experience and her questions from the field.[45] It did not allow her to trace how deeply the colonial settlement had shaped the assumptions still in play when scripture was read around her. It did not allow her to ferret out harmful assumptions about scripture's plot, about the purpose of reading or about the objectivity of the exegesis provided by White, Western, male, middle-class scholars and leaders. Dube therefore 'journeyed with some sense of injustice and emptiness in … academic biblical studies'.[46] Something more was needed – and what was needed was not a more diligent pursuit of the settlement's existing disciplines, but a disruption of the settlement itself.

Such a disruption is made possible by the hearing of Dube's own voice, and of voices similar to hers. These are not the voices that she and others have been granted within the existing structures of the colonial settlement, and within the disciplines of scriptural reading as they exist in that settlement. They are, instead, the voices with which they have learnt to speak out against that settlement from the midst of their own experience. Having discovered how to speak in their own voices, they are in a position to begin naming some of the many ways in which the bible has been read to support their oppression. They can begin identifying some of those elements of the text that lend themselves to colonial reading. They can begin unpicking the colonial assumptions made by interpreters, and the colonial readings given of specific passages. They can begin calling out some of the ways in which oppressive reading is perpetuated by the rules for reading and the ways of imagining reading that help to hold this settlement in place. And they are in a position to begin, positively, imagining what it might be to read differently, to live with the text differently, to experiment differently in faithfulness.[47]

The kind of critique that Dube champions can strike deeply into patterns of reading that at first seem innocuous or even salutary. Consider, for instance, Jennifer Harvey's analysis of the reading habits of some of her students, students who are clearly interested in social justice, and committed to fighting against racism, who see that

---

[44] Ibid., 13–15.
[45] Ibid., 23, 13.
[46] Ibid., 13.
[47] Ibid., 23.

commitment as a natural part of their discipleship, and as something demanded of them by scripture. We might seem to be a world away from the colonialist and racist reading practices that Dube critiques, and yet Harvey explores the ways in which these students have been habituated into asking the question, 'What would Jesus do?' and allowing that question to frame their approach to the text. While agreeing that this can be an important and even perhaps a necessary question, she points out that it is also a question that places the reader who asks it at the centre of the narrative. And that is a problem.

'One of the many effects of whiteness', Harvey says, 'is that it always already locates white people at the center of most narratives and structures. Such positioning is mitigated by class, gender and sexual orientation, but when racial difference is present white people tend to be positioned as primary actors in whatever location we find ourselves.'[48] For such White readers to identify too quickly with Jesus can be poisonous: 'It just so happens that identifying with or as the central agent in the narratives we embody is one of the broken ways of being toward which white people are prone. It just so happens that being inclined to do "for" in postures that are paternalistic is another damaged side-effect of white racialization.'[49] Asking the 'What would Jesus do?' question, it turns out, can end up paradoxically subverting readers' commitment to the justice that they see Jesus embodying. 'In this move by the white Christian to identify with Jesus, the centrality and power of the white actor is reiterated and reaffirmed. Simply put, identifying with the divine is about the last thing that a white person whose life is embedded in white supremacist structures should be doing.'[50] It might be better, instead, Harvey argues, for such readers to begin by asking, 'What would Zacchaeus do?' – learning first to identify with someone in the text who 'had forsaken brotherhood and sisterhood, and been seduced into allegiance with death-dealing power structures', and who was called by Jesus to repentance and to restitution, and to the active betrayal of those structures.

The identification of this problem was not something at which Harvey arrived on her own. Just as Dube tells her own story, Harvey tells hers – and tells how she was challenged by engagement with Black students and faculty at Union Theological Seminary, by reading works of Black theology and critical analyses of Whiteness, and how she was helped by some of her own students to imagine forms that a Zacchaeus-like response might take.

Dube's and Harvey's works provide just two examples from a much wider range of forms of critique that press around dominant Christian forms of reading at present. All forms of Christian reading are open to criticism, but the patterns of distortion and brokenness that afflict settlements other than the ones that Dube and Harvey had

---

[48] Jennifer Harvey, 'What Would Zacchaeus Do?' in *Christology and Whiteness: What Would Jesus Do?* ed. George Yancy (London: Routledge, 2012), 94. In talking about Whiteness, Harvey is talking about the complex and various systems of power that, in racialized societies like hers (in the United States) and mine (in the United Kingdom), position people differently according to the perceived colours of their skins. These systems of power are contingent, but they are deeply rooted, and those perceived to be White can benefit from them in multiple ways without being aware of them, or even while fighting against them.

[49] Ibid.

[50] Ibid., 95.

discussed will be different; each settlement is shaped by its own mixture of misplaced assumptions and unseen biases. The brokenness of all our patterns of reading runs deep, however, and we cannot overcome it simply by an act of will – not even an act of good will. To identify the problems, to begin unpicking them, to call out the ways in which they are perpetuated by our rules for reading and our ways of imagining our reading, we need each other's help – and we need each other's help to begin imagining how we might read differently.

Evolving settlements

I have so far in this chapter explored the idea that the church is called into a particular kind of reading. I have argued that the rule of faith and the subsequent doctrinal tradition call the church to a form of reading within which it can encounter scripture's Christ-centred objectivity, and so hear the voice of God as gift and challenge. Yet Dube's work, and Harvey's, and similar work by many others show us that deeply oppressive patterns of reading have been able to flourish in this soil, and that they have not been rooted out simply by the diligent application of the church's familiar forms of self-discipline. Such work therefore pushes us to revise the picture of reading that I have been painting.

My suggestion is, however, that challenges like Dube's and Harvey's do not pull the church away from the encounter with scripture's objectivity, nor from the expectation that the church will hear the voice of God there. Instead, challenges like this can be precisely the means by which the Spirit enables the church to see more of the rich objectivity of scripture, and so hear more of the divine word spoken through it as challenge and gift. Such challenges can be a means by which God's gift of scripture is unwrapped, or unleashed, and the invitation deeper into God's love heard more clearly.

I am going to begin, however, with much smaller scale, much more prosaic changes than the ones that Dube and Harvey discuss, because understanding the dynamics of these small-scale changes can help us make sense of more thoroughgoing disruptions.

The church's scriptural settlements are always mobile, always changing. People are always coming to see new things in the text, or questioning what they previously thought they had seen. Consider what it is like, for instance, to hear someone say something unexpected about a particular scriptural text, or to see them do something different with it. You might hear a sermon, see a comment on social media, have a conversation with a friend or read a book, and quite suddenly see in a new light the text concerned. What we see in the text shifts as the conversations in which we are involved move on, and as we move to engage in new circumstances. New people, with new questions, convictions and habits, arrive in our lives. New situations, new questions, new urgencies, new relationships arise – and, consciously or unconsciously, we find ourselves seeing and responding to the text in new ways. This process is always going on, and even if it is normally an unnoticed or a barely noticed process it can sometimes be much more explicit, much more like the sudden turning on of a lamp.[51]

---

[51] See Harvey, *Believing and Belonging*, 24.

Sometimes, we will be able to locate the new reality we have encountered on our existing maps. Living with scripture in some new context might involve no more than drawing in familiar ways upon what we have already seen in the text. Sometimes, however, the new situation or the new experience will call for a more obviously creative, a more obviously improvisatory process. Think of a preacher faced with an apparently unhelpful lectionary reading on the Sunday after a tragedy, and of the way in which her labour to find something to say will also be a labour of creative composition. The preacher may feel unable simply to apply existing rules, drawing something appropriate from the expository filing cabinet. What might emerge from her creative labour is not simply a thoughtful sermon, but a new way of seeing the text in question, identifying in it something more or something different from what she had seen before.

Such processes of change might involve no more than the realization that one can do new things with a familiar text. They might, however, involve coming to realize that the text has objective features that one has simply never registered before. Your attention is drawn, say, to the way in which the opening three petitions of the Matthean Lord's prayer – hallowed be your name, your kingdom come, your will be done – parallel one another. That might persuade you to read the first petition slightly differently, but also and more fundamentally it might become part of what you see or hear when you see or hear this text.[52] Your attention is drawn to features of the text that you had not registered before, perhaps even to features of a kind that you had not registered before. By such means, different aspects of the text come to appear as features, as signal rather than noise. They bed down in our ways of reading, and become part of what we encounter when we encounter the text. To the extent that they do, they become part of what this text is, for us. We are grasped by the text in new ways. And this is always going on, for individuals and for whole communities.

At the other end of the scale, consider the process that stands right at the origin of the Christian reading of scripture. The followers of Jesus read the Hebrew scriptures in the light of their continuation in Jesus – the use that Jesus made of them, the way he inhabited them – and so they read them differently. Their sense of the purpose, the plot and the yield of scripture changed dramatically as they experienced what God was doing through Jesus and in raising Jesus from the dead. They saw different features in the text by means of the light cast back from him. Different texts became salient. Different patterns linking multiple texts came into view – in fact, whole different kinds of pattern became visible. The text became, for them, the field of such features. They sought to justify Jesus's continuation of the story by pointing out these features to those who did not share their reading, but there was a slowly growing sense that they and their interlocutors saw different things when they looked at the text. What was to them a set of features patent in the text looked to their interlocutors like

---

[52] The Greek is ἁγιασθήτω τὸ ὄνομά σου· ἐλθέτω ἡ βασιλεία σου· γενηθήτω τὸ θέλημά σου (Mt. 6.9-10). My attention was drawn to this by Ian Paul, in a blog post on 'The Poetic Structure of Jesus' Teaching', *Psephizo*, 27 June 2013. Available online at www.psephizo.com/biblical-studies/the-poetic-structure-of-jesus-teaching/; cf. 'Why we need a new Lord's Prayer', *Psephizo*, 2 October 2018; www.psephizo.com/biblical-studies/why-we-need-a-new-lords-prayer/ (both accessed 4 December 2019). Ian Paul's attention was drawn to it by David Wenham, in 'The Sevenfold Form of the Lord's Prayer in Matthew', *Expository Times* 121 (2010): 373–82.

no more than strained interpretations, structures shakily built over the text. The sense that they were engaged in a shared argument over scripture, as participants in a single settlement, fractured.

This transformation happened both suddenly and slowly. It was slow in that it was prepared for by long habits of reading, the steeping in scripture of the culture within which Jesus's first disciples had grown up. It was also slow in that, once they had encountered and accompanied Jesus, there remained a long labour of reading and re-reading as these disciples learnt into what new pattern of reading they had been tipped. It was slow, in that it involved the growth of a whole new culture of scriptural reading – new sensibilities, new practices, new institutions.[53] It was, however, sudden, in that the disciples seem very quickly to have been compelled by Jesus's re-reading (and their own re-reading) of certain luminous passages. They recognized, with their scripture-soaked imaginations, that God was dramatically at work in Jesus – and that recognition in part took the form of being struck by select passages that made sense in the light of Jesus, and that allowed them to make sense of him. These passages were catapulted by the disciples' experience of Jesus into the centre of their reading of scripture as a whole, landing with a disruptive splash in the midst of their once settled habits.

The working out of this new way of reading played out over years, over decades and over centuries. It was a matter of learning whether and how the rest of scripture could be read around these now central passages, and around these readers' shared grasp of the decisiveness of God's action in Jesus. In the process of this working out, the very form of this community's reading was altered. Christians were led to give new prominence to the literal reading of certain portions of scriptural narrative. They were led to explore various kinds of spiritual reading that enabled them to weave other parts of scripture around the narrative of Jesus. They found ways of accommodating texts made suddenly awkward because this new construal of scripture's plot cut across their grain.

There was, of course, a sense in which the new insight that had triggered this whole process of re-reading was tested by means of it. It was tested to ensure that it could indeed make sense as a reading of the whole of scripture. It was not the case, however, that the new insight could simply be tested by an existing pattern of responsible exegesis.[54] The change brought about by Jesus's life, death and resurrection involved not simply altered claims about the meaning of specific texts, but an altered sense of how reading should work. The disciples' claims were bound to look flimsy when judged by the settled and deeply rooted reading habits of existing settlements – and it was a long time before the disciples found replacements of comparable scope for those habits. The new patterns of Christian reading proved compelling and habitable well before those who pursued them knew what to do with much of scripture, or how to treat those texts that sat most awkwardly with their new understanding. The promise that the whole of scripture might be seen afresh in the new light that had fallen across it remained just that – a promise – for a very long time.

---

[53] It might be more accurate to say that it led to the growth of several overlapping new cultures. See Chapter 8 on the essentially contested nature of Christian interpretation.
[54] Nor was the canon of texts that would constitute 'the whole of scripture' a foregone conclusion.

The changes in reading triggered by Jesus's life, death and resurrection are unique, and they remain as central to Christian readings of what now became the Old Testament as they were to the production of the New. They have, however, been echoed, again and again, in smaller scale revolutions throughout Christian history. Time after time, readers have been brought to see new things in scripture, and so to see scripture anew – to read it in new ways.[55] And time after time, the process has been similar: sudden and slow, instantly compelling but only gradually convincing, a change of minds that has involved the spread of new practices and the growth of new institutions. The changing of settlements is seldom straightforward.

This process can begin in a moment of eruptive disruption. It can begin with excited delight: there is something new here, something that compels one's attention and promises to set off a cascade of new connections, new readings.[56] It can also, sometimes simultaneously, be a matter of painful challenge and uncertainty. A settled habit of reading, in its way comfortable and reassuring, might suddenly cease to be available, because one has been brought to see one of the texts on which it relies in a new way, or to realize the acute angle that it makes with a text now central for one's faith, or to see the ways in which one's settled habit is deeply complicit in harm. The floor on which one stands lurches, and one no longer knows how to remain upright.

There is something more here than diligent discipline, a process in which the accent falls on what we do and are capable of doing. There is an event, something happening to us – something breaking out from the text, in part by means of the text. It can leave us stuttering to a halt, unsure for now how to go on, how to test what we now think we have seen. It can leave us incomprehensible to family and friends, even to ourselves, as we struggle to express something for which there is no obvious home in our existing language.

Such disruption can happen despite us. It is also, however, a possibility towards which we can lean, towards which we can orient ourselves, to an extent, or towards which we might be oriented by the Spirit. Such an orientation, though it will need to involve a constantly renewed attention to the text, will not be reducible to patient labour. It will need, beyond that, to involve a certain kind of watchful waiting, an air of expectation, a readiness for the unexpected – what Reinhard Hütter calls an 'active waiting for God's activity', or Andrew Louth 'waiting on God, openness to God of the whole person in stillness'.[57]

Considered from one direction, such openness will, above all, be a matter of prayer. Prayer is not a technique. It is not a form of diligence that guarantees progress or security, nor does its absence guarantee stasis. Rather, prayer is, in this context, simply a continually renewed petition for God's expansion of our senses and interruption of

---

[55] See my brief discussion of the Jerusalem 'Council' from Acts 15, in Chapter 4, pp. 81, 84.
[56] I first learnt about this from the band Fat and Frantic, in 1987. 'She told me heaven's not a party in the sky. / She said the rich folks put it up there, but it's just another lie. ... Now I've stopped running round in circles and I'm getting organized, / 'cos the Old Testament seems full of stuff I'd never realised. / Now people tell me "Boy, for man to see / *shalom* is just a fantasy", / but I pray "May your kingdom come", and that I plan to see.' 'Take me Home', on the album *Aggressive Sunbathing* (I'll Call You Records, 1987).
[57] Reinhard Hütter, *Suffering Divine Things: Theology as Church Practice* (Grand Rapids, MI: Eerdmans, 2000), 72; Andrew Louth, *Theology and Spirituality*, revised edn (Oxford: SLG, 1978), 3.

our habits, and a continually renewed waiting. One might think of this prayer as a form of contemplation: an eagerly expectant watching of the surface of scripture, waiting with patient impatience to be shown more.[58]

Considered from another direction, such openness will be a matter of movement. The process by which new light breaks out of the text is seldom simply solitary. The characteristic form of the outbreaking of new light is not the lonely reader locked in his tower with the text. Sometimes, of course, the origin of a given transformation will be hard to pin down: it will be a move of the Spirit that seems to blow in from nowhere. It can strike like lightning from a clear sky. Sometimes, it might be provoked by some quite simple change in our situation, or some new experience.[59] Often, however, the transformation of our vision will be promoted by an encounter with others, by the growth of a new relationship, by our hearing, and learning to attend to, a new voice.

This is what both Dube's and Harvey's testimonies point us towards: the disruption to a settlement that is made possible when voices are heard that until now have been excluded or marginalized – voices that, at times, can break out against our existing settlements and tip us into revolution. This, too, is no simple matter. Before such hearing can happen in any serious way, there might need to be changes in the structures within which our conversations about scripture happen, changes in the patterns of relationship that grow within those structures, changes to who is allowed to speak, changes to people's sense of the voices in which they can speak, changes to who is listening – and so on. All of these changes might be tangled together, each both edging the others forward and being held back by them at different points.

We should therefore be wary of saying that we already know how to listen. To reach the point where we are hearing voices previously excluded or ignored is not simply a matter of our good will; it takes more than a benign readiness to pay attention. It might involve learning new practices and forms of engagement; it might involve learning new languages (literally and metaphorically); it might involve institutional and structural change – and we may need the help of others for each of these forms of learning. Hearing may emerge from an ongoing process of struggle and negotiation.[60]

To say that the transformation of our vision or of our hearing can be prompted by new encounters or relationships is, then, a shorthand way of describing what can be a much more complex process. But light does break out, in part, as we learn to read the text in new company. We wait for such illumination, not on our own and with eyes and ears closed to the world, but with a form of contemplative attention that is earthy, dialogical and involved.

---

[58] Cf. Andrew Prevot, *Thinking Prayer: Theology and Spirituality and the Crises of Modernity* (Notre Dame, IN: University of Notre Dame Press, 2015), 329, on being 'actively open to … gifts that come from a divine anteriority that outstrips all possible finite recollection. … [T]here is always more to be desired in the infinite divine mystery.'

[59] Anselm Atkins, 'Religious Assertions and Doctrinal Development', *Theological Studies* 27, no. 4 (1966): 527, speaks of 'the inventive thrust of theological clarification' as being 'like the process of an amoeba on the move, is guided by chance encounter with obstacles'.

[60] I am grateful to Jenny Leith for helping me understand this point. See also Chapter 9, pp. 229–30.

The scintillating text

Earlier parts of this chapter might have suggested that Christian reading is a steady excavation of the text, disciplined, diligent and continuous. The last few pages might have suggested, instead, a process pulled this way and that, shapeshifting and unstable. My claim, however, is that the transformations of vision or hearing that I have just been discussing are no distraction from reading. They are means by which the Spirit can open the eyes and ears of the church more fully to scripture's rich objectivity, and so lure the church more deeply into the abundance of God whose gift scripture is.[61]

If you look at a glowing ember in the heart of a mature fire you can often see a kind of liquid scintillation playing across its surface. As the currents of air shift, whipped into turbulence by the fire's heat, different parts of the ember suddenly brighten. Over time, more of its shape is revealed. That might be an appropriate image of scripture: the text is present as a richly structured object, only some aspects of which are ever in view. As the Spirit plays across its surface, different aspects of its content and structure become visible. This is what I mean by the text's 'rich objectivity'.[62]

The text of scripture is given but not possessed.[63] It is given, in the sense that the text is there in front of us, quite open and complete. It is all on the surface, all exposed to the fire. Jesus says, in Mt. 5.18, that 'not one letter, not one stroke of a letter, will pass from the law until all is accomplished'; Rev. 22.19 condemns anyone who 'takes away from the words of the book of this prophecy'. Yet what is given has an unending complexity to it. The surface of scripture is not smooth; it is not the kind of object that one can take in at a glance, or possess fully by means of a summary. It does not have the kind of shape that could be generated by the application of a formula. One always has to reckon with what Owen Chadwick calls 'the rugged, the unexpected, the anfractuous'.[64] There are always shadows from which something unexpected can emerge.[65]

To discover more of this rich objectivity may be disturbing. We might be drawn into a deeper attentiveness to the tensions marking scripture's surface. We might be drawn to hear how one part of scripture questions or undercuts another. We might be alerted to dangers and learn to face texts of terror. We might learn to acknowledge that some

---

[61] 'The miracle of the Bible is … that it is inexhaustible' (The Doctrine Commission of the Church of England, *Christian Believing: The Nature of the Christian Faith and Its Expression in Holy Scripture and Creeds* (London: SPCK, 1976), 31).

[62] The picture I paint of scripture here has parallels with a more general accounts of texts common in the Gadamerian tradition. Dunne, summarizing Gadamer, says that a text 'is charged with possibilities of meaning that become actual only in virtue of movements in the rest of the field. It is the dynamism of history that constitutes this field and within it there is the never fully completed process of bringing to light different aspects of the meaning of the text' (*Back to the Rough Ground*, 118). The text, he says, 'has its *being* in the conversations in which it is brought into partnership' (121, emphasis in original). Or as I put it in 'Whose Psalm Is It Anyway? Why Christians Cannot Read Alone', 88, the text 'is what it is in all the company it keeps'.

[63] To borrow a phrase of Medi Ann Volpe, Christian reading is 'more pilgrimage than possession' (*Rethinking Christian Identity*, 34).

[64] Owen Chadwick, *From Bossuet to Newman*, 2nd edn (Cambridge: Cambridge University Press, 1987), 10.

[65] Ben Quash, *Found Theology: History, Imagination and the Holy Spirit* (London: Bloomsbury, 2013), 9, says that scripture 'will elude any possessive appropriation, and it is constantly liable to be discovered somewhere other than where we thought we had put it for safekeeping'.

texts simply remain perplexing. To have our eyes and ears opened more fully to this text does not mean being drawn to any sanitized image of it. It means being drawn by our encounters in the world to trace again and again the ways in which the words of this text actually run.

The lure into the rich objectivity of the text is not, for Christian reading, a matter of its inherent fascination. The journeys of discovery on which the Spirit leads the church are not undertaken for the sake of the text, but for the sake of God. In the *Analogy of Religion*, Joseph Butler says that,

> as it is owned the whole scheme of Scripture is not yet understood, so, if it ever comes to be understood before the restitution of all things, and without miraculous interpositions, it must be in the same way as natural knowledge is come at: ... by particular persons attending to, comparing, and pursuing intimations scattered up and down it, which are overlooked and disregarded by the generality of the world. ... Nor is it at all incredible that a book, which has been so long in the possession of mankind, should contain many truths as yet undiscovered. ... And possibly it might be intended that events, as they come to pass, shall open and ascertain the meaning of several parts of scripture.[66]

Butler appears to be describing a process that is entirely naturally intelligible, just what one would expect when exploring a complex historical text: 'Nor is it at all incredible,' he says. This is not, however, a perfect analogy, as he hints in the final sentence: 'And possibly it might be intended ...'. The process by which the text of scripture is opened up to the church in the course of 'events, as they come to pass' has something providential, something divinely ordered about it.

To put it more boldly, the ongoing reception of God's gift, the uncovering or illuminating of scripture's rich objectivity, the challenging and overthrowing of our misapprehensions, takes place as scripture's readers are drawn onward by the Spirit. In the words of Dan Hardy, our exploration of this rich objectivity is a matter of 'allowing our imaginations to be drawn forward by divine attraction: an ongoing process of envisioning and re-envisioning, so that we are stretched forward by the divine purposes ... an abduction that grabs you into the spirit's wind and pulls you along in the direction of the divine movement'.[67] Christians hold fast to this text, and keep on looking for the Spirit to unfold it to them, because – in words that I have already quoted from Katherine Sonderegger – 'we meet God there, the very One who chose and formed and taught the People Israel, and the very One who came among us in the Son, mighty to save.'[68]

Ben Quash explores just this territory. He imagines a reader, steeped in what I have called a scriptural settlement, meeting something new: a new person, a new situation,

---

[66] Joseph Butler, *The Analogy of Religion, Natural and Revealed, to the Constitution and Course of Nature* (London: J.M. Dent, 1906), 151, emphasis removed.
[67] Daniel W. Hardy, with Deborah Hardy Ford et al., *Wording a Radiance: Parting Conversations on God and the Church* (London: SCM, 2010), 77.
[68] See n. 1.

a new object – 'some found thing'.[69] In that encounter, the reader will face the task of seeing whether they 'can think this event and think Christ together in some way'.[70] They will depend upon the Spirit who can lure them into 'new sorts of Christian thought … new forms of action, relationship and institution: new alignments of people, place and time'.[71] Each of these new developments is a genuinely creative response to a situation in part unprecedented. Each at the same time is a re-reading of what has already been given – a reading with new eyes, but of the existing text. It is in the interaction of the given and the found, an interaction that will bear some of the marks of the re-reading of scripture triggered by the advent of Jesus, 'that revelation is constituted'. That is, it is in the interaction of the given and the found that the given is unveiled.[72] This is not simply a trust in the capacities of a classic text to speak meaningfully in new situations. It is not simply a claim about the inherent dynamics of reading. It is a claim about God's word spoken to the world in Jesus, and about the scriptures that God has given to draw us into that word.[73] 'The historical work of the Spirit is a constant proving of the fundamental Christian wager, namely that the "foundational story" of Jesus Christ, with all its particularities of place, time and religious context, can be shown to be "at home" with all the varying enterprises of giving meaning to the human condition.'[74]

The same Spirit who was at work in the formation of scripture, ensuring that, as a creaturely object, produced by a complex web of creaturely causes, it was apt for this ongoing revelatory work, is also at work in the church's ongoing reading, opening believers' eyes and ears to read and read again, beckoning them further in and further up into the truth. Amplifying the hint that we heard in Butler, Quash says that history – the history of found encounters by which our eyes and ears can be opened to scripture's richness – can therefore be understood as 'the gift and the medium of the Holy Spirit'.[75]

> God's revelation in Christ is not compromised by – indeed, precisely implies – an ongoing historical dynamic whereby, in God, human beings are constantly invited to relate the given to the found. The givens come alive only in this indefinitely extended series of encounters with new circumstances, and the Christian assumption ought to be that no new found thing need by construed as a threat to what has been given, for we have to do with the same God both in the given and in the found.[76]

---

[69] Quash, *Found Theology*, 17.
[70] Ben Quash, *Theology and the Drama of History* (Cambridge: Cambridge University Press, 2005), 207.
[71] Ibid., 211.
[72] Quash, *Found Theology*, 17.
[73] A fuller exposition of the Christological aspects of the abundance and inexhaustibility that I am describing here would need to tease out (a) the inexhaustible historical particularity of Jesus's human nature; (b) the continued liveliness of Jesus as one who is resurrected and ascended; and (c) the inexhaustible abundance of the Logos to which the human nature was and is hypostatically united.
[74] Quash, *Found Theology*, 28.
[75] Ibid., xvi, emphasis removed.
[76] Ibid., xiv, emphasis removed.

Christians should therefore 'do what they can to widen the range of their encounters in Christ's name'.[77] They should go out beyond the edges of the settlements within which they might otherwise remain undisturbed, and put themselves in the way of encounters and relationships beyond the familiar – or, rather, allow themselves to be led out into the world by the Spirit. In the words of Dan Hardy, they should be 'a walking Church', who 'wander first and then think theologically and practically in response to what they have found. Whoever or whatever turns up as they walk, whatever they find as they go along, these become the found realities in response to which they think and act.'[78] Such walking always brings Christians into specific locales, each of which has its own fractal complexity, and in each of which the Spirit is already at work, forming life that echoes the life of God. In each of these locales, Christians are to pursue

> the enacting of holiness, not as something general and timeless but as what is the 'refining fire' of Christ in this place, in this set of circumstances, for these people, and through them all others, now; and the effects of this holiness are to be seen in the energizing of these people for and within the holiness of God as that reaches the whole world in its complexity. Hence it is an occasion of performing – and thus learning – the quality of God's holiness in action, whose implications are seen as it reconstitutes the life of those involved, forming their multifold interactions with others.[79]

The walking and engagement that Hardy describes, and the finding that Quash describes, are not distractions from scripture, but are the condition for committed attentiveness to it. They are the shape of the journey on which the Spirit draws out the riches of the text.[80] This journey won't necessarily be smooth: it is sometimes a matter of hairpin bends and sudden drops – challenges and revolutions. And it certainly is not finished. Christians have not been led from ongoing reception to full possession. They should therefore, says Quash, be 'provisional by instinct', and 'energetically opposed to models of doctrine that assume for it any sort of ahistorical completeness'. '[T]he God to whom Scripture witnesses is better gestured to in this never-completeness than in the presumed fixity of a particular linguistic matrix.'[81]

---

[77] Ibid., 24.
[78] Hardy, *Wording a Radiance*, 86.
[79] Hardy, *Finding the Church*, 21.
[80] Healy, *Church, World and the Christian Life*, says that 'We witness to our dependence upon the Other, upon God and his presence in others, by seeking out and listening to those, within and outside the church, who challenge the adequacy of our ecclesial action. When we need to, we contritely abandon a practice, or modify it or engage in bricolage to develop a better one' (151). That means also attending to those who 'live ... more at the cultural borderlands, at those places where the Christian tradition must engage with other forms of inquiry and their embodiments' (177). 'Since the church can at times learn from the work of the Spirit working in what is non-church, it seems reasonable to propose that the church should make a habit of listening to the non-church, of trying to discern the Spirit's action in its challenges, of seeking out its wisdom in case Christ's word is spoken there' (69). Cf. Stephen E. Fowl and L. Gregory Jones, *Reading in Communion: Scripture and Ethics in Christian Life* (London: SPCK, 1991), 29.
[81] Quash, *Found Theology*, xiv, 1, 80.

The love of God is infinitely rich; it is unplumbable. Every discovery truly made in creaturely life of how to respond to and communicate God's love is a finite image of that love. No creaturely image, however, and no ensemble of such images, provides an exhaustive map of the original. Every image is partial, every one fractured, every one in need of supplementation and correction. There is always more to know, and although each image is sustained by some familiar way of living with scripture, we can always be drawn back to scripture again, and taught to read differently. The scintillating abundance of the text, its endless openness for such rediscovery, its rich objectivity, is a gift from the divine abundance, a witness to it, and an invitation into it. This is what it means to say, with Sonderegger, that 'we are brought into the fiery Presence of the Lord through this earthen vessel'.[82]

Conclusion

Doctrinal theology explores what the church has seen or heard in scripture. The first and simplest thing to say about the relationship between doctrine and scripture is that doctrinal statements are intended to summarize the central plot that Christian readers have found together in scripture in the course of their proclamation, confession, teaching and controversy – the plot that forms the context for all of Christian life.

Yet doctrinal theologians don't simply create such summaries; they use them to think with. They explore the connections and the implications of the central ideas that they have found in scripture. As they pursue that task, they often find themselves exploring implications, or making connections, or insisting on distinctions, that are not themselves directly discussed in scripture. They do this because they believe that the materials that God has given them in scripture enable this kind of exploration, and that – as we saw in Chapter 4's discussion of teaching – scripture itself calls for it.

Doctrinal theology does not, however, simply summarize what it finds in scripture, or work with those summaries. In its various forms in different times and places, it helps to hold in place the church's ways of reading. It identifies constraints upon the church's ongoing engagement with scripture, and it provides imaginative resources for that engagement. Specifically, it can call the church to seek in scripture an ongoing encounter with the Jesus whose identity is rendered for us in the gospels, and it can invite the church to recognize its reading as a spiritual discipline, undertaken in the power of the Spirit who draws people to this Jesus in a journey of purification and ascent, on the way further up and further in to the abundant love of God. By calling it into this kind of reading, doctrinal theology can help to make possible the church's ongoing engagement with scripture's objectivity.

The work of doctrinal theology is itself properly tested by the church's ongoing reading. In part this means that it is tested by the diligent pursuit of the practices of reading that it helps to hold in place – and in that sense it sets the terms of its own testing. Yet doctrinal theology can also help to hold in place an expectation of challenge

---

[82] See n. 1.

that goes beyond this. It can help to hold in place a trusting expectation that the Spirit will break out against the church's settlements by means of scripture, including against the church's present apprehensions of scripture, and the church's present habits of reading. Doctrinal theology can help to hold in place the expectation that the Spirit can and will break out against even the expectations that doctrinal theology helps to hold in place. The Spirit can break out against doctrinal theology, against the traditions of doctrinal reflection on behalf of which doctrinal theologians speak, and even at times against the doctrinal formulations that anchor those traditions. Doctrinal theology can help to hold in place the expectation that the Spirit will, by means of scripture, call for the refinement, the alteration, even at times the transformation of doctrine.

The reading practices to which the church is called, and which doctrinal theologians are to accompany, are practices of reading while walking. That is, they are practices of re-reading in the light of the new situations, the new encounters and the new relationships into which the Spirit leads scripture's readers. Above all, they are practices of re-reading in the company of those who suffer and are oppressed, those who are marginalized and excluded, those who are harmed by the church's present settlements. They are practices in which those in positions of hermeneutical power and privilege sit at the feet of those who read from the margins, to listen, to learn, to accompany and in time to converse. The Spirit can open the eyes and ears of readers more fully to scripture, and enable them to hear, see and dwell in the word of God more richly, by means of these situations, encounters, relationships and conversations. If doctrinal theology is to play a role here, it will be by keeping the church to this kind of reading and walking, by holding open space for the conversations that emerge, and by exploring the challenges and suggestions that are generated by those conversations.

There are several aspects of this picture that I need to discuss more fully in the remaining chapters of this book. In Chapter 10, I will explore what it might mean in practice, in my own church's life, for doctrinal theologians to accompany the church's walking and reading. In Chapter 9, I will dig much more fully into the hints I have dropped here about the refinement, alteration or transformation of the church's doctrinal claims. Before we get to those conversations, however, I need to delve into another topic that makes the account I have given in this chapter considerably more difficult: the pervasive phenomenon of Christian disagreement. What sense can we make of the idea that the Spirit is opening believers' eyes and ears to the scriptures, and drawing them on journeys of discovery, when those believers, pervasively, disagree about what it is that they see, and about how it is that they are seeing it?

8

Doctrine and disagreement

Introduction

Christian life, in all its lively and disquieting variety, is a collective exploration of discipleship, a bazaar of experiments in following Jesus. Though each experiment is mixed, each in some ways a failure, each also embodies and displays something of the love of God. Together, they display something of that love's abundance. The Spirit is at work throughout all this life, beckoning God's people further up and further in to the source of their faith by enticing them out beyond the boundaries of their existing settlements.

Whatever may be suggested by my language of 'exploration', and my descriptions of the Spirit's beckoning, the life of the church does not take the form of a single, continuous pilgrimage, a constant journey of enrichment on which the church uncovers more and more of what is meant by discipleship. Such a picture would omit three unmistakable features of Christian life.

First, it ignores Christian forgetfulness. In the words of the Church of England's Doctrine Commission, 'Much of the history of theology has been characterized by forgetting as well as by learning, with the result that instead of an accumulation of knowledge and understanding we see only the replacement of one partial insight by another equally partial.'[1] Any serious backward look at earlier generations of Christianity will encounter, at least in part, strangeness: a foreign people speaking a language now forgotten.

Second, it ignores Christian repentance. The history of Christianity is marked by repeated moments in which Christians have concluded that they have inherited broken and harmful patterns of discipleship. Any serious look at the history of Christianity will find a history of changes of direction, of deliberate unpickings and reformations – and of trajectories still demanding reversal.

Third, it ignores Christian difference. The church is, as I said in Chapter 4, polycentric. If we are telling the story of the church in enough detail to pick out what is known of the love of God in particular experiments, then there is not one story but a multitude. Different experiments in worship, witness and discipleship happen around the world, wherever Christianity has spread. And the differences that cross this mosaic of Christian life often take the form of disagreement. Christianity past and present

---

[1] The Doctrine Commission of the Church of England, *Christian Believing*, 4.

is fractious and disunited, far beyond the limits of any picture of mutually enriching variety. Any serious look at the history or present shape of Christianity will need to do justice to its deeply contested nature.

It is this third reality, of disagreement, that will be my focus in this chapter; forgetfulness and repentance will largely have to wait until the next. I will begin by drawing attention to just how constant and how pervasive disagreement has been in Christianity, right down from the time when an argumentative band of disciples accompanied Jesus on the road to Jerusalem. I will ask what it means that some of these disagreements are intractable: differences that cut deeply into the possibility of shared worship, witness and discipleship, and for which no realistic route to reconciliation seems to exist. I will discuss how these intractable disagreements can be bound up with differing apprehensions of scripture, and different narrations of tradition, leaving no easy way of deciding between them. I will look at the ways in which doctrinal theology and doctrinal statements are caught up in the history of Christian disagreement, as products of it, as responses to it and as strategies for either sharpening or overcoming it. And I will suggest that doctrinal theology can sometimes serve other purposes in this divided body: it can destabilize entrenched positions enough to make movement possible even when reconciliation remains unavailable, it can make boundaries just porous enough to enable certain kinds of learning to flow across them without erasing them, or it can simply provide a means for the divided parties to understand one another more deeply. I will suggest that the pursuit of these purposes might be part of what it means to hold on, in the face of our deep-riven divisions, to a vision of the polycentric church as a single body led by the Spirit in shared and creative exploration of God's abundant gift.

Christian disagreement

I argued in Chapter 6 that the church is always discovering the meaning of discipleship by means of local improvisation. Christian life does not evolve according to some deductive or organic logic, but by means of inventive judgement or creative construal in the face of new situations. As soon as there is more than one situation – which means as soon as there is more than one moment, let alone more than one place – the possibility of difference arises. It comes with the very processes by which Christianity exists as a reality with extension in space and time. Christianity is 'always already a multiplicity'.[2]

Multiplicity does not have to mean disagreement or separation. It is a result both of the unending particularity of creaturely existence – different in every moment and every location – and the unending abundance of God. On the one hand, no two creatures, precisely because they are creatures, can inhabit and express the love of God identically. On the other, the love of God always exceeds its embodiment in any one location, and calls forth other embodiments.[3] All the members of the church, and all

---

[2] Burrus, 'History, Theology, Orthodoxy, Polydoxy', 11; cf. Tanner, *Theories of Culture*, 159.
[3] Jesus embodies the love of God perfectly not by containing it in one location, but in a life that cannot be contained. Jesus rises from the tomb, and draws all people to himself (Jn 12.32).

the communities, networks and traditions that it comprises, have been on different journeys, and have been led to the discovery of something different from God's inexhaustible abundance.

Nevertheless, there was never a moment in Christian history when some of this diversity did not already take the form of dispute.[4] Even on the road with Jesus, the disciples argued with one another (Mk 9.34) and with him (Mk 8.32-33). We are told that, after Pentecost, 'the whole group of those who believed were of one heart and soul' (Acts 4.32), but also that there was disagreement between the Hellenists and the Hebrews (Acts 6.1). Then Jesus's followers were scattered across Judaea and Samaria (Acts 8.1), Galilee (Acts 9.31), Phoenicia, Cyprus and Antioch (Acts 11.19), and their discipleship took different forms as they spread (Acts 11.19-20), leading to 'no small dissension and debate' (Acts 15.2).

The impact of Jesus upon his immediate followers, and upon those with whom they shared their faith, was, as Stephen Sykes put it, 'inherently disputable'. The pages of the New Testament show us a Christian faith 'unprotected from the eruption of disputes both about its content and about the practice of Christian discipleship', disputes that pushed beyond any 'easy toleration of diversity'.[5] The disciples had received a complex inheritance that took the form not of a bare and closely defined principle, or a rigidly worked out rule of life, but of a whole jumble of stories and sayings, of memories and impressions, events and practices. There was no way of using this inheritance, no way of seeking to make sense of it and to live in accordance with it, that did not involve active construal: a debatable identification of the patterns that held it together. Different acts of construal produced different descriptions of what mattered most in this inheritance, and so different identifications of the criteria that could be used to judge faithfulness to it.[6] And this proliferation of different uses unavoidably became disputatious, precisely because the different parties considered themselves to be about the same task: they were contesting a shared inheritance, seeking to understand what it meant to be followers of the same Lord. As Kathryn Tanner says, 'What unites Christian practices is not ... agreement about the beliefs and actions that constitute true discipleship; but a shared sense of the importance of figuring it out.'[7]

Recognizing its contested nature should prevent us from slipping into certain familiar ways of telling the story of Christianity. I am thinking of descriptions in which

---

[4] See the Faith and Order Commission report, *Communion and Disagreement*, §§1-2 for the history of Christian disagreement, and Jeremy Worthen's comments in the supporting papers for the report, §§5.27-28, on the difference between forms of diversity we can 'affirm as *gift*' and forms that 'can be borne as *challenge and task*' (emphasis in original).

[5] Sykes, *The Identity of Christianity*, 19-23 (and cf. the Doctrine Commission, *Christian Believing*, 4). Sykes (ibid., 256, 264) draws on W. B. Gallie's account of 'essentially contested concepts', from *Philosophy and the Historical Understanding* (London: Chatto and Windus, 1964). See also David Collier, Fernando Daniel Hidalgo and Andra Olivia Maciuceanu, 'Essentially Contested Concepts: Debates and Applications', *Journal of Political Ideologies* 11, no. 3 (2006): 211-46.

[6] The texts that form scripture themselves bear the traces of this contestation, and become the sources of contestation. Vanhoozer, *The Drama of Doctrine*, 31, says that 'Scripture itself is an ongoing canonically embodied argument into the meaning and significance of what God was doing in Jesus Christ' (emphasis removed).

[7] Tanner, *Theories of Culture*, 153. The central affirmations of Christianity 'are so vague that they amount, in practice, to a project requiring a solution' (cf. 158-9).

the narrator assumes an easy capacity to identify Christianity's original meaning, and then to sort developments according to whether they preserve or distort that meaning. No such attempt sits above the contestation that it describes. Christianity is, as Denise Kimber Buell says, a 'strategic, contingent and mutable' concept, and we need to approach it 'not as an essence but as a contested site – one defined and claimed by competing groups and individuals – and Christian history not as an evolving totality but rather as a series of ongoing struggles, negotiations, alliances, and challenges'.[8]

Intractable disagreements

Many of the differences that mark Christian life don't become, or don't persist as, disputes. Many of them can be welcomed or celebrated, or may simply enrich Christian life without being much noticed. Even when we are considering differences that are hard to see in this positive light, however, the people involved mostly find some way of rubbing along together that doesn't require them to resolve, or perhaps even to acknowledge, the problem. All of Christian life (including the life of each individual believer) is marked by inconsistencies, unevenness, questions that have not been faced, differences that have not come to a head. It is marked by workarounds, coping strategies and tactical silences. It is marked by conscious and unconscious acquiescence in difference.[9]

Some of the differences that emerge in Christian life do become disputes, however.[10] Situations arise in which some of those involved don't believe that a bearable modus vivendi has been found. They try to persuade others to change what they say and do, or agitate for some new shared settlement to be adopted. Some such disputes turn out to be soluble or tractable. There is enough agreement in practice among the disputants about how to tackle this kind of disagreement – the procedures that should be followed, the arguments that are relevant, the evidence that is telling within those arguments – and it proves possible for the people involved to work together towards a solution.

Intractable disagreements are those that run deeper than this: differences where there is little shared sense of how the disagreement should be faced, where different parties appeal habitually to different kinds of argument and evidence, and where enough

---

[8] Denise Kimber Buell, *Why This New Race: Ethnic Reasoning in Early Christianity* (New York, NY: Columbia University Press, 2005), 29. I am grateful to Marika Rose for this reference.
[9] Nicholas Rescher, 'Is Consensus Required for a Benign Social Order', in *Pluralism: Against the Demand for Consensus* (Oxford: Clarendon Press, 1993), 164, says that '*Acquiescence* ... is not a matter of *approbation*, but ... of a mutual restraint which, even when disapproving and disagreeing, is willing (no doubt reluctantly) to "let things be", because the alternative – actual conflict or warfare – will lead to a situation that is still worse' (emphasis in original). Cf. Nicholas Adams, 'New Plural Settlements: The Secular and Secularisation', *Journal of Scriptural Reasoning* 15, no. 2 (2016); available online at jsr.shanti.virginia.edu/back-issues/volume-15-number-2-november-2016/ (accessed 6 December 2019).
[10] Timothy Jenkins, *An Experiment in Providence: How Faith Engages with the World* (London: SPCK, 2006), 18, argues that 'God is ... to be encountered in epiphanies: glimpses given to us that change us, gather us into new groupings, and set us on to new tasks – the new both recasting the past and being made sense of in the light of it.' Yet the patterns of life into which such epiphanies call us 'can be incompatible with one another, for the apprenticeship of one system may block that of another' (ibid., 19).

is at stake that it is hard simply to ignore the situation. Intractable disagreements are those in which the participants often feel, however strong they think the case for their side is, that they never seem to make any headway with their opponents.[11]

Intractable difference and scripture

Many intractable disputes in the life of the church are powered, in part, by an irresolvable disagreement over scripture. That disagreement need not necessarily appear irresolvable. There might appear to be a genuine shared conversation about scripture going on, which has the capacity (if people would only take it seriously enough) to resolve the dispute. Perhaps one more book, or one more article, or one more argument will finally make the case. After all, on the various sides, people are appealing to the same scriptures, and they are making use of many of the same tools. They are discussing the text's historical contexts, the meanings that key terms would have had for the original authors and recipients, the shape of the arguments present in the text and so on – and they all seem to be claiming that the dispute could in principle be resolved by these means. Yet resolution never arrives. There is little sense of an emerging consensus, and little sense that many people's minds are being changed by all these arguments.

The fact that an apparently shared practice of reasoning leads people to (or leaves them with) such different conclusions has consequences. It tends to lead, for instance, to suspicions of insincerity. Suppose that you and I are both looking at the same text, and using similar kinds of argument about that text, and yet you are refusing to come to the conclusion that to me seems to be so plainly demanded. I am likely to think that your conclusion is actually being shaped by something else. Unlike me, I will think, you must only be pretending to base your conclusions on the text; you must be twisting the text to some preconceived agenda. Such suspicions of insincerity are a characteristic feature of intractable disagreements.

Such suspicions, however, often rest on a mistake. The apparent commonality in our forms of argument disguises much deeper differences in our apprehensions of scripture. Those deeper differences call into question the claim that we are all really 'looking at the same text'. In the sense explained in Chapter 7, the various parties to the dispute actually see different things when they turn to scripture; the text has different features for them. Their ways of reading are shaped by different patterns of imagination, and held in place by different apprenticeships. They inhabit different scriptural settlements.[12]

This pattern is visible in the disagreements about same-sex relationships that have been taking place in the Church of England. Those disagreements are certainly not a

---

[11] It is, in general, 'quite impossible to find a *general principle*' – that is, a principle readily acceptable to all parties – 'for deciding which of two contestant uses of an essentially contested concept really "uses it best"' (Gallie, *Philosophy*, 184).

[12] According to Stephen E. Fowl, *Engaging Scripture: A Model for Theological Interpretation* (Oxford: Blackwell, 1998), 59, each of the church's conflicting practices of interpretation can be given an account 'both rigorous and clear and in each case capable of evaluation', but that does not mean that reading is one thing, the standard of judgement singular. Cf. Fossett, *Upon This Rock*, 170–1.

straightforward contest between two sides; there are multiple parties, multiple different approaches, multiple attitudes to scripture involved. Nevertheless, in simplified form, one of the aspects of the debate illustrates my point about scripture.[13]

For one party, it is clear that scripture provides consistent teaching on key moral issues. Various passages need to be read together, and one passage may qualify or supplement another; there may be elements of a developmental story to tell across various passages, and individual passages certainly need to be read within the framework provided by scripture as a whole. Nevertheless, on the whole, the moral teaching provided in scripture is harmonious and clear. Scripture is a coherent act of communication by a communicative God, a God who graciously tells us how we should live.

For another party, it is no less clear that scripture is marked by deep tensions, by a combination of luminous witness to God and the repeated demonstration of humanity's capacity for horror. Texts that display the love of God jostle with texts of terror, and the whole of scripture is marked by the interaction of those two voices.[14] Learning to read scripture well means facing up to this complexity. It involves bringing each text to the foot of the cross in order to discern how it speaks for, and how it speaks against, the love of God that is enacted perfectly in Jesus. Scripture is a witness to that love, but it is a witness in an earthen vessel. Readers encounter God more fully the more they learn to read with such discernment.

By setting out the options like this, I may appear to be granting myself a privileged position above the fray. That would be a far from neutral position, however. By focusing attention on the sincerity of both sides, I might serve to hold the dispute in stasis. In other words, my analysis might undercut the impetus to change, and so turn away from those longing for it – especially those LGBTIQ+ people who are crying out against the suffering that they experience in the current state of the church's life. I hope that it will be clear from the remainder of this chapter and the next that preserving the status quo is not my purpose. Recognizing that this dispute is, in my sense of the word, intractable does not mean that we can only leave things as they are. It does, however, mean recognizing that the typical forms of argument that tend to be flung between the various sides in this dispute are not themselves likely to be the forces that generate change.

As with many intractable disagreements, the differences involved in this dispute are easy to misdiagnose. People involved on either side may not realize just how thoroughly their apprehension of scripture is shaped by a particular settlement. They may miss how deeply rooted their apprehension is in their imaginations and the patterns of their feelings. They may miss how much it is sustained by the style of preaching they hear, the exemplars of interpretation that they value and the wider pattern of Christian life that it helps to hold in place. Those in the first party really do hear harmony and cohesion when they listen to scripture, and they love what they hear. To them, those in the second party who claim not to be struck by it must be constructing artificial arguments

---

[13] There are other axes to the debate about scripture in this context, such as that between conservative and inclusivist evangelicals. For a useful analysis of the main parties, see Alasdair Rogers, *To What Extent Is George Lindbeck's 'Postliberal' Approach to Doctrine Helpful for the Resolution of Contemporary Christian Controversies?* (PhD thesis, Chester University, 2018).

[14] I am alluding, of course, to Phyllis Trible, *Texts of Terror: Literary-Feminist Readings of Biblical Narratives* (Philadelphia, PA: Fortress, 1984).

in order to avoid scripture's plain and compelling teaching. Those in the second party really do hear, and feel, the tensions and the terrors when they listen to scripture. To them, those in the first party who claim not be struck by them must be deliberately ignoring them, constructing a sanitized version of scripture in their minds to avoid hearing the difficulties so plainly audible in the text. People in both parties may listen to their opponents' arguments carefully, and be willing to have their minds changed if only those arguments will anchor themselves to the plain features of the text. They will think it clear, however, that their opponents are only sustaining their position by refusing to read with open-minded diligence. There is no real shared argument here. In the midst of this kind of intractable disagreement, appeal to scripture is likely only to reinforce, not to resolve division.

Contested hindsight

Intractable disagreements can also be marked by rival narrations of history. Though all sides supposedly share a past, within any one narration it will typically seem that only the narrator's party can claim to have remained faithful to that past.[15] Just as the development of a settlement involves habituation into a particular apprehension of scripture, so it involves habituation into a particular apprehension of the tradition. In that apprehension, only certain features are registered, and only the present position that preserves or builds on those features is believed to honour the past. Other features are registered only as background noise, if at all.[16]

Take the disagreement between Irenaeus and the Valentinians discussed in Chapter 7. There is, as I noted, an unavoidable circularity to that story: Irenaeus draws the rule of faith from scripture by reading scripture in a certain way, but this way of reading is then itself held in place by the rule. The Valentinians read differently, but their way of reading too is supported by what they read. The same circularity affects attitudes to the history of interpretation on both sides. For Irenaeus, it was clear that his way of reading stood in continuity with the practice of the apostles, but the Valentinians were in their own way no less traditional. Their approach to the text, as a repository of encoded mysteries, built on uses of scripture visible in the New Testament itself. As John Behr puts it 'Valentinus did not feel the need to close a body of fixed authoritative writings, but rather continued to reuse, imaginatively and creatively, texts and images from Scripture in much the same way that the New Testament had used the Old Testament.'[17]

The form of the continuity that the Valentinians may have seen between their own practice and that of earlier generations would also have been different from the form that Irenaeus claimed to see. The kind of continuity proper to the passing on of esoteric insight is different from the kind proper to the passing on of a publicly visible narrative.

---

[15] See Chapter 2, p. 29.
[16] Cf. Rosemary B. Kellison, 'Tradition, Authority, and Immanent Critique in Comparative Ethics', *Journal of Religious Ethics* 42, no. 4 (2014): 718: 'Given that traditions are made only through the process of retrospective reconstruction, there is always the possibility that the narratives could be told differently – and given what we know of the diversity of traditions, they often are.'
[17] Behr, *The Formation of Christian Theology 1*, 20; cf. Young, *Biblical Exegesis and the Formation of Christian Culture*, 15–16.

An appeal to the history of interpretation cannot provide an antidote to intractable disagreement, because that appeal takes different forms for the different sides.

The classic version of this whole process is perhaps the formation of the canon of scripture itself. Like many others, John Webster insists that, although the choice of just these books to serve as the church's scripture is an act of the church, it is not the church's 'whim' or even the church's 'judgment' or 'decision'. It is an act of acknowledgement, of 'normed compliance'.[18] These texts are not granted authority by the church, but rather the church in the act of canonization recognizes that they already bear that authority. Yet the capacity for that recognition was not there in the church from the beginning, fully formed and simply waiting to be applied. There is a history to its formation woven in with the history of the formation of the canon. When Webster says that the history of canonization is the work of the Spirit, this must include the work of the Spirit in granting to the church 'the sense for the truly apostolic' that is put to use in canonization.[19] From a human point of view, that history could have gone quite differently, and yet looked in retrospect no less consistent, no less necessary. The end point of such a history is a community with a fixed canon, and with standards of judgement formed by immersion in that specific canon. Of course this community will find that the texts of its canon are just the ones that meet these standards of judgement. There is no way of turning that retrospective sense of inevitability around, and claiming that the process had to unfold as it did, except by appeal to the work of the Spirit – and that pneumatological move is clearly one that deserves further interrogation. I will be returning to it later in the chapter.

The same logic that we find in descriptions of the emergence of the canon can be found in descriptions of doctrinal development. It is not uncommon to find accounts that explain how, once a particular question had been posed with clarity, the orthodox answer was inevitable. Such narrations are often, however, framed in terms that assume the development they describe.

One typical example can be found in David Yeago's article, 'The New Testament and the Nicene Dogma'. The New Testament displays, Yeago says, patterns of judgements made by the early Christians. We find, in various forms, the founding Christian affirmation that 'The God of Israel, the God in whose name Jesus of Nazareth claimed to speak, has raised him from the dead and exalted him as Lord.'[20] The unique and incomparable God of Israel, jealous of all idolatry, 'comes to his rightful, exclusive sovereignty over the whole creation … precisely through creation's acknowledgement of the lordship of the particular person Jesus'. Henceforth 'it is not possible to turn to the God of Israel without at the same time turning to Jesus.' 'This remarkable identification', Yeago says, 'reflects the inner logic of the church in the Spirit.' What happened at Nicaea was that a question was posed that could, in the light of these judgements embodied in scripture, only properly be answered in one way once it had been asked. 'The affirmation that this God has so radically identified himself with Jesus can rhyme with Israel's confession of the singularity and incomparability of God if

---

[18] Webster, *Holy Scripture*, 62.
[19] Ibid., 60.
[20] David Yeago, 'The New Testament and the Nicene Dogma', *Pro Ecclesia* 3, no. 2 (1994): 154.

and only if their relationship is eternal.' Their relationship must in some sense 'always have been intrinsic to YHWH's identity'.[21] Yeago quotes N. T. Wright's exegesis of Philippians 2 to provide the turning point in his argument:

> For consider: if the God who will not share his glory with another has now shared it with Jesus ... then there are only three possible conclusions that can be drawn. It might be the case that there are now two Gods. Or Jesus – who up until then had been a man and nothing but a man – might now have been totally absorbed into the one God without remainder (so to speak). Or there might be a sense – requiring fuller investigation, exploration, and clarification, no doubt – in which Jesus ... is receiving no more than that which was always, from before the beginning of time, his by right.[22]

We might have trouble with this argument at four different levels. We might dispute the reasons that Wright and Yeago give for the option that they choose. We might dispute whether the list of options that they present exhausts the possibilities for reconciling the initial assumptions. We might dispute the terms that have been used to frame all of the options on offer. Or we might dispute whether the whole approach of framing disjunctive logical possibilities for the reconciling of propositionally framed initial statements is an appropriate method in the first place. My questions hover between the fourth and the third of these levels.

To set this game up in the first place, Wright and Yeago must assume that we know roughly what we are talking about when we talk about 'sharing glory'. They must also assume that we know roughly what it would mean to count gods – that is, to assert or deny that there are 'now two Gods'. Their confidence in framing the available options therefore draws power from their ability to distinguish between what might be shared and who it might be shared among. In other words, their whole framing draws power from a distinction between substance and person – yet this is a Nicene distinction. Wright's trilemma is a way of framing the question that is only likely to have been advanced by someone schooled in the Nicene tradition.

And this schooling goes deeper. The scriptural texts selected, the features highlighted in their exegesis, the relative emphasis given to those features, the ways in which the ensemble of such texts is summarized – their whole way of telling the story leading up to the Nicene decision is shaped by a Nicene imagination. From the vantage point provided by that imagination, the whole development looks inevitable, but it has the inevitability of a retrospective reconstruction. It remains possible that a theologian sitting downstream of a different, non-Nicene settlement, would tell the whole story differently, and with no less tight a narrative of necessary development.[23]

The reason I have introduced this example by way of Yeago's article rather than the book of Wright's that he cites is because of a telling shift in wording in the quote I gave

---

[21] Ibid., 155–7, emphases removed.
[22] N.T. Wright, *The Climax of the Covenant Christ and the Law in Pauline Theology* (Minneapolis: Fortress Press, 1993), 94, quoted in Yeago, 'Nicene Dogma', 156–7. Yeago does not regard the second of these options as a viable interpretation of Philippians 2.
[23] See the discussion of Robert Brandom's work in Chapter 6, p. 128.

earlier. 'The affirmation that this God has so radically identified himself with Jesus can *rhyme* with Israel's confession of the singularity and incomparability of God *if and only if* their relationship is eternal.'[24] The word 'rhyme' here suggests an aesthetic grasp that has creatively found a way of holding together the materials at its disposal. The phrase 'if and only if' is, by contrast, the language of logical deduction.

John Milbank provides a rather different account of the emergence of decisions like those made at Nicaea, and unlike Yeago he does not turn rhyming into deduction. He notes that 'It is when interpretative doubts set in about the permanent "setting" assumed for the human drama [of scripture, and of the church's life], that a theoretical, doctrinal, level tends to "take off" from the level of narrative.'[25] At such times, a doctrinal account may be offered that not only articulates the implicit structures of the existing narrative but 'emphatically pronounces with regard to doubts that narrative and practice do not clearly resolve'.[26] There is in such pronouncements 'a radically "inventive" moment'. That invention is justified not by deduction from the pre-existing data, but by 'the redoubled force' that it gives 'to existing Christian practice', and the coherence and harmony of the picture of God and God's work that it provides.[27] To someone who internalizes the picture formed in this way, this compelling coherence and harmony – the 'rhyme' of the emergent solution – is liable to leave them thinking that the picture could not have been painted otherwise. They are likely to think the development logical rather than aesthetic. The creativity and the contingency of the process of doctrinal development are easily forgotten.[28]

John Henry Newman provides one of the clearest discussions of this retrospective logic. By way of illustration, he asks us to think of the way in which we typically re-read a person's history in the light of their later conduct.

> [I]t is plain that a person's after course for good or bad brings out the passing words or obscure actions of previous years. Then we make the event a presumptive interpretation of the past, of those past indications of his character which were too few and doubtful to bear insisting on at the time, and would have seemed ridiculous had we attempted to do so. And the antecedent probability is found to triumph over contrary evidence, as well as to sustain what agrees with it.[29]

Newman's account of the development of doctrine does not start, as it were, from the beginning of the story, and seek to demonstrate that at every point in the growth to full flowering the story had to unfold as it did. He begins instead with the end already in

---

[24] Yeago, 'Nicene Dogma', 157, emphasis changed.
[25] John Milbank, *Theology and Social Theory: Beyond Secular Theory*, 2nd edn (Oxford: Blackwell, 2006), 385.
[26] Ibid., 384–5. Contrast John Webster, *Holiness* (London: SCM, 2003), 16, for whom 'Holy reason is not a *poetic* but a *receptive* enterprise'.
[27] Milbank, *Social Theory*, 386.
[28] Cf. Volpe, *Rethinking Christian Identity*, 5, 85, 93. Milbank (*Social Theory*, 382) describes theology as 'the constant re-narration of [ecclesial] practice as it has historically developed' – and argues that the nature of 'reason' is itself re-narrated in this process.
[29] John Henry Newman, *An Essay on the Development of Christian Doctrine*, 1845 edn, ed. J.M. Cameron (Harmondsworth: Penguin, 1974), 179–80.

view: with a grasp of how impressive is the array of doctrines displayed in the Catholic Church: 'their high antiquity yet present promise … their harmonious order'.[30] This must 'affect the imagination most forcibly towards the belief that a teaching so young and so old, not obsolete after so many centuries, but vigorous and progressive, is the very development contemplated in the divine scheme'.[31] Therefore, 'in proportion as there are reasons for presuming the correctness of the existing developments of Christianity, shall we dispense with a formal historical argument in their favour, and content ourselves with such accidental corroborating evidences as the stream of time has washed upon our shores'.[32] The explicit articulation of arguments provides at best a secondary support for what was grasped by other means: 'logic is brought in to arrange and inculcate what no science was employed in gaining.'[33]

Newman made his arguments very much in favour of one of the Christian settlements available in his own day. I am exploring these matters in order better to understand the relation between multiple settlements. In situations of intractable difference, members of each party are likely to claim, sincerely and with good reason, that scripture and tradition support their approach. Given what they see in scripture and in the tradition, decisions had to unfold as they did. My argument has been that such claims only work retrospectively: they do not provide the knock-down arguments against alternative possibilities that they seem to offer. This is not, however, an argument that each settlement is simply arbitrary. The different features that are seen in scripture and tradition from within differing settlements might well be objective features in the sense discussed in Chapter 7. A settlement may be creative, contingent and held in place by arguments that only work retrospectively, but that does not stop it from being genuinely insightful. A contingent and contested settlement – held in place by a pattern of doctrinal statements – can still be one in which something of the abundant gift of God has been received.

Beyond separation

Doctrinal decisions

Christianity, then, is pervasively marked by difference, and among those differences by numerous intractable disagreements. The story of Christian doctrine is often told as a story of authoritative decisions made in the context of such disagreements. The story goes like this: as Christianity spread and diversified, controversies arose as to the compatibility of its various forms, and as to their faithfulness to Jesus. As each controversy came to a head, some authoritative meeting of bishops – that is, precisely of those charged with oversight of Christian faithfulness – would be convened to pronounce upon the issues at stake. After appropriate deliberation, and the occasional

---

[30] Ibid., 182.
[31] Ibid.
[32] Ibid.
[33] John Henry Newman, *An Essay on the Development of Christian Doctrine*, 1887 edn (London: Longmans, Green, and Co., 1909), 190.

punch-up, these bishops would produce a statement excluding some of the positions in play. Formal doctrinal statements of the kind found in creeds and confessions are expressions of such decisions. Nicaea, Constantinople, Ephesus, Chalcedon: authoritative doctrinal statements emerge in the context of theological controversy, and each further defines the limits of faithfulness.

In such a decision-focused account of the emergence of doctrine, doctrinal statements are best understood as boundary markers, even when they are framed as positive statements. W. R. Matthews writes, for instance, that the 'primary intention' of dogmas 'is to rule out certain lines of thought rather than to give a coherent conspectus of Christian truth'; Stylianos Harkianakis writes that 'the decrees of the ecumenical synods or councils signify a "setting of boundaries" or an intellectual "enclosure", so that the mind may not go beyond certain boundaries, but rather be guided on the true path where living waters are found'.[34]

The generation of such doctrinal decisions involves construal and commensuration. The council finds a way of construing the debate that frames it as a sharp decision. They find terms that can be used to articulate both the position of those deemed orthodox and the position of some group deemed heretical, with the heretical group denying something that the orthodox affirm. This commensuration brings the controversy to a head: a complex negotiation of differing forms of Christian life and speech becomes a decision for or against a certain proposition.[35]

An illustration of this can be provided by returning to Sarah Coakley's discussion of Chalcedon, already quoted in an earlier chapter. As she reads it, the Chalcedonian definition 'sets a "boundary" on what can, and cannot, be said, by ... ruling out three aberrant interpretations of Christ (Apollinarianism, Eutychianism, and extreme Nestorianism)' and it provides 'an abstract rule of language (*physis* and *hypostasis*) for distinguishing duality and unity in Christ'.[36]

These two moves are closely interrelated, and the second is the central act of construal. The profusion of Christian language about Christ – the language of Scripture, the language of liturgy and prayer, the language of ordinary catechesis and proclamation, the language of earlier controversy – is construed as having a certain underlying shape to it, which can be named by means of a carefully specified technical vocabulary. That process of construal then powers the other move: these same technical terms

---

[34] Matthews, 'The Nature and Basis of Dogma', 7; Stylianos Harkianakis, 'Dogma and Authority in the Church', in *The Task of Theology Today*, ed. Victor Pfitzner and Hilary Regan (Edinburgh: T&T Clark, 1998), 63; cf. Colin E. Gunton, 'Dogma, the Church and the Task of Theology', in *The Task of Theology Today*, ed. Pfitzner and Regan, 3–4.

[35] Rowan Williams argues that 'doctrinal definitions, Chalcedon above all, and the subsequent Christological clarifications of the Byzantine period, are indeed not *simply* regulative stipulations (no more ontologically bold than the rules of tennis), but the result of applying regulative principles to the more chaotic language of pre-dogmatic *doctrina* ... the whole complex of practices, verbal and non-verbal, moral, imaginative, devotional, and reflective, which embody "the church's conviction" about Jesus' ('Doctrinal Criticism: Some Questions', 250–1, Williams's emphasis).

[36] Coakley, 'What Does Chalcedon Solve and What Does It Not? Some Reflections on the Status and Meaning of the Chalcedonian "Definition"', 161. Cf. Orr, who (in *The Progress of Dogma*, 27) sees Chalcedon as, 'if not a final formulation – for what formulation on such a subject can be regarded as final – at least marking off the bounds within which a true doctrine of our Lord's Person must move.'

can be used to describe Apollinarianism, Eutychianism and extreme Nestorianism, and to name them as rejections of orthodox affirmations. This act of construal and commensuration serves to mark a line within which the ongoing deployment of orthodox Christian language can take place. It marks out the boundaries within which truth lies, without foreclosing the ongoing discovery of truth within those boundaries.

The process of construal involved in a decision like this is continuous with a process deeply embedded in Christian life. To be able to improvise, one must see what one has inherited as having a shape. That is, one must see the Christian life that one has received as more than a collection of equally weighted imperatives, an indivisible structure the alteration of any part of which can only be thought of as vandalism. One must be able, instead, to see it as having depths and shallows – as having, perhaps, a spirit animating the letter of its practices. That makes it possible for the shallower elements to be amended in ways that continue to do justice to the deeper.[37] One need not do exactly what one's forebears have done in order to remain true to the tradition that animated them. Yet any such construal is always implicitly negative as well as positive. By identifying what is at stake in the inherited faith, it both underpins the freedom to improvise and indicates paths that should not be taken.

The very processes by which Christianity spreads into new contexts therefore necessitate practices of construal, and the discernment of some kinds of boundary. In one sense, then, the kind of formal doctrinal controversy that I have been describing does not demand or create an entirely new dynamic, but it certainly pushes this dynamic to a new pitch. It demands that construal becomes more articulate and more precise. It shifts more of the weight from the front foot to the back – from the enabling of faithfulness to the identification of unfaithfulness. And it takes this drawing of boundaries from the context of local improvisation to the realm of high ecclesiastical politics, which is the realm of permanent exclusion and schism.

In this telling of the story of doctrinal development, then, moments of doctrinal decision are thought of as steps in the progressive clarification and purification of the church's teaching, an ever more precise identification of the proper and permanent boundaries to exploration. Doctrinal decisions enable us to draw lines across the map of possible construals of the gospel, and to colour in pink the territory within which true Christian life is to be lived.

What such a telling of the story of doctrine misses, however, is that the moments in which major doctrinal articulations are produced were very often not moments in which the disputants resolved their disagreement – by means of a 'sentence of judgment' which 'finished their strife', in Richard Hooker's words[38] – but moments in which negotiations collapsed, and the disputants separated. One side does not accept the decision of the other, or it disputes the terms in which that decision has been made. A boundary is erected, but it is a boundary that leaves people living on both sides. The history of doctrinal articulation is less a history of decision than a history of division – and what it leaves us with is not an ever more precisely defined territory within which

---

[37] See Chapter 9, pp. 226–8. Cf. Tanner, *Theories of Culture*, 162, for caution about this idea of depth.
[38] Hooker, *Of the Laws of Ecclesiastical Polity*, Preface, 6.3, in the modern spelling edition by Arthur Stephen McGrade, vol. 1 (Oxford: Oxford University Press, 2003), 25.

truth can be found, but an ever crazier patchwork of differing construals, crossed by lines of hostile separation.

Orthodoxy and separation

It may sound, at this point, as though I am throwing the whole idea of orthodoxy – perhaps the whole idea of doctrinal theology – under the bus. That is not, however, my intention. I, and the church of which I am a part, sit downstream of a whole history of doctrinal developments. I believe that those developments have enabled us to register, and to inhabit, something of the deep truth of God's gift in Christ. Our doctrinal statements help us to name and to be accountable for what we have registered. We cannot simply walk away from all that just because we now see more clearly the contingent and problematic nature of the history by which it arose. That would be to walk away from what we have seen and cannot unsee. It would be to walk away from the (partial and imperfect but, we trust, real) unfolding of the Word into which the Spirit has led us.[39]

Furthermore, there is no place for us to stand that is simply above the contestation and division that mark Christianity. There is no place from which impartially to survey all the different seeings spread across its life. Any such position that we thought we could occupy would inevitably turn out to be yet another defended territory in contest with all the others, no less partial, and no less fraught with its own idiosyncratic history. The question is not how (impossibly) to escape, but how to inhabit some position on this landscape gracefully, without closing our eyes to what we know of the landscape as a whole, and without denying the possibility of movement.

The whole discourse of Christian theology – the articulation and exploration of the truth that Christians believe they are discovering under the Spirit's guidance – involves the making of distinctions. The whole discourse is shaped by some variant or other of the idea of orthodoxy, even among those who most vehemently reject it. There are things that we should and should not do, things that we should and should not say, as disciples of Christ.

The idea of orthodoxy is, however, a complex one. It is, first of all, unavoidably shaped by the idea of naming and defending a specific territory within the patchworked landscape of Christian disagreement. Doctrine and division are, in effect, made for one another, and the history of doctrine provides ample demonstration of the connection.[40] There is also, however, a second impetus entangled with this first, because the idea of orthodoxy also springs from a concern for communion.

Rowan Williams speaks about this when asking whether there was such a thing as 'pre-Nicene orthodoxy'. He describes the wide diversity of second- and third-century Christianity, and then argues that, within this diversity, it is possible to identify a particular widespread network that was held together by 'what can sometimes seem

---

[39] That is not to say that it is impossible to walk away. It happens all the time.
[40] The claims I am making about 'the landscape as a whole' are, of course, not neutral. They will make more sense to inhabitants of some settlements than others. This is not a neutral overview: it is a proposal for a way forward, made from and to a specific nested set of contexts.

like an almost obsessional mutual interest and interchange'. This network was bound together by letters and visits and arguments – expressions of a deep concern with the versions of Christianity taking root in different locales, and with the question of 'how far they [were] answerable to each other or share[d] an identifiable point of reference'.[41] Over time, Williams argues, these bonds of mutual interest and exchange formed a webbing thick enough to allow the communities and individuals involved to see each other as about the same task, and as inhabitants of the same world.[42]

The emergence of this interest and interchange is, he argues, no accident. Among the various communities of this Christian diaspora evincing 'some sort of commitment to or dependence on the figure of Jesus', there were two broad approaches. For some, Jesus was, as it were, 'absorbed into the community's experience of enlightenment and liberation'.[43] What mattered was what happened here, in their own developing life, and the connection that this life might bear to what was happening elsewhere or had happened in the past was secondary. There were others, however, whose faith centred on connection to a Jesus who retained a certain kind of objectivity or distance over against their life. For them, the communication of the story of Jesus was about 'the bringing of the hearer into "dramatic" relation with the subject of the story – offering the hearer a new self-definition determined by his or her stance toward Jesus, offering a place within the story itself, as recipient of forgiveness and of judgment, as colluding with the betrayal of Jesus and sharing in the power of the risen Lord'.[44]

For these latter communities, it was natural to be concerned with the faithful transmission of Jesus's story, its ability to connect believers to him. He was not their possession, nor any other community's possession, but Lord of them all. '[F]or that hearing to go on being a hearing of the *same* story, canons of authorization are necessary for those who tell it or enact it; otherwise the story loses its distance or difference, and so its converting power, by becoming simply a story I choose to tell to myself.'[45] All those communities who shared this pattern of belief saw themselves as having to do with the same Jesus, as working out in their own distinct locations what it meant to be obedient to the same Lord, and as needing therefore to be held to account by those others who looked to the same source and to hold them to account in turn. It made sense for them to have an interest in the connection between their own obedience and the obedience of the other scattered communities of Jesus's followers.

From one point of view we must say that this difference identified by Williams, between those who were part of the proto-orthodox network and those who were not, is simply another of the distinctions that cross the emerging and cacophonous life associated with early Christianity. This network might be called 'proto-orthodox' insofar as it in some sense provided the soil in which post-Nicene orthodoxy grew, but that in itself does not allow a historian today to identify this network as authentic

---

[41] Williams, 'Does It Make Sense to Speak of Pre-Nicene Orthodoxy?' 11, 12, 9. Cf. Burrus, 'History, Orthodoxy', 11–12.
[42] Ibid., 10. Cf. Larry Hurtado, 'Interactive Diversity: A Proposed Model of Christian Origins', *Journal of Theological Studies* 64, no. 2 (2013): 445–62.
[43] Williams, 'Pre-Nicene Orthodoxy', 10.
[44] Ibid., 15–16.
[45] Ibid., 16, emphasis in original.

over against their supposedly inauthentic gnostic opponents. We might identify some strong forms of continuity between first-century Christianity and this network of second- and third-century communities, but there is no particular reason to focus on those rather than on all the other processes by which in this period many other forms of Christianity developed.

I read this history, however, as someone who does not stand to one side of it as an observer, but within it. I am someone who accepts that his task and the task of his community is the discovery of faithful discipleship to Jesus – the one whose identity is rendered for us in the gospels. That has been the frame for my whole presentation in this book so far, and those are the deepest terms I know in which to name what we are about. And that means that I and my community are heirs to this 'almost obsessional mutual interest and interchange' that Williams names. I am a member of a community held together by a common interest in Jesus, and therefore by interest in one another's discipleship, and I and my particular community are engaged in this task alongside countless others who are responding to, and responsible to, the same source – and who can hold us to account before that source. We are followers of Jesus together, and it is for that reason that we also have to consider the possibility of irresponsibility, and can't avoid making distinctions of some kind between faithfulness and betrayal. The emergence of the web of accountability holding together the multiple centres of the church's life was at the same time the emergence of the process of decisive boundary-drawing, of the formalizing of disavowal and exclusion. It was the emergence of orthodoxy as a habit of division – and we are unavoidably heirs to that, too.

Recognizing this dual character to the emergence of orthodoxy suggests, however – even if only very schematically at this point – a possible way of inhabiting it differently. It is not possible, as I have said, to commit together to discipleship without making distinctions, without saying 'no' as well as 'yes', without finding limits to what we can recognize as a faithful following of Jesus. But it is possible, in the entanglement between the seeking of communion and the making of distinctions, to order the two differently. The tendency in Christian history has often been to subordinate communion to differentiation. That is, the tendency has been to let the boundaries defined by doctrinal decisions mark out the only Christian community worth considering – to let them mark a boundary beyond which there need be no bonds of mutual accountability, only antagonism or indifference. It is possible, however, to order these two principles the other way around.[46] That is, it is possible to read the decisions and separations of orthodoxy as serious disagreements within a deeper communion. The whole scattered diversity of Christianity is a single unruly conversation, an argument marked by sharp and proliferating disagreements, and by all kinds of failure, more and less disastrous, but an argument nevertheless about a common subject matter. It is an unruly conversation about Jesus, and about what it means to follow him.

---

[46] This is a proposed 'repair' of this tradition: a rethinking of what I take to be a shallower component in the light of a deeper. For something like this sense of repair, see Nicholas Adams, 'Reparative Reasoning', *Modern Theology* 24, no. 3 (2008): 447–57. I will have more to say about this kind of process in Chapter 9.

My suggestion, then – though it is one that I will need to explore and justify more fully in the remainder of this chapter – is that faced with the convoluted landscape of Christian agreement and disagreement, we should recognize that 'separation', in any final sense, is simply not one of the responses available to us.[47]

The Spirit and the church

Newman's account of the development of doctrine, already mentioned earlier, provides a contrast that can clarify the move I want to make. Underlying his articulation of the several forms of continuity that connect contemporary Catholicism to the apostolic church are a small number of basic convictions. The first is simply that 'the idea of Christianity as originally revealed, cannot but develop'.[48] Christians are not gathered around an abstract principle, but around an incomparably rich gift the depth and beauty of which it takes time to see. The word 'idea', for Newman, does not name an essence that can be grasped all at once, still less something capturable in a proposition; it names the whole way of seeing that can unfold out of the original gift. As Nicholas Lash explains it, for Newman 'Christianity is an "idea" inasmuch as it is the human apprehension of that "fact" which is christianity considered as God's word, or self-disclosure of his will and purposes for man.'[49] Development is nothing other than the unwrapping of this gift.

The second conviction is that there is a 'high antecedent probability that Providence would watch over His own works'. The giver of this gift wants it unwrapped, and has provided for its unwrapping.[50] The development of doctrine is 'informed and quickened by what is more than intellect, by a Divine Spirit'.[51] The history of doctrine can be seen as the faithful development of the church's apprehension of the original gift because Newman can trust that the Spirit of Christ is at work in and through the human processes by which the unfolding takes place.

Newman's third conviction is an ecclesiological one. It is that the Spirit works in and through the teaching authority of the church. When he speaks of the 'high antecedent probability that Providence would watch over His own works', he explains that this means not only that God would 'direct' the development of doctrine but that he would 'ratify' it.[52]

> [I]n proportion to the probability of true developments of doctrine and practice in the divine scheme, is the probability also of the appointment in that scheme of an external authority to decide upon them, thereby separating them from the mass of

---

[47] Cf. Tanner, *Theories of Culture*, 155, on avoiding situations in which parties 'fall irretrievably out of the arena of further Christian consideration'. Graham Ward, *How the Light Gets In*, 116, speaks of the need not to be driven by 'a fear of being seriously attentive to the other, to difference' which means that 'we continue to produce and so pass on the violences of denominationalism and sectarianism'.
[48] Newman, *Development* (1845), 182.
[49] Lash, *Newman on Development*, 52.
[50] Newman, *Development* (1845), 193; cf. 163.
[51] Ibid., 149.
[52] Ibid., 193.

mere human speculation, extravagance, corruption, and error, in and out of which they grow. This is the doctrine of the infallibility of the Church; for by infallibility I suppose is meant the power of deciding whether this, that, and a third, and any number of theological or ethical statements are true.[53]

The fourth conviction is simply that the contemporary Catholic Church displays such a richly developed array of doctrine, such a beautiful embodiment of the Christian idea, that it must be the Church capable of this ratification. 'I think very few persons', Newman says, ingenuously, 'will deny the very strong presumption which exists that, if there are developments in Christianity, the doctrines propounded by successive Popes and Councils, through so many ages, are they.'[54]

Newman's account of development, then, rests upon a picture of the abundance of God's gift, which cannot be grasped all at once but needs to unfold in time, upon a picture of God's active work in and through the course of that unfolding, upon a picture of the church's relation to that unfolding, and upon a deep sense of where the unfolded gift is to be found in the contemporary church. These pictures arise together, and support one another; indeed, they are elements of a single composition.

My account rests upon a different composition, but it is built from similar elements. Newman was captivated by the telling resemblance between the Catholic Church and the apostles, and by a deep-rooted grasp that the one is connected to the other by a thick rope of continuity. I am captivated by the kind of picture I have been trying to paint in this chapter. It is a picture of multiple histories and locations of Christian development, from within each of which it is possible to tell a story of the same form that I can tell in mine. Each is shaped by a history of improvisation by means of which God's abundant gift in Jesus Christ has been explored. Where Newman saw a rope linking one contemporary communion to the past, I see a spider's web of threads spreading out from the past to more contemporary contexts than I can count.

Newman was convinced of the calm unfolding of the truth by a succession of popes and councils, and allowed his telling of the detailed history to be held in place by that underlying conviction. I have a basic apprehension of the messy humanity of the history of unfolding. The history of doctrine is always and everywhere a history of thoroughly human action, with all its convolutions, all its gradients of power, all its misrecognitions and bewilderments. It is a history of discovery, but also of forgetting, repenting and disagreeing.[55]

Newman rested his confidence upon a trust that the Divine Spirit has both prompted the emergence of developments among the faithful and appointed the magisterium of the Catholic Church to the task of ratifying and guarding it. I am convinced of a different pneumatology. The Spirit is at work across the whole surface of the divided church. The Spirit is at work wherever two or three are gathered together in Jesus's

---

[53] Ibid., 168.
[54] Ibid., 183.
[55] Ephraim Radner, *A Brutal Unity: The Spiritual Politics of the Christian Church* (Waco, TX: Baylor University Press, 2012), 231–2, provides a good description of the messy humanity of the Council of Chalcedon, for instance. As he says (ibid., 283), councils never live up to the image that conciliarists have of them. Cf. Ward, *Light*, 13.

name. The Spirit is at work wherever anyone declares that Jesus is Lord. The Spirit is at work reminding us of all that Jesus taught, and leading us into that teaching.[56] The Spirit is at work, in other words, wherever anything of the abundance of Christ's love is being discovered, wherever local improvisation is generating insight into the gift that founded the church. The Spirit's work is the unfolding of the abundant word, wherever it takes place.[57]

Given the presence of all the deep and shallow disagreements that craze the surface of the church, this claim about the Spirit's ubiquitous presence cannot mean that we simply declare all development to be true development. Not everything that glitters is gold. All gatherings in Jesus's name are partly faithless, all declarations of his lordship partly misspoken, all explorers of the abundance of God's gift get lost, sometimes very lost, along the way. All the experiments of Christianity are failed experiments, even though the Spirit has been at work within them. As I shall be saying at much more length in Chapter 9, the Spirit is also and vitally at work in raising up witnesses to the truth beyond the life of the church, in convicting the church of error, and in calling the church to repentance. Nevertheless, we have no shortcut to delimit where in the fractured landscape of the church's life we should look for the Spirit's work. We have no quick way of drawing a line across the map in order to concentrate only on the territory to one side of it, consigning everything on the other to our antagonism or indifference. Whatever doctrinal decisions mean in the history of the church, whatever work they do to name and protect what has been shown of God's gift to a given community, they do not establish boundaries around the work of the Spirit.

Doctrinal disagreements are (sometimes, at least) serious. They have to do (sometimes, at least) with matters of life and death. Christians have proven capable, too many times to enumerate, of enshrining as an interpretation of the gospel and encoding in their doctrinal statements teachings that betray the kingdom of heaven, that turn away from Christ's love and that divert our worship towards idols. Disagreements about these matters matter, and matter deeply, but those disagreements – including the ones which are most intransigent – are disagreements *within* the whole body that is animated by the one Spirit.

At times, scripture urges separation. In 1 Corinthians, Paul tells his addressees 'not to associate with sexually immoral persons' (5.9), and to drive out the wicked person from among them (5.13). They need to do this, in part, for the sake of purity: they must not let the contamination spread. 'Do you not know', he says, 'that a little yeast leavens the whole batch of dough? Clean out the old yeast so that you may be a new batch' (5.6-7). This is not, however, a matter of the church's separation from the world; it is an action directed towards a member of the community: 'For what have I to do with judging those outside? Is it not those who are inside that you are to judge?' (5.12).

---

[56] Matthew 18.20 (I am taking Jesus's presence to be his presence by the Holy Spirit); 1 Cor. 12.3.
[57] John Flett's work, *Apostolicity: The Ecumenical Question in World Christian Perspective* (Downers Grove, IL: InterVarsity Press, 2016), is important here. He seeks to move away from a linear picture of apostolicity, which seeks to delimit where in the present faithfulness is to be found, to attention to the processes of creative translation by which Christianity has taken root in the multiple centres of world Christianity.

Paul does not temper his words 'Do not even eat with such a one' (5.11), he says; 'hand this man over to Satan for the destruction of the flesh' (5.5): he is to be severed from the community, to suffer the outworking of his wickedness. This act of separation is, however, oriented towards the salvation of the one excluded. It is carried out 'so that his spirit may be saved on the day of the Lord' (5.5).[58] It is an action undertaken against someone who is inside, and it is ordered towards his restoration, whether that restoration is expected eschatologically or temporally. The one excluded still has a place, however tenuous and precarious, within the community of those oriented towards salvation.

Furthermore, although Paul's insistence upon separation appears to have arisen in a context in which he and the Corinthians disagreed about whether a particular form of behaviour was permitted in their community (5.2), it does not appear to have been a response to a situation in which two different factions had emerged within the church. That kind of situation, by contrast, is described earlier in the letter: 'Now I appeal to you, brothers and sisters, by the name of our Lord Jesus Christ, that all of you should be in agreement and that there should be no divisions among you, but that you should be united in the same mind and the same purpose' (1.10). Different leaders were building in different ways on the foundation provided by Christ, some with gold and silver, some with wood, hay, straw (3.12). All those materials were mixed inextricably together. The purification of this edifice, the stripping away of the elements built with baser materials, awaited the eschaton, when 'the work of each builder will become visible, for the Day will disclose it, because it will be revealed with fire, and the fire will test what sort of work each has done' (3.13). Even then, those who have built with straw will be saved (3.15). Until then, the church is built of mixed materials, true and false, and it is that mixed church of which Paul says, 'Do you not know that you are God's temple and that God's Spirit dwells in you? If anyone destroys God's temple, God will destroy that person' (5.16-17). The one who destroys the temple of God, the one who impugns its holiness, is not the one who builds with wood and straw – material that will be destroyed on the Day of the Lord – but the one who divides. The fate of those who boast in one leader rather than another (5.21-22) sounds considerably worse than the fate of the immoral person discussed earlier.

Ephraim Radner has been one of the most insistent proponents of something like this vision. 'Churches cannot properly put other churches out of communion with themselves, except according to worldly structures, because true communion – if providence is to have its say! – is in any case a matter of mutual suffering and is thus, paradoxically, embraced in its fullness precisely when communion's brokenness is purely suffered.'[59] He insists that 'The truthful witness of Jesus to the Father is given precisely in the refusal to part with the perpetrators of deceit and the willingness to share communion, in the literal sense even of the Lord's supper, with contradictors of

---

[58] In 1 Tim. 1.19-20, we find a similar harsh-worded exclusion, and it is similarly ordered towards the good of those excluded: 'By rejecting conscience, certain persons have suffered shipwreck in the faith; among them are Hymenaeus and Alexander, whom I have turned over to Satan, so that they may learn not to blaspheme.'

[59] Radner, *Hope among the Fragments*, 74.

that truth.'[60] Radner has in mind the specific narrative of Judas – the Judas who, already set upon his path of betrayal, is still welcomed to the table in the upper room, who still has his feet washed by Jesus, and who is still given the bread and wine, the body and blood of the one he is betraying. 'Judas', says Radner, 'is "one of us", not some other.'[61]

If this is the story of the church, then that story 'is the story of the self-giving of Jesus to the apostles and betrayers and indifferent altogether'.[62] 'Those who claim … that there are peculiar moments when the virtues of (doctrinal) truth claim precedence over the demands of (ecclesial) unity, or vice versa, are called to subject themselves to the shape of those Scriptural narratives that describe, in their corporate application, the form of Jesus' singular embrace of these two aspects together.'[63]

We do need to tread carefully at this point, however. On the one hand, I can insist at a high level of generality that all Christian disagreements are disagreements within the body of Christ. I can try to shift away from a pattern of imagination in which the history of doctrinal decisions marks out ever more precisely a territory separated from error. I can try to shift towards a picture in which those decisions mark out divisions across the body, always involving complex gains and losses, and always leaving misapprehension, disappointment and failure on both sides of the divide. I can try to shift towards a picture in which doctrinal decisions do not sever the bonds of mutual accountability.

On the other hand, Christians are, in practice, always negotiating specific forms of life in particular locales, with the resources we have available to us. We are always already engaged in a complex overlapping and nested set of contexts from the local to the global, caught in a web of existing relationships and responsibilities that pull us in multiple directions at once. We are engaged in trying to do justice, in the midst of all this, to whatever we believe we have already understood of God's abundant word spoken in Jesus, thanks to the Spirit's guidance. We are always engaged in drawing some kinds of boundaries, trying to exclude some kinds of speech and action from the life that we are negotiating. We are always faced with responding to the multiple forms of harm that we see being done by Christians in circles of which we are a part, and in others with which we have less to do: working out how to protect ourselves and others from them, how to avoid complicity in them, how to overcome them, how to protest against them. We always have limited resources of time, money, energy and emotional resilience to spend on all this work of negotiating a life together.

It makes sense for us in the midst of these negotiations to be eager to be drawn deeper into the abundant love of God by the work of the Spirit. It makes sense to deny that our location in the body has granted us any peculiar access to the Spirit, or given us peculiar possession of God's gift. It makes sense to refuse to countenance final separation from any of those involved in exploring the same gift, or to deny that the same Spirit is at work among them. It makes sense to believe that we are always called by the Spirit out beyond the confines of our current settlements, into engagement with others who will challenge, unsettle and enrich us in ways that we can't yet predict.

---

[60] Ibid., 116.
[61] Radner, *Brutal*, 120.
[62] Ibid., 153.
[63] Radner, *Hope*, 118.

We are, nevertheless, always having to make decisions about who to talk to, where to look, where to invest time and energy, and the costs that we and those around us can and should be asked to bear. We are always having to make fallible discernments about where it is that the Spirit might be leading us to look next. There is no route that will take us from where we are now to an overview, only a continued journeying in which what we have learnt will always be partial, always marked with attendant misapprehensions and insensitivities, and always still in need of gifts that lie beyond the boundaries we have drawn.[64]

Facing disagreement

Whatever the route we find ourselves taking, it will involve discovering how to live with, and learn from, Christians from whom we are at present deeply divided. In the remainder of this chapter, therefore, I am going to ask what help doctrinal theologians might be able to offer, as the church negotiates such disagreements. I should acknowledge straight away that, in relation to many disagreements, the answer may be 'very little indeed'. In fact, in many situations, the most appropriate ambition for doctrinal theologians may simply be, 'Try not to make things worse!' Nevertheless, there are times when they may have something more positive to contribute. I am going to look at four main possibilities: the resolution of a disagreement, persuasion across an intractable divide, receiving gifts across such a divide and promoting deeper understanding while such divides persist.

Though the differences that divide the church are multiple and entangled, I am for the sake of clarity going to work with a simplified picture: of two households, both alike in dignity, separated perhaps by ancient grudge or fresh mutiny but certainly by deep disagreement. I am thinking of a situation in which there is open dispute within the church, and in which that dispute has become so polarized that most participants see it as a battle between two sides (even if that actually means that a clear majority think themselves part of the small minority who stand somewhere in the middle). While recognizing how artificial this is, I will therefore speak, in this section, as if there were two reasonably well-defined 'traditions' in play: two communities or networks, with differing habits of thought, speech and action, different sensibilities and assumptions.

I am thinking of a situation in which the dispute between these two sides is stuck axle-deep in mud because they each have a different way of making up their minds. Within each tradition, different things are generally found salient, different patterns of argument are deployed and different languages of persuasion are spoken.[65]

I am imagining that, on both sides, there are doctrinal theologians. They are able to set out some of the reasons people have in their tradition for thinking and acting as they do, and some of their reasons for disagreeing with the other tradition. The accounts that these doctrinal theologians offer are of course their own creative construals, and

---

[64] I am grateful to Frances Clemson for helping me think through these issues.
[65] I explored some of this material in 'Making our minds up', *Kai Euthus*, 15 October 2017, mikehigton.org.uk/making-our-minds-up/ (accessed 6 December 2019).

they capture only something of their tradition's thinking, but I am imagining for now that their accounts are recognizable to many other members of their traditions.

I am imagining a situation in which the dispute between these traditions is sustained and pursued in part by a trade in doctrinal reasoning, even if that is mixed with other kinds of reason, exegetical, philosophical, historical and scientific, and even if much of what shapes people's minds happens somewhere to one side of reason. I am imagining people from both traditions presenting doctrinal claims and arguments in attempts to persuade the church in one direction or another.

In such a situation, there can be a temptation – an element of the intellectualism I discussed in Chapter 5 – for doctrinal theologians to think that their work will be able to resolve the dispute. Their concepts provide the tools needed to grasp what is going on, and the leverage needed to tip people towards consensus (if only people would pay sufficient attention). In a situation of intractable disagreement, however, even if their most lurid dreams of influence should come true doctrinal theologians will suffer from the same problem that afflicts everyone else. The doctrinal considerations that are telling for people on one side of the division will fail to persuade those on the other. The two sides appeal to different doctrinal statements, to different degrees, in different ways. They draw on doctrinal theologies that differ in method as well as substance. They disagree about doctrinal theology's proper sources, about the kind of exegesis that should underpin it and about what counts as a fundamental matter and what as a thing indifferent. Within each tradition, doctrinal argument is undertaken by different kinds of people, with different positions in relation to the wider life of the church, for different purposes. Doctrinal theology is no one thing, and it will seldom supply the missing discourse that allows intractably divided sides to argue to a settled conclusion.[66]

Worse still, attempts at doctrinal resolution sometimes make things worse. Many of the tools of doctrinal argument were forged as weapons. I noted earlier that the decisions involved in the development of doctrine tend to have demanded some level of commensuration: an attempt to find a set of common terms that can be used to name positions that are to be separated. In cases of intractable difference, however, the parties involved are unlikely to have agreed about these terms. One side, say, thinks that all sides' claims can be rephrased using the terms *physis* and *hypostasis*. Those on other sides may think, however, not that the formula that describes their positions in these terms should win, but that this whole way of framing the debate is wrongheaded. Doctrinal theology inherits multiple sets of terms that promise to allow commensuration and differentiation across a wide territory of disagreement – but that are themselves disputed. To think that these terms can be pressed into service to help secure consensus is often to mistake swords for ploughshares.

---

[66] Mallock, *Doctrine and Doctrinal Disruption*, 30–1, gave a description of debates in his own day which could well be applied to debates in ours: 'The magnitude of the differences between the doctrinal conclusions of our various Church parties is such as to show they must be due, largely if not entirely, to corresponding differences in the premises from which the various parties derive them.' '[E]ach school starts with some different conception of what the authorities and proofs are, from which the doctrines of Christianity are derived and by which their truth is established.'

Seeking resolution

Of course, some doctrinal disagreements do turn out to be resolvable at a propositional level, by theologians working with the church's existing doctrinal statements, and the logical elaborations to which they lend themselves. An effort at disambiguation, the clarification of terms, the specification of domains of applicability and the correction of erroneous inferences might be enough to allow claims previously thought incompatible to be integrated.

The embeddedness of these claims in the different patterns of life on either side of the debate might well, in such an approach, recede into the background – but that could be precisely the source of this approach's power. Theologians from both sides might construe their two traditions' complex patterns of Christian life, which in practice grate against one another in all kinds of awkward ways, as powered by commitment to two differing systems of doctrine. They might then demonstrate the conceptual compatibility of those systems, and perhaps issue some kind of joint declaration proclaiming their achievement. That might, conceivably, make it possible for inhabitants of those two traditions to imagine themselves with new force as sharing a common life. That might in turn unlock possibilities of practical coexistence previously thought unavailable. Of course, a lot will depend on how inhabitants of these two traditions relate to their theologians. It will depend on whether and in what way those theologians are understood to speak on behalf of the community, and on the patterns of deferral that link the believing of the wider community to them. Nevertheless, some genuine forms of resolution take this form.

Some doctrinal disagreements might be resolvable in a different way, especially when conceptual reconciliation is not obviously on offer. The doctrinal statements that seem to differ might be understood as rules for Christian practice. It might be argued that although these statements seem incompatible when considered in the abstract, when considered as instructions for practice they might prove compatible. I discussed earlier George Lindbeck's attempt to translate classical incarnational doctrine into regulative terms.[67] It is possible that more elaborate regulative interpretations could be given of, say, Chalcedonian Christology and of a monophysite alternative, and that we could discover that there was nothing about the first rule of life that would prevent someone who followed it from also committing to the second, and vice versa.

A regulative reconciliation like this would still be one carried out at the level of statements. It is now, however, statements in the form of rulings for practice that are to the fore, and the logic governing the reconciliation of such statements is distinctive, and requires some practical imagination as well as logical facility. No less than in cases of propositional reconciliation, however, the success of any such resolution will depend upon the attitudes of those involved in the divided life of the church to their doctrinal theologians' work. It would demand, in particular, that people on both sides recognized the regulative translation of their doctrine as capturing what mattered

---

[67] See ch. 6, pp. 113–14.

about it for them. Such a resolution might, nevertheless, sometimes unlock genuine possibilities of coexistence.[68]

Agreements of both kinds are possible, and they may at times be effective. The history of formal ecumenical dialogues might give us some reasons for hope, even if it also suggests that such strategies are not universal solvents, or at least that they are eating their way through the church's dividing walls only very slowly.

Persuasion

In less tractable disagreements, there may be no shared language within which the separated sides can pursue these kinds of resolution. However, the fact that it is possible for someone on one side of the debate to learn the language used by their opponents, and vice versa, might allow for certain forms of persuasion. It makes it possible, at least in principle, for inhabitants of each tradition to experiment in the other tradition's discourse, and so to try drawing members of that tradition closer from within.

Suppose that you and I inhabit opposing traditions. If I, as a doctrinal theologian, have articulated my tradition's stance, and displayed our grounds and modes of argument, you may see whether you can, using those grounds and modes, persuade me towards a conclusion closer to your position. I might try something similar in return. The articulation of reasons and patterns of argument in each case creates the possibility that we might temporarily inhabit each other's ways of reasoning – or at least inhabit a publicly available simulation of them. Doctrinal theology, precisely because it is a way of articulating our reasons and patterns of argument, might make such persuasion possible.[69]

This kind of persuasion can often be more complex, and more creative, however. As I articulate my tradition's position, I may present a tolerably clear sense of the norms underpinning it, of their ordering and interconnection. The processes by which that kind of articulation is developed, deployed and discussed are, however, inherently flexible. The life of Christian thought and speech is always richer than the doctrinal articulations in which we seek to capture it, and it is always more various. Even within a single tight-knit community it is likely that a range of articulations will circulate, differing visibly or invisibly, the more so if the tradition in question is lively and fractious. In fact, as a doctrinal theologian in a living tradition, I am likely to always hover between various overlapping ways of articulating it. Perhaps without noticing it, I will be capable of deploying subtly different articulations in different contexts. And each articulation, precisely by being made articulate, calls forth from within my own tradition revisions, improvements, criticisms and counterproposals. Those differing articulations will be likely to resemble one another in their identification and ordering of norms, but they won't coincide completely. I might, therefore, as a doctrinal theologian, try to speak for my tradition, and say, 'Here we stand!' – but on closer inspection 'here' will turn out to be the name of a complex space of possible positions.

---

[68] For an interesting attempt in this direction, see Alasdair Rogers thesis, cited in n. 13.
[69] See my discussion in *A Theology of Higher Education*, ch. 9, pp. 247–50.

If you are sufficiently attentive, you might see something of the complexity, mobility and uncertainty with which I and others in my tradition articulate our stance. You might see the disagreements that it generates, the confusions that it leaves in its wake, and you might decide to experiment with this mobility. You might play with the possibilities that we are already exploring in our tradition's conversations, perhaps even pushing further in directions we have already opened up, in order to see if you can argue from some version of this tradition that we might find recognizable to conclusions that you value for reasons internal to your own tradition. You might see, let us say, that we differ among ourselves in the extent to which we are willing to admit figural reading as a strategy for making sense of scripture, and you might push at the boundary of our conversation, suggesting still fuller versions of the figural approach, and rubbing away at the boundary we still tend to draw between the figural and the allegorical. You might, by means of such experimentation, be able to propose to us in our own terms an approach that resembles your tradition's full-blooded use of allegorical reading.[70]

Such approaches are not uncommon, and they can be powerful. It is perhaps worth noting, however, that they are beset by a problem, similar to the problem of apparent insincerity that I noted earlier.[71] Recognizing, at some level, that your way of making up your mind is different from mine, I may try to persuade you by arguing on what I understand to be your grounds, or something like them. Consciously or unconsciously, I might use forms of argument and cite kinds of evidence that resemble those I have seen you employing, even though they are not my own. Should you defeat those arguments, however, it will not change my commitment to my own position, because that position is not for me directly supported by the arguments that I have been using to sway you. From your point of view, I may then seem to lack integrity: to be refusing the consequences of the argumentative game I have agreed to play. Such accusations are common in situations of intractable disagreement.[72]

---

[70] I have been strongly influenced here by Menachem Fisch and Yitzakh Benbaji, *The View from Within: Normativity and the Limits of Self-Criticism* (Notre Dame, IN: University of Notre Dame Press, 2011). Fisch and Benbaji examine possibilities of argument between rival 'normative systems' in a scientific context. They explore what happens when an advocate of one system tries to persuade an advocate of another by arguing on that person's terms. 'She will try to frame her argument from a perspective as similar as possible to his, yet sufficiently (and subtly) different from it to enable her to make her case' (257). To hear such an argument can be transformative: 'What a good trusted critic allows us to experience and ponder is ... a significantly different yet recognisable *version of ourselves*' (264, emphasis in original). '[N]ormative criticism leveled at us by others allows us a glimpse, not merely of how we outwardly look or sound to them, but of how they think we think and should be thinking. The better informed and more trustworthy we deem them to be, the more profound the disorienting sense of self-estrangement they are capable of arousing' (250).

[71] See p. 174.

[72] Mallock, *Doctrinal Disruption*, 8–10, sees such questions of integrity arising in his context, with people of various parties in the Church of England all trying to demonstrate that the Articles supported or at least allowed their position, without necessarily resting anything upon that demonstration. Something similar is visible in some of the debates in my church about sexuality and gender, in which a lot of the argument takes place in exegetical terms, without those exegetical arguments mattering to all sides in the same way.

Receptivity

Alongside or instead of seeking resolution or persuasion, there is another stance I might take towards those on the other side of an intractable divide. I have been arguing that our separated positions are, in whatever flawed and broken ways, responses to the gift of God in Christ, into which the Christians on either side have been led by the Spirit (however wayward and erratic their following). If that is true, then it makes sense for me to face across the disagreements between us asking what there might yet be for me to receive from you of that abundant gift, even while our disagreements remain in place.

At this point, I draw inspiration from Receptive Ecumenism, a practice of ecumenical conversation in which agreement is not the main goal, and even the attempt to persuade one's conversation partners to move is not primary.[73] Paul Murray, whose work underpins Receptive Ecumenism, writes that 'ecumenical encounter, ecumenical engagement, ecumenical responsibility and calling can be privileged contexts for promoting the process of personal and ecclesial growth into more intensely configured communion in Christ and the Spirit'.[74] A Receptive Ecumenism is 'about the integral refreshment and renewal of what … one's community already has in the light of what can be appropriately received'.[75] The receptive approach is to ask, '"What, in any given situation, can one's own tradition appropriately learn with integrity from other traditions?" and, moreover, to ask this question without insisting, although certainly hoping, that these other traditions are also asking themselves the same question.'[76] The church, precisely because it is always being purified by the Spirit, 'can properly appreciate and receive from the aspects of catholicity present in other traditions which … may be being lived there more adequately'.[77] This is

> not about becoming less Catholic (or less Methodist, less Anglican, or whatever) … but about becoming more deeply, more richly, more fully Catholic (more fully Methodist, more fully Anglican, etc), precisely though a process of imaginatively explored and critically discerned receptive learning from others' particular gifts.

---

[73] Behind Receptive Ecumenism, I am also drawing on the inter-faith reading practice called Scriptural Reasoning. Nicholas Adams, 'Long-Term Disagreement: Philosophical Models in Scriptural Reasoning and Receptive Ecumenism', *Modern Theology* 29, no. 4 (2013): 154, argues that both Receptive Ecumenism and Scriptural Reasoning are 'strategies for dealing with long-term disagreement … that do not seek to preserve or promote such disagreement, but which face it in a non-utopian manner and seek to maintain a concern with truth while taking questions of tradition seriously'. See the chapters on Scriptural Reasoning in Higton and Muers, *The Text in Play*, ch. 8–16.

[74] Paul Murray, 'Receptive Ecumenism and Catholic Learning: Establishing the Agenda', in *Receptive Ecumenism and the Call to Catholic Learning: Exploring a Way for Contemporary Ecumenism*, ed. Paul Murray (Oxford: Oxford University Press, 2008), 7. See also his 'Living Catholicity Differently: On Growing into the Plenitudinous Plurality of Catholic Communion in God', in *Envisioning Futures for the Catholic Church*, ed. Staf Hellemans and Peter Jonkers (Washington, DC: The Council for Research in Values and Philosophy, 2018), 109–58. For a detailed discussion of Murray's thinking, see Greg Ryan, *Receptive Integrity and the Dynamics of Doctrine: A Study in the Hermeneutics of Catholic Ecclesial Learning* (PhD thesis, Durham University, 2018).

[75] Murray, 'Receptive Ecumenism', 8.

[76] Ibid., 12.

[77] Ibid., 13.

It is about the intensification, complexification, and further realization of Catholic identity, not its diminishment and loss.[78]

The simplest versions of such reception have a clear enough logic to them. You show me something that makes sense on your tradition's grounds, and I, with a mind formed within my own tradition, see it as attractive or telling. My eye is drawn, say, by your use of scripture to something that, by my own existing lights, I could and should take into account, even though I have not yet done so. Or perhaps you raise a question about practice that, even though I had not yet heard it posed from within my own tradition, makes quick sense in my tradition's own terms. There is no difficulty in accounting for this: in no living tradition has every claim been made or every question been asked that can already make sense in that tradition's terms.

The logic of reception goes deeper than this, however, as Murray suggests. Reception has 'the potential to take each tradition with integrity to a different place than at present; one resulting ... from the creative expansion of current logic rather than its mere clarification, extrapolation, and repetition'.[79] The scenario described in the previous paragraph left my tradition's patterns of reasoning undisturbed. Disturbance of those patterns might, however, be precisely what reception has to offer. As I attend to the way of being Christian fostered in your tradition, I might seek to imagine what it would be like to inhabit that way, or whether there are at least aspects of it that I can inhabit, and whether there are elements of it that I find attractive, even compelling. At the same time, I might also, as I described in the previous subsection, be imagining slightly different ways of construing my own tradition: slightly different ways of performing the creative task of summarizing and articulating the structures of our belief and the commitments that hold it in place. I might be involved in the mobile and disputatious processes of articulation sustained by my tradition, and know (or have a feel for) something of their latitude and their intransigence, their capacity to generate versions of myself between which I am not normally forced to choose. An element of your believing might, as it were, exercise a magnetic pull which draws me across the space of possible versions of myself that I already inhabit. I might find that I can justify adopting something from you if I inhabit some of those versions of my tradition but not others. Indeed, the very fact that I have seen that element of your tradition as attractive in the first place – the fact that I catch its scent, am tickled by its touch – might be a sign that I have already shifted my weight. I might already, perhaps in as yet unconscious ways, be sensing the world from one side of the space of possibilities that I have hitherto been inhabiting.

That space is defined by experimentation with different articulations of the norms of my tradition. To be drawn across that space might mean being drawn to less familiar, more playful articulations of those norms – and it might entice me to further experimentation in a similar direction. What happens if I reorder some of the norms that I have taken to underpin my tradition? What happens if I start seeing a particular norm as more local, more context-specific than I used to? What happens if I allow

---

[78] Ibid., 17.
[79] Ibid., 14.

another norm to weaken or even vanish? How recognizable would I still be to myself and to other members of my tradition? How much of what we care about could I still say? How much can I perhaps say even more clearly than before? What are the losses, and how much do they matter?

In the light of the account I have been giving in this book so far, I can understand such a process to be – potentially – a matter of catching a glimpse, hearing an echo, of something of the abundance of God's gift of love in Jesus, something that is new to me however deeply it has already shaped your own inhabitation of that gift. There is something new there that I might learn to see or hear, while remaining – just about – recognizable to myself. What I feel in that moment of attraction or compulsion might be the touch of the wings of the Spirit. I can't know that simply by the tug of attraction that I feel; there is still a process of discernment to go through, and even that does not pre-empt the Day in which the straw will be separated from the gold – but the possibility of movement is there.

Doctrinal theology can therefore at times play a destabilizing role, helping to clarify the ways in which a community does not occupy a punctiliar position in the landscape of Christian possibilities, but hovers over a neighbourhood of possibilities, of overlapping versions of itself. Doctrinal theology is powered by a kind of uncertainty principle, by which its attempts to pin down where exactly in this neighbourhood a community properly sits themselves generate responses which position the community differently. Articulation generates conversation that may perturb and extend the boundaries of possibility. Doctrinal theology can therefore help to enable the process by which a community is drawn, magnetically, to and beyond the edge of its current possibilities by something that has been glimpsed or heard in the life of its neighbours.

Doctrinal theology, then, can play a role in making the divisions between traditions porous, allowing the differing apprehensions of the Word that each tradition inhabits to circulate more freely around the body. We might learn to hear, even from a tradition that we continue to think deeply mistaken in its way of apprehending that abundant gift, something of that gift that we had not already taken in.[80]

Seeking understanding

Sometimes, the role that doctrinal theology can play will be more limited than all the options I have explored so far. There may be no visible routes open to resolution, to persuasion or even to reception. In such situations, the best that doctrinal theologians can do might simply be to pursue deeper understanding of the doctrinal traditions involved.[81] That does not mean simply learning to rehearse doctrinal claims made in one's own and others' traditions, or gaining a facility in comparing the propositions

---

[80] At times, the division between my own tradition and another will be so deep that the forms of holding together available to us will attenuate to little more than protest, and I may find that the only gift I can see how to receive from that tradition's grasp of the Word is to recognize in myself some echoes of the disastrous misapprehension I see written so clearly in it. The protest or avoidance which might be, for now, the dominant form of my relation to them remain, however, strategies undertaken within the body. Cf. Tanner, *Theories of Culture*, 154.

[81] Cf. Faith and Order Commission, *Communion and Disagreement*, §13.

involved.[82] To understand doctrinal claims more deeply, one's own and others', one needs to understand what Christians who hear the claim in question are being asked to think, say and do – and what it might look like in practice to heed this call. One needs to explore how the terms being used make sense in the context of a web of practices (or the overlap of various differing webs). One needs to see who makes these doctrinal claims, on whose behalf, within what networks of deferral, in what contexts, and for what purpose. One needs to understand what is being protected, and in what way is it seen as precious, or what is being attacked, and why is it seen as a threat. One needs to know what questions are being answered by the making of this claim.[83] One needs to grasp what attempts at commensuration (for the sake of alliance or separation) are involved. One needs to attend to the mobile variety of ways in which the tradition from which these claims come is being articulated: the differing ways in which the norms of that tradition are being identified and ordered. One needs to gain a sense for this tradition's flexibility, and its limits. One needs to know its live questions, its areas of perplexity, the unresolved alternatives that persist side by side within it.[84] One needs to look for the ways in which these doctrinal claims are supported, for their adherents, by more than visible evidence and explicit arguments, looking for the patterns of imagination, the shapes of feeling and the habituation to worry about some questions rather than others, which hold them in place. One needs to be alert to the ways in which those are knotted to gradients of privilege and power.

All these forms of understanding can be deepened by engagement across the boundaries of intractable disagreement. It is not just that it is hard to see the contours of one's own tradition until they are illuminated by the contrast of another; it is that the pull and push of what one finds attractive and repulsive in another tradition tug at the connections that hold one's own tradition together, and draw them into visibility.

---

[82] We should heed the advice of Mark Chapman, in the supporting papers for the report cited in the previous footnote, §4.3, that 'things are seldom what they seem'. We don't know what we are dealing with until we know how it is entangled with a community's whole life.

[83] '[Y]ou cannot find out what a man means by simply studying his spoken or written statements, even though he has spoken or written with perfect command of language and perfectly truthful intention. In order to find out his meaning you must also know what the question was (a question in his own mind, and presumed by him to be in yours) to which the thing he has said or written was meant to be an answer.' (R.G. Collingwood, *An Autobiography* (Oxford: Clarendon, 1978 (1939)), 31.) 'No two propositions can contradict one another unless they are answers to the same question' (ibid., 33). 'Meaning, agreement and contradiction, truth and falsehood, none of these belonged to propositions in their own right, propositions by themselves; they belonged only to propositions as the answers to questions' (ibid.). Cf. Anthony C. Thiselton, *The Hermeneutics of Doctrine* (Grand Rapids, MI: Eerdmans, 2007), 5. Liam J. Fraser, 'A Tradition in Crisis: Understanding and Repairing Division over Homosexuality in the Church of Scotland', *Scottish Journal of Theology* 69, no. 2 (2016): 155–70, provides a Collingwoodian analysis of disagreements about sexuality in the Church of Scotland.

[84] 'Angling for change, the theologian determines which theological materials do the most work in a particular theological configuration and how much interpretive leeway already surrounds them' (Tanner, *Theories of Culture*, 90). Nicholas Adams, in his discussion of Scriptural Reasoning and Receptive Ecumenism, suggests that one can pursue three grades of engagement. The first level 'is reached when a member of one tradition can rehearse the claims made by a member of another tradition', the second 'when a member of one tradition can identify and rehearse disagreements within another tradition', and the third 'when a member of one tradition is able to identify and rehearse the obscurities that mark another tradition' – the 'zones of experimentation, paradox and wilful self-contradiction' ('Long-term Disagreement', 169–70).

We can know any tradition – our own and others' – better in conversation than we can alone.[85]

Of course, this kind of deeper understanding of one's own tradition and of others won't necessarily make relations between traditions any easier; it won't necessarily do anything to remove the intractable differences that separate one group from another, or to help any of the traditions involved move or grow. It might very well make things more rather than less difficult. To the extent, however, that the patterns of doctrine that we explore really are ingredient in the life of the relevant communities, and to the extent that the kinds of understanding that we pursue spread, this kind of work might help overcome certain caricatures and misunderstandings – including those generated in the history of our doctrinal disputes. It might make the relationship more truthful, and it might allow certain kinds of recognition across our divides. It might enable one to see that one's interlocutors are not, in fact, playing badly the game that one is playing oneself, or playing it while refusing to abide by its rules; they are playing a different game altogether. It might enable members of one tradition to see the different way in which another is rooted (or in which its inhabitants can, with integrity, believe it to be rooted) in God's abundant word. It might enable one to see one's opponents' way of proceeding as an essay in faithfulness, however mistaken or distorted one continues to think the form that this faithfulness takes.

This kind of deeper understanding might, conceivably, if it spreads, change the texture of the possibilities for coexistence that members of the two traditions can register together. This, however, is where we reach the limits of the entirely artificial picture I have been using, of two traditions facing one another across a neat divide, effectively delegating management of that divide to their doctrinal theologians. That is very seldom how the life of the church works. The church is much more often faced, instead, with the complex practical task of negotiating overlapping and interacting forms of life, and with discovering how people who differ in complex ways can best share space with one another. Doctrinal theologians are largely, and rightly, bit-part players in these negotiations and discoveries.

What counts as a shared life is difficult to pin down. It depends on the context and on the scale to which we are attending. The kind of practical coexistence that one might find within a single congregation is different from the kind one might find within a number of congregations of different denominations working together in some locality. Both are different from the kind that one might find among people who belong to the same denomination but who are scattered over a wide geographical area. Understanding what 'shared life' means for any two groups of people is also inherently multifaceted. What resources – including property and money – are shared, and how?

---

[85] The bishops gathered at the second council of Constantinople in 553 recognized the necessity of debate: 'The truth cannot be made clear in any other way than when there are debates about questions of faith, since everyone requires the assistance of his neighbour' (cited in Pelikan, *Credo: Historical and Theological Guide to Creeds and Confessions of Faith in the Christian Tradition*, 186). A much later council echoed their words: '[I]t would probably be true to say that authority on the Church works *through* rather than in spite of disagreement' (*The Lambeth Conference 1988: The Reports, Resolutions and Pastoral Letters from the Bishops* (London: Church House Publishing, 1988), 104). See Radner, *Brutal Unity*, 303 for a caution about such claims.

Are there any shared processes for decision making? Do they have shared structures for ministry or leadership? Are these people able to celebrate the sacraments together, and do they do so in practice? Do they pray with one another? Are there common figures acknowledged as teachers? Do they work alongside one another, and, if so, on what? Do they use similar patterns of speech when talking about their faith? Are they able to argue with one another in such a way that they find at least some of each other's arguments telling? How dense is the network of relationships and interactions that joins members of one group to members of another, and what form do those relationships and interactions take? As Christians negotiate these questions together, their understanding of each other's doctrinal beliefs certainly can play a role – but it is only one thread in a complex tangle of considerations.[86]

Conclusion

In a divided church, what one hopes for from doctrinal theologians will be limited.

For one thing, doctrinal theology is only one ministry among others in the body of Christ. For another, it is not easy to predict the role played in the life of that body by theologians' articulations and discoveries. It will depend upon the nature of their authority, on the patterns of deferral within which they are situated, on the recognizability to their community of what they say, and on the processes of reception by which their contributions might spread and mutate.[87] For another, doctrinal theology, at its best, captures only some aspects of a particular tradition's life. It attempts to summarize and articulate the truths by which members of that tradition understand themselves to be bound. It expresses something of what they see of the one word of God from within their tradition – what they express and seek to hold themselves accountable to by their doctrinal formulations. The life that is being summarized and articulated, however, always exceeds the doctrinal diagram drawn of it. It is shaped by connections and by possibilities, by features of God's abundant gift, that the doctrinal theologian simply does not register. To argue about the compatibility of doctrinal systems is only ever a partial proxy for the discovery of possibilities of coexistence between forms of Christian life and of fruitful discovery together of the abundance of God's love.

Sometimes, the contribution of doctrinal theologians to such engagements will be worse than a distraction. Our doctrinal language has been shaped by conflict, and is oriented towards separation. We deploy schemes of categories that we take to be calmly comprehensive, but we forget the histories of dispute and exclusion from which these schemes come. The joy of learning and deploying doctrinal language is mixed. It combines a joy in the features of God's gift that those words allow one to name and to celebrate, and a more dangerous joy in purity and separation.

Doctrinal theology can therefore be thought of as suspended between two forms of the passion for truth. On the one hand, there is a passion to hold fast to what we have

---

[86] Cf. Radner, *Brutal Unity*, 170, 221–67; Faith and Order Commission, *Communion and Disagreement*, §43.
[87] Cf. Fisch and Benbaji, *View*, 292.

been shown, both to the features of the truth that have become visible to us and the forms of error that we have learnt to identify and to avoid.

Yet as doctrinal theologians in a polycentric church and a divided church, none of us stands in or speaks on behalf of the centre. We each stand in one peripheral, diasporic territory, one failed experiment among others. We stand within particular Christian communities, each shaped by what it has truly received of God's gift in Christ, but each also shaped by what we have missed, and what we have misunderstood. On the other hand, therefore, doctrinal theology is properly marked by a hunger oriented towards the abundance of God's gift, its infinite exceeding of our grasp. And that abundance is, in part, reflected or exhibited in the diversity of the church – for all its many failings and errors. It is echoed in the diverse church's capacity to surprise, unsettle, disturb, challenge and excite. Each of our traditions stands in need of the rest of this body, and of the gifts that our fellow members bear. We witness to the truth that exceeds us, the truth of the Word to which we are all accountable, by holding together, searching for the gifts that we might have to receive from one another. In always contingent and ramshackle configurations, the product of happenstance, self-protection and the limitations of our resources as much as of any carefully planned engagement, we hold on to one another as a way of waiting upon the Spirit, holding on for a blessing.

There is therefore a proper curiosity to doctrinal theology, a pleasure in encounter and discovery, which will and should always be looking beyond the boundaries erected by our doctrinal decisions, with a magpie's eye for the glint of something bright that has not yet been grasped. In the conditions of confusion in which we all live, it might even be that my neighbours' error – a real error, one that does real harm – anchors their capacity to see something in the Word that I have missed, or to see the error in my own way of seeing. We should not so hold on to what we believe we have already been shown as to defend ourselves from all possibility of seeing more.

This is the deeper reality pointed to by Vincent of Lérins, when he declared that Christian truth is that which is taught *ubique semper, et ab omnibus*; everywhere, always and by everyone.[88] For Vincent, this meant that, as Thomas Guarino puts it, we will not find the truth by looking to teachings 'confined to one geographical area, to one time period, or to a small group of believers'; heresy is characteristically innovative, and local.[89] The thoroughly non-Vincentian recognition that, in fact, *all* Christian teaching is innovative and local need not lead us to abandon his insight altogether. It really is the whole body constituted by this polycentric diversity – everyone, everywhere, always – that is the form taken in the world by the imperfect, error-riddled and fissile but rich, complex and beautiful apprehension of God's abundant gift in Christ.[90]

---

[88] Vincent of Lérins, *Commonitorium* 2.5, cited in Thomas C. Guarino, *Vincent of Lérins and the Development of Christian Doctrine* (Grand Rapids, MI: Baker Academic, 2013), 4.
[89] Guarino, *Vincent*, 5, 11.
[90] Flett, *Apostolicity*, 321, writes that 'the multiple histories of world Christianity find their possibility in the one history of Jesus Christ, for in this history they are redeemed. It is in the integration of particular histories in the one living history of Jesus Christ that the community provisionally represents the alteration of the world that has taken place in him.'

9

Doctrine and change

Introduction

With all its divisions, and in all its diversity, the Christian church is being beckoned by the Spirit into the discovery of God's abundant gift in Jesus Christ. Its life is a collection of experiments in which the abundant love of God is explored and embodied. Yet in every part of the church the reception and embodiment of that gift is partial and fallible, damaged and damaging. In Chapter 8, I argued that each part of the church therefore stands in need of the challenge and gift of every other. The Spirit also, however, beckons the church further up and further in to this abundant gift by beckoning it to the margins of its current existence, and on out into the world. The Spirit continually draws the church into fresh contexts and relationships, which call for new responses, new experiments in love. And in each such experiment the church can learn to grasp differently its inheritance of faith. That is the subject of the present chapter.

When Christians heed the call of the Spirit, their journey into the abundance of God's gift is not always smooth. It does not always take the form of new wisdom and insight added to old. Often, a Christian community discovers as it moves that it has been passing on a broken inheritance, and its journey takes the form of turning, of conversion. Even then, however, the next step at any given moment is made possible – and has to be made possible – by what has gone before. It is as people formed by their histories, by the faith passed on to them in all its ambivalence, that members of the church sense where next they might put their feet. And that is true even when they find themselves called to change that upsets the very terms in which they currently name their faithfulness.

I am reluctant to call such change the 'development of doctrine'. That phrase can suggest that doctrine changes according to some dynamism of its own – deductive, organic or dialectical. It tends to suggest, in other words, that it is primarily the doctrine that does the developing. It is, however, the church that changes, as it is drawn by the Spirit into new configurations in new times and places, in new encounters and in response to new challenges. Those within it who engage in doctrinal thinking, or who produce and consume doctrinal statements, get caught up in such change, their work sometimes enabling and sometimes impeding it.[1]

---

[1] Given that the life of the church is the embodiment of its exegesis, we can also think of the development of doctrine as the history of the reading and re-reading of scripture. Cf. Bradford Hinze, 'Narrative Contexts, Doctrinal Reform', *Theological Studies* 51 (1990): 418.

In this chapter, I will be asking what it means for this changing church to be faithful to the God who called it into being. I will argue that it always includes both faithfulness to what God has already enabled the church to know and faithfulness to the God who always has more to give. I will begin with the sinfulness of the church, which both makes change necessary and makes it difficult. It is not simply that there are many sinful people within the church, who neglect or refuse to follow its teachings; it is not simply that the church fails to live up to what it knows. Rather, the church in all its instantiations, in every time and place, is sinful even in its teachings and the central practices that surround them. What the church passes on, even at its best, is both damaged and damaging. To illustrate this claim, I will look at George Lindbeck's account of supersessionism: a murderous distortion, passed on not just in the aberrant action of some Christians, but deep in the doctrinal grammar of the church, and crying out for reformation.

I then distinguish between forms of change that the church in any given place already, in principle, knows how to pursue and forms that it does not yet know, and needs to be taught. The church in any of its settlements already has access to disciplines of attention, of self-criticism and of learning that in various ways enable it to change, aligning itself more fully to what it can already see of God's gift in Jesus. But there is always more to that gift than the church can yet see, and God can call the church into that excess by calling it out beyond its current disciplines. In language I develop in dialogue with Karl Barth, I argue that the church therefore lives both under discipline and under judgement – or rather, that it lives in the space between its existing disciplines and the Spirit's interruption of its life.

I next turn to a trio of authors each of whom calls the church to inhabit that space in a particular way, and each of whom can expand our sense of the possible prompts, dynamics and character of doctrinal change. I look at the work of David Ford, who describes Christian wisdom developing in response to cries that erupt wherever life exceeds our existing framings – and who, although he focuses on cries of suffering, also points to cries of joy and wonder as drivers of the church's rethinking of its tradition. I look at Linn Marie Tonstad's critique of the masculinist assumptions knotted into the church's trinitarian language, and at her call to the church to turn from a dogged reproduction of what it already knows towards a delighted openness to difference. And I look at Willie James Jennings's call to root out the racism and imperialism that are borne by the doctrinal heritage of the European church, and at the role of intimacy in making such change possible.

Finally, I try to gather together and line up all the hares that these various explorations have set running. The kinds of change that I am trying to describe are triggered when Christians in some particular time and place sense that God might be calling their church forward, speaking to it through cries, through encounters, and through improvisations. The challenges and changes set off by this call can provoke a creative re-construal of their church's belief – an attempt to understand what in that belief is deeper and what shallower, and to re-evaluate the latter in terms of the former. Those re-construals in turn provoke processes of reception, in which members of this church discover whether, as they learn to inhabit some new construal, they are still recognizable to themselves as disciples of the same Jesus. In this way, challenges heard from beyond the life of their church, or from what many of its members currently think of as its margins, can become internal. They can become challenges that this church learns to speak to itself, and to recognize as calls into a deeper faithfulness than it knew. The call out into the world can be a call further up and further in to the word that God spoke to the world in the life, death and resurrection of Jesus, who was and is and is to come.

I finish by discussing where, exactly, doctrinal theologians might fit in this whole picture of change. I will suggest that they are not normally its heroes, but that they can play supporting roles in the story, for good or ill. I will ask what the temptations and possibilities are that face them as they pursue those roles, and I will suggest that they can, at their best, help the church to articulate what it already knows, help it playfully to explore possible re-orderings of that knowledge, and help it listen out for the call of God luring the church beyond that knowledge, further up and further in to God's abundant life.

Reforming the sinful church

The church is sinful. That sinfulness is not simply a matter of particular individuals and groups departing from the inheritance of faith. It is a matter of distortions passed on in and with that inheritance. In any given time and place, the church's teaching, the church's deep habits, the things that the church believes it knows about God – all that the church diligently passes on is, in part, damaged and damaging.[2] It has been and is frequently murderous. Lauren Winner argues that there are 'deformations of Christian practices that are characteristic of the practices themselves', deformations that those practices attract, and are prone to pass on – 'because nothing apart from God (not church, not sacraments, not saints) is exempt from the damage produced by the Fall'.[3] Diligent pursuit of the church's inherited practices and diligent internalization of its teachings are not themselves a sufficient bulwark against sin; they can be the very means by which it takes deeper root.[4]

The church is always, in its practices, passing on more than it knows, and less than it hopes. Luke Bretherton writes, for instance, of the ways in which, in many contexts, the church's liturgy 'reproduces and reinforces class conflict';[5] a matter of 'how we sit, talk, dress, and comport ourselves, as well as what and where we sing, read, and speak in

---

[2] Cf. Healy, *Church, World and the Christian Life*, 17.
[3] Lauren F. Winner, *The Dangers of Christian Practice: On Wayward Gifts, Characteristic Damage, and Sin* (New Haven, CT: Yale University Press, 2018), 14, 16.
[4] Winner speaks, for instance, of 'the curious optimism, almost magical thinking' by which some postliberal theologians 'ask the Eucharist to do a lot of work: to make possible a set of behaviours and actions that are decidedly at odds with the behaviours and actions invited by late capitalism and her coercive handmaiden, the nation state; to make possible hospitality, abundance, and peace' (ibid., 40).
[5] Luke Bretherton, 'Sharing Peace: Class, Hierarchy, and Christian Social Order', in *The Blackwell Companion to Christian Ethics*, 2nd edn, ed. Stanley Hauerwas and Samuel Wells (Oxford: Blackwell, 2011), 337.

worship'.⁶ He writes that 'Class as a phenomenon directly affects our common worship, as the form, timing, order, language and aesthetic of worship are often determined in unacknowledged ways by class rather than theological commitments.'⁷ The final clause of that sentence, however, suggests too easy an escape route. In most of these contexts, the church's theological commitments, too, are shaped by class. Theology's attempts to shape the church reproduce and reinforce class conflict, as well as many other forms of distortion.

Ephraim Radner presses this point in relation to the Rwandan genocide. 'There is no longer any question', he writes, 'but that elements of Christian theological understanding and practice – and not only discrete (and somehow Christianly uninformed) acts by Christians – motivated these killings, if in ways that were hardly exhaustive.'⁸ We cannot free the church from sin simply by insisting on the diligent pursuit of its core practices, not even the church's forms of self-scrutiny and repentance. As Winner says, even 'repentance has its own deformations'.⁹

Doctrinal claims, and doctrinal theology, insofar as they are means that the church in any given time and place employs to help hold in place and to pass on what it thinks it has received, stand under the same judgement. They help to reproduce the existing life of the church and so to propagate all the distortions that afflict our vision, and to reinforce the damage that we do.¹⁰

George Lindbeck

One account of the sinfulness of the church can be found, perhaps surprisingly, in the work of George Lindbeck – surprisingly, that is, given his reputation as a theologian interested in holding in place the patterns of the church's life. Lindbeck both identifies a particular pattern of sin deeply rooted in the life of the church and argues that this pattern has prevented the church taking its own sinfulness seriously.¹¹

As we have seen, Lindbeck argues that classic incarnational doctrine calls the church to participate in an ongoing tradition of Christian reading. In that reading,

---

⁶ Bretherton, 'Sharing Peace', 337. Cf. John Flett's description, *Apostolicity*, 29, of what is passed on by Western church: a foreignness in 'dress, liturgy, order, architecture and the framing of space, patterns of ministry, hymnology, theological questions and idiom, and even the imported structures of schism'; 'the institutions regarded as basic to the visible continuity of the church are, in fact, derived from Western culture.'

⁷ Bretherton, 'Sharing Peace', 331.

⁸ Radner, *A Brutal Unity*, 39.

⁹ Winner, *Dangers*, 157. Not even lament is exempt (160). Nicholas Healy notes that although there are many ways for individuals to acknowledge their sin, 'there are few social practices which embody and make public the church's belief in its corporate sinfulness, whereby it could witness to its dependence solely upon the cross of Jesus Christ' (*Church, World*, 12).

¹⁰ The Church of England's *Articles of Religion* say of General Councils – those bodies that have defined the church's doctrine – that, 'when they be gathered together (forasmuch as they be an assembly of men, whereof all be not governed with the Spirit and Word of God,) they may err, and sometimes have erred, even in things pertaining unto God'. From Article XXI; available online at www.churchofengland.org/prayer-and-worship/worship-texts-and-resources/book-common-prayer/articles-religion (accessed 9 December 2019).

¹¹ I developed some of the material in this section in 'George Lindbeck and the Christological Nature of Doctrine', 47–62.

the Jesus whose identity is rendered in the gospels is understood as 'the unsurpassable and irreplaceable clue to who and what the God of Israel and the universe is'.[12] To read in this way involves Christians reading themselves into the story set out in the bible. Lindbeck certainly supposes that this practice of reading will be a dynamic affair, because 'the worlds in which we live change. They need to be inscribed anew into the world of the text'.[13] Nevertheless, much of the time it sounds as though the church is already in secure possession of that 'world of the text' and so of the criteria by which all those changes can be judged.

At the heart of his work in the years after *The Nature of Doctrine*, however, is a passionate plea for change to the patterns of Christian reading. He insists that, in order to continue faithfully as followers of Jesus, Christians need now to rethink how they read their own story in relation to the story of Israel. The God of Jesus Christ is both the God of the church and the God of Israel, and some account of the church's relation to Israel is therefore unavoidable in Christian theology. In the present post-Holocaust situation, however, it has become appallingly clear just how murderous many of the dominant accounts of that relationship are. They have, for much of the history of the Christian church, underwritten widespread and inventive cruelty; they have fostered lies, thefts, evictions, oppression, murder and torture, and they have taught their perpetrators to see them as righteousness. Continuing to read faithfully as followers of Jesus in the light of that belated and horrific realization requires the church to turn decisively and penitently against those dominant accounts. The church must repent of its supersessionism.[14]

This claim has deep roots in Lindbeck's work. As far back as the 1960s, when looking for ways of making sense of the church's post-Christendom situation, he had been attracted by the Second Vatican Council's emphasis on the church as the people of God. He warmed to the idea that 'the church is the people of God in the same thoroughly concrete way that Israel is'.[15] As his thought became more explicitly scriptural from the time of *The Nature of Doctrine* onwards, this morphed into an emphasis on 'the messianic pilgrim people of God typologically shaped by Israel's story', and on the insistence that God, in gathering the church, is 'doing in this time between the times what he has done before: choosing and guiding a people to be a sign and witness in all that it is and does, whether obediently or disobediently, to who and what he is'.[16]

It is impossible to explore those kinds of claim in any depth, however, without facing the question of the church's relationship to Judaism. Lindbeck became convinced that two quite different answers to this question have structured Christian life, and Christian

---

[12] Lindbeck, 'The Story-shaped Church', 164.
[13] George A. Lindbeck, 'Barth and Textuality', *Theology Today* 43, no. 3 (October 1986): 375.
[14] Cf. Bradford Hinze, 'Ecclesial Repentance and the Demands of Dialogue', *Theological Studies* 61 (2000): 237, and Radner, *Church*, 9, 127.
[15] George A. Lindbeck, 'Ecclesiology and Roman Catholic Renewal', in *New Theology 2*, ed. Martin Marty and Dean Peerman (New York, NY: Macmillan, 1965), 194; cf. 'A Protestant View of the Ecclesiological Status of the Roman Church', *The Journal of Ecumenical Studies* 1 (1964): 249. See also my discussion of Lindbeck's catholic sectarianism in 'Reconstructing *The Nature of Doctrine*', 11–12.
[16] Lindbeck, 'The Church', in his *The Church in a Postliberal Age*, ed. James J. Buckley (Grand Rapids, MI: Eerdmans, 2002), 146, 157.

practices of reading. In the first, Christians regard themselves as sharing (rather than fulfilling) the story of Israel. Israel and the church are not related as type and antitype, but rather 'the kingdom already present in Christ alone is the antitype, and both Israel and the church are types'. The creation of the church is 'not the formation of a new people but the enlargement of the old'.[17] Yes, in this pattern, the Jews are an unfaithful people – but so is the church. Yes, in this pattern, the church is the recipient of God's irrevocable promises, of God's Spirit, of God's gracious acceptance – but so are the Jews.

Lindbeck tells the story, however, of the emergence of a second answer in place of the first. In this second answer, the church is the antitype of Israel as type. Israel is faithless, the church faithful; Israel rejects grace, the church basks in it; Israel lacks the Spirit, the church is the Spirit's community. And this construal, which became the dominant one for most of Christian history, has had 'monstrous offspring'.[18] It entails the denial that, after the coming of Christ, Jews outside the church are the people of God. The church's *appropriation* of the story of Israel becomes *expropriation* – and violent expropriation at that. And this makes possible 'the ecclesiological triumphalism of a *theologiae gloriae*' in which the church's purity is emphasized by contrast with Israel's sinfulness.[19] It fosters so close an identification between Christ and the church that Christ's capacity to challenge the church is muted, his lordship over the church undermined.[20] The church claims to speak for Christ while ignoring his voice, and claims to act for him while murdering his kin.

Lindbeck insists that this second, supersessionist pattern of reading must be rejected in favour of a version of the first, in which the church joins Israel, alongside the Jews.

> Israel's Messiah, Jesus the Christ, has made it possible for gentiles while remaining gentiles to become citizens of the enlarged commonwealth of Israel. ... Israel does not 'rise to life in the church' (as Barth supersessionistically puts it), but rather the church of Jews and Gentiles exists as a transforming and serving movement within the messianically enlarged Israel in this time between the times. ... One might say that the church ... exists for Israel, not Israel for the church.[21]

For Lindbeck, we are now in a position to see that some such decision is needed both to repair the deadly sinfulness of the church's attitude to Jews and to clarify and secure the church's basic affirmation that Jesus is Lord. It is needed to avoid a theology of glory in which trust in Christ alone is displaced by trust in the church. Lindbeck believes that, by attending to the cry of Jewish people, and seeing the harm that has been done

---

[17] Ibid., 166, 168.
[18] Lindbeck, 'The Story-shaped Church', 171; see also 'The Church as Israel: Ecclesiology and Ecumenism', in *Jews and Christians: People of God*, ed. Carl E. Braaten and Robert W. Jenson (Grand Rapids, MI: Wm. B. Eerdmans, 2003), 78–94.
[19] George A. Lindbeck, 'Ecumenical Directions and Confessional Construals', *Dialog* 30, no. 2 (1991): 120.
[20] Ephraim Radner, in *Brutal Unity*, 124, makes a similar case.
[21] Lindbeck, 'Response to Michael Wyschogrod's "Letter to a Friend"', *Modern Theology* 11, no. 2 (1995): 206–7.

to them by the teaching and practice of the church, the church can be drawn not away from but deeper in to the gift of God in Jesus Christ.[22]

For my purposes in this chapter, three things are salient about Lindbeck's call to overcome supersessionism. First, it is a call for change that reaches deep into the patterns of the church's teaching. It calls for the overthrow of a structure of thought that has, for most of Christian history, and in most places where the church has taken root, been a deep but deadly shape of the church's inhabited grammar.

Second, it is a call to rediscover a pattern of thought that allows the sinfulness of the church to be acknowledged. It draws attention to the way in which the church has maintained its sense of purity by projecting faithlessness onto Israel, and then onto countless others that were read into Israel's position – all too often with similarly deadly consequences. As Radner notes, Israel has since at least the fourth century been used 'as the type for the Church's heretical offspring and enemies'.[23] The very form of the doctrinal tradition, insofar as it involves the marking out of the space of the church's purity by means of the identification of heresy, is challenged by the repudiation of supersessionism.

Third, Lindbeck's call for change is driven both by the cries of Jewish suffering and by what he discovers in Christian scripture and tradition when he examines them in the light of those cries. Here, however, I want to draw attention to a lack in Lindbeck's approach. The response to supersessionism that he advocates is very largely generated by Christian reflection. The 'Jews' who appear in that response are still Jews defined by a story told by Christians – albeit now a story less horrific than the ones Christians have told in the past. There is no space left open for Jewish people to interrupt the claims made on their behalf with claims of their own – claims about their faithfulness and sinfulness, their relation to the Spirit and to God's promises, or their understanding of where Christians fit within Jewish stories. Lindbeck's is certainly a repair of the Christian tradition prompted by Jews, and oriented towards Jews – but it is not a repair carried out in the company of Jews.[24] In this regard, as later portions of this chapter will show, Lindbeck's approach to repair itself stands in need of repair.

Diligence and disruption

The kind of change that Lindbeck sets out, and more generally the kind that I have in mind in this chapter, does not involve starting again from scratch. It does not declare a year zero. Change happens in the midst of things. It is made possible in part by our existing habits, and by what they have enabled us to see or hear of God's gift. We can only see with the eyes, or hear with the ears, that we have been given. And yet the

---

[22] For Peter Ochs, this is central to Lindbeck's postliberalism: 'His surprising discovery is that the church can neither repair its relation to the academy nor achieve ecclesial unity until it repairs its relation to the people Israel' (*Another Reformation: Postliberal Christianity and the Jews* (Grand Rapids, MI: Baker Academic, 2011), 39).
[23] Radner, *Brutal Unity*, 80. Radner traces this move back to Epiphanius's *Panarion*, written in the last quarter of the fourth century.
[24] Cf. Ochs, *Another Reformation*, 28.

change made possibly by our inheritance might be a change that challenges deeply what we have inherited – a change that calls us to see and hear very differently.[25]

There are some straightforward ways in which our Christian formation can enable us to see or hear challenges, interruptions and surprises. We inherit practices of attention that, if pursued with the diligence that our traditions try to teach us, do bring us up against difficult and demanding material. Most obviously, we inherit practices of reading that bring us up against the angular surface of scripture. And we inherit practices of self-examination and of repentance that ask us to amend our lives in the light of what our attention discovers.

To the extent that our doctrinal theologies help to hold in place such practices of attention, self-examination and penitence, they bind us in to a life of ongoing conversion. 'A creed', says John Webster, 'does not ensure the church's safety from interruption – quite the opposite: it exposes the church to the need for an unceasing renewal of confession of the gospel, of hearing, obedience, and acknowledgement of that which the formula indicates.'[26] Some change in the church can be driven by diligent pursuit of just those disciplines that the church already knows.

Sometimes, however, as with Lindbeck and supersessionism, our formation enables us to hear challenges in a different way. To an extent, any formation that we have received teaches us what to expect. We inherit a loose set of narratives, schemas, patterns and systems within which we can (roughly and flexibly, most of the time) arrange what we know of our lives, what we encounter in the world and what we discover in our texts. Precisely by teaching us such expectations, however, our formation can allow us to register – with more or less discomfort or dissonance – something that does not fit. Of course, we also inherit, and are diligent in pursuing, any number of strategies for ignoring exceptions, or for squeezing unruly realities into our more familiar categories. There is nothing inevitable about our capacity to acknowledge the awkward, and our inventiveness when our comfort is at stake is boundless. Nevertheless, the possibility is there, shadowing more or less visibly the formation of our expectations, of noticing what we did not expect – potentially tipping us into a questioning and rethinking of what we have received.[27] Lindbeck's search for a response to the cries of Jewish suffering might be seen as one such example.

This suggests, in a way that I hope the rest of this chapter will justify, that Christians need to adopt a double attitude towards the formation that we have received.[28] On the

---

[25] Daniel Hardy, speaking specifically of Anglicans, writes that 'Our way is to take things as we find them and then work in relation to them ... a willingness to live within the historical situation in which the Church finds itself, and to wait for change to come through the long term of history.' (Hardy, with Deborah Hardy Ford et al., *Wording a Radiance*, 76).

[26] John Webster, 'Confession and Confessions', 123.

[27] Philip Ziegler writes: 'A Christian theology funded by a fresh hearing of New Testament apocalyptic will stress the unexpected, new, and disjunctive character of the divine work of salvation that comes on the world of sin in and through Christ.' (*Militant Grace: The Apocalyptic Turn and the Future of Christian Theology* (Grand Rapids, MI: Baker Academic, 2018), 27). He stresses that this re-hearing of the New Testament can drive change that is not a matter of 'mere repair, development, or incremental improvement within a broadly stable situation' (28).

[28] Basil Mitchell, 'I Believe, We Believe', in The Doctrine Commission of the Church of England, *Christian Believing: The Nature of the Christian Faith and Its Expression in Holy Scripture and Creeds* (London: SPCK, 1976), 21, writes that 'The individual believer's commitment to the tradition and

one hand, we have to trust what we have received – to trust that the Spirit has been at work in the processes by which this tradition was formed and by which it has formed us, and to trust that we have not been rendered wholly insensitive, but have indeed been enabled to hear, see or sense something of God's gift in Christ. To trust what we have received is to trust that we have already grasped something of God's gift, and to commit ourselves to it in faithful determination. We have been shown something of God's love, and what we have been shown helps us to make some sense of our existence.[29]

On the other hand, we need to accept that our current grasp of God's gift is partial and distorted.[30] However diligent we may have been in holding fast to what we have been shown, however faithfully determined, we are not freed from the fact that all our understanding is marbled with sin. The church in every time and place is broken; it inhabits teachings and practices that do harm. In facing what we have inherited and are passing on, it is therefore necessary to be sharply suspicious. In binding ourselves to what we think we have heard from God, we might be (and in some ways certainly will be) binding ourselves to idols.

If we look at this double attitude simply in relation to the tradition within which we stand, it may seem like a paradox. We are called both to trust and to be suspicious of that tradition, caught like a Pushmi-pullyu between opposing demands. Our trust, however, is properly not in our tradition or in our theology but in God. We trust the giver. Trusting the giver implies trust in the gift given, but it does not imply unqualified trust in any aspect of our reception of that gift. We can, instead, trust the giver both to give and to judge and repair our reception of the gift. Both our holding fast to our formation and our openness to judgement breaking out against it are forms of our one trust in God, and the instability with which we are saddled by this tension is a proper consequence of our trust in God.

Another way of grasping the connection between the two aspects of this attitude is to ask what distortions stand on either side of it. In one direction stands an easily imaginable overconfidence in what we have grasped of God's gift. Trust in God can become, by easy steps in that direction, trust in ourselves. Yet in the other direction, even if a little more obscurely, a very similar overconfidence waits: the belief that we

---

the Church's commitment to it both involve a certain acceptance of the provisional nature of what is believed, together with an underlying faith in the truth it is believed to point to.'

[29] Romand Coles, *Beyond Gated Politics: Reflections for the Possibility of Democracy* (Minneapolis, MN: University of Minnesota Press, 2005), xiii, sets out a similar pattern of thought not in relation to the Christian tradition (he is not a theologian), but in relation to the radical democratic tradition: 'I am particularly interested in the tensions between cultivating what appears to be the best of the received wisdom of a tradition and cultivating a readiness for reformation in the face of others and new circumstances. In the stretching that occurs when we are discrepantly drawn by different considerations, concerns, insights, and bodily locations, our receptive capacities can acquire a depth, multidimensionality, and supple mobility without which we tend to do poorly in our relations with others.'

[30] Colin Gunton, 'Dogma, the Church and the Task of Theology', 16, sees dogmas as 'acts of faith on the part of the church whose coherence with one another and with Scripture can only be decided provisionally; that is, under eschatological proviso'. The Doctrine Commission of the Church of England, 'We Believe in God', in *Contemporary Doctrine Classics from the Church of England*, 12, insists that the interaction of revelation, reason and experience will always 'yield only a provisional result, since the conversation is still ongoing and will continue to do so for as long as the Church exists'.

already securely possess some other standard by which the deliveries of our faith can be judged and sorted, that we already know quite well enough how to identify and to eradicate the distortions present in our inheritance.[31] The unstable centre is where we land when we turn away from both of these forms of trust in ourselves.

Our doctrinal language is caught up in this tension. On the one hand, it is supposed to be an identification of the deepest context for our lives, and so of the deepest bases for our judgement. Rowan Williams writes that

> If we treat our doctrinal language as revisable in the same sense as our talk about polity, we risk treating our human ends as negotiable, as potentially under human control or at the mercy of human circumstance. ... Doctrine is about our end (and our beginning); about what in our humanity is not negotiable, dispensable, vulnerable to revision according to political convenience or cultural chance and fashion.[32]

Yet that does not mean that we are left with nothing but the stable deliveries of our faith. Later in the same book, Williams writes that

> There can be an assumption that scriptural or doctrinal language stands before us as straightforwardly the product of a process now definitively past ... [but] this will tend to neglect the unfinished business of the tradition's language, the questions and issues raised in a process that does not find a simple closure in the production of the formulae. When that unfinished business is recognised, Scripture and Creed become something more like reports of where the labour has arrived so far within a project that continues.[33]

Karl Barth

Something like this double attitude is displayed in the opening pages of Karl Barth's *Church Dogmatics*. The first volume opens with the thesis statement: 'As a theological

---

[31] Carl Braaten, 'The Role of Dogma in Church and Theology', in *The Task of Theology Today*, ed. Victor Pfitzner and Hilary Regan (Edinburgh: T&T Clark, 1998), 26, warns against making the facilitation of emancipation, rather than faithfulness to Christ, the core criterion of doctrinal truth. I would rather warn against the assumption that we already know in full what emancipation means. Trust in Christ is precisely the trust that we are being taught the nature of emancipation as the Spirit leads us on into reception of God's gift of love in Jesus. Subject to that proviso, facilitation of emancipation, as the Spirit has so far led us to grasp it, certainly is a criterion for doctrinal truth.

[32] Rowan Williams, *Anglican Identities* (London: DLT, 2004), 54, 55. This is Williams speaking about Richard Hooker. Typically, it is not easy to detect quite where Hooker stops, and Williams starts.

[33] Williams, *Anglican Identities*, 83, this time on Brooke Foss Westcott. The bluntest form of the tendency he rejects here is visible in statements like this, from Franz Pieper: '[T]here cannot be a development of Christian doctrine, because Christian doctrine is an entity that was completely closed with the doctrine of the apostles, which is not to be developed in the course of time, but to be preserved and taught utterly without change' (*Christliche Dogmatik I* (St Louis, MO: Concordia, 1924), 148; translated in Jaroslav Pelikan, *Development of Christian Doctrine: Some Historical Prolegomena* (New Haven, CT: Yale University Press, 1969), 23).

discipline dogmatics is the scientific self-examination of the Christian Church with respect to the content of its distinctive talk about God.'[34] Dogmatic theology works upon the speech about God that takes place in the lives of individual believers, in the church's activities of worship, mission and 'works of love', and especially in the church's preaching and administration of the sacraments.[35] The church is called into being by God's word in Christ, and commissioned to proclaim that word through all these forms of its speech. Dogmatic theology asks whether and how well the church is fulfilling that commission. It is, as it were, a critical commentary, an interlinear gloss, upon the church's proclamation.

All of the church's proclamation is fallible human speaking; the church grasps only inadequately what it is called to proclaim. Hence the need for dogmatic theology to ask its questions: it seeks to measure the fallible ways in which the church says 'Jesus is Lord' against the standard to which, in saying it at all, the church points. But dogmatic theology is itself fallible human talk.[36] The dogmatic theologian does not have somewhere independent to stand, from which to survey the church's proclamation, nor some 'higher or better source of knowledge'.[37] Dogmatic theologians grasp only inadequately the standard by which they are measuring the church.

It might be tempting to think that the pursuit of dogmatic theology could move in a spiral. The church's present understanding of what it means to say 'Jesus is Lord' brings with it certain ways of asking the question of the church's faithfulness. Dogmatic theologians might take their stand within that existing understanding, and pose those questions as diligently as they can. Their work might then lead the church to say 'Jesus is Lord' differently, but that will also alter the form of the question of faithfulness, which in turn will alter the work of questioning that dogmatic theology has to do. There is a circularity here, but it need not be a vicious one. We might think that, by running through this cycle again and again, asking and re-asking the dogmatic question in evolving forms, the church could be led safely to ever more adequate forms of discipleship.

Barth, however, says that dogmatics must be 'a laborious movement from one partial human insight to another with the intention though *with no guarantee of advance*'.[38] Dogmatic theologians can hope and trust that, by standing in and with the church, and committing themselves to what the church grasps of God's word, they might have some capacity to draw the church deeper into faithfulness to that word. They can't, however, plant their feet on any foundation that will guarantee the success of their work – not even the assumption that God must guarantee the general drift of their work over time. Their hope and trust in the validity of their own work has to be surrounded, and destabilized, by a deeper hope and trust that God will correct the church, and if necessary overthrow the church's dogmatic theology. The primary response to the fallibility and distortion of the church's proclamation is not dogmatic theology,

---

[34] Karl Barth, *Church Dogmatics I/1: The Doctrine of the Word of God*, trans. G. W. Bromiley (Edinburgh: T&T Clark, 1975), 3.
[35] Ibid.
[36] Ibid., 3–4.
[37] Ibid., 80.
[38] Ibid., 12, emphasis mine.

therefore, but prayer – earnest petition for God to reform the church, whether that is by means of or against the work of its theologians.[39]

In effect, then, for Barth the church stands both under discipline and under judgement. On the one hand, members of the church are called to pursue, as diligently as they can, the forms of self-criticism made available to them by their existing grasp of God's word. The church lives under this discipline. Yet, on the other hand the church must acknowledge that the truth of its speech about God cannot be guaranteed by any discipline that it knows. Truth is not something producible; it is not something that lies within the church's – or dogmatic theology's – power. The church is always in need of interruption and redirection by the judgement of God. It stands under judgement, and prays for it.

My claim in this chapter is that there are ways of inhabiting the space that Barth marks out here between dogmatic discipline on the one hand and prayer as sheer petition for interruption on the other. In particular, we can inhabit that space by listening – listening to the voices of others, and especially to their cries of suffering, and attending to the challenge that those voices bear for our existing ways of thinking and speaking. Barth himself, for all the depth of his listening to scripture, and the seriousness with which he attended to voices from the theological tradition, was disastrously inattentive to the voices of the women in his own household; he had an unpunctured confidence in his ability to tell the story of their lives in his own dogmatic theological voice. The pain that he caused to his wife, Nelly Barth, and to his secretary and mistress, Charlotte von Kirschbaum, and the damage he did to their lives were in part enabled by his failure to think that their voices might interrupt his theology and call him to account.[40]

Inhabiting the space between dogmatic discipline and petition for the Spirit's interruption is, I will suggest, in significant part a matter of listening, and of thinking again in company with others. It is a matter of dwelling openly, expectantly and penitently in what we have inherited, while putting ourselves in the way of the challenges and gifts that others might bring, and that might be the Spirit's means for leading us further up and further in to God's gift. Yet our listening is itself caught between discipline and judgement. It can sound as though it is simply a form of discipline that lies within our power, as if what is needed to put us on the right track is simply that we adopt the right attitude of openness, or pursue the appropriate practices of attention. Yet – in different ways in different parts of the church – none of us yet knows how to listen as we ought. We all need to be taught how to listen by the Spirit. Even for our ability to listen, we are dependent upon help that we cannot give ourselves, and that we cannot secure by our own efforts.[41]

Learning to listen might demand changes in the patterns of our expectations and imagination; it might involve rethinking the institutions and arrangements within

---

[39] Ibid., 75
[40] See Christiane Tietz, 'Karl Barth and Charlotte von Kirschbaum', *Theology Today* 74, no. 2 (2017): 86–111; Stephen Plant, 'When Karl Met Lollo: The Origins and Consequences of Karl Barth's Relationship with Charlotte von Kirschbaum', *Scottish Journal of Theology* 72, no. 2 (2019): 127–45, and Muers, 'The Personal Is the (Academic-)Political: Why Care About The Love Lives of Theologians?', *Scottish Journal of Theology*, forthcoming.
[41] I am grateful to Jenny Leith for helping me recognize this point.

which we do our theology; it might mean confronting the forces and structures that keep us, like Barth, locked into destructive habits of inattention. Listening is not simply a matter of our attitudes; it is a matter of the cultures, the forms of sociality and the structures of power and privilege that shape our lives. Listening as we already know how to listen, within the structures and processes that we already inhabit, should perhaps itself be thought of as a form of enacted prayer for the Spirit to break in and disrupt that habitation.

Cries, feasting and intimacy

In order to explore the possibility that I have just sketched, I am going to look at the work of three very different theologians, each of whom attends to this space between what we already know and what we hope to be shown – the space between the tradition that we inhabit and the change to which we are called.

David Ford

I begin with the work of my own teacher, David Ford. Peter Ochs has aptly said that 'One ubiquitous characteristic of David Ford's work has been joy: the joy of the Spirit's outpouring in all of creation, in prayer, song, speaking, love, friendship, feasting.' For Ford, 'the Spirit's superabundance is displayed through a variety of faces, each one naming a locus, manner, and mood of God's fluid presence.'[42]

Ford speaks of the ways in which our Christian lives, and our theologies, are interrupted by the cries 'that arise from the intensities of life – in joy, suffering, recognition, wonder, bewilderment, gratitude, expectation or acclamation'. 'Christian wisdom', he says, 'is discerned within earshot of such cries', and hearing such cries 'refuses to allow it to rest in any closure'.[43]

The central example of this in Ford's book on *Christian Wisdom* is Job's cry of suffering. The book of Job is, Ford says, 'a text that is simultaneously set within a tradition to which it contributes, yet also open across its own tradition's boundaries in such a way as … to open itself to radical critique and transformation.'[44] Job is wise, but he does not yet know how to be wise in his new situation. He is wise, but 'the scope of wisdom is the scope of God', and so there is more of that wisdom to discover.[45]

As Ford reads it, the central question in the book is 'Does Job fear God for nothing?'[46] In part, that means that the text asks whether Job honours God only because of what God does for him. Does Job's God fit neatly within a scheme that Job can grasp, providing him with a platform on which he can build his security? Is he willing to

---

[42] Ochs, *Another Reformation*, 195–6.
[43] David Ford, *Christian Wisdom: Desiring God and Learning in Love* (Cambridge: Cambridge University Press, 2007), 53.
[44] Ibid., 96.
[45] Ibid., 99.
[46] Ford explains (ibid., 100) that 'for nought' translates the Hebrew חנם (*hinnam*) 'meaning fortuitously, for no purpose, without cause', and that the Septuagint translation is δωρεάν (*dōrean*), 'as a gift'.

trust, instead, a God who exceeds his grasp – who is beyond any finite calculation or predictable benefit? In the body of the book, Job is faced with this question by unmerited suffering – a breach of the covenant he thought God had made, in which obedience was inseparable from reward, and punishment from disobedience. Specifically, Job is faced with a breach of 'the sort of understanding of God and the covenant with Israel given in the book of Deuteronomy and associated biblical writings'. That scheme, which had until now allowed Job to make sense of his life and his world in relation to God, collapses. It is the same scheme that continues to be upheld by his friends.[47]

In the face of his suffering, Job can find no other sense to make, and so he rejects both his senseless life and the senseless world, desiring their end. God, in response, draws Job to see creation's 'life, superabundance and uncontainability', its 'riotous particularity', its existence as 'a manifold of intensities'.[48] Such a vision 'not only rules out seeing creation in terms of human utility, control or even comprehensibility; divine utility, a "role" for creation in the purposes of God, does not figure either'. But rather than making creation senseless, it grants it 'a dignity, freedom, beauty, mystery and intense life of its own'.[49] There is more to the world than Job knows, and more than he can know – and, just so, more to God. Neither creation nor Creator can be confined within the kind of scheme to which Job had clung. They are beyond not just Deuteronomic thinking, but any human sense-making.

In all this, no sense is made of Job's suffering. 'There is no denial of the trauma and its terrible inexplicability; but alongside it is an affirmation of a creation that cannot be drawn into trauma without remainder, and of a God who can, through being questioned and questioning, open the eyes of the afflicted to who he is for his own sake.'[50] Although he despaired of his life and of his world, Job refused to give up on God. Even if only in the form of crying out in distress and protest, demanding an answer, he continued to call upon God, 'reaching out for more from God even when the only sign of the "more" is his own crying out' – unlike his friends, who refused to believe that there could be any more, and insisted upon making Job 'fit the procrustean bed of their wisdom'.[51]

There is a drama here of a clash between the inherited tradition and the discovery of what lies beyond it – a drama of the given and the found. Job's Deuteronomic wisdom is broken down; suffering is the form taken by this breaking; and the reformation of Job's theology emerges from this suffering. Yet there is a deeper dynamic, too: the discovery of abundance, the unending fact of the 'more' of God displayed in the 'more' of creation. Job's passage through suffering indicates one of the forms that, in a fallen world, the discovery of that abundance might take – but it is neither the only nor the primary form.

That is why, for Ford, the cries that matter for wisdom are not restricted to cries of pain, but include cries of recognition, wonder, bewilderment, gratitude, expectation

---

[47] Ibid., 96. For the account below, see also Susannah Ticciati, *Job and the Disruption of Identity: Reading beyond Barth* (London: T&T Clark, 2005).
[48] Ford, *Christian Wisdom*, 109.
[49] Ibid., 113–14.
[50] Ibid., 115.
[51] Ibid., 132, 126.

or acclamation – cries that mark sites of intensity, of places where life overflows the bounds that we have come to expect. Doctrinal change properly happens within earshot of all these cries; they mark out the unstable place where doctrinal theology belongs.

Linn Marie Tonstad

Linn Marie Tonstad pursues another critique of inherited tradition. Specifically, she examines the ways in which trinitarian theology has become 'a way to enjoin practices of sacrifice and submission', 'a masculinist discourse of mastery over the mystery of God in the voice of feminine submission'.[52] Even among those theologians who insist most firmly that their theologies imply subordination neither among the divine persons nor among human beings, she finds that the metaphors they use, the deep assumptions they appear to be making and the insights they claim into the texture of the divine life belie their stipulations. She reads their texts not 'with a first naïveté, which assumes the innocence and transparency of theological argument' but with strategies designed to 'make visible what stipulation naturalizes'.[53]

Much of her critique falls on patterns of theological description in which 'good relations between persons (divine or human)' seem to always involve one person 'making room for another … through sacrificial forms of (something like) suffering', and this not simply as a result of sin, but as the inherent nature of identity and relationship.[54] Tonstad argues, for instance, that for Graham Ward 'the nature of bodied personhood' is 'a practice of making room for the invasion of the other', because 'it seems that bodies must … stretch to incorporate each other – must, indeed, *penetrate* each other in order to relate to each other – because matter signifies irreducibility, thus protecting the particularity of bounded and finite identities'.[55] She finds something similar in the work of Sarah Coakley: 'Humans practice self-erasure so that God may move in, for true humanity means ceding to the divine'.[56]

Her criticism is that, in these theologians (and many others), 'The trinitarian bodies – the images, symbols, and vivifications that theologians use to explicate the shape of [divine and divine–human] relationships … remain penetrated and penetrating bodies, bodies that must make room for each other since they cannot be in the same place at the same time, their transformations amounting to no more than cycles of penetrating and being penetrated'.[57] This is a pattern of imagination that, despite the intentions of these theologians, sacralizes sacrifice and suffering; it is complicit in subordination, violence and abuse.

Yet this pattern of imagination, deeply rooted though it might be in the doctrinal tradition, runs against other strands of that tradition. For instance, 'The utter gratuity

---

[52] Tonstad, *God and Difference*, 1.
[53] Ibid., 2, 3. For more on the strategy of denaturalization, see her *Queer Theology* (Eugene, OR: Cascade, 2018), 56.
[54] Tonstad, *God and Difference*, 13.
[55] Ibid., 85, emphasis in original.
[56] Ibid., 99.
[57] Ibid., 106.

of creation, its ex nihilo status, entails that the world is not made out of God's kenotic self-emptying.'[58] God does not need to get out of the way in order to make space for creation; there is not (and cannot be) less of God, nor any competition for space between creation and God.[59] Similarly, Tonstad insists that in God's good and abundant creation, human relationships do not need to be imagined in terms of dispossession and penetration. 'One need not move aside to make room for the other, for there is enough space for all.'[60] To cede to the other, to make space, to turn away from oneself in order to give way to the other – Tonstad argues that all these are secondary forms of relationality, made necessary at times only by the sinful distortion of creaturely life. More fundamental is the possibility of flourishing together, of being drawn by our relationships with each other on journeys of delighted growth, discovering together what is made possible by all that we are and have been. 'God comes close in love to transform human difference from its seemingly inevitable, sinful tendency to turn into competition necessitating self-sacrifice into the possibility of table fellowship in friendship with each other and Jesus, as adoptive children of God all seated around the banquet table enjoying the overflow that characterizes the life given by God.'[61] In the light of God's abundance, Christians do not need to imagine their existence as a response to scarcity. 'The shape of Christian existence is celebration of the presence of Christ at a banquet.'[62]

This vision has implications for doctrinal theology. The church, Tonstad argues, is living towards a future it does not yet know and certainly cannot control, because it is being drawn into God's abundance. It always has more of that abundance to receive. This does call for a certain kind of dispossession, but what the church needs to lose is its sense of completeness, a sense of 'its own purity of achievement' – and so a sense that its duty is the stolid reproduction of its own existing life. Tonstad therefore criticizes 'reproductive ecclesiologies' which 'show exaggerated optimism about the church's ability to monitor its own adherence to a form of God's promised kingdom'. Instead, 'our faithfulness ... depends on a relationship to a Jesus whom we fail to recognize', and who we will be taught to recognize more and more fully only in company with others. The church therefore 'cannot close its borders for fear of shutting Christ out'.[63] The church is called to receive more of Christ, continually, in relationships of 'intimacy without distance, differentiation without fracture, difference without competitive multiplicity, and gratuity without sacrifice or suffering'.[64]

There are, then, two elements to Tonstad's critique of the doctrinal tradition she has inherited, and they are visible in the double use that she makes of queer theory. On the one hand, queer theory provides her with a range of tools and techniques that she can use in criticizing what she has inherited – tools such as 'mimetic, over-literalizing, and imagistic interpretive methods' that help her uncover the dangerous depths of

---

[58] Ibid., 81.
[59] Ibid., 47.
[60] Ibid., 239.
[61] Ibid., 238.
[62] Ibid., 239.
[63] Ibid., 270, 276.
[64] Ibid., 85.

theological texts. On the other, it provides her with glimpses of patterns of relation no longer bound by gendered separation, subordination and competition: glimpses of 'the truth of complexity, of partiality, of existence without finality, transparency, and self-possession'.[65]

First, then, she seeks to root something out from her tradition, standing on some elements of what she has inherited while she dislodges others. This is a work of repair, provoked by cries of suffering: Tonstad construes the tradition differently, in order to overcome the harm that she sees being done by the tradition as it is. Second, however, she offers a different vision of what the work of doctrinal theology might be more generally. It should not be a means for the church to lock down the reproduction of its present life, or to ensure the purity of succession. It should, instead, be a labour undertaken on behalf of those who inhabit the tradition but who have found themselves attracted by new possibilities of life together, new realizations of feasting that go beyond their present restricted imaginings – and who are asking whether and how that feasting might be possible for them as Christians.[66] It is as it turns towards those possibilities of feasting that doctrinal theology is destabilized, and made into something new.

Willie James Jennings

Wille James Jennings writes about the Portuguese chronicler Gomes Eanes de Zurara (*c.* 1410–*c.* 1474), and his presence, on 8 August 1444, at the landing in Lagos of 235 Black African slaves. Zurara sees the slaves, some with their heads bowed, some groaning, some 'crying out loudly, as if asking help of the Father of nature. … And though we could not understand the words of their language, the sound of it right well accorded with the measure of their sadness.' Zurara responded to this cry with tears of his own: 'their humanity maketh mine to weep in pity for their sufferings … seeing before my eyes that miserable company, and remembering that they too are of the generation of the sons of Adam.' He manages to quieten himself, however, with thoughts of providence, the God who 'doest and undoes, compassing the matters of this world as pleaseth thee', who is capable of consoling these slaves with 'some understanding of matters to come', and who has arranged all this for 'the salvation of those souls that before were lost'.[67]

---

[65] Tonstad, *Queer Theology*, 94. For a more concrete description of one of these positive glimpses of life beyond the church's failures, see her Twitter thread on 'what church promised me and the dancefloor gave me', @Pennamiriel, 19 September 2019, twitter.com/Pennamiriel/status/1174726366996180992 (accessed 9 December 2019).

[66] Romand Coles (see n. 29) says of the democratic tradition that, at its most fruitful, it 'has always hinged upon those who sensed, in their myriad insurgent, inventive, and receptive capacities, that democracy was, is, and will be significantly beyond democracy as "we" "know" it in its dominant forms: beyond the arbitrary exclusions, subjugations, and dangers that accompany every democratic "we" and their "knowing" and disclose complacency toward present practices as a sham' (*Beyond Gated Politics*, xi).

[67] Gomes Eanes de Azurara, *The Chronicle of the Discovery and Conquest of Guinea* (London: Hakluyt Society, 1896–99), 81–3; quoted in Jennings, *The Christian Imagination*, 18–19.

Jennings asks how Zurara, and those like him, could have learnt to be undisturbed by the cries of these slaves. He explores Zurara's arrangement of the slaves on a scale from those who were 'White enough' to those he found demonically Black, an aesthetic partly learnt from existing imagined geographies, and partly from the distinctions White Christians had learnt to employ in order to distinguish from themselves *moriscos* (converted Muslims) and *conversos* (converted Jews). He explores the theology that said that 'the pope, servant of the servants of God, for the sake of Christ and through Christ, lays claim to the entire world', and so had the jurisdiction to award to Portugal (and to other European powers) rights to African and American territories.[68] And he explores a set of convictions that were rooted in the doctrine of *creatio ex nihilo*. When looked at in the light of that doctrine, no creature has its own stability; stability comes only in relation to God. Zurara had watched as the families of these displaced Africans were separated in front of him, but he believed the bonds of place, tribe and family entirely secondary to the tie that binds each person to God. '[P]eoples exist without a necessary permanence either of place or identity. ... The essential characteristic of people is their need – for pardon and life, that is, for salvation from God.' And because that need has been met in Christ, Christ's representatives on earth can – and must – override all the demands of geography and kinship in order to save souls. '[N]ative identities, tribal, communal, familial and spatial, were constricted to simply their bodies, leaving behind the very ground that enables and facilitates the articulation of identity.'[69]

Jennings looks back to the supersessionist roots of this vision, in a way that partly echoes and partly supplements Lindbeck's concerns discussed earlier. The church has, in a vision like Zurara's, displaced the Jewish people completely as the locus of salvation – and so can all too easily (when it so desires) define itself over against the Jewish people's obligations to kin, to land and to the physical particularities of a specific place. It has also so displaced the Jewish people that its White European members can no longer recognize themselves as gentile. That is, they can no longer see themselves as recipients of the gospel who had to learn to respond to Christ in their own specific way, alongside others who responded differently.[70] They can only read their own response to the gospel as Christianity *simpliciter*, and themselves as the standard by which others must be judged.

In brief, Zurara is armoured against his own tears by a whole doctrinal settlement, and by the racist and colonialist imagination that it helps to hold in place.

I have already touched on Jennings's account of J. W. Colenso, and Colenso's failure to understand how deeply his Christianity might be challenged and changed by the Africans among whom he worked.[71] Jennings argues that Colenso's supersessionism (his belief in 'a God who is not only beyond but in some sense opposed to the strictures of Jewish identity') was entangled with his colonial imagination: his ability 'to universalize the earth, that is, to free it from the strictures of particular ways

---

[68] Jennings, *Christian Imagination*, 23, 32–3, 26.
[69] Ibid., 28, 43.
[70] Ibid., 98. Cf. the discussion of conversion in Chapter 4, p. 81.
[71] See Chapter 2, p. 34.

of life'.⁷² Colenso could not, therefore, imagine Christianity differently: he mistook his particular settlement for Christianity's universal essence. He believed that 'All theological identity is essentially the same, Jewish, Christian, or Zulu' but 'What looks like a radical antiracist, antiethnocentric vision of Christian faith is in fact profoundly imperialist'.⁷³

Colenso's approach to the Zulu people 'did not deny cultural particularity' but it did deny 'that it mattered theologically'.⁷⁴ He missed an 'invitation to a process of concurrency, not simply linguistic, social, or cultural, but also theological'.⁷⁵ That is, he missed the possibility of the kind of deeper encounter with the Zulu people that might have allowed him to imagine Christianity taking root differently, in the 'inner logics' of their world. And he missed the opportunity to see from that vantage point the contingency and particularity of the way in which Christianity had taken root in European soil. He missed the processes of mutual learning by which the Zulu people among whom he worked might have discovered their own way of being Christian in relationship with him, and by which he in turn might have discovered from them how to be Christian differently in his own location. He did not envisage 'the joining of peoples in the struggle to learn each other's languages in the process of lives joined, lives lived together in new spaces, and constituting a new history for a new people'.⁷⁶

In a way that could be understood to build on Lindbeck's critique of supersessionism, Jennings critiques deep patterns of Christian doctrinal thinking that have helped to create and sustain the horrific suffering of the slave trade, and of anti-Black racism. There is a difference, however. For Lindbeck, the process of change was prompted by the cries of Jewish suffering but then continued primarily through the Christian theologians' work of re-reading scripture in the light of those cries. Jennings, by contrast, insists that the process of re-reading needs to take place in a context of relationship – in the context, that is, of a life joined with the lives of those who cried. 'The problem', he says,

> is not simply in what or how theologians write. ... The problem is not one of contextuality or insensitivity to situatedness, or of attending to difference, otherness, or alterity in the writing of theological texts; ... The problem is in imagining whom we theologians belong to as we write, as we think, as we pray. The problem has fundamentally to do with a world formed and continuing to be formed to undermine the possibilities of Christians living together, loving together, and desiring each other ... the necessary beginning for overturning the remade world.⁷⁷

We need 'deep abiding intellectual joining, not only of ideas but of problems, not only of concepts but of concerns, not only of beliefs and practices but of common life, and

---

⁷² Jennings, *Christian Imagination*, 146.
⁷³ Ibid., 145.
⁷⁴ Ibid., 147.
⁷⁵ Ibid., 154.
⁷⁶ Ibid., 160–1.
⁷⁷ Ibid., 202.

all of it of the multitude of many tongues'. We need a 'mutual enfolding', a 'struggle toward cultural intimacy'.[78]

To inhabit the space of expectancy – to make the work of doctrinal theology a prayer for the Spirit to interrupt us and to lead us onward – therefore demands two things. First, it demands this intimacy: 'I yearn', says Jennings, 'for a vision of Christian intellectual identity that is compelling and attractive, embodying … the power of love that gestures toward joining, toward the desire to hear, to know, and to embrace.'[79] Doctrinal theology belongs in the conversation between different peoples, a conversation that demands immersion in the different languages spoken, the different demands and possibilities of life in play. It is in such spaces that doctrinal theologians might be taught to distinguish between their culture and their faith, between Christ and their own identities – and so learn how to avoid universalizing themselves.

Second, however, this work demands attention to all the ways in which the world is formed, and continues to be formed, to undermine this possibility. Zurara's and Colenso's failures were not theirs alone. They inherited patterns of imagination, and patterns of theological practice, that were entangled with the structures of empire, with arrangements of power, with the flow of commodities, with accumulations of wealth, with the overlapping of ecclesiastical and political power. For intimacy to become possible demands more than individual good will and determination. It involves attention to the ways in which doctrinal theological imagination and practice is still held back from intimacy by the structures within which it lives.[80]

The dynamics of change

Christians are called to inhabit a space between continuity and discontinuity – holding fast to what they have already received of the gift of God in Jesus Christ, and hoping for the Spirit to lead them further in to that gift. They pursue what they think they have already been shown of the love of God, seeking to embody it, and they wait to be shown more of that love, or shown it differently.

The distortions that beset the life of the church differ from place to place and time to time; the forms of holding fast and hoping for change differ, too; the work that the Spirit undertakes to sanctify the church is specific to each location in its polycentric life. When change comes as a result of that work, it can unfold in all kinds of ways; it is normally multifaceted and resistant to brief description. We can, nevertheless, distinguish three broad movements that tend to characterize such change, wherever it happens: a call forward, a process of re-construal and a process of recognition. We have seen the first two of these in the work of Ford, Tonstad and Jennings. Each of

---

[78] Ibid., 202 (see also 248), 273, 271.
[79] Ibid., 289.
[80] Nicholas Lash, *Theology on Dover Beach* (London: Darton, Longman and Todd, 1979), 71–4, argued that dethroning White Europeans from 'the centre of the universe of meaning' is a process that 'calls in question our self-understanding, … that structure of feeling, that culture, of which our theoretical activities and positions are a secondary and derivative expression' and 'calls in question those organizational patterns in which our present self-understanding is embodied'.

them highlighted some of the calls that the church in his or her own context can hear; each showed how those calls could and should trigger processes of rethinking. In this section, I examine all three movements more closely, asking both what they involve in the life of the church and what role doctrinal theologians might play in relation to them.

The call forward

The first movement is the call forward. Imagine a church inhabiting some relatively settled construal, some particular grasp, of God's abundant gift – inevitably a mixture of insight and inattentiveness, truth and distortion. We might be talking about a little local community, or a whole denomination; the scale does not particularly matter. Imagine that the people in this church tend to project some roughly coherent and stable sense of who 'we' are, and what 'our' way of life and thought is or should be. There might be all kinds of variations and recusal, but there is something like a dominant discourse that frames many of the deliberations and decisions that shape this community's life.

Any such community faces a question because there is always more of God's abundance to discover, and the 'more' of God calls them onward and upward. For this group to hear and answer God's call forward will mean being called beyond or away from the present form of their existence. It will mean the unsettling of their dominant sense of 'our' way of life and thought, and perhaps of their current sense of the boundaries that mark out 'us'. Given how knotted into multiple forms of failure every Christian settlement is, God's call will often be heard as a call to repentance, a call to turn away from distortion and damage. The deeper form of the call is, however, always a call forward: a call to discover more of God's love together. It is a call deeper into God's gift, and the reception of that gift – even if it comes by means of profound repentance and thoroughgoing reconstruction – will ultimately involve neither the abnegation of the self nor the destruction of the church, but their true flourishing.

God's call might reach this church in multiple ways. Some forms of it will already be audible within the habits to which this church is collectively committed. The church will, for instance, have habitual ways of reading scripture together, and the diligent pursuit of those habits will enable them to hear words that challenge them and draw them onwards. Means of discovery are already in their hands. My focus in this chapter, however, falls on other ways in which God's call might be heard.

God's call reaches this church through cries: cries that mark places where life exceeds its existing frames of reference. Most sharply, the call reaches the church through cries of suffering – cries from those injured, marginalized, erased, ignored or forced into passivity by the existing patterns of this church's speech and action. These may be the cries of those who are already visibly part of the life of this church; they may be the cries of those on or beyond what are currently thought of as its edges – but wherever they come from, these cries break in on the church's present life, posing questions and demanding re-evaluation. Can they do justice to the lives from which these cries emerge?

God's call might reach this church through encounters, especially when those encounters deepen into intimacy. All the members of this church live within different tangles of relationships, and the patterns of their relationships change over time. They are constantly meeting, and engaging with, and living with, others who live, speak and think differently – others within and beyond the church. They hear the voices of people who speak different languages from the ones that this church fosters, sometimes sharply different, and many of them learn to speak or already speak some of those languages themselves. As they negotiate these languages, learning to translate between them, learning to speak about their faith, their obligations and the life of their church in them, they might hear the call to think their faith differently.

God's call might also reach this church through the improvisations in following Jesus in which its members are involved, as they find themselves in new situations – both the improvisations in which each individual participates and the improvisations by which this community develops new corporate forms and collective activities. Such improvisations are always happening at the edges between the familiar and the unfamiliar – and in reality the whole of the church's life is edge, even if some edges are more of a bump to cross than others. People in this church might hear God's call by attending to the new forms of speech and practice that are emerging within each improvisation.

God's call forward reaches the church through all these means – and they are not distinct, but overlapping and entangled aspects of its life. The church can inhabit the space between continuity and discontinuity more fully the more these cries become audible in its life, and two things are needed for that audibility: the life of this community must bring it into contact with more of these cries, and these cries must have the capacity to shake, to unsettle, to question, to entice the community as a whole.

Doctrinal theologians might, at times, be able to serve this process in two ways: by listening out for such calls and by learning to speak what they hear into the life of the church.[81] The political philosopher Romand Coles suggests something of the activity that the first of these might involve. He is a non-Christian philosopher discussing the relationship of theorists to the radical democratic tradition, but his description transfers easily to Christian theologians in relation to the church. We need, he says, extended and open-minded encounter with people involved in a wide variety of practices and experiments, especially practices and experiments taking place in situations marginalized by existing patterns of power and privilege. We need to engage in movement from context to context – margin to margin, edge to edge – listening to and joining in with the endeavours that we find, including endeavours that are uncomfortable or, in the terms of the theory we already know, wayward. We need to attend to the dynamics that action has taken on in specific locales, amid specific constraints. That lived experimentation, which goes far beyond anything that theorists might invent on their own, is the primary source of both critique and discovery. If we remain aloof from it, we will 'miss subtlety, critiques of power, and paradoxes painfully obvious to many and carefully negotiated by far more people than we recognize'.[82]

Many of those who are, or who become, doctrinal theologians will already be involved in these contexts – they will have come from them, or found their ways

---

[81] For a reminder of what I mean by 'doctrinal theologian', see p. 38.
[82] Coles, *Beyond Gated Politics*, xvi.

into them, and will enter the practices of doctrinal theology from that direction. The diversity of the community of doctrinal theologians matters deeply – and the stark lack of diversity that marks this community in many of the church and university contexts that I know best undermines all the doctrinal theological work undertaken in those contexts.

Nevertheless, far more is always going on than is already carried by the voices of doctrinal theologians or embodied in them – and the question of diversity among theologians needs to broaden into the question of whose company doctrinal theologians keep, the question of who it is that they are thinking with and for. There is always more to hear, and some – especially among those who pursue doctrinal theology in positions of privilege and power – will be called to travel to new contexts, participate in new experiments, join new conversations. And what matters is not that any individual theologian become a virtuoso of such travelling, but that the community of doctrinal theologians be a network of people who together are involved in many such contexts, so that 'each of us may be fed variously by the energies, comparisons, collaborations, insights, and wonder of others who theorize attentively in relation to journeys in proximate or distant places tabooed, maligned, or ignored'.[83]

Second, in addition to such an active listening, attending to all these forms of call demands learning – and multiple kinds of learning. It requires, as I have said, much more than good will, and more than a curious gaze. We need, for instance, to learn where to look – discovering, over time, where generative and challenging developments are happening. For many of us, there will be a temptation always to focus on what looks exciting from our current perspective – and so, implicitly, to look for situations that confirm what we have already begun to think. Learning to look elsewhere, and what to make of others' estimates of where we should look, might take time.

We also need to learn the languages that will allow us to make sense of what we find, or what we are involved in – both the languages spoken in the context in which we find ourselves and the theoretical languages that will enable us to articulate well what we find, and speak from these contexts into the wider life of the church. Those languages can be as demanding and as time-consuming to learn as the Greek and Hebrew that biblical scholars know they need.

We may also, however, need to learn what in our habits and assumptions, and in the structures within which we work, holds us back from serious engagement – from attention, from discovery, from intimacy. This learning might take a particular form for those pursuing doctrinal theology in Western academic contexts, for instance. I discussed in Chapter 3 some of the ways in which the very processes of academic engagement (the research interview, for instance) can reinforce a set of entangled binaries (critical versus naive, male versus female, White versus Black) that lead to the misrecognition of what we hear. In Chapter 5, I discussed the way in which doctrinal theologians can be tempted to misread ordinary practice as the inconsistent application of badly grasped intellectual principles, rather than understanding the sense that it

---

[83] Romand Coles, *Visionary Pragmatism: Radical and Ecological Democracy in Neoliberal Times* (Durham, NC: Duke University Press, 2016), 13, emphasis removed.

makes in its own terms.[84] Learning to attend seriously means learning to attend in ways that can challenge not only our descriptions but the categories built in to the forms of investigation that we use, and the institutional spaces that we inhabit. Attending is not something that we can do simply by deciding to do it, and there are no guarantees that we will learn to do it well.

Re-construal

The second moment in change is that of attempted re-construal. To hear the call forward – or to think that we might be hearing it – is to hear a question posed to our existing life. We might be asked whether there is something that we should stop doing or saying, or some new habit or concern that we should adopt; we might be asked whether the boundaries we have drawn around 'us' are in the wrong place. In small ways or more sharply, we are asked whether the configuration of our worship, witness and discipleship should shift. We are asked to receive a new vision of ourselves.

These kinds of question are being faced and answered all the time, without any help from doctrinal theologians. People find ways of responding in new circumstances; they reach new settlements; they experiment, and some of their experiments stick. As I said in Chapter 6, 'It might be a matter of hesitation and agonized deliberation; it is no less likely to be a matter of barely recognized skill, even of flair.'[85] People find ways forward that are 'fitting' – and what they deem 'fitting' will seldom be capable of analysis into a finite number of explicit reasons. It will be a matter of the stories people tell, their aesthetic grasp of a whole situation, the patterns of their feeling, the nature of their relationships, the responsiveness of their institutions and so on and on. It will, as I said, be 'worked out on a middle-distance scale of practical arrangements and promises, habits and adjustments'. And that is just as it should be.

Sometimes, however, the question will be asked and answered more explicitly. People will give one another reasons for the way forward they think appropriate; they will explain how it makes sense in relation to the church's commitments and sources of authority. This may happen before, during or after the change has taken hold. That is, it may help to make a change imaginable, it may cement one already taking place or it may follow it as a post hoc rationalization. It may be surrounded by complex patterns of deferral, in which most of those involved in the change trust that someone with the relevant authority has already done the thinking required.[86] It may simply be a performance that helps calm dissatisfaction while having little substantive impact on the decisions made. When I talk in the paragraphs that follow about the processes of reasoning involved in re-construal, I don't mean to assume too much about whether, where and with what effect these processes might actually take place.

Nevertheless, the central form that reasoning to change takes is simple enough. We judge that we are free to change some feature of our existing settlement while remaining faithful disciples, because the features we want to change are inessential.

---

[84] See Chapter 3, pp. 49–50, Chapter 5, p. 99.
[85] See Chapter 6, p. 127.
[86] See Chapter 6, pp. 121–3.

They are not, we now realize, among the deeper features of our discipleship, and we reason that we can be as true, or truer, to those deeper features if we change these shallower ones. The belief that we are remaining faithful – that we remain disciples of Jesus Christ, that we remain true to the tradition that we have inherited and the gift that we have been given – rests upon this continuity in the depths.[87]

To say this is not, however, a way of saying that proper change is superficial – that it is a cosmetic rearrangement that does not disturb business as usual. In my context, for instance, I believe that the Spirit continues to speak out against the church through the cries of Jews calling out against the church's supersessionism, of Muslims against the church's Islamophobia, of Black people against the church's racism, of women against the church's misogyny, of the disabled against the church's ableism and of LGBTIQ+ people against the church's cis- and heteronormativity. These are the cries of people who, around the world, in our own society, and in and by the churches, are being subjected to marginalization, to exclusion, to bullying, to violence, to abuse; they are at times the cries of those who are being killed or driven to suicide. The failings of the church are deep, and they are deadly, and the urgent change that these cries should trigger will be a very long way from being easy or comfortable. To say that it rests upon a continuity in the depths is to say that my church is called to pursue the breaking down and remaking of the structures and habits of our life together by the same Jesus that we read about in the bible and worship in our liturgies, and that it will be driven by the same Spirit whose presence and power we invoke in our prayers.

To the extent that we reason out such change explicitly, we rely upon the possibility of construing the inherited elements of the tradition – the materials from which our community's settlement has been constructed – as standing at different depths. We rely, that is, upon the deployment of some kind of scale that will allow us to speak meaningfully about 'shallower' and 'deeper'. That we can think in such terms is not automatic. It is true that, as they inhabit any settlement, people will in practice tend to treat their various commitments as being flexible to different degrees. That does not automatically mean, however, that they will have a discourse for articulating these commitments that arranges them against any consistent scale of depth. This is, rather, a way of thinking that comes into its own, or is even called into being, precisely within processes of change. We see Jesus, for instance, in the midst of his polemic against the scribes and Pharisees, distinguishing the 'weightier matters of the law' from 'the others' (Mt. 23.23); elsewhere he identifies the central commandments on which all the others hang (Mt. 22.34-40). These are acts of construal that accompany his proclamation of a new settlement. Similarly, Paul, writing to enable distant churches to discover faithful responses to new situations, persuades them that they have deep resources – stories, principles and habits – from which they can reason to resolve shallower issues – what to do, say, with meat sacrificed to idols. Claims about depth are strategic moves in processes of persuasion.

---

[87] Rose, *A Theology of Failure*, 150, speaks of an 'infidel fidelity', one 'that betrays certain aspects of Christian tradition in the name of faithfulness to others'. 'To love the church is to be willing to put it to death, to betray it in the name of what we love in it' (ibid., 178). Nicholas Adams, 'Reparative Reasoning', *Modern Theology* 24, no. 3 (2008): 451, frames this in terms of what we take to be axioms and what we take to be hypotheses capable of modification in the light of those axioms.

Re-construal is a creative act.[88] Beliefs and practices don't come labelled with a precise and objective indication of their depth. Arranging them in even a rough hierarchy involves a contingent act of construal of elements that could well have been arranged otherwise. When we think of the creativity involved in construal, however, we should not think first of all of the lone genius, engaged in deliberate invention.[89] If anyone is in a position to offer a fresh construal of what a community has inherited, they will have been enabled to see that inheritance differently, to grasp a different possible construal, by all that surrounds and shapes them. Creativity happens to us and among us as much as being something achieved by us.

Re-construal normally happens in a context in which multiple construals are already circulating. The story of the faith gets told differently on different occasions; different reasons get offered for habits and imperatives; different claims become the focus of attention on different occasions. The life of any reasonably complex Christian community is likely to involve a mobile and fluid circulation of construals, all of them partial and most of them inchoate. Someone who takes on the task of explicit construal, for the sake of change, will normally be drawing on and intervening in that mix of possibilities.[90]

The act of re-construal might take a form already described in Chapter 8. The call that I hear might exercise a magnetic pull which draws me (whether I notice it or not) across the space of possible construals already circulating in my community. Indeed, the very fact that I think I have heard a call might indicate that such perturbation has already been happening: that I have been drawn towards a construal of our faith that stands at one edge of the field of possibilities in circulation. A call animates re-construal; it is named as a call in the light of re-construal.

The purpose of all this re-construal is the same. It offers to this community of people a new account of who they are – of what they have been involved in together, of what their scriptures say, of what are the deepest truths they know and inhabit together. It asks for the community's recognition of that account: their agreement that that can see themselves, their past and their scriptures, in this description. And it shows that some change, some repentance, some venture, some new relationships make sense in the light of this account. If this is who we are, if this is what we believe, then this change is demanded of us.

---

[88] Tanner, *Theories of Culture*, 93.
[89] Such creative re-construal is going on all the time, as people of all kinds discover different ways of living their faith. Rosemary B. Kellison writes, in 'Tradition, Authority, and Immanent Critique in Comparative Ethics', *Journal of Religious Ethics* 42, no. 4 (2014): 717, that 'Each time [one] applies a concept or endorses a norm, one participates in … reconstruction of a tradition. Whether implicitly or explicitly, each new use of a traditional concept tells a story of how that concept came to contain determinate normative content; no matter how faithful one attempts to be to the tradition, in the very act of telling the story from and for one's particular context, one changes it.'
[90] Rose (*Theology of Failure*, 13) speaks of fidelity 'to the church understood in a material sense not as an idea or a set of ideas but as a particular group of people, a particular set of institutions, a particular collection of texts and practices. It is fidelity to a body, therefore, that is as ill-defined, fluid, and mutable as any other body – which always exceeds and undermines any particular interpretation, any attempt to identify the universal core of Christianity.'

Recognition

This brings me to the third element of reasoning towards change: recognition. For change to take place, the re-construal that makes sense of it must 'take' – must catch on, spread and bed down in the community.[91]

To be recognizable in a particular community, a construal does not need simply to be a repetition of what that community already says. It does, however, need to provide a shape capable of gathering up significant parts of what members of that community already value.[92] It needs to do justice to much of what they already think and feel about the weight of their commitments. As I have already said, people inhabiting a settlement are likely, on the whole, to behave as if there were some very rough hierarchy to their belief – some elements that, in practice, they sit more lightly to than others, some which can be challenged or changed with less drama than others. Attention to their habits is likely to reveal a flexible, partial, unevenly shared and perhaps inconsistent structure – a matter of their emotional ties to different elements, of the characteristic patterns of their imagination and of the depth with which different habits have been written into their bodies. Someone proposing a re-construal within such a community is playing with all of that material, its resistances and possibilities.

The process of recognition can be slow and uneven. It seldom takes the form of a single act of proposal followed by a single wave of acceptance. In response to a call, a re-construal of the community's commitments might be offered which is, at first, very partial and very blunt – perhaps convincing only to a few already caught up in hearing and responding to the call in question. It may be at this early stage a construal patently incapable of doing justice to much of what the community currently values, or incapable of doing justice to much of scripture, or much of the tradition, as members of this community currently read them. It may take a long time, and much controversy, before a more compelling and comprehensive version of this re-construal emerges – before it looks, to those with eyes inclined to be sceptical, like a serious contender over against construals that have had enough time to become habitual or even invisible.

This whole process may be acted out explicitly in argument and counterargument, or it may take place in more subterranean ways, in the slow emergence and spread of new patterns of speech and thought. It might be less a matter of the persuasion of those who currently hold power in the community, and more a matter of their retirement, and the arrival of a new generation. The process of recognition might hinge more on the composition of appointment panels than on the settling of arguments. It might be a matter of the building of new institutional spaces in which the new construal can be incubated. It might involve pursuing informal and formal research projects that slowly establish how much more of Christian life, of scripture and of the tradition, can be

---

[91] 'If my arguments are not judged by others to be justified – to be skilful reconstructions of the tradition – they will be inconsequential and will not be taken as authoritative by others' (Kellison, 'Tradition', 718). 'There is no point in academic theology's making a proposal for change if it does not address people where they already are theologically' (Tanner, *Theories of Culture*, 85).

[92] For a given construal we can ask, 'How well does that organization make sense of the different things that Christians have been prone to say and do? Does it make sense of the things that Christians tend to value most? What is lost when materials are organized in that way? What is gained, in apparent truth, beauty, intelligibility, or the advancement of the good?' (Tanner, *Theories of Culture*, 163).

re-read in this new construal's terms. And it might be that the speaking and publishing of doctrinal theologians play a role in all of this – though it is unlikely to be the main means by which change arrives.

There is no guarantee that recognition will take place. The community may, rightly or wrongly, fail to discern in what they have heard a true call deeper into the truth to which they are committed. The church might divide, yet again, into those who do and those who do not discern such a call. It may be that a new community forms around the new construal, leaving its parent community with the old. Where recognition does take place, however, it often means that an external impetus has become internal, or a marginal impetus central. That is, it means that some call from outside the community or from what the community had thought of as its margins – a call heard in some cry, or encounter, or improvisation – has become the word that reshapes this community's life. It has become a call that this community can repeat to itself, in language that it now recognizes as its own, a call that its members together recognize as the voice of God.

Conclusion

In the light of all this, what can we say about the role of doctrinal theologians in the life of the church? As before, I suggest that someone is acting as a doctrinal theologian to the extent that they are involved in the explicit articulation of belief, exploring its sources, its connections and its implications, and if their articulations draw on doctrinal statements or explore the major topics touched on in such statements. I use it more specifically for those who have fairly intensive involvement in this kind of work, who do it in some kind of direct conversation with what in Chapter 6 I called the 'articulate tradition', and who hope by it to help shape or nourish the life of the church.

Doctrinal theologians deal in summary articulations or construals of belief. They produce them, discuss them and dissect them – testing the roots of belief in scripture, exploring belief's structure and implications in conversation with the varied voices of the tradition, the contemporary church and the wider world. They construe the ordering of that belief, positioning its elements at different depths and exploring the dependencies between them.

For good or ill, this is work that tends to play a role in the reproduction of the life of the church. It can play a role in holding the church to what it has already seen or heard in God's abundant gift – to those features of scripture that stand out to it, to some of the constraints that make for fruitful articulation, to some of the resources that give belief its reach and power. It also, inextricably from that, plays a role in holding the church to the deformations and insensitivities that mar its life. Doctrinal theology is involved in the reproduction of failure.

This tendency to reproduce failure is, perhaps, strongest in situations in which a church and the doctrinal theologians within it have forgotten the contingent and partial nature of their understanding. Doctrinal theologians can be the custodians of that forgetfulness, making seem inevitable what was contingent, re-narrating messy processes of historical change as the necessary unfolding of ideas. They can sometimes see themselves, or present themselves, as speaking masterfully on behalf of the tradition and its proper ordering, obscuring the specificity of their own location, and obscuring the ways in which they are passing on only the way the faith looks from a single position of power.

Even when doctrinal theologians adopt their calmest air of sobriety, however – setting out with unflappable authority the one true ordering of the faith – there remains an almost ineradicable playfulness to their work. To pronounce a construal invites critique and counter-construal. It invites variation. Doctrinal theology has an inbuilt tendency (even though it is one that is often strenuously resisted) to explore and to expand the space of possible construals of belief, even if the gamut explored in any particular location is limited.

To an extent, doctrinal theologians can be rescued from their inattentiveness and from the indiscriminate conservatism that is one of their besetting temptations by pursuing the disciplines that they understand to be called for by the belief they articulate. They can read their scriptures more diligently; they can pursue their historical work with greater attention; they can press at the connections of their articulations more critically – and from time to time this may yield a question or a challenge, and place the doctrinal theologian not so much in the role of the guardian of the church's continuity, but as a critic.

The gamut of their explorations will be wider, however, their playfulness more fruitful, and their diligent disciplines more likely to yield surprises, the more they attend to those who disagree with them, the more they listen to cries, put themselves in the way of encounters, or join in with improvisations. It will be still wider if they accompany and attend to others in their communities and among their colleagues who pursue such engagement beyond their own capacity or experience. Listening, pilgrimage and experiment are tasks of the whole body of Christ, and the whole ecclesial task certainly does not fall on the head of doctrinal theologians. Doctrinal theologians can, however, focus on the specific task of investigating the re-construals of the faith that might be triggered by taking these engagements seriously – asking what it would mean for their community's pattern of belief to be transformed in their light. In this way they can, at times, play a role in the kinds of process of change that I have described in this chapter, or the kinds of process of engagement across ecclesial differences that I described in Chapter 8. They can help the church to hear calls that it might have missed; they can help the church rethink its life in relation to those calls.

There are dangers here too, however. If those doctrinal theologians who are themselves privileged in the present ordering of the church's life – who are comfortable, who are accorded a voice, who are in a position to be taken seriously – take it upon themselves to speak on behalf of those who cry out, or those who are encountered or those who are engaged in improvisation, they can all too easily become ventriloquists: holding up their own model of the people that they have encountered, and speaking through that model with their own voice. They can allow themselves too easily to mute, or to make safe, the challenge that they are supposedly passing on – or to assimilate it too easily to regnant fashions of critique. And even those theologians who can speak about some call directly from their own experience, and who embody in their own lives the challenge that this call presents to the church, can be drawn into a problematic relation to their own experience by the very processes by which they gain the kind of voice recognized in the wider church.[93]

Doctrinal theology does not and cannot capture the whole of belief, or the whole of the lives that surround belief. Even when it is done well, it articulates only a part of what is going on; it deals in diagrams or cartoons, while belief is an impressionist painting. Doctrinal theologians therefore need to cultivate practices of speech that don't hog the microphone: they can gloss and comment and query and advocate, but they should do so only in such a way that their audience's attention is turned towards the lives about which they are speaking, and the voices of those from whom they have been learning.

The work of doctrinal theologians can be at its most ambivalent when they end up acting as gatekeepers. They can, certainly, play a role in calling the church to be faithful to what it has seen of God's abundant gift, and to guard against ways in which that gift is being lost or distorted. A doctrinal theologian might, for instance, play a role in calling the church back to the ongoing task of taking seriously the humanity of Christ, and insisting that unity with Christ takes place in our full humanity, embodied, relational, historical, affective and intellectual. A doctrinal theologian might, in various contexts and in various ways, take up the role of examining the life of the church for signs of its perennial tendency to deny this truth, sounding the alarm when those signs are detected. This is important work, and it can be fruitful.

The always-attendant danger of such gatekeeping, however, is that the doctrinal theologian might help to close the gates of the church in such a way as to shut Christ out – to shut out the disruptive potential of the scriptures and of the tradition, and to shut out the cries, the encounters and the improvisations through which God is calling the church further in to God's own love. Precisely because and to the extent that they become involved in gatekeeping, doctrinal theologians are called to a self-critical attentiveness – to a speculative, 'what if' interrogation of the voices they criticize. What if this voice is saying something more challenging, more reformatory, than they had realized? What if, even if in the midst of the moves that the doctrinal theologian continues to regard as mistakes, this person or group has seen or heard something in God's word to which the theologian has hitherto been oblivious? The further the voice in question is from the forms of privilege and power that attend the theologian's gatekeeping role, the more this work of experimental re-construal is called for.[94]

There is, of course, no formula that will guarantee that doctrinal theologians will hear what ought to be heard, that they will open all the gates that should be opened, or close only those that ought to be closed. The work of doctrinal theologians will always, like the life of the churches that they serve, be a failure. The doctrinal theologian is therefore always thrown back upon prayer – not as a technique that might somehow provide the missing guarantee, but as a form of recognition that we simply do not

---

[93] See my discussion of the emergence of intellectualism in Chapter 5, pp. 97–9.
[94] Anthony Reddie, *Theologising Brexit: A Liberationist and Postcolonial Critique* (Abingdon: Routledge, 2019), 149, asks 'how successfully can the subaltern reimagine the substantive meaning of the Christian faith in general and the Bible in particular when the dictates of what is constructed as orthodoxy and normativity were produced in epochs and contexts that resonate with the power of the centre and not the margins?'

have it in us to ensure the righteousness of our action. We are thrown back upon the recognition not just that we might, but that we are failing and will fail.

Doctrinal theologians are nevertheless also called to pray that God might use their work, might turn it into one among the diverse gifts that the Spirit is giving to the church, as the Spirit leads the church into the truth of what it has been given. And they might offer their diligence – in pursuit of the disciplines proper to their work, in playfulness, in attending to voices that might be the call of God upon them – as an element of their praying.

Doctrinal theologians are not the heroes of the church's story. They are not virtuosos of the faith, from whose sheer intellectual creativity we can expect reformation, nor is their work unusually dangerous, always courting damnation. Forget the chiaroscuro. Doctrinal theology is one ordinary ministry among others in the life of the church, and – to the very limited extent that such distinctions are at all meaningful – it is not the most important. Doctrinal theologians are not those in whom the mind of the church specially resides – which is to say, we are not the head of this body.[95] Instead, we are people with a particular set of roles to play in the life of the body, roles that matter, and that it is worth trying to play well. At our best, we can assist with some of the processes by which the church holds fast to what it has already seen, heard or tasted of the gift that God has given to the world. We can assist with some of the processes by which the church grubs out the distortions and restrictions that mar its reception of that gift. We can assist with some of the processes by which the church in deep engagement with the world discovers just how much more it has yet to know, as it journeys deeper into the abundant love that God has opened for the world in Jesus of Nazareth. And that is more than enough.

---

[95] There might be a temptation to think that we are, if not the brain, then at least the kidneys in this body, filtering its blood, identifying and removing the toxins. Even that is still a bit too self-aggrandizing for my tastes. I prefer to think of us as the spleen: we have something of a filtering role, we store some resources, we are useful in fighting off a certain range of infections – and not many people know with any accuracy what our work is for. The trick, of course, is to inhabit this role without becoming splenetic.

10

Coda

Serving the church

Introduction

In this final, brief chapter, I ask what it means for doctrinal theology to serve the church. I begin by summarizing the account that I have been developing over the past six chapters, of doctrinal theology as one form of support for ordinary belief. I then suggest that, in practice, the support that doctrinal theologians can offer to ordinary belief will take four overlapping forms – encouraging, amplifying, resourcing and challenging – with all four necessarily animated by an ongoing process of listening and re-construal. Finally, I illustrate this account by turning back to the Church of England, and looking at three locations in which doctrinal theology becomes visible: the work of bishops, of commissions and of Theological Education Institutions. None of these is the source from which the church's believing flows, or the space within which the church's knowledge of God is held, but each, I suggest, can fruitfully be understood as one form of support for the church's ongoing discovery of the abundant love of God.

Serving ordinary belief

Doctrinal theology exists for the sake of ordinary belief – for the sake of lives of worship, witness and discipleship negotiated in particular places, in the midst of complex circulations of production and consumption and jagged landscapes of power. It is one ministry among others in the body of Christ, and its aim is to build up that body, 'until all of us come to the unity of the faith and of the knowledge of the Son of God, to maturity, to the measure of the full stature of Christ' (Eph. 4.13). Doctrinal theology is, in other words, a form of life support for the knowledge of God that lives in the church.

That does not mean – or it should not mean – that doctrinal theology is dedicated to the reproduction of the church's present life, or that it serves the maintenance of the church's present distributions of power. Instead, it exists to serve the church's ongoing exploration and embodiment of the abundant love of God, and that exploration will often involve penitence and sharp changes of course. Doctrinal theology aims at the building up of the body, but the building up that it pursues will often demand a breaking down. Doctrinal theology serves the church's ongoing journey into the surprising and challenging abundance of God's gift in Christ.

In each context in which we find the church, its life is an experiment in love. In each of these experiments something of the love of God is grasped, inhabited and handed on; in each that love is also misunderstood, ignored and betrayed. Each experiment is a pragmatic settlement between multiple different patterns of imagination, multiple different forms of practical wisdom, rubbing along together coherently enough to sustain for a while a pattern of shared life. Each is an arrangement of bodies, a way of organizing time, a set of habits and practices, a distribution of money and resources and energy, a tangle of power relationships, a grid of inclusions and exclusions. The church's patterns of imagination and practical wisdom show up in the shapes taken by this material life, the embodied forms of its worship, discipleship and witness.

Doctrinal theology exists for the sake of this ongoing embodied experimentation. It exists to help all those who participate in the church's life discover more together of God's love for them – to grasp more of its breadth and length and height and depth. It exists to help them discover more of how they might live that love out in the world, in the midst of all the relationships – local, political and cosmic – in which they find themselves. Doctrinal theology, if it is done well, contributes to the church's imagination and to its practical wisdom.

Dimensions of the task

All kinds of people are involved in sustaining, enriching and challenging the life of the church. All the participants in that life are constantly learning from and responding to one another, both consciously and unconsciously. In addition, all kinds of people play distinctive roles in teaching, guiding and informing that life.

In the midst of all this learning and teaching, there are some who focus on doctrinal theology – people who have some kind of formal responsibility for or professional interest in it, or who simply devote their time and energy to it. They contribute to the negotiations of the church's life, more or less directly, by exploring the ideas about God and God's ways with the world that might shape those negotiations, and by drawing on the wider conversations of the church within which those ideas have been explored and elaborated.

The support that such doctrinal theologians can offer to the life of the church takes four overlapping forms: encouraging, amplifying, resourcing and challenging.

Encouraging. The life of ordinary believing, and the learning and negotiation by which it develops over time, are always already going on, before doctrinal theologians speak or write a word. If all those who dedicate their time and energy to the explicit pursuit of doctrinal theology were to turn off their computers and lock up their libraries tomorrow, the life and learning of the church would continue. Ideas about God and God's ways with the world – articulations of the plot of Christian belief, identification of its characters, claims about the tenor and tendency of the life for which it calls – are always already in play, and people are always already thinking with them, deploying them and shaping their lives around them. Part of the role of a doctrinal theologian is simply to notice this, to name it, to celebrate what people already know and to encourage them to carry on.

Amplifying. To celebrate the doctrinal thinking that is already taking place in the church means drawing attention to it. Doctrinal theologians can help those involved in some particular experiment in faithfulness to notice what they are up to – drawing attention to the ways in which they are deploying ideas about God and God's ways with the world. Doctrinal theologians can also help people in other contexts hear what is going on in this experiment, disseminating the thinking that is emerging so that others can learn from it, and can improvise upon it. Doctrinal theologians can describe, articulate and draw attention to what is exciting about this experiment, naming the way in which the Christian story is being told here recognizably but differently. Doctrinal theologians are often people who have been handed some kind of platform for public speech; part of their role is handing that platform over to others.

Resourcing. This work of amplifying shades over into resourcing. Doctrinal theologians can draw the attention of those involved in the church's present negotiations to others whose experiments in faithfulness, whose ways of telling the Christian story, are powerful and challenging. They can draw attention to compelling ways of imagining God and God's ways with the world, and to the different visions of worship, witness and discipleship that flow from them. They can draw on voices from the wider church, voices from the longer tradition and voices from scripture, articulating and developing what they find, and offering resources that might enrich the improvisation, and extend the imaginative repertoires, of their churches today.

Challenging. In doing this, doctrinal theologians might also draw attention to voices, insights and discoveries that will challenge, unsettle or warn their churches. They might help the church to identify its involvement in destructive and harmful patterns of life and thought, its betrayals of the love of God. Doctrinal theology might be involved in calling the church to repentance, or in advocating significant change in its policies and practices, especially in the light of challenges from those who have been marginalized in, excluded from or harmed by its life.

The work of doctrinal theologians is always, however, fallible and ambiguous. They can only encourage and amplify what they currently recognize as good; they can only draw on resources that they currently value, or challenge what they currently discern to be harmful. Like therapists who need themselves to be in therapy, they need their work to be embedded in processes of learning and ongoing revision. They need to be listening for the call of God that might be audible in cries, encounters and improvisations. They need to be continually experimenting with re-construal in the light of the calls that they hear, revisiting the scriptures and the tradition, and the stories that they and their churches have woven around them, to see if they might need to be told differently in response to God's call. Doctrinal theologians are not guardians of the given, but people caught up in the reaction between the given and the found – their work one of the sites in which that reaction can occur.

Doctrinal theology is therefore a work of encouraging, amplifying, resourcing and challenging, set in the midst of listening and re-construal. As such, it is necessarily driven by attention paid in numerous directions, by a wide variety of interacting and entangled conversations. No one individual can do this work comprehensively. It has to emerge from the interaction between many people, each of whom is paying attention to different conversation partners, different cries, encounters and improvisations, different voices in the tradition, different discoveries in scripture. The work of doctrinal theology takes place as those who pursue it encourage one another, amplify one another, resource one another and challenge one another, and the good that it can do is tied to the quality of those interactions.[1]

Illustrations from the Church of England

I can illustrate these dimensions of the work of doctrinal theology by turning back briefly to the Church of England, and indicating how certain of the locations in which doctrinal theology is particularly visible in its life – the work of bishops, of commissions and of TEIs – might look in the light of my account.

Bishops

In the Church of England, bishops have a particular role as doctrinal theologians. Canon law says that it appertains to the office of bishops 'to teach and to uphold sound and wholesome doctrine, and to banish and drive away all erroneous and strange opinions'. In their consecration services, each new bishop is asked, 'Will you teach the doctrine of Christ as the Church of England has received it, will you refute error, and will you hand on entire the faith that is entrusted to you?', and the bishop replies, 'By the help of God, I will.'[2]

Bishops play this role in the midst of a church in which teaching and learning are always already taking place, in all manner of ways – in parishes, chaplaincies, fresh expressions, schools, religious orders, charities and mission societies. It is no slight on episcopal authority to say that, like all doctrinal theologians, their role as teachers is secondary to this life; their role is to serve and support it. Bishops are, however, given an unusual opportunity to discover the variety, richness and complexity of the learning and teaching taking place across the church, and to exercise oversight in relation to

---

[1] 'Progress in apprehension of the truths of the Gospel must chiefly come by the intercourse of minds united in friendship, so that they can do that most difficult thing to which St Paul refers as though it ought to come naturally – "speaking the truth in love".' William Temple, 'Chairman's Introduction', in *Doctrine in the Church of England: The Report of the Commission on Christian Doctrine Appointed by the Archbishops of Canterbury and York in 1922* (London: SPCK, 1938), 1.

[2] *The Canons of the Church of England: Canons Ecclesiastical Promulgated by the Convocations of Canterbury and York in 1964 and 1969 and by the General Synod of the Church of England from 1970* (London: Church House Publishing, 2012), C18.1; 'Ordination of a Bishop', available online at www.churchofengland.org/more/policy-and-thinking/canons-church-england/canons-7th-edition; Common Worship: Ordination Services, available online at www.churchofengland.org/prayer-and-worship/worship-texts-and-resources/common-worship/ministry/common-worship-ordination-services (both accessed 9 December 2019). I am drawing, in this section, on material I prepared for the Church of England's *Living in Love and Faith* project.

it – upholding what they discover to be good, and 'refuting' or 'banishing' what they find to be erroneous.

In my terms, their role is precisely one of encouraging, amplifying, resourcing and challenging. One of the most powerful actions available to a bishop is to bless: to attend to the teaching and learning going on in the church that they serve, to identify as best they can where the Spirit is at work luring people deeper in to the love of God and to acknowledge, celebrate and amplify what they have found. This role might at times be hidden behind the bureaucratic language of 'identifying and sharing best practice', but it is more than that: it is an act of discernment of the Spirit, and of inviting the wider church to give thanks for and to learn from the Spirit's work.

Bishops are teachers in their own right, and are given a wide variety of opportunities to preach, speak and write. Their resourcing of the church's conversations can draw on their own learning and their own capacity to articulate what they have learnt. As those with a ministry of oversight, however, they also have a deeper role in asking how richly resourced is the whole life of teaching in the church. They are granted an unusual vantage point from which to see those institutions, networks and individuals that are doing most to root the teaching of the church in scripture, to connect it to the wider conversations of the tradition and to draw on the insights of the church across the world; they are able to see more than most of where the church is being shaped by attention to cries, encounters and improvisations. They can, therefore, more directly than most, ask after the health of this whole ecclesial ecology of conversation and engagement. They can ask how well the church recognizes, encourages, resources, and makes use of these institutions, networks and individuals; they can commission, promote and support.

Bishops also play a role in challenging, as they seek to 'banish and drive away all erroneous and strange opinions'. As they exercise oversight of the teaching and learning of the Church, they can ask how that teaching and learning relates to the limits that earlier generations of the church have identified as necessary to the overall health of the Christian faith. Their work might involve admonishing individuals in private, speaking out publicly against certain developments and contributing to debates in synods and other deliberative and decision-making processes.

As with all other forms of doctrinal theology, however, this episcopal work of encouraging, amplifying and resourcing cannot be undertaken alone – and that is especially true in relation to the work of challenging erroneous teaching. As with all other forms of doctrinal theology, the work of bishops needs to be embedded within processes of ongoing listening and re-construal, in which there is a real possibility of their being led to see differently by the challenge of others. Bishops are enabled to play their role as teachers by being members of communities of conversation and exploration that can encourage them, resource them and challenge them – and especially by being members of communities that can read scripture with them, and inspire them to read it differently. In particular, their ability to 'uphold sound and wholesome doctrine' will be directly proportional to their ability to hear the call of God in cries, encounters and improvisations – because those are the means that the Spirit characteristically uses to draw the church deeper in to the sources of its faith.

I have, for some years, experienced one model for this kind of ongoing learning. Twice a year, a small 'theological retreat group' of which I am a member has met with a particular bishop for twenty-four hours. We do not discuss urgent practical matters on this bishop's agenda, but background themes that might shape his ministry – everything from poverty to marriage, money to holiness. We read scripture together; we discuss what we think are the most important relevant developments in doctrinal theology; we argue. We are a collection of doctrinal theologians and biblical scholars, from a range of ecclesial and academic contexts – and, to an extent (though this could be pursued much more deliberately and intensively) we include people who can speak from a range of contexts at the edges of the Church of England's current distributions of power. We don't develop policy, or publish papers; we are simply there to talk, and to help the bishop think. This is one way in which the doctrinal theological work of a bishop can be embedded in processes of listening and re-construal.

Commissions

At any given moment in the life of the Church of England, there are always multiple report-writing commissions at work – whether permanent bodies like the Faith and Order Commission and the Liturgical Commission, working on multiple projects at a time, or temporary bodies with a single task, like the Living in Love and Faith group, working on a specific topic (in this case, marriage, sexuality and gender). These commissions are one of the most visible spaces in the life of the church in which doctrinal theology is pursued.

My discussion of the nature of doctrinal theology suggests two conditions that the work of these commissions needs to satisfy. First, it needs to avoid disconnection from the life of ordinary believing. At their worst, commissions can become spaces in which people speak a peculiar dialect, a language that one learns by reading reports and practices by writing them; they can end up speaking only to an audience of other report-writing commissions, and to the kind of people who get invited onto those commissions. Yet if their work is meant, at whatever remove, to enrich and resource ordinary belief, it needs to be informed by careful attention to that belief – and by attention that goes beyond anecdote and caricature.

The Doctrine Commission's 1991 report, *We Believe in the Holy Spirit*, provides one example of such attention. It includes a chapter on 'Charismatic Experience: Praying "in the Spirit"', largely the work of Sarah Coakley, which is based on participant observation in charismatic worship, and on 'a number of in-depth interviews with Anglican charismatics from a particular church which was deemed to be representative of the development of the movement within the Church of England'.[3] The Commission were clear that 'The material gleaned from the interviews and the participant observation cannot in itself, and without further reflection, solve ... hard questions about the nature of the Spirit' – but this material does help show what is at stake in those questions, and how ordinary believers are inhabiting significantly different pneumatologies, and experiencing the tensions between them.[4] That provides one model for the kind of

---

[3] Doctrine Commission of the Church of England, 'We Believe in the Holy Spirit', in *Contemporary Doctrine Classics from the Church of England*, 146.
[4] Ibid., 156–7.

attentiveness that needs to feed the work of the Church's commissions – and it is an example worth improvising upon.

The second condition for the health of the work of these commissions is that they be spaces within which a wide variety of voices can be heard. This is not simply a matter of ensuring that they have a membership that is seen to be representative of major parties in the church, achieving a political balance that allows their work to be taken seriously. It is a matter of ensuring that their deliberations are habitually interrupted, challenged and informed by voices from beyond the institutional Church's comfort zone. Part of a commission's task is to listen for the call of God in cries, encounters and improvisations – and to be a space for experimenting with the re-construals that such calls can trigger. They can be spaces for the negotiation between the given and the found.

Informed by this listening and re-construal, such commissions can play a role in encouraging, amplifying, resourcing and challenging the wider church, in precisely the sense described earlier in this chapter. They are not the primary spaces in which the church's doctrinal thinking is done: they are spaces for reflection upon the doctrinal thinking that is taking place all around the church – for drawing attention to it and celebrating its vitality, for brokering conversation between divergent strands of it, for making sure that the challenges that it yields are heard more widely around the church and for assisting with the process of re-reading the scriptures, the tradition and the church's existing teaching in the light of all those challenges.

Theological Education Institutions

My final example is the teaching of doctrine in the Church's TEIs – that diverse collection of institutions which train people for ordination and for other forms of ministry in the Church of England and in various ecumenical partner churches.

Students who enter the doctrine classrooms of the Church's TEIs are already involved in believing. They already inhabit forms of imagination and practical wisdom, ways of telling the story of God and God's ways with the world. The doctrinal education they experience in their TEIs is meant to connect to and enrich that believing. As far as possible, they should be enabled to see how the doctrinal ideas that they encounter in their classrooms and their reading connect to, and give them language for, their existing involvements, commitments and concerns. They are not being introduced to a knowledge of God that is foreign to them or to the communities from which they come; they are encountering a form of support for an exploration of the knowledge of God in which they are already engaged. They should therefore experience their doctrinal education as – among other things – a form of encouragement.

The doctrinal teaching that they encounter does, however, draw their existing exploration of the knowledge of God into a set of wider conversations – helping them to recognize that they are discovering that knowledge alongside a vast community of others, whose explorations can enrich and challenge them. Especially when they are being drawn into encounter with the articulate tradition, their engagement with this wider community of believing might be mediated by technical terminology and detailed argument; it may require the learning of languages of explanation and argument that can seem foreign to the life of embodied belief. The point of those tools should always be, however, to articulate patterns of imagination and wisdom that embodied belief can inhabit. Helping students to keep on making that connection – to see what difference each doctrinal claim makes, and why it matters – is one of the deep challenges of doctrinal teaching.

Doctrinal teaching is meant to draw students not only into encounters with the articulate tradition but into encounter with the voices of those who live belief differently – especially those who have been marginalized within or excluded from the life of the church. This can't be kept as a secondary and subordinate part of their education – a few weeks in the midst of their doctrinal education in which they undertake a Cook's tour of exotic voices. The processes of listening and re-construal are, as I have tried to say throughout this book, crucial to the health of doctrinal theology and the church. Doctrinal teaching can, at its best, help students understand – help habituate them to – the processes of listening for the call of God in cries, encounters and improvisations, and exploring the re-construals of their faith that such calls can trigger.

All of this is meant to make a difference to the life that students will lead once they finish their formal education. It is meant to make a difference to the communities that they serve. It matters to the extent that it enriches their and their communities' imaginations and improvisations. Doctrine teachers don't need to shy away from the question, 'What use will this be in my ministry?' There may not be a short-term, instrumental answer to that question, but if we cannot show why the ideas and the conversations that we are exploring can and should make a difference to the life of embodied belief, we should pack up and go home.

Doctrinal theological education is not about training the individual virtuoso. It is not about training the individual who has internalized enough of the articulate tradition, and enough of the theological conversation of the contemporary church, to be a rich resource for the communities they serve through all the remaining years of their ministry. It is, instead, about drawing students more deeply into an ongoing conversation – helping them become more consciously members of a community of people who can encourage, amplify, resource and challenge one another's belief. And that means that doctrinal teachers need to have an eye to the spaces within which that ongoing conversation takes place, and the means by which it occurs. They are preparing their students not only to preach and to teach but to carry on reading and thinking, to participate more richly in theological conversation on social media, to respond thoughtfully to the output of the Church's commissions, to sustain communities of conversation at the level of the parish, the deanery and the diocese – to be involved in their own distinctive ways in the whole doctrinal ecology of the Church.

Conclusion

I said in Chapter 2 that I am writing from one side stream in the braided delta of church history. This stream is not, however, stagnant. It is not a finished settlement, but a Church that is now, as always, involved in an ongoing process of discovering how to live. Its life is now, as always, being animated by new people, new conversations, new experiments – and marked by new misunderstandings and failures. Like the rest of the worldwide church, we in the Church of England are engaged together, fallibly and unevenly, in the discovery and embodiment of the abundant love of God.

As someone who aims to serve this Church, but does so from an academic context, I am, on the whole, encouraged by the state of the doctrinal theology that I see around me. I see vast energies being poured into the exploration of the articulate theological tradition, discovering more of why the ideas discussed in it matter, and of what they have to offer to the life of belief in the present. I see a dramatic growth in the attention being paid to the connections between doctrinal ideas and the life of ordinary belief, and to the richness and complexity of that believing. Above all, I see encouraging signs that the doctrinal theological conversations in which I am involved are becoming more diverse, and less dominated by privileged voices like mine. It is easier now than it was when I first entered the world of academic doctrinal theology to encounter people with very different kinds of experience and different kinds of relation to the life of the churches, and to hear a range of sharper challenges to 'business as usual'. There is of course very much more to do, and there is no justification for complacency – but there are also many hands to do that work, and I am hopeful for the future.

Doctrinal theology is, however, a work wholly dependent upon the grace of God for any good service that it can do for the church. Doctrinal theologians might do all in our power to pursue the forms of engagement, attentiveness and deliberation that we already know – but we cannot pursue the forms that we do not yet know. We are surrounded by lives in which the Spirit of God is at work in ways that we do not yet know how to recognize – and we need the grace of God to enable us to hear that work and to be transformed by it. Our work makes sense only as an earnest petition for the ongoing breaking in of this convicting and animating grace, in ways that go beyond anything that our labour can produce.

Doctrinal theology is only one ministry in the life of the church. There is only so much that it can do, and it is as flawed and fallible as any other aspect of the church's life. Whether it will, in fact, do any good depends entirely upon the grace of God. But, trusting in that grace, it does seem that there is work to do – and that it is work worth doing.

Bibliography

Adams, Nicholas. 'Long-Term Disagreement: Philosophical Models in Scriptural Reasoning and Receptive Ecumenism'. *Modern Theology* 29, no. 4 (2013): 154–71.
Adams, Nicholas. 'New Plural Settlements: The Secular and Secularisation'. *Journal of Scriptural Reasoning* 15, no. 2 (2016). Available online: jsr.shanti.virginia.edu/back-issues/volume-15-number-2-november-2016/ (accessed 6 December 2019).
Adams, Nicholas. 'Reparative Reasoning'. *Modern Theology* 24, no. 3 (2008): 447–57.
Allegro, John M. *The Sacred Mushroom and the Cross*. London: Hodder and Stoughton, 1970.
Andrews, James A. *Hermeneutics and the Church: In Dialogue with Augustine*. Notre Dame, IN: University of Notre Dame Press, 2012.
Anglican-Oriental Orthodox International Commission. *Christology: Agreed Statement* (2014). Available online: www.anglicancommunion.org/media/103502/anglican-oriental-orthodox-agreed-statement-on-christology-cairo-2014.pdf (accessed 30 November 2019).
Anglican-Roman Catholic International Commission. *Salvation and the Church: An Agreed Statement* (1986). Available online: www.anglicancommunion.org/media/105239/ARCIC_II_Salvation_and_the_Church.pdf (accessed 30 November 2019).
Archbishops' Commission on the Organisation of the Church of England. *Working as One Body*. London: Church House Publishing, 1995.
Archbishops' First Committee of Inquiry. *The Teaching Office of the Church*. London: SPCK, 1919.
Arendt, Hannah. *The Human Condition*. Chicago: University of Chicago Press, 1958.
Astley, Jeff. 'Ordinary Theology as Lay Theology: Listening to and Learning from Lay Perspectives'. *Marriage, Families & Spirituality* 20, no. 2 (2014): 182–90. A pre-print version is available online at humanities.exeter.ac.uk/media/universityofexeter/collegeofhumanities/theology/centreforbiblicalstudies/Astley_2014_preprint_INTAMS_2018290.pdf (accessed 30 November 2019).
Astley, Jeff. *Ordinary Theology: Looking, Listening and Learning in Theology*. London: Routledge, 2002.
Atkins, Anselm. 'Religious Assertions and Doctrinal Development'. *Theological Studies* 27, no. 4 (1966): 523–52.
Avis, Paul. '1662 and All That'. *Ecclesiology* 9, no. 2 (2013): 157–60.
Avis, Paul. *The Identity of Anglicanism: Essentials of Anglican Ecclesiology*. London: T&T Clark, 2007.
Avis, Paul. 'Theology in Dogmatic Mode'. In *Companion Encyclopedia of Theology*, edited by Peter Byrne and Leslie Houlden, 976–1000. London: Routledge, 1995.
Ayres, Lewis. 'Augustine on the Rule of Faith: Rhetoric, Christology, and the Foundation of Christian Thinking'. *Augustinian Studies* 36, no. 1 (2005): 33–49.
Ayres, Lewis. 'Irenaeus versus the Valentinians: Toward a Rethinking of Patristic Exegetical Origins'. *Journal of Early Christian Studies* 23, no. 2 (2015): 153–87.

Ayres, Lewis. *Nicaea and Its Legacy: An Approach to Fourth-Century Trinitarian Theology*. Oxford: Oxford University Press, 2004.

Ayres, Lewis. 'On the Practice and Teaching of Christian Doctrine'. *Gregorianum* 80, no. 1 (1999): 33–94.

Ayres, Lewis. 'The Soul and the Reading of Scripture: A Note on Henri De Lubac'. *Scottish Journal of Theology* 61, no. 2 (2008): 173–90.

Ayres, Lewis. '"There's Fire in That Rain": On Reading the Letter and Reading Allegorically'. *Modern Theology* 28, no. 4 (2012): 616–34.

Ayres, Lewis. 'What Is Catholic Theology?' In *The Oxford Handbook of Catholic Theology*, edited by Lewis Ayres and Medi-Ann Volpe with Thomas L. Humphries, 5–41. Oxford: Oxford University Press, 2019.

Azariah, Vedanayagam Samuel. 'The Problem of Co-operation between Foreign and Native Workers'. In *World Missionary Conference, 1910, The History and Records of the Conference: Together with Addresses Delivered at the Evening Meetings*, 306–15. Edinburgh: Oliphant, Anderson & Ferrier, n.d.

de Azurara, Gomes Eanes, *The Chronicle of the Discovery and Conquest of Guinea*, translated by Charles Raymond Beazley and Edgar Prestage. London: Hakluyt Society, 1896–99.

Barrett, Al. *Interrupting the Church's Flow: Engaging Graham Ward and Romand Coles in a Radically Receptive Political Theology in the Urban Margins*. PhD thesis, Vrije Universiteit, Amsterdam, 2017.

Barrett, Richard. *Enquirers' Courses*. Diocese of Lichfield, 2016. Available online at cofelichfield.contentfiles.net/media/documents/document/2016/12/Enquirers_Courses_2016.pdf (accessed 30 November 2019).

Barth, Karl. *Church Dogmatics I/1: The Doctrine of the Word of God*, translated by G. W. Bromiley. Edinburgh: T&T Clark, 1975.

Barton, Mukti. *Rejection, Resistance and Resurrection: Speaking Out on Racism in the Church*. London: Darton, Longman and Todd, 2005.

Behr, John. *The Formation of Christian Theology 1: The Way to Nicaea*. Crestwood, NY: St Vladimir's Seminary Press, 2001.

Bennett, Zoë. 'Finding a Critical Space: Scripture and Experience in Practical Theology'. In *Theologians on Scripture*, edited by Angus Paddison, 23–35. London: Bloomsbury, 2016.

Birkett, Kirsten. 'The Theological Curriculum for Twenty-First Century Ministry: A UK Perspective'. *Practical Theology* 12, no. 4 (2019): 402–14.

Bloch, Maurice. 'Deference'. In *Theorizing Ritual: Issues, Topics, Approaches, Concepts*, edited by Jess Kreinath, Jan Snock and Michael Stausberg, 495–506. Leiden: Brill 2006.

Bokedal, Tomas. 'The Early Rule-of-Faith Pattern as Emergent Biblical Theology'. *Theofilos* Supplement 7, no. 1 (2015): 57–75.

Bourdieu, Pierre. 'The Scholastic Point of View'. In *Practical Reason: On the Theory of Action*, translated by Loïc Wacquant, 127–40. Cambridge: Polity Press, 1998.

Bowden, John. 'The Future Shape of Popular Theology'. In *Theology and Change: Essays in Memory of Alan Richardson*, edited by R. H. Preston, 11–24. London: SCM, 1975.

Braaten, Carl. 'The Role of Dogma in Church and Theology'. In Pfitzner and Regan, *The Task of Theology Today*, 23–54.

Brandom, Robert B. *Reason in Philosophy: Animating Ideas*. Cambridge, MA: Harvard University Press, 2009.

Brandom, Robert B. *Tales of the Mighty Dead: Historical Essays in the Metaphysics of Intentionality*. Cambridge, MA: Harvard University Press, 2002.

Bretherton, Luke. *Christ and the Common Life: Political Theology and the Case for Democracy*. Grand Rapids, MI: William B. Eerdmans, 2019.
Bretherton, Luke. 'Sharing Peace: Class, Hierarchy, and Christian Social Order'. In *The Blackwell Companion to Christian Ethics*, 2nd edn, edited by Stanley Hauerwas and Samuel Wells, 329–43. Oxford: Blackwell, 2011.
Briggs, Richard S. *Words in Action: Speech Act Theory and Biblical Interpretation*. Edinburgh: T&T Clark, 2001.
British Academy. *Theology and Religious Studies Provision in UK Higher Education*. London: 2019. Available online at www.thebritishacademy.ac.uk/sites/default/files/theology-religious-studies.pdf (accessed 30 November 2019).
Brown, Peter. *Power and Persuasion in Late Antiquity: Towards a Christian Empire*. Madison, WI: University of Wisconsin Press, 1992.
Bryant, M. Darrol, ed. *The Future of Anglican Theology*. New York: Edwin Mellen, 1984.
Buell, Denise Kimber. *Why This New Race: Ethnic Reasoning in Early Christianity*. New York, NY: Columbia University Press, 2005.
Bulgakov, Sergius. 'Dogma and Dogmatic Theology' (1937), translated by Peter Bouteneff. In *Tradition Alive: On the Church and the Christian Life in Our Time: Readings from the Eastern Church*, edited by Michael Plekon, 67–80. Lanham, MD: Rowman and Littlefield, 2003.
Burrus, Virginia. 'History, Theology, Orthodoxy, Polydoxy'. *Modern Theology* 30, no. 3 (2014): 7–16.
Burton, Sarah. 'The Monstrous "White Theory Boy": Symbolic Capital, Pedagogy and the Politics of Knowledge'. *Sociological Research Online* 20, no. 3 (2015): 1–11.
Butler, Joseph. *The Analogy of Religion, Natural and Revealed, to the Constitution and Course of Nature*. London: J.M. Dent, 1906.
Butterworth, Nick, and Mick Inkpen. *Stories Jesus Told*. London: Marshall Pickering, 1994.
Caird, G. B. *Paul's Letters from Prison*. Oxford: Oxford University Press, 1976.
Chadwick, Owen. *From Bossuet to Newman*, 2nd edn. Cambridge: Cambridge University Press, 1987.
Chadwick, Owen. *The Victorian Church*. London: Adam & Charles Black, 1966–70.
Chapman, Mark D. *Anglican Theology*. London: Bloomsbury T&T Clark, 2012.
Chapman, Mark D. 'Essays and Reviews 150 Years On' in Percy and Slocum, *Point of Balance*, 67–74.
Chapman, Mark D. 'F.D. Maurice and Reciting the Creeds'. In *Bishops, Saints and Politics: Anglican Studies*. London: T&T Clark, 2007.
Charry, Ellen T. *By the Renewing of Your Minds: The Pastoral Function of Christian Doctrine*. New York: Oxford University Press, 1997.
Charry, Ellen T. 'The Moral Function of Doctrine'. *Theology Today* 49, no. 1 (1992): 31–45.
Christian, William A. *Doctrines of Religious Communities: A Philosophical Study*. New Haven: Yale University Press, 1987.
Christie, Ann. *Ordinary Christology: Who Do You Say I Am?* Aldershot: Ashgate, 2012.
Church of England. *The Canons of the Church of England: Canons Ecclesiastical Promulgated by the Convocations of Canterbury and York in 1964 and 1969 and by the General Synod of the Church of England from 1970*. London: Church House Publishing, 2012. Available online at www.churchofengland.org/more/policy-and-thinking/canons-church-england/canons-7th-edition (accessed 9 December 2019).
Church of England. *Common Worship: Ordination Services*. Available online at www.churchofengland.org/prayer-and-worship/worship-texts-and-resources/common-worship/ministry/common-worship-ordination-services (accessed 9 December 2019).

Church of England. *Formation Criteria with Mapped Selection Criteria for Ordained Ministry in the Church of England* (2014). Available online at www.churchofengland.org/sites/default/files/2017-10/formation_criteria_for_ordained_ministry.pdf (accessed 30 November 2019).

Clements, Keith W. *Lovers of Discord: Twentieth Century Theological Controversies in England*. London: SPCK, 1988.

Clutterbuck, Richard. *Handing on Christ: Rediscovering the Gift of Christian Doctrine*. London: Epworth, 2009.

Coakley, Sarah. *God, Sexuality, and the Self: An Essay 'On the Trinity'*. Cambridge: Cambridge University Press, 2013.

Coakley, Sarah. *Powers and Submissions: Spirituality, Philosophy and Gender*. Oxford: Blackwell, 2002.

Coakley, Sarah. 'What Does Chalcedon Solve and What Does It Not? Some Reflections on the Status and Meaning of the Chalcedonian "Definition"'. In *The Incarnation: An Interdisciplinary Symposium on the Incarnation of the Son of God*, edited by Stephen T. Davis, Daniel Kendall and Gerald O'Collins, 143–63. Oxford: Oxford University Press, 2002.

Cocksworth, Ashley. 'Theorizing the (Anglican) *Lex Orandi*: A Theological Account'. *Modern Theology*, forthcoming.

Cocksworth, Christopher. 'Preface'. In Faith and Order Commission, *The Gospel, Sexual Abuse and The Church*, 6–9.

Coles, Romand. *Beyond Gated Politics: Reflections for the Possibility of Democracy*. Minneapolis, MN: University of Minnesota Press, 2005.

Coles, Romand. *Visionary Pragmatism: Radical and Ecological Democracy in Neoliberal Times*. Durham, NC: Duke University Press, 2016.

Collingwood, R. G. *An Autobiography*. 1939. Oxford: Clarendon, 1978.

Collingwood, R. G. *Principles of Art*. Oxford: Clarendon, 1938.

Collins, Jeffrey R. 'The Church Settlement of Cromwell'. *History* 87, no. 285 (2002): 18–40.

Common Awards. *Preface to the Common Awards in Theology, Ministry and Mission* (2012). Available online at www.churchofengland.org/sites/default/files/2018-07/Preface%20to%20the%20Common%20Awards%20in%20Theology%2C%20Ministry%20and%20Mission.pdf (accessed 30 November 2019).

Common Awards. *A Vision for Theological Education in the Common Awards* (2016). Available online at www.dur.ac.uk/theology.religion/common.awards/projects/theological.agenda/ (accessed 30 November 2019).

Cornwall, Susannah. 'Identity and Formation in Theological Education: The Occasion of Intersex'. *Journal of Adult Theological Education* 12, no. 1 (2015): 4–15.

Cosin, John. *The Correspondence of John Cosin, D.D.*, vol. 1. Durham: Andrews etc., 1869.

Cox, Jeffrey. 'The Dialectics of Empire, Race, and Diocese'. In *The Oxford History of Anglicanism V: Global Anglicanism, c. 1910–2000*, edited by William L. Sachs, 25–49. Oxford: Oxford University Press, 2018.

Craigo-Snell, Shannon. 'Tradition on Fire: Polydoxy, Orthodoxy, and Theological Epistemology'. *Modern Theology* 39, no. 3 (2014): 17–33.

Crockett, William. 'The Hermeneutics of Doctrine'. In Bryant, *Future of Anglican Theology*, 59–71.

Cross, Claire. *Church and People: England 1450–1660*, 2nd edn. Oxford: Blackwell, 1999.

Daley, Brian E. '"In Many and Various Ways": Towards a Theology of Theological Exegesis'. *Modern Theology* 28, no. 4 (2012): 597–615.

Daston, Lorraine, and Peter Galison. *Objectivity*. New York: Zone Books, 2007.

Davidowski, Wiesław. 'Regula Fidei in Augustine: Its Use and Function'. *Augustinian Studies* 35 (2004): 253–99.

Davie, Grace. *Religion in Britain: A Persistent Paradox*, 2nd edn. Chichester: Wiley, 2015.

Davies, Douglas J. 'Anglican Soteriology: Incarnation, Worship, and the Property of Mercy'. In *Salvation in Christ: Comparative Christian Views*, edited by Roger R. Keller and Robert L. Millet, 53–67. Provo, UT: Religious Studies Center, Brigham Young University, 2005.

Day, Abby. *Believing in Belonging: Belief and Social Identity in the Modern World*. Oxford: Oxford University Press, 2011.

Day, Abby. *The Religious Lives of Older Laywomen: The Last Active Anglican Generation*. Oxford: Oxford University Press, 2018.

Dickens, A. G. *The English Reformation*. London: Batsford, 1964.

Doctrine Commission of the Church of England. *Believing in the Church: The Corporate Nature of Faith*. London: SPCK, 1981.

Doctrine Commission of the Church of England. *Christian Believing: The Nature of the Christian Faith and Its Expression in Holy Scripture and Creeds*. London: SPCK, 1976.

Doctrine Commission of the Church of England. *Doctrine in the Church of England: The Report of the Commission on Christian Doctrine Appointed by the Archbishops of Canterbury and York in 1922*. London: SPCK, 1938.

Doctrine Commission of the Church of England. *We Believe in God*. London: Church House Publishing, 1987. Reprinted in *Contemporary Doctrine Classics from the Church of England*, 1–128. London: Church House Publishing, 2005.

Doctrine Commission of the Church of England. *We Believe in the Holy Spirit*. London: Church House Publishing, 1991. Reprinted in *Contemporary Doctrine Classics from the Church of England*, 129–272. London: Church House Publishing, 2005.

Drosnin, Michael. *The Bible Code*. London: Weidenfeld & Nicolson, 1997.

Dube, Musa W. 'Toward a Post-Colonial Feminist Interpretation of the Bible'. In *Postcolonial Feminist Interpretation of the Bible*, edited by Musa W. Dube, 11–26. St Louis, MO: Chalice, 2000.

Duffy, Eamon. 'The Shock of Change: Continuity and Discontinuity in the Elizabethan Church of England'. In Platten, *Anglicanism and the Western Christian Tradition*, 42–64.

Dunne, Joseph. *Back to the Rough Ground: Practical Judgment and the Lure of Technique*. Notre Dame, IN: Notre Dame University Press, 1993.

Elbourne, Elizabeth. *Blood Ground: Colonialism, Missions, and the Contest for Christianity in the Cape Colony and Britain, 1799–1853*. Montreal: McGill University Press, 2002.

Emery, Gilles. 'Thomas Aquinas, Postliberal? George Lindbeck's Reading of St. Thomas', translated by Matthew Levering. In Gilles Emery, *Trinity, Church, and the Human Person: Thomistic Essays*, 263–90. Naples, FL: Sapientia Press, 2007.

Faith and Order Commission of the Church of England. *Communion and Disagreement*. Church of England, 2016. Available online at www.churchofengland.org/sites/default/files/2017-10/communion_and_disagreement_faoc_report_gs_misc_1139.pdf (accessed 9 December 2019).

Faith and Order Commission of the Church of England. *Forgiveness and Reconciliation in the Aftermath of Abuse*. London: Church House Publishing, 2017. Available online at www.churchofengland.org/sites/default/files/2017-10/forgivenessandreconciliation_0.pdf (accessed 30 November 2019).

Faith and Order Commission of the Church of England. *The Gospel, Sexual Abuse and the Church: A Theological Resource for the Local Church*. London: Church House

Publishing, 2016. Available online at www.churchofengland.org/sites/default/files/2017-10/theologicalresourcefaocweb.pdf (accessed 30 November 2019).

Farrer, Austin. *Lord I Believe: Suggestions for Turning the Creed into Prayer*. 2nd edn. London: SPCK, 1962.

Fergusson, Everett. *The Rule of Faith: A Guide*. Eugene, OR: Cascade, 2015.

Fiddes, Paul S. 'The Great Ejection of 1662: The Effect of the Act of Uniformity on Baptists and Its Ecumenical Significance for Baptists today, 1662–2012'. *Ecclesiology* 9, no. 2 (2013): 183–204.

Fielding, Harold. *The Hearts of Men*. New York: Macmillan, 1901.

Fisch, Menachem, and Yitzakh Benbaji. *The View from Within: Normativity and the Limits of Self-Criticism*. Notre Dame, IN: University of Notre Dame Press, 2011.

Flett, John. *Apostolicity: The Ecumenical Question in World Christian Perspective*. Downers Grove, IL: InterVarsity Press, 2016.

Flynn, Gabriel, and Paul Murray (eds). *Ressourcement: A Movement for Renewal in Twentieth-Century Catholic Theology*. Oxford: Oxford University Press, 2011.

Ford, David F. *Christian Wisdom: Desiring God and Learning in Love*. Cambridge: Cambridge University Press, 2007.

Ford, David, and Mike Higton. 'Religious Literacy in the Context of Theology and Religious Studies'. In *Religious Literacy in Policy and Practice*, edited by Adam Dinham and Matthew Francis, 39–54. Bristol: Polity Press, 2015.

Fossett, Robert L. *Upon This Rock: The Nature of Doctrine from Antifoundationalist Perspective*. Eugene, OR: Pickwick, 2013.

Fowl, Stephen E. *Engaging Scripture: A Model for Theological Interpretation*. Oxford: Blackwell, 1998.

Fowl, Stephen E., and L. Gregory Jones. *Reading in Communion: Scripture and Ethics in Christian Life*. London: SPCK, 1991.

Fraser, Liam J. 'A Tradition in Crisis: Understanding and Repairing Division over Homosexuality in the Church of Scotland'. *Scottish Journal of Theology* 69, no. 2 (2016): 155–70.

Frei, Hans W. 'Conflicts in Interpretation'. In Hans W. Frei, *Theology and Narrative*, edited by George Hunsinger and William C. Placher, 153–66. New York and Oxford: Oxford University Press, 1993.

Frei, Hans W. *The Eclipse of Biblical Narrative: A Study in Eighteenth and Nineteenth Century Hermeneutics*. New Haven: Yale University Press, 1974.

Frei, Hans W. *The Identity of Jesus Christ: The Hermeneutical Bases of Dogmatic Theology*. Philadelphia: Fortress Press, 1975.

Frei, Hans W. 'The "Literal Reading" of Biblical Narrative in the Christian Tradition: Does It Stretch of Will It Break?' In *The Bible and the Narrative Tradition*, edited by Frank McConnell, 36–77. Oxford: Oxford University Press, 1986. Republished in *Theology and Narrative*, 117–52.

Frei, Hans W. 'Theology and the Interpretation of Narrative: Some Hermeneutical Considerations'. In Hans W. Frei, *Theology and Narrative*, edited by George Hunsinger and William C. Placher, 95–116. New York and Oxford: Oxford University Press, 1993.

Frei, Hans W. *Theology and Narrative*, edited by George Hunsinger and William C. Placher. New York and Oxford: Oxford University Press, 1993.

Frei, Hans W. *Types of Christian Theology*, edited by George Hunsinger and William C. Placher. New Haven: Yale University Press, 1992.

Fulford, Ben. *Divine Eloquence and Human Transformation: Rethinking Scripture and History through Gregory of Nazianzus and Hans Frei*. Minneapolis, MN: Fortress, 2013.

Furlong, Monica. *C of E: The State It's In*. London: Hodder and Stoughton, 2000.
Gallie, W. B. *Philosophy and the Historical Understanding*. London: Chatto and Windus, 1964.
Gathercole, Simon J. 'The Christ of the Canonical Gospels and the Christs of the Apocryphal Gospels'. In *The Oxford Handbook of Christology*, edited by Francesca Murphy, 531–48. Oxford: Oxford University Press, 2015.
Gilbert, Margaret. 'Collective Epistemology'. *Episteme* 1, no. 2 (2004): 95–107.
Gore, Charles. 'Dogma in the Early Church'. In W. R. Matthew et al., *Dogma in History and Thought: Studies by Various Writers*, 51–81. London: Nisbet, 1929.
Goulder, Michael, ed. *Incarnation and Myth*. London: SCM, 1979.
Green, Michael, ed. *The Truth of God Incarnate*. London: Hodder and Stoughton, 1977.
Guarino, Thomas C. *Vincent of Lérins and the Development of Christian Doctrine*. Grand Rapids, MI: Baker Academic, 2013.
Guest, Mathew, Kristin Aune, Sonya Sharma and Rob Warner. *Christianity and the University Experience: Understanding Student Faith*. London: Bloomsbury, 2013.
Guest, Mathew, Sonya Sharma and Robert Song. *Gender and Career Progression in Theology and Religious Studies*. Durham: Durham University, 2013. Available online at trs.ac.uk/wp-content/uploads/2013/11/Gender-in-TRS-Project-Report-Final.pdf (accessed 30 November 2019).
Gunstone, Pete. *Penal Substitution in the Worship of the Church of England: Historic Texts and Contemporary Practice*. MA diss., Durham University, 2019.
Gunton, Colin E. 'Dogma, the Church and the Task of Theology'. In Pfitzner and Regan, *The Task of Theology Today*, 1–22.
Haenchen, Ernst. *The Acts of the Apostles: A Commentary*. Oxford: Basil Blackwell, 1971.
Hall, Edward. *Hall's Chronicle*. 1548. London: J. Johnson et al., 1809.
Hampton, Stephen. 'Confessional Identity'. In Milton, *Oxford History of Anglicanism I*, 210–27.
Hanson, Anthony Tyrrell. *Beyond Anglicanism*. London: Darton, Longman & Todd, 1965.
Hardy, Daniel W. *Finding the Church: The Dynamic Truth of Anglicanism*. London: SCM, 2001.
Hardy, Daniel W. *God's Ways with the World: Thinking and Practicing Christian Faith*. Edinburgh: T&T Clark, 1996.
Hardy, Daniel W., with Deborah Hardy Ford et al. *Wording a Radiance: Parting Conversations on God and the Church*. London: SCM, 2010.
Harkianakis, Stylianos. 'Dogma and Authority in the Church'. In Pfitzner and Regan, *The Task of Theology Today*, 55–78.
Hartog, Paul. 'The "Rule of Faith" and Patristic Biblical Exegesis'. *Trinity Journal* 28, no. 1 (2007): 65–86.
Harvey, Anthony E. 'Attending to Scripture'. In Doctrine Commission of the Church of England, *Believing in the Church*, 25–44.
Harvey, Anthony E. *Believing and Belonging: The Practice of Believing in the Church*. London: SPCK, 1984.
Harvey, Anthony E., ed. *God Incarnate*. London: SPCK, 1981.
Harvey, Jennifer. 'What Would Zacchaeus Do?' In *Christology and Whiteness: What Would Jesus Do?* edited by George Yancy, 84–100. London: Routledge, 2012.
Hauerwas, Stanley. 'On Doctrine and Ethics'. In *The Cambridge Companion to Christian Doctrine*, edited by Colin E. Gunton, 21–40. Cambridge: Cambridge University Press, 1997.
Hays, Richard B. *Echoes of Scripture in the Gospels*. Waco, TX: Baylor University Press, 2008.

Hays, Richard B. *Echoes of Scripture in the Letters of Paul*. New Haven: Yale University Press, 1989.

Healy, Nicholas M. *Church, World and the Christian Life: Practical-Prophetic Ecclesiology*. Cambridge: Cambridge University Press, 2000.

Heard, James. *Inside Alpha: Explorations in Evangelism*. Eugene, OR: Wipf and Stock, 2012.

Hefling, Charles. 'The "Liturgy of Comprehension"'. In *The Oxford Guide to the Book of Common Prayer: A Worldwide Survey*, edited by Charles Hefling and Cynthia Shattuck, 61–3. Oxford: Oxford University Press, 2006.

Hefling, Charles. 'On "Core" Doctrine: Some Possibly Relevant Soundings'. *Anglican Theological Review* 80, no. 2 (1998): 233–49.

Helmer, Christine. *Theology and the End of Doctrine*. Louisville, KY: Westminster John Knox, 2014.

Henson, Hensley. *The Church of England*. Cambridge: Cambridge University Press, 1939.

Herbert, George. *The Temple: Sacred Poems and Private Ejaculations*. London: Pickering, 1838.

Heyduck, Richard. *The Recovery of Doctrine in the Contemporary Church: An Essay in Philosophical Ecclesiology*. Waco, TX: Baylor, 2002.

Heywood, David. 'Educating Ministers of Character: Building Character into the Learning Process in Ministerial Formation'. *Journal of Adult Theological Education* 10, no. 1 (2013): 4–24.

Hick, John, ed. *The Myth of God Incarnate*. London: SCM, 1977.

Hidalgo, Daniel, and Andra Olivia Maciuceanu. 'Essentially Contested Concepts: Debates and Applications'. *Journal of Political Ideologies* 11, no. 3 (2006): 211–46.

Higton, Mike. 'Apophaticism Transformed'. *Modern Theology* 31, no. 3 (2015): 511–16.

Higton, Mike. *Christ, Providence and History: Hans W. Frei's Public Theology*. London: T&T Clark, 2004.

Higton, Mike. 'Doctrine and Prayer'. In *The T&T Clark Companion to Christian Prayer*, edited by Ashley Cocksworth and John C. McDowell. London: Bloomsbury, forthcoming.

Higton, Mike. 'Foreword'. In Hans W. Frei, *The Identity of Jesus Christ: The Hermeneutical Bases of Dogmatic Theology*, revised and updated edition, xi–xix. Eugene, OR: Cascade, 2013.

Higton, Mike. 'George Lindbeck and the Christological Nature of Doctrine'. *Criswell Theological Review* 13, no. 1 (2015): 47–62.

Higton, Mike. 'Making Our Minds Up'. *Kai Euthus*, 15 October 2017. Available online at mikehigton.org.uk/making-our-minds-up/ (accessed 6 December 2019).

Higton, Mike. 'One-Bit Word Game'. 27 May 2018. Available at www.stbrandon.org.uk/wp-content/uploads/2018/05/2018-05-Trinity-Sermon.pdf (accessed 2 December 2019).

Higton, Mike. 'Patterns of Interfaith Reading I: Scriptural Settlements'. In Higton and Muers, *The Text in Play*, 115–18.

Higton, Mike. 'Reason'. In *The Routledge Companion to the Practice of Christian Theology*, edited by Mike Higton and Jim Fodor, 9–22. London: Routledge, 2015.

Higton, Mike. 'Reconstructing *The Nature of Doctrine*'. *Modern Theology* 30, no. 1 (2014): 1–31.

Higton, Mike. 'Scriptural Reasoning and the Discipline of Christian Doctrine'. *Modern Theology* 29, no. 4 (2013): 120–37.

Higton, Mike. 'Theological Education between the University and the Church: Durham University and the Common Awards in Theology, Ministry and Mission'. *Journal of Adult Theological Education* 10, no. 1 (2013): 25–37.

Higton, Mike. *A Theology of Higher Education*. Oxford: Oxford University Press, 2012.

Higton, Mike. 'Whose Psalm Is It Anyway? Why Christians Cannot Read Alone'. In Higton and Muers, *The Text in Play*, 71–92.

Higton, Mike. *Why Doctrine Matters*. Cambridge: Grove, forthcoming.

Higton, Mike, and Steve Holmes. 'Meeting Scotus: On Scholasticism and Its Ghosts'. *International Journal of Systematic Theology* 4, no. 1 (2002): 67–81.

Higton, Mike, and Rachel Muers. *The Text in Play: Experiments in Reading Scripture*. Eugene, OR: Wipf and Stock, 2012.

Hinze, Bradford. 'Ecclesial Repentance and the Demands of Dialogue'. *Theological Studies* 61 (2000): 207–38.

Hinze, Bradford. 'Narrative Contexts, Doctrinal Reform'. *Theological Studies* 51 (1990): 417–33.

Holland, Henry Scott. 'The Ministry of the Word (i)'. In Archbishops' First Committee of Inquiry, *Teaching Office of the Church*, 72–5.

Hooker, Richard. *Of the Laws of Ecclesiastical Polity*, edited by Arthur Stephen McGrade. Oxford: Oxford University Press, 2003.

House of Bishops of the General Synod. *Eucharistic Presidency: A Theological Statement*. London: Church House, 2014.

Hughes, Ann. 'The Cromwellian Church'. In Milton, *Oxford History of Anglicanism I*, 444–56.

Hunsinger, George. 'Truth as Self-Involving: Barth and Lindbeck on the Cognitive and Performative Aspects of Truth in Theological Discourse'. *Journal of the American Academy of Religion* 61, no. 1 (1993): 41–56.

Hunt, Cherryl. 'Be Ye Speakers of, and Listeners to, the Word: The Promotion of Biblical Engagement through Encountering the Scriptures Read Aloud'. *The Expository Times* 129, no. 4 (2018): 149–57.

Hunt, Cherryl. 'People of the Book? Responses to the Bible as "Big Story" or "Drama"'. *The Expository Times* 130, no. 8 (2019): 337–44.

Hunt, Cherryl. *Promoting Biblical Engagement among Ordinary Christians in English Churches: Reflections on the Pathfinder Project*. PhD thesis, University of Exeter, 2016.

Hunt, Cherryl. 'Seeing the Light: Ordinary Christians Encountering the Bible through Video'. *The Expository Times* 129, no. 7 (2018): 307–16.

Hurtado, Larry. 'Interactive Diversity: A Proposed Model of Christian Origins'. *Journal of Theological Studies* 64, no. 2 (2013): 445–62.

Hurtado, Larry. *Lord Jesus Christ: Devotion to Jesus in Earliest Christianity*. Grand Rapids, MI: Eerdmans, 2003.

Hussey, Robert. *Reasons for Voting upon the Third Question to be Proposed in Convocation on the 13th inst*. Oxford: J.G.F. and J. Rivington, 1845.

Hütter, Reinhard. *Suffering Divine Things: Theology as Church Practice*. Grand Rapids, MI: Eerdmans, 2000.

Inter-Anglican Standing Committee on Unity Faith and Order. *Towards a Symphony of Instruments: A Historical and Theological Consideration of the Instruments of Communion of the Anglican Communion* (2012). Available online at www.anglicancommunion.org/media/209979/Towards-a-Symphony-of-Instruments-Web-Version.pdf (accessed 30 November 2019).

James VI and I. 'Directions for Preachers' (1622). In *The Oxford Handbook of the Early Modern Sermon*, edited by Hugh Adlington, Peter McCullough and Emme Rhatigan, 557–9. Oxford: Oxford University Press, 2011.

Jenkins, Timothy. 'Anglicanism: The Only Answer to Modernity'. In *Anglicanism: The Answer to Modernity*, edited by Duncan Dormor, Jack McDonald and Jeremy Caddick, 186–205. London: Continuum, 2003.

Jenkins, Timothy. *An Experiment in Providence: How Faith Engages with the World.* London: SPCK, 2006.

Jenkins, Timothy. 'Fieldwork and the Perception of Everyday Life'. *Man* 29, no. 2 (1994): 433–55.

Jennings, Willie James. *Acts*. Louisville, KY: Westminster John Knox, 2017.

Jennings, Willie James. *The Christian Imagination: Theology and the Origins of Race*. New Haven, CT: Yale University Press, 2010.

Jervell, Jacob. *The Theology of the Acts of the Apostles*. Cambridge: Cambridge University Press, 1996.

Johnson, Luke Timothy. *The Acts of the Apostles*. Collegeville, MN: Liturgical Press, 1992.

Jowett, Benjamin. 'On the Interpretation of Scripture'. In *Essays and Reviews*, 330–433. London: John W. Parker and Son, 1860.

Keener, Craig S. *Acts: An Exegetical Commentary 1: Introduction and 1:1–2:47*. Grand Rapids, MI: Baker Academic, 2012.

Kellison, Rosemary B. 'Tradition, Authority, and Immanent Critique in Comparative Ethics'. *Journal of Religious Ethics* 42, no. 4 (2014): 713–41.

Kelly, J. N. D. *Early Christian Creeds*, 3rd edn. Harlow: Longmans, 1972.

Kerr, Nathan R. *Christ, History and Apocalyptic: The Politics of Christian Mission*. London: SCM, 2008.

Kinzig, Wolfram, ed. *Faith in Formulae: A Collection of Early Christian Creeds and Creed-related Texts*. Oxford: Oxford University Press, 2017.

Knox, Ronald. 'Tendencies of Anglicanism'. *Dublin Review* 162 (1918): 25–40.

Konolige, Kit and Fredeerica. *The Power of Their Glory: America's Ruling Class: The Episcopalians*. New York, NY: Wyden, 1978.

Lake, Peter. 'The "Anglican Moment?" Richard Hooker and the Ideological Watershed of the 1590s'. In Platten, *Anglicanism and the Western Christian Tradition*, 90–121.

Lake, Peter. *Anglicans and Puritans? Presbyterianism and English Conformist Thought from Whitgift to Hooker*. London: Unwin Hyman, 1988.

Lambeth Commission on Communion. *The Windsor Report*. London: The Anglican Communion Office, 2004.

Lambeth Conference 1958: The Encyclical Letter from the Bishops together with the Resolutions and Reports. London: SPCK / Greenwich, CT: Seabury, 1958.

Lambeth Conference 1988: The Reports, Resolutions and Pastoral Letters from the Bishops. London: Church House Publishing, 1988.

Lambeth Conferences of 1867, 1878, and 1888, edited by Randall T. Davidson. London: SPCK, 1889.

Lampe, G. W. H. 'The 1938 Report in Retrospect'. In *Doctrine in the Church of England*, ix–lx. London: SPCK, 1982.

Lash, Nicholas. *Newman on Development: The Search for an Explanation in History*. London: Sheed and Ward, 1975.

Lash, Nicholas. *Theology on Dover Beach*. London: Darton, Longman and Todd, 1979.

Ledger-Lomas, Michael. 'Mass Markets: Religion'. In *The Cambridge History of the Book in Britain 6: 1830–1914*, edited by David McKitterick, 324–58. Cambridge: Cambridge University Press, 2009.

Le Guin, Ursula K. 'Brin Mawr Commencement Address'. In *Dancing at the Edge of the World: Thoughts on Words, Women, Place*, 147–60. New York: Grove, 1989.

Leith, Jennifer. *Between Church and World: Anglican Formation of Christian Political Identity*. PhD thesis, Durham University, 2020.

Levine, Amy-Jill. 'Introduction'. In *A Feminist Companion to the Acts of the Apostles*, edited by Amy-Jill Levine and Marianne Blickenstaff. London: T&T Clark, 2004.

Lindbeck, George A. 'Atonement and the Hermeneutics of Intertextual Social Embodiment'. In *The Nature of Confession: Evangelicals and Postliberals in Conversation*, edited by Timothy Phillips and Dennis Okholm, 221–40. Downers Grove, IL: IVP, 1996.

Lindbeck, George A. 'Barth and Textuality'. *Theology Today* 43, no. 3 (1986): 361–76.

Lindbeck, George A. 'The Church'. In *Keeping the Faith: Essays to Mark the Centenary of Lux Mundi*, edited by Geoffrey Wainwright, 179–208. London: SPCK, 1989. Reprinted in Lindbeck, *The Church in a Postliberal Age*, edited by James J. Buckley, 145–65. Grand Rapids, MI: Eerdmans, 2002.

Lindbeck, George A. 'The Church as Israel: Ecclesiology and Ecumenism'. In *Jews and Christians: People of God*, edited by Carl E. Braaten and Robert W. Jenson, 78–94. Grand Rapids, MI: Wm. B. Eerdmans, 2003.

Lindbeck, George A. 'Discovering Thomas (1): The Classical Statement of Christian Theism'. *Una Sancta* 24, no. 1 (1967): 45–52.

Lindbeck, George A. 'Ecclesiology and Roman Catholic Renewal'. *Religion in Life* 33 (1963): 383–94. Reprinted in *New Theology 2*, edited by Martin Marty and Dean Peerman, 183–97. New York, NY: Macmillan, 1965.

Lindbeck, George A. 'Ecumenical Directions and Confessional Construals'. *Dialog* 30, no. 2 (1991): 118–23.

Lindbeck, George A. 'Justification and Atonement: An Ecumenical Trajectory'. In *By Faith Alone: Essays on Justification in Honor of Gerhard O. Forde*, edited by Joseph A. Burgess and Marc Kolden, 183–219. Grand Rapids, MI: Eerdmans, 2004.

Lindbeck, George A. *The Nature of Doctrine: Religion and Theology in a Postliberal Age*. Philadelphia, PA: Westminster, 1984.

Lindbeck, George A. 'A Protestant View of the Ecclesiological Status of the Roman Church'. *The Journal of Ecumenical Studies* 1 (1964): 243–70.

Lindbeck, George A. 'Reply to Avery Cardinal Dulles'. *First Things* 139 (2004): 13–15.

Lindbeck, George A. 'Response to Bruce Marshall'. *The Thomist* 53, no. 3 (1989): 403–6.

Lindbeck, George A. 'Response to Michael Wyschogrod's "Letter to a Friend"'. *Modern Theology* 11, no. 2 (1995): 205–10.

Lindbeck, George A. 'The Story-shaped Church: Critical Exegesis and Theological Interpretation'. In *Scriptural Authority and Narrative Interpretation*, edited by Garrett Green, 161–78. Philadelphia, PA: Fortress Press, 1987.

Lindbeck, George A. 'Unbelievers and the "*Sola Christi*"'. *Dialog* 12 (1973): 182–9. Reprinted in Lindbeck, *The Church in a Postliberal Age*, edited by James J. Buckley, 77–87. Grand Rapids, MI: Eerdmans, 2002.

Litton, E. A. *Introduction to Dogmatic Theology on the Basis of The Thirty-Nine Articles*. London: Elliot Stock, 1882–1892.

Lloyd, Vincent. 'Virtue against Domination'. *Syndicate*, 23 September 2019. Available online at syndicate.network/symposia/theology/the-character-of-virtue/ (accessed 3 December 2019).

Lloyd, Vincent. 'What Love Is Not: Lessons from Martin Luther King, Jr.'. *Modern Theology* 36, no. 1 (2020): 107–20.
Long, Thomas G. *1 & 2 Timothy and Titus*. Louisville, KY: Westminster John Knox, 2016.
Longley, Clifford. 'Are the Gospels a "Myth?"'. *The Times*, 1 July 1977, 18.
Longley, Clifford. 'Theological War Opens over Divinity of Christ'. *The Times*, 29 June 1977, 1.
Loughlin, Gerard. 'The Basis and Authority of Doctrine'. In *The Cambridge Companion to Christian Doctrine*, edited by Colin E. Gunton, 41–64. Cambridge: Cambridge University Press, 1997.
Louth, Andrew. *Theology and Spirituality*, revised edn. Oxford: SLG, 1978.
MacCulloch, Diarmaid. *All Things Made New: The Reformation and Its Legacy*. Oxford: Oxford University Press, 2016.
MacCulloch, Diarmaid. 'Church of England 1533–1603'. In Platten, *Anglicanism and the Western Christian Tradition*, 18–41.
MacCulloch, Diarmaid. 'The Myth of the English Reformation'. *Journal of British Studies* 30, no. 1 (1991): 1–19.
MacCulloch, Diarmaid. '*Our Church* by Roger Scruton – Review'. *The Guardian*, 19 June 2013.
Maiden, John G. *National Religion and the Prayer Book Controversy, 1927–1928*. Woodbridge: Boydell, 2009.
Mallock, W. H. *Doctrine and Doctrinal Disruption: Being an Examination of the Intellectual Position of the Church of England*. London: Adam and Charles Black, 1900.
Maltby, Judith. *Prayer Book and People in Elizabethan and Early Stuart England*. Cambridge: Cambridge University Press, 1998.
Maltby, Judith. 'Suffering and Surviving: The Civil Wars, the Commonwealth, and the Formation of "Anglicanism", 1642–1660'. In *Religion in Revolutionary England*, edited by Christopher Durston and Judith Maltby, 158–80. Manchester: Manchester University Press, 2006.
Maltby, Judith, and Alison Shell. 'Introduction: Why Anglican; Why Women; Why Novelists?' In *Anglican Women Novelists: From Charlotte Brontë to P.D. James*, edited by Judith Maltby and Alison Shell, 1–14. London: T&T Clark, 2019.
Markschies, Christoph. *Christian Theology and Its Institutions in the Early Roman Empire: Prolegomena to a History of Early Christian Theology*. Waco, TX: Baylor University Press, 2015.
Marshall, Bruce. 'Aquinas as Postliberal Theologian'. *The Thomist* 53, no. 3 (1989): 353–402.
Martin, Jessica. 'Early Modern English Piety'. In Milton, *The Oxford History of Anglicanism I*, 395–411.
Mascall, E. L. *Theology and the Gospel of Christ: An Essay in Reorientation*. London: SCM, 1984.
Mascall, E. L. 'Whither Anglican Theology?' In *When Will Ye Be Wise? The State of the Church of England*, edited by Anthony A. Kilmister. London: Blond and Briggs, 1983: 30–49.
Matthews, W. R. 'The Nature and Basis of Dogma'. In W. R. Matthews et al., *Dogma in History and Thought: Studies by Various Writers*, 1–26. London: Nisbet, 1929.
Maughan, Stephen. *Mighty England Do Good: Culture, Faith, Empire, and World in the Foreign Missions of the Church of England, 1850–1915*. Grand Rapids, MI: William B. Eerdmans, 2014.

Maurice, Frederick Denison. *The Kingdom of Christ: Or, Hints on the Principles, Ordinances and Constitution of the Catholic Church. In Letters to a Member of the Society of Friends*, 2nd edn. London: J.G.F. and J. Rivington / Darton and Clark, 1842.
Maurice, Frederick Denison. *The Prayer Book: Considered Especially in Reference to the Romish System: Nineteen Sermons Preached in the Chapel of Lincoln's Inn*. London: John W. Parker, 1849.
McCabe, Herbert. *God Matters*. London: Continuum, 2005.
McClendon, James Wm., Jr. *Systematic Theology 2: Doctrine*. Nashville, TN: Abingdon, 1994.
McGrath, Alister E. 'An Evangelical Evaluation of Postliberalism'. In *The Nature of Confession: Evangelicals and Postliberals in Conversation*, edited by Timothy Phillips and Dennis Okholm, 23–44. Downers Grove, IL: IVP, 1996.
McGrath, Alister E. *The Genesis of Doctrine: A Study in the Foundation of Doctrinal Criticism*. Grand Rapids, MI: Eerdmans, 1990.
McIntosh, Ian. 'Formation in the Margins: The Holy Spirit and Living with Transitions in Part-Residential Theological Education'. *Journal of Adult Theological Education* 11, no. 2 (2015): 139–49.
McIntosh, Mark A. *Mystical Theology*. Oxford: Blackwell, 1998.
McMichael, Ralph. 'What Does Canterbury Have To Do with Jerusalem? The Vocation of Anglican Theology'. In *The Vocation of Anglican Theology*, edited by Ralph McMichael, 1–34. London: SCM, 2014.
Methodist Conference. *The Constitutional Practice and Discipline of the Methodist Church*, vol. 2. London: Methodist Publishing, 2017.
Middleton, Robert Dudley. 'Tract Ninety'. *Journal of Ecclesiastical History* 2, no. 1 (1951): 81–101.
Milbank, John. *Theology and Social Theory: Beyond Secular Theory*, 2nd edn. Oxford: Blackwell, 2006.
Milton, Anthony. 'Arminians, Laudians, Anglicans, and Revisionists: Back to Which Drawing Board?' *Huntingdon Library Quarterly Review*, 78, no. 4 (2015): 723–43.
Milton, Anthony. 'Introduction: Reformation, Identity, and "Anglicanism"', c. 1520–1662'. In Milton, *Oxford History of Anglicanism I*, 1–27.
Milton, Anthony, ed. *The Oxford History of Anglicanism I: Reformation and Identity, c.1520–1662*. Oxford: Oxford University Press, 2017.
Moss, Claude Beaufort. *The Christian Faith: An Introduction to Dogmatic Theology*. London: SPCK, 1943.
Mitchell, Basil. 'I Believe, We Believe'. In The Doctrine Commission of the Church of England, *Believing in the Church*, 9–24.
Muers, Rachel. 'The Personal Is the (Academic-)Political: Why Care about The Love Lives of Theologians?' *Scottish Journal of Theology*, Forthcoming.
Murray, Paul. 'Living Catholicity Differently: On Growing into the Plenitudinous Plurality of Catholic Communion in God'. In *Envisioning Futures for the Catholic Church*, edited by Staf Hellemans and Peter Jonkers, 109–58. Washington, DC: The Council for Research in Values and Philosophy, 2018.
Murray, Paul. 'Receptive Ecumenism and Catholic Learning: Establishing the Agenda'. In *Receptive Ecumenism and the Call to Catholic Learning: Exploring a Way for Contemporary Ecumenism*, edited by Paul Murray, 5–25. Oxford: Oxford University Press, 2008.

Myers, Ben. 'Idiosyncratic Dogmatics'. *Faith and Theology*, 10 March 2006. Available online at www.faith-theology.com/2006/03/idiosyncratic-dogmatics.html (accessed 30 November 2019).

Newman, John Henry. *Discussions and Arguments on Various Subjects*. London: Longmans, Green, and Co., 1907.

Newman, John Henry. *An Essay on the Development of Christian Doctrine*. 1845, edited by J. M. Cameron. Harmondsworth: Penguin, 1974.

Newman, John Henry. *An Essay on the Development of Christian Doctrine*. 1887. London: Longmans, Green, and Co., 1909.

Newman, John Henry. *Tract 90*. London: J. G. F and J. Rivington, 1841.

Newman, John Henry. *The Via Media of the Anglican Church*, vol. 1. London: Longmans, Green and Co., 1901.

Nichols, Aidan. *The Panther and the Hind: A Theological History of Anglicanism*. Edinburgh: T&T Clark, 1993.

Nussbaum, Martha C. *Love's Knowledge: Essays on Philosophy and Literature*. New York, NY: Oxford University Press, 1990.

Oakley, Ann. 'Interviewing Women: A Contradiction in Terms'. In *Doing Feminist Research*, edited by H. Roberts, 30–61. London: Routledge and Kegan Paul, 1981.

Oakley, Ann. 'Interviewing Women Again: Power, Time and the Gift'. *Sociology* 50, no. 1 (2016): 195–213.

Ochs, Peter. *Another Reformation: Postliberal Christianity and the Jews*. Grand Rapids, MI: Baker Academic, 2011.

'Old Tactics from New Vinedressers'. *Third Way* 1, no. 14 (14 July 1977): 12.

Oliver, Simon. *Creation: A Guide for the Perplexed*. London: Bloomsbury, 2017.

Origgi, Gloria. 'Croyance, Déférence et Témoignage'. In *Philosophie Cognitive*, edited by J. Proust and E. Pacherie, 167–83. Paris: Éditions Ophrys / Éditions de la Maison des Sciences de l'Homme, 2004.

Orr, James. *The Progress of Dogma*, 4th edn. London: Hodder and Stoughton, 1901.

Owen, D. R. G. 'Is There an Anglican Theology?' In Bryant, *Future of Anglican Theology*, 3–13.

Page, Sydney H. T. 'Whose Ministry? An Appraisal of Ephesians 4:12'. *Novum Testamentum* 47, no. 1 (2005): 26–46.

Papanikolaou, Aristotle. *The Mystical as Political: Democracy and Non-Radical Orthodoxy*. Notre Dame, IN: University of Notre Dame Press, 2012.

Patterson, Neil. *Ecclesiastical Law, Clergy, and Laity: A History of Legal Discipline and the Anglican Church*. London: Routledge, 2018.

Paul, Ian. 'The Poetic Structure of Jesus' Teaching', *Psephizo*, 27 June 2013. Available online at www.psephizo.com/biblical-studies/the-poetic-structure-of-jesus-teaching/ (accessed 4 December 2019).

Paul, Ian. 'Why We Need a New Lord's Prayer', *Psephizo*, 2 October 2018. Available online at www.psephizo.com/biblical-studies/why-we-need-a-new-lords-prayer/ (accessed 4 December 2019).

Peake, F. A. 'The Anglican Ethos'. In Bryant, *Future of Anglican Theology*, 27–41.

Pelikan, Jaroslav. *Credo: Historical and Theological Guide to Creeds and Confessions of Faith in the Christian Tradition*. New Haven, CT: Yale, 2003.

Percy, Martyn. 'Afterword'. In Percy and Slocum, *Point of Balance*, 131–5.

Percy, Martyn. 'Engagement, Diversity, and Distinctiveness: Anglicanism in Contemporary Culture'. In Percy and Slocum, *Point of Balance*, 13–27.

Percy, Martyn. '*The Gift of Authority* in the Church of England: Sketching a Contextual Theology'. In Faith and Order Group of the Church of England, *Unpacking the Gift: Anglican Resources for Theological Reflection on The Gift of Authority*, 76–93. London: Church House Publishing, 2002.

Percy, Martyn. *Words, Wonders and Power: Understanding Contemporary Christian Fundamentalism and Revivalism*. London: SPCK, 1996.

Percy, Martyn, and Robert Boak Slocum, eds. *A Point of Balance: The Weight and Measure of Anglicanism*. Harrisburg, PA: Morehouse, 2012.

Petrenko, Ester. *Created in Christ Jesus for Good Works: The Integration of Soteriology and Ethics in Ephesians*. Milton Keynes: Paternoster, 2011.

Pfitzner, Victor, and Hilary Regan, eds. *The Task of Theology Today*. Edinburgh: T&T Clark, 1998.

Pieper, Franz, *Christliche Dogmatik I*. St Louis, MO: Concordia, 1924.

Plant, Stephen. 'When Karl Met Lollo: The Origins and Consequences of Karl Barth's Relationship with Charlotte von Kirschbaum'. *Scottish Journal of Theology* 72, no. 2 (2019): 127–45.

Platt, Jane. *Subscribing to Faith? The Anglican Parish Magazine 1859–1929*. Basingstoke: Palgrave Macmillan, 2015.

Platten, Stephen, ed. *Anglicanism and the Western Christian Tradition: Continuity, Change and the Search for Communion*. Norwich: Canterbury Press, 2003.

Podmore, Colin. 'The Governance of the Church of England and the Anglican Communion' (2009). Available online at www.speakcdn.com/assets/1145/governance_of_the_coe_and_ac.pdf (accessed 30 November 2019).

Pratt, Mary Louise. *Imperial Eyes: Travel Writing and Tranculturation*, 2nd edn. London: Routledge, 2008.

Prevot, Andrew. *Thinking Prayer: Theology and Spirituality and the Crises of Modernity*. Notre Dame, IN: University of Notre Dame Press, 2015.

Price, H.H. *Belief: The Gifford Lectures delivered at the University of Aberdeen in 1960*. London: Allen and Unwin, 1969.

Quash, Ben. *Found Theology: History, Imagination and the Holy Spirit*. London: Bloomsbury, 2013.

Quash, Ben. *Theology and the Drama of History*. Cambridge: Cambridge University Press, 2005.

Quilty-Dunn, J., and E. Mandelbaum. 'Against Dispositionalism: Belief in Cognitive Science'. *Philosophical Studies* 175, no. 9 (2018): 2353–72.

Radner, Ephraim. *A Brutal Unity: The Spiritual Politics of the Christian Church*. Waco, TX: Baylor University Press, 2012.

Radner, Ephraim. *Church*. Eugene, OR: Cascade, 2017.

Radner, Ephraim. *Hope among the Fragments: The Broken Church and Its Engagement of Scripture*. Grand Rapids, MI: Brazos Press, 2004.

Radner, Ephraim. *Time and the Word: Figural Reading of the Christian Scriptures*. Grand Rapids, MI: William B. Eerdmans, 2016.

Ramsey, Michael. *The Gospel and the Catholic Church*. London: Longmans, Green, 1936.

Reddie, Anthony. *Theologising Brexit: A Liberationist and Postcolonial Critique*. London: Routledge, 2019.

Rescher, Nicholas. 'Is Consensus Required for a Benign Social Order?'. In *Pluralism: Against the Demand for Consensus*, 156–85. Oxford: Clarendon Press, 1993.

Rogers, Alasdair. *To What Extent Is George Lindbeck's 'Postliberal' Approach to Doctrine Helpful for the Resolution of Contemporary Christian Controversies?* PhD thesis, Chester University, 2018.

Rogers, Andrew P. *Congregational Hermeneutics: How Do We Read?* London: Routledge, 2016.

Rogers, Eugene F., Jr. *After the Spirit: A Constructive Pneumatology from Resources outside the Modern West.* London: SCM Press, 2006.

Rose, Marika. *A Theology of Failure: Žižek against Christian Innocence.* New York: Fordham University Press, 2019.

Rush, Ormond. *The Reception of Doctrine: An Appropriation of Hans Robert Jauss' Reception Aesthetics and Literary Hermeneutics.* Rome: Gregorian University Press, 1997.

Ryan, Greg. *Receptive Integrity and the Dynamics of Doctrine: A Study in the Hermeneutics of Catholic Ecclesial Learning.* PhD thesis, Durham University, 2018.

Ryle, Gilbert. *The Concept of Mind.* London: Hutchinson, 1949.

Ryrie, Alec. 'The Reformation in Anglicanism'. In *The Oxford Handbook of Anglican Studies*, edited by Mark D. Chapman, Sathianathan Clarke and Martyn Percy, 34–45. Oxford: Oxford University Press, 2016.

Sanneh, Lamin O. *Disciples of All Nations: Pillars of World Christianity.* Oxford: Oxford University Press, 2008.

Sanneh, Lamin O. *Translating the Message: The Missionary Impact on Culture*, 2nd edn. Maryknoll, NY: Orbis, 2009.

Sarisky, Darren. *Scriptural Interpretation: A Theological Exploration.* Oxford: Wiley-Blackwell, 2013.

Scharen, Christian B., ed. *Explorations in Ecclesiology and Ethnography.* Grand Rapids, MI: Wm. B. Eerdmans, 2012.

Scharen, Christian B. *Public Worship and Public Work: Character and Commitment in Local Congregational Life.* Collegeville, Minnesota: Liturgical Press, 2004.

Schlink, Edmund. 'The Structure of Dogmatic Statements as an Ecumenical Problem'. In *The Coming Christ and the Coming Church*, translated by I. H. Neilson et al., 16–95. Edinburgh: Oliver and Boyd, 1967.

Schwitzgebel, Eric. 'A Phenomenal, Dispositional Account of Belief'. *Noûs* 36, no. 2 (2002): 249–75.

Shuger, Debora. '"Societie Supernaturall": The Imagined Community of Hooker's Laws'. In *Richard Hooker and the Construction of Christian Community*, edited by A. C. McGrade, 307–29. Tempe, AZ: Medieval & Renaissance Texts & Studies, 1997.

Slee, Nicola M., Leslie J. Francis and Ferelith Eccles Williams. *The Windy Day: Teddy Horsley Celebrates Pentecost on Whit Sunday.* London: Collins, 1983.

Slocum, Robert Boak. 'The Bonds and Limits of Communion: Fidelity, Diversity, and Conscience in Contemporary Anglicanism'. In Percy and Slocum, *Point of Balance*, 5–11.

Smith, Claire S. *Pauline Communities as 'Scholastic Communities': A Study of the Vocabulary of 'Teaching' in 1 Corinthians, 1 and 2 Timothy and Titus.* Tübingen: Mohr Siebeck, 2010.

Sonderegger, Katherine. 'Holy Scripture as Sacred Ground'. In *The Task of Dogmatics: Explorations in Theological Method*, edited by Oliver Crisp and Fred Sanders, 131–45. Grand Rapids, MI: Zondervan, 2017.

Sonderegger, Katherine. *Systematic Theology 1: The Doctrine of God.* Minneapolis, MN: Fortress Press, 2015.

Stanley, Brian. *The World Missionary Conference, Edinburgh 1910*. Grand Rapids, MI: William B. Eerdmans, 2009.

Sterba, Richard F. *Reminiscences of a Viennese Psychoanalyst*. Detroit: Wayne State University Press, 1982.

Stevenson, W. Taylor. 'Is There a Characteristic Anglican Theology?' In Bryant, *Future of Anglican Theology*, 15–26.

Stout, Jeffrey. *Ethics after Babel: The Languages of Morals and Their Discontents*. Boston: Beacon, 1988.

Strong, Rowan. *Anglicanism and the British Empire, c. 1700–1850*. Oxford: Oxford University Press, 2007.

Strong, Rowan. 'Series Introduction'. In Milton, *Oxford History of Anglicanism I*, xvii–xxvi.

Sullivan, Francis A. *Creative Fidelity: Weighing and Interpreting Documents of the Magisterium*. New York: Paulist, 1996.

Swinton, John. 'The Body of Christ Has Down's Syndrome: Theological Reflections on Vulnerability, Disability, and Graceful Communities'. *Journal of Pastoral Theology* 13, no. 2 (2003): 66–78.

Swinton, John. 'From Inclusion to Belonging: A Practical Theology of Community, Disability and Humanness'. *Journal of Religion, Disability and Health* 16, no. 2 (2012): 172–90.

Swinton, John. 'Restoring the Image: Spirituality, Faith, and Cognitive Disability'. *Journal of Religion and Health* 36, no. 1 (1997): 21–7.

Swinton, John. *Resurrecting the Person: Friendship and the Care of People with Mental Health Problems*. Nashville, TN: Abingdon, 2000.

Swinton, John. 'Who Is the God We Worship? Theologies of Disability; Challenges and New Possibilities'. *International Journal of Practical Theology* 14 (2011): 273–307.

Swinton, John, Harriet Mowat and Susannah Baines. 'Whose Story Am I? Redescribing Profound Intellectual Disability in the Kingdom of God'. *Journal of Religion, Disability and Health* 15, no. 1 (2011): 5–19.

Sykes, Stephen W., ed. *Contemporary Doctrine Classics from the Church of England*. London: Church House Publishing, 2005.

Sykes, Stephen W. 'Foreword', in *Contemporary Doctrine Classics from the Church of England*, xv–xxxiv.

Sykes, Stephen W. 'The Genius of Anglicanism'. In *The English Religious Tradition and the Genius of Anglicanism*, edited by Geoffrey Rowell. Wantage: Ikon / Nashville, TN: Abingdon, 1992.

Sykes, Stephen W. *The Identity of Christianity: Theologians and the Essence of Christianity from Schleiermacher to Barth*. London: SPCK, 1984.

Sykes, Stephen W. *The Integrity of Anglicanism*. New York: Seabury, 1978.

Tanner, Kathryn. *Jesus, Humanity, and the Trinity: A Brief Systematic Theology*. London: T&T Clark, 2001.

Tanner, Kathryn. *Theories of Culture: A New Agenda for Theology*. Minneapolis, MN: Fortress, 1997.

Taylor, Charles. *Sources of the Self: The Making of the Modern Identity*. Cambridge: Cambridge University Press, 1989.

Taylor, Charles. 'To Follow a Rule'. In *Philosophical Arguments*, 165–80. Cambridge, MA: Harvard University Press, 1997.

Temple, William. 'Chairman's Introduction', in Doctrine Commission of the Church of England, *Doctrine in the Church of England*, 1–17.

Temple, William. *Nature, Man and God*. London: Macmillan, 1956.

Thiel, John E. *Senses of Tradition: Continuity and Development in Catholic Faith*. Oxford: Oxford University Press, 2000.

Thiselton, Anthony C. *The Hermeneutics of Doctrine*. Grand Rapids, MI: Eerdmans, 2007.

Thiselton, Anthony C. 'Knowledge, Myth and Corporate Memory'. In Doctrine Commission of the Church of England, *Believing in the Church*, 45–78.

Thompson, David M. 'The Great Ejection of 1662: Memories, Interpretations and Justifications within Protestant Dissent, 1662–2012'. *Ecclesiology* 9, no. 2 (2013): 161–82.

Thornton, Ed. 'Campaigners Seek to Change the System'. *Church Times*, 30 November 2012. Available online at www.churchtimes.co.uk/articles/2012/30-november/news/uk/campaigners-seek-to-change-the-system (accessed 30 November 2019).

Ticciati, Susannah. *Job and the Disruption of Identity: Reading beyond Barth*. London: T&T Clark, 2005.

Ticciati, Susannah. *A New Apophaticism: Augustine and the Redemption of Signs*. Leiden: Brill, 2013.

Ticciati, Susannah. 'Response to Mike Higton'. *Modern Theology* 31, no. 3 (2015): 517–22.

Tietz, Christiane. 'Karl Barth and Charlotte von Kirschbaum'. *Theology Today* 74, no. 2 (2017): 86–111.

Tilling, Chris. '"Knowledge Puffs Up, But Love Builds Up": The Apostle Paul and the Task of Dogmatics'. In *The Task of Dogmatics: Explorations in Theological Method*, edited by Oliver Crisp and Fred Sanders, 87–106. Grand Rapids, MI: Zondervan, 2017.

Tonstad, Linn Marie. *God and Difference: The Trinity, Sexuality, and the Transformation of Finitude*. New York, NY: Routledge, 2016.

Tonstad, Linn Marie. *Queer Theology: Beyond Apologetics*. Eugene, OR: Cascade, 2018.

Tonstad, Linn Marie. 'The Real Problem of Abstraction in Systematic Theology'. Paper presented to the Society for the Study of Theology, 2019.

Townes, Emilie. 'Thin Human Imagination: Searching for Grace on the Rim Bones of Nothingness'. Paper presented to the Society for the Study of Theology, 2019.

Trible, Phyllis. *Texts of Terror: Literary-Feminist Readings of Biblical Narratives*. Philadelphia, PA: Fortress, 1984.

TRS UK. Constitution (no date). Available online at trs.ac.uk/about-trs/ (accessed 30 November 2019).

Twelftree, Graham H. *People of the Spirit: Exploring Luke's View of the Church*. Grand Rapids, MI: Baker Academic, 2009.

Tyacke, Nicholas. 'Anglican Attitudes: Some Recent Writings on English Religious History, from the Reformation to the Civil War'. In *Aspects of English Protestantism, c. 1530–1700*, 176–202. Manchester: Manchester University Press, 2001.

Tyacke, Nicholas. *Anti-Calvinists: The Rise of English Arminianism c. 1590–1640*. Oxford: Clarendon, 1987.

Vanhoozer, Kevin J. *The Drama of Doctrine: A Canonical-Linguistic Approach to Christian Doctrine*. Louisville, KY: Westminster John Knox, 2005.

Village, Andrew. 'Assessing Belief about the Bible: A Study among Anglican Laity'. *Review of Religious Research* 46, no. 3 (2005): 243–54.

Village, Andrew. *The Bible and Lay People: An Empirical Approach to Ordinary Hermeneutics*. Aldershot: Ashgate, 2007.

Village, Andrew. 'Does Higher Education Change the Faith of Anglicans and Methodists Preparing for Church Ministries through a Course Validated by a UK University?' *Practical Theology* 12, no. 4 (2019): 389–401.

Village, Andrew. 'Factors Shaping Biblical Literalism: A Study among Anglican Laity'. *Journal of Beliefs & Values* 26, no. 1 (2005): 29–38.

Volpe, Medi Ann. *Rethinking Christian Identity: Doctrine and Discipleship*. Oxford: Blackwell, 2013.

Wainwright, Geoffrey. 'Does Doctrine Still Divide?' *Ecclesiology* 2, no. 1 (2005): 11–34.

Walker, Arthur. 'The Creed of the Average Englishman'. *Modern Churchman*, 11, no. 8 (1921): 405–11.

Walls, Andrew F. 'Converts or Proselytes: The Crisis over Conversion in the Early Church'. *International Bulletin of Missionary Research* 28, no. 1 (2004): 2–6.

Walsham, Alexandra. *Charitable Hatred: Tolerance and Intolerance in England, 1500–1700*. Manchester: Manchester University Press, 2006.

Ward, Graham. *How the Light Gets In: Ethical Life 1*. Oxford: Oxford University Press, 2016.

Ward, Kevin. *A History of Global Anglicanism*. Cambridge: Cambridge University Press, 2006.

Ward, Pete. 'Affective Alliance or Circuits of Power: The Production and Consumption of Contemporary Charismatic Worship in Britain'. *International Journal of Practical Theology* 9, no. 1 (2005): 25–39.

Ward, Pete. *Liquid Ecclesiology: The Gospel and the Church*. Leiden: Brill, 2017.

Ward, Pete, ed. *Perspectives on Ecclesiology and Ethnography*. Grand Rapids, MI: Wm. B. Eerdmans, 2011.

Ward, Pete. *Selling Worship: How What We Sing Has Changed the Church*. Bletchley: Paternoster, 2005.

Ward, Pete. 'Spiritual Songs as Text: Genre and Interpretation'. *Journal of Youth and Theology* 1, no. 1 (2002): 49–64.

Webster, John. 'Confession and Confessions'. In *Nicene Christianity: The Future for a New Ecumenism*, edited by Christopher R. Seitz, 119–31. Grand Rapids, MI: Brazos, 2001.

Webster, John. *Holiness*. London: SCM, 2003.

Webster, John. *Holy Scripture: A Dogmatic Sketch*. Cambridge: Cambridge University Press, 2003.

Webster, John. 'Theological Theology'. In *Confessing God: Essays in Christian Dogmatics II*, 11–31. London: T&T Clark, 2005.

Webster, John. 'What Makes Theology Theological?' *Journal of Analytic Theology* 3 (2015): 17–28.

Wenham, David. 'The Sevenfold Form of the Lord's Prayer in Matthew'. *Expository Times* 121 (2010): 373–82.

Westcott, Brooke Foss. *The Historic Faith: Short Lectures on the Apostles' Creed*. London: Macmillan, 1883.

Westra, Liuwe H. *The Apostles' Creed: Origin, History, and Some Early Commentaries*. Turnhout: Brepols, 2002.

White, Peter. *Predestination, Policy, and Polemic: Conflict and Consensus with the English Church from the Reformation to the Civil War*. Cambridge: Cambridge University Press, 1992.

Wigg-Stevenson, Natalie. *Ethnographic Theology: An Enquiry into the Production of Theological Knowledge*. London: Palgrave, 2014.

Williams, Anna. *The Architecture of Theology: Structure, System, and Ratio*. Oxford: Oxford University Press, 2011.

Williams, Rowan. *Anglican Identities*. London: DLT, 2004.

Williams, Rowan. 'Doctrinal Criticism: Some Questions'. In *The Making and Remaking of Christian Doctrine: Essays in Honour of Maurice Wiles*, edited by Sarah Coakley and David A. Pailin, 239–64. Oxford: Clarendon Press, 1993. Reprinted as 'Maurice Wiles and Doctrinal Criticism'. In *Wrestling with Angels: Conversations in Modern Theology*, edited by Mike Higton, 275–99. London: SCM, 2007.

Williams, Rowan. 'Does It Make Sense to Speak of Pre-Nicene Orthodoxy?' In *The Making of Orthodoxy: Essays in Honour of Henry Chadwick*, edited by Rowan Williams, 1–23. Cambridge: Cambridge University Press, 1989.

Williams, Rowan. 'Foreword to the Series'. In Percy and Slocum, *Point of Balance*, ix–xii.

Williams, Rowan. 'Newman's *Arians* and the Question of Method in Doctrinal History'. In *Newman after a Hundred Years*, edited by Ian Ker and Alan Hill, 263–85. Oxford: Oxford University Press, 1990.

Williams, Rowan. 'Unity and Universality, Locality and Diversity in Anglicanism', 2009. Available online at aoc2013.brix.fatbeehive.com/articles.php/2287/unity-and-universality-locality-and-diversity-in-anglicanism (accessed 30 November 2019).

Winner, Lauren F. *The Dangers of Christian Practice: On Wayward Gifts, Characteristic Damage, and Sin*. New Haven, CT: Yale University Press, 2018.

Witherington, Ben, III. *The Letters to Philemon, the Colossians, and the Ephesians: A Socio-Rhetorical Commentary on the Captivity Epistles*. Grand Rapids, MI: Eerdmans, 2007.

Woodhead, Linda, and Andrew Brown. *That Was the Church That Was: How the Church of England Lost the English People*. London: Bloomsbury, 2016.

Woods, Eric. 'Innumerable Benefits: The Soteriology of the Book of Common Prayer'. *Faith and Worship* 65–66 (2010): 23–38.

World Missionary Conference, 1910. *Report of Commission I: Carrying the Gospel to all the Non-Christian World*. Edinburgh: Oliphant, Anderson & Ferrier, n.d.

Wright, N.T. *The Climax of the Covenant Christ and the Law in Pauline Theology*. Minneapolis: Fortress Press, 1993.

Yeago, David. 'Jesus of Nazareth and Cosmic Redemption: The Relevance of Maximus the Confessor'. *Modern Theology* 12, no. 2 (1996): 163–93.

Yeago, David. 'The New Testament and the Nicene Dogma'. *Pro Ecclesia* 3, no. 2 (1994): 152–64.

Young, Frances M. *The Art of Performance: Towards a Theology of Holy Scripture*. London: Darton, Longman and Todd, 1990.

Young, Frances M. *Biblical Exegesis and the Formation of Christian Culture*. Cambridge: Cambridge University Press, 1997.

Young, Frances M. *The Making of the Creeds*. London: SCM Press, 1991.

Young, Frances M. 'Paideia and the Myth of Static Dogma'. In *The Making and Remaking of Christian Doctrine: Essays in Honour of Maurice Wiles*, edited by Sarah Coakley and David A. Pailin, 265–81. Oxford: Clarendon Press, 1993.

Zahl, Simeon. 'Tradition and Its "Use": The Ethics of Theological Retrieval'. *Scottish Journal of Theology* 71, no. 3 (2018): 308–23.

Ziegler, Philip. *Militant Grace: The Apocalyptic Turn and the Future of Christian Theology*. Grand Rapids, MI: Baker Academic, 2018.

Zimmerman, John D. 'A Chapter in English Church Reform: The Enabling Act of 1919'. *Historical Magazine of the Protestant Episcopal Church* 46, no. 2 (1977): 215–25.

Index

Abell, Thomas 23 n.31
ableism 123, 227
abundance. *See also* gift of God; word of God
  of God 8, 83, 93, 102, 111, 138, 140–1, 163 n.58, 164, 171–2, 180, 187, 196, 198, 200–3, 205, 215–16, 218, 223, 235
  of God's love 9, 103–4, 141, 156, 168, 170, 188, 190, 198, 201, 203, 233–4, 242
  of God's word 86, 94, 166 n.73, 190, 200
  of scripture 141, 168
abuse 17, 54, 67–8, 217, 227
accountability 92, 95, 116, 136, 184–5, 190, 201–2
Acts of Uniformity 24, 27
Adams, Nicholas 173 n.9, 185 n.46, 196 n.73, 199 n.84, 227 n.87
Allegro, John M. 149 n.21
Alpha Course 55–7
amplification 9, 232, 234–41
Ananias 84
Andrewes, Lancelot 29
Andrews, James 154
angels 76–8, 80, 97
Anglican Communion 6, 18, 33–5, 37, 39–40, 66
Anglican Consultative Council 66
Anglicanism 16 n.1, 17, 28, 29, 32, 68
  doctrinal diffidence 19–25
  identity 25 n.42, 26–7, 29, 36–44, 99–101, 210 n.25
Anglican-Oriental Orthodox International Commission 4, 71
Anglican-Roman Catholic Internatonal Commission 68–9
anglo-catholicism 31, 36–7, 46–7, 52 n.37
Anselm of Canterbury 96 n.3

anti-Semitism. *See* supersessionism
apocalyptic 81 n.14, 86, 210 n.27
apostles 77, 84, 91, 102, 128–9, 190. *See also names of particular individuals*
Apostles' Creed 89 n.33, 155
apostolicity 77, 138, 143, 176–7, 186–7, 188 n.57, 212 n.33
Aquinas, Thomas 152 n.31
Arendt, Hannah 127
argument 3, 10, 12, 25, 38–9, 41–3, 56, 63, 75, 92–6, 174–6, 191–2, 194–5, 201, 229, 239–40
  constitutive of tradition 59, 130 n.68, 135, 161, 185
  in scripture 84–5, 146, 148, 172 n.6
Arminianism 25
art 107, 126–7, 155–6
Articles of Religion. *See* Thirty-Nine Articles
articulate tradition 60, 98–9, 101, 131, 135–6, 139, 230, 240–2
articulation 4, 7, 45–53, 75, 87–92, 94, 98–101, 104, 107, 109, 133, 152, 179–83, 194, 197, 201–2, 205, 225, 227, 230–2, 235–6, 238, 241
  playfulness 194–5, 198, 228, 231
Astley, Jeff 46, 49
Atkins, Anselm 163 n.59
attention 61, 117, 127, 162, 186 n.47, 204, 210, 214, 224–6, 232, 236. *See also* contemplation; inattention
  to encounters 163, 238
  to God 39, 153, 233
  to Jesus 39, 48, 79, 124
  to ordinary belief 63, 242
  to others 195, 197, 199, 208, 231, 237
  to scripture 142–4, 148–51, 153, 155, 160, 164, 167
Augustine of Canterbury 17 n.2
Augustine of Hippo 99 n.14, 153–4
Aune, Kristin 64 n.65

Index

Austen, Jane 54
authority 136, 184, 226, 229 n.91, 231
  apostolic 92
  cosmic 102–3
  ecclesiastical 13, 38–9, 41, 62 n.61, 66, 101, 136, 180–1, 186, 200 n.85, 237
  political 23–4, 136
  of scripture 46, 134, 143 n.7, 152, 155 n.40, 176–7
  of statements 12
  theological 38–41, 42, 122, 134–5, 192 n.66, 201
  of tradition 152
  of women 88
Avis, Paul 16 n.1, 20, 22, 27 n.52, 36 n.97, 37, 39–40, 42, 101 n.24
Ayres, Lewis 87 n.25, 128–9, 152–4
Azariah, Vedanayagam Samuel 35–6

Baines, Susannah 123–4
banqueting. *See* feasting
baptism 3, 89 n.31, 90
Barnabas, companion of Paul 85, 129
Barnes, Robert 23 n.31
Barrett, Al 136 n.83
Barrett, Richard 55 n.46
Barth, Karl 204, 208, 212–15
Barth, Nelly 214
Barton, Mukti 17–18
Behr, John 152 n.29, 154 n.38, 176
belief
  conceptual structure 111, 118, 120–1, 125, 131, 133–4
  and dispositions 7, 111, 118–20, 125
  ordinary 4, 6, 9, 10, 43–4, 45–61, 63–72, 98–101, 106–9, 111, 114, 118, 128, 130–8, 156, 225, 234–6, 239–42
  social structure 111, 118, 121–3, 125, 133–4, 138
Benbaji, Yitzakh 195 n.70
Bennett, Zoë 146 n.14
Bhatti, Deborah 45 n.1
Bible. *See* scripture
Birkett, Kirsten 61 n.57
bishops 9, 24, 29, 28, 31 n.65, 40, 60, 64, 67, 72, 93, 156 n.42
  in Anglican Communion 33–5
  as doctrinal teachers 45, 65–6, 180–1, 200 n.85, 237–9
blessing 51, 76–7, 103, 202, 238
Bloch, Maurice 122 n.37, 123 n.41
bodies 50–1, 56–7, 82, 86, 105, 124–5, 126 n.56, 129–30, 135, 217, 231–2, 235
  and belief 39, 82, 122, 125, 137, 155, 181, 240–1
  and discipleship 94–5, 124
  and knowledge of God 4–5, 113, 140
  and love 4, 99, 109, 141, 170–1, 203, 222, 234, 242
  and scripture 144, 156, 203 n.1
body of Christ 8, 95, 99, 101–5, 136–8, 171, 188, 190 198, 201–2, 228 n.90, 231, 233–5. *See also* church
body of Jesus 82, 95, 158, 190
Bokedal, Tomas 152 n.29
Book of Common Prayer 26, 27 n.52, 29–30, 40, 69
Bourdieu, Pierre 50 n.26, 99 n.12
Bowden, John 14
Braaten, Carl 212 n.31
Brandom, Robert 128, 178 n.23
Bretherton, Luke 20, 205–6
Briggs, Richard S. 89 n.30, 91 n.40
British Academy 61, 62 n.60
Brown, Andrew 37
Brown, Peter 99 n.14
Buell, Denise Kimber 173
Bulgakov, Sergius 138 n.85
Bultmann, Rudolf 71
Burrus, Virginia 90 n.39, 171, 184 n.41
Burton, Sarah 98 n.9
Butler, Joseph 165–6
Butterworth, Nick 53

Caird, G. B. 130–31
calling forward 204, 222–6, 229
Calvin 152 n.30
Calvinism 25, 27 n.48, 100
Cambridge Inter-faith Programme 11
Cameron, Helen 45 n.1
caring 5, 51, 53, 93, 99, 124
catechesis 90, 93, 181. *See also* teaching
Catholic Church 17, 21, 24–5, 27, 30, 68, 180, 186–7, 196–7
catholicity 82, 86, 196

Centre for Catholic Studies 11
Chadwick, Owen 31 n.68, 164
Chalcedon, Council of 4, 71, 114 n.14, 132, 181, 187, 193
challenging 8–9, 41, 52, 72, 82, 138, 140, 142, 144, 148, 159, 162, 165, 167–9, 190, 202–5, 208–10, 214, 220, 223, 226, 231–2, 234–42
Chapman, Mark 20, 23 n.35, 24 n.39, 26 n.46, 29, 31, 36 n.96, 90 n.38, 199 n.82
charismatic movement 56, 239
Charles I 24–5
Charry, Ellen T. 92 n.42, 104, 131 n.72
Christian, William A. 14 n.15
Christie, Ann 48–51
Christology 47–50, 71–2, 76 n.1, 89 n.33, 90, 113, 151, 166 n.73, 177–9, 181–2, 232. *See also* Chalcedon, Council of
church. *See also* apostolicity; catholicity; division; journeying; polycentricity; reproduction; sin
   believing 3–4, 72, 98, 234
   communicative 90–1
   and doctrine 4, 7, 9, 12–15, 42, 55, 58, 72, 75–7, 86, 94, 156, 206, 210, 230–7, 242
   and Israel 207–9
   learning 5, 8–9, 15, 69, 79, 93, 104, 134, 182, 203–5, 218
   messy 3, 5, 13, 101, 189, 200
   and the resurrection 5, 7, 75, 83, 86
   and word 5, 78, 84, 94, 137
   and world 3, 9, 52, 54, 188
   and scripture 140–4, 149–51, 156, 159, 164–6, 168–9
   and Spirit 8, 77, 80, 83, 138, 140, 165, 169–70, 177, 186–8, 196, 203–4, 222–5
Church Assembly 65, 69
Church Missionary Society 32 nn.71–2, 33
Church of England 6–7, 9–10, 16–72, 75, 100–1, 174–6, 195 n.72, 234–42
   and state power 17, 23, 28, 36, 65–6, 69
circularity 14, 153, 176, 213. *See also* retrospective inevitability
circulation 12–13, 45 n.1, 52–8, 64–5, 70–2, 131, 194, 198, 228, 234
class 5 n.2, 17, 36, 44, 62, 98, 135, 157–8, 205–6
Clements, Keith W. 71 n.84
Clemson, Frances 59 n.54, 191 n.64
Clutterbuck, Richard 12 n.9, 14 n.15, 90 n.38, 98 n.8
Coakley, Sarah 20, 106–7, 131–2, 181, 217, 239
Cocksworh, Ashley 43 n.128
Cocksworth, Christopher 67
Codrington, Christopher 32 n.72
coexistence 193–4, 200–1
Coggan, Donald 70
Colenso, J. W. 34, 220–2
Coles, Romand 211 n.29, 219 n.66, 224–5
Collier, David 172 n.5
Collingwood, R. G. 126, 199 n.83
Collins, Jeffrey R. 26 n.44, 27 n.51
colonialism 6, 17, 31–7, 85, 90, 93, 156–8, 204, 220–2
commensuration 181–2, 192, 199
Common Awards 10, 60 n.57
confession 3, 7, 75, 86, 88–90, 92–6, 117, 131, 168
Constantinople, Council of 181, 200 n.85
construal 8–9, 88, 129, 133, 139, 151, 156, 171–2, 181–3, 204, 226–32
   of Anglican history 25, 42
   and depth 121, 182, 197–8, 204, 227–8, 236, 238–41
   and disagreement 191, 193, 197
   of scripture 154, 161, 168, 181
contemplation 106, 153, 163
controversy 3, 7, 29–31, 71 n.84, 75, 90–6, 131, 168, 180–2, 229
Conventical Act (1664) 27
conversation 3, 12, 21, 58–64, 67–8, 86, 133–4, 138–9, 159, 174, 198–200, 230, 235–8, 240–2
   and disagreement 39–40, 42, 44, 185, 196
   and exclusion 32–4, 36
   in the world 14, 52–3, 159, 169, 222, 225

conversion 81, 84, 91, 184, 203, 210.
    See also proselytizing
Convocation 65
Cornelius the centurion 81–2
Cornwall, Susannah 60 n.57
Corporation Act (1661) 27
correspondence 112–17, 132 n.74.
    See also truth
Cosin, John 25
councils 12, 39, 87 n.25, 93, 156 n.42,
    180–3, 187, 206 n.10. *See also*
    Chalcedon; Constantinople; Nicaea;
    Vatican II
Cox, Jeffrey 17, 32 n.71, 32 n.75, 35
Craigo-Snell, Shannon 99 n.11
Cranmer Hall 11
creation 12–13, 54, 77, 82, 87, 89 n.33,
    112–14, 136, 154, 215–18, 220
creativity 126 n.53, 129–30, 139, 160,
    166, 171, 176, 179–80, 188 n.57,
    191, 197, 204, 228, 233. *See also*
    invention
creeds 12–13, 19, 45 n.1, 48, 51, 87
    n.25, 88 n.27, 89–90, 101, 155, 181,
    210, 212. *See also* Apostle's Creed;
    Chalcedon, councils; doctrinal
    statements; Nicaea
cries 5, 8, 204, 208–10, 214–17, 219–21,
    223–4, 227, 230–2, 236–8, 240–1
Crockett, William 12 n.10
Cross, Claire 27
Crowther, Samuel Ajayi 33
Cyril of Alexandria 4

Daley, Brian E. 154 n.36
Daston, Lorraine 149 n.18
Davidowski, Wiesław 152 n.29
Davie, Grace 122 n.37
Davies, Douglas J. 69 n.78
Day, Abby 48 n.17, 50–3, 119 n.30
deferral 122–3, 133–5, 193, 199, 201, 226
desire 101–2, 106, 119, 163 n.58
development of doctrine 12, 60, 69,
    80–1, 89–90, 97, 113 n.6, 136, 169,
    173–83, 186–8, 192, 203, 212 n.212,
    239
diaspora 82, 184, 202
Dickens, A. G. 23
disability 62, 123–5. *See also* ableism

disagreement 52, 95, 145, 169–202, 231.
    See also controversy
  in Church of England 10, 25, 28–31,
    37–43
  intractable 8, 171, 173–80, 191–2,
    198–201
  and scripture 161, 171, 172 n.6,
    174–6
discernment 38–9, 44, 130, 133, 167
    n.80, 175, 182, 191, 196–8, 230,
    236, 238
discipleship 3–4, 7, 14, 38–9, 51, 59, 75–
    83, 91–5, 97, 102, 104 n.31, 107–8,
    114–16, 123, 130, 135, 137, 139,
    142, 158–9, 160–1, 170–2, 183–5,
    204, 207, 213, 224--7, 234–6
diversity 5, 62, 76 n.2, 92, 172, 183–5,
    202–3, 224–5, 240, 242
division 8, 85, 95, 103, 111, 171, 176,
    182–2, 185, 189–202, 230. *See also*
    argument; disagreement; separation
doctrinal commissions 9, 45, 64, 66,
    72, 234, 237, 239–41. *See also*
    Anglican–Oriental Orthodox
    International Commission;
    Anglican–Roman Catholic
    Internatonal Commission;
    Doctrine Commission; Faith
    and Order Commission; Inter-
    Anglican Standing Committee
    on Unity Faith and Order;
    Inter-Anglican Theological and
    Doctrinal Commission; Liturgical
    Commission
doctrinal ecology 6, 72, 91, 238, 241
doctrinal reasoning. *See* articulation;
    argument; commensuration;
    construal; conversation; persuasion;
    receptivity; repair; resolution;
    stipulation; summarizing;
    understanding
doctrinal statements 7, 12, 86, 87 n.25,
    89, 181, 183, 188, 203, 230. *See also*
    creeds
doctrinal theology. *See also* challenging;
    encouraging; proposing;
    resourcing; warning
  as academic discipline 10–13, 16, 21,
    46, 48–9, 51–2, 58–64, 67, 225, 242

as ministry   9, 95, 136, 138, 201, 233–4, 242
doctrine. *See also* development of doctrine
  decline   97–8
  nature   4, 7, 11–12, 42, 75, 97, 104
  in other religions   13–14
  regulative account   113–14, 117, 131–2, 181 n.35, 193 (*see also* grammar)
  unnaturalness   75, 87, 91
Doctrine Commission of the Church of England   6, 20, 64, 66, 68–71, 164 n.61, 170, 172 n.5, 211 n.30, 239
dogmatic theology   13, 20–1, 97, 213–14
Drosnin, Michael   146 n.16
Dube, Musa   156–9, 163
Duce, Catherine   45 n.1
Duffy, Eamon   24–5
Dunne, Joseph   126–7, 164 n.62

eating   5, 78, 80 n.10, 85, 93
ecclesiology   38–40, 56, 99, 186, 207–9, 218
ecumenism   21–2, 40, 62, 66, 111, 194. *See also* Receptive Ecumenism
Edward VI   23
Elbourne, Elizabeth   32 n.76
Elizabeth I   6, 23–4
Elizabethan settlement   22, 24–5, 27, 29
embodiment. *See* bodies
Emery, Gilles   112 n.5
Emmaus, road to   76, 79, 83
encounter   5, 8, 34, 76, 71 n.14, 82, 105, 117–18, 121, 130, 136, 141, 146 n.14, 163, 165–9, 190, 202–4, 210, 223–4, 230–2, 236–8, 240–2
encouraging   9, 108, 141, 234–41
Epiphanius   209 n.23
Essays and Reviews   30–1
essentially contested concepts   161 n.53, 172 n.5, 174 n.11
ethnography   45, 47 n.10, 63, 148. *See also* Day, Abby; Ward, Pete
Eucharist   3, 69, 76, 189–90, 205 n.4
Eunice, mother of Timothy   142–3, 145, 147
evangelicalism   31, 36, 46–7, 50, 56–7, 100, 175 n.13

exclusion   4, 6, 8, 17, 19, 27, 26, 42, 44, 52, 57–8, 62, 72, 86, 92, 94, 109, 111, 123, 141, 156 n.42, 163, 169, 182, 185, 189, 201, 219 n.66, 227, 235–6, 241. *See also* ableism; colonialism; homophobia; Islamophobia; marginalisation; misogyny; racism; supersessionism; transphobia
expectancy   162–3, 169, 210, 214–16, 222
experience   7, 13 n.10, 38, 50, 78–9, 83–4, 119, 124, 160–1, 163, 184, 211 n.30, 239
experiments in following Jesus   4, 41, 75, 92–3, 107, 138, 140–1, 144–5, 157, 170, 188, 203, 224–6, 231, 235–6, 241

failure   4–5, 7, 85, 93 n.46, 108–9, 111, 138, 140–1, 144–5, 170, 185–6, 190, 202–4, 223, 227, 230, 232–3, 241
Faith and Order Commission of the Church of England   20, 66–8, 172 n.4, 198 n.81, 201 n.86, 239
faithfulness   87 n.26, 94, 127, 172, 176, 180–7, 204–5, 213, 218, 226–7, 228 n.90, 232, 236. *See also* apostolicity
Farrer, Austin   106 n.39
Fat and Frantic   162 n.56
feasting   215, 218–19
feeling   43, 48, 50, 52, 55, 56–7, 78, 89, 115–16, 118–20, 122, 124, 134–5, 146, 175–6, 199, 222 n.80, 226, 229, 232
Fergusson, Everett   90 n.35, 93 n.45, 152 n.29
Fetherstone, Richard   23 n.31
Fiddes, Paul   27 n.52
Fielding, Harold   115 n.15
figural interpretation   84, 154, 195
Fisch, Menachem   195, 201 n.87
fittingness   129, 134, 138, 179, 226
Five Mile Act (1665)   27
Flett, John   188 n.57, 202 n.90, 206 n.6
Ford, David   11 n.7, 63 n.63, 204, 215–17, 222
forgetfulness   170–1, 187, 201, 230
forgiveness   68, 77, 121, 184

Fossett, Robert L.   117 n.24, 143 n.7, 174 n.12
Fowl, Stephen E.   167 n.80, 174 n.12
Francis, Leslie   53
Fraser, Liam J.   199 n.83
Frei, Hans   8, 11, 143, 149–52
Freud, Sigmund   9
friendship   35–6, 124–5, 215, 218, 237 n.1. *See also* intimacy
Fulford, Ben   150 n.23, 150 n.26, 151 n.27
Furlong, Monica   18, 23 n.31, 31 n.67, 37, 70 n.83

Gadamer, Hans-Georg   164 n.62
Galison, Peter   149 n.18
Gallie, W. B.   172 n.5, 174 n.11
Garrard, Thomas   23 n.31
Gathercole, Simon J.   89 n.33
gender   9, 49, 50–2, 54, 62, 106, 135, 143, 158. *See also* misogyny
General Synod of the Church of England   6, 64–6, 70–71
gentiles   79, 81–2, 102, 129, 208, 220
gift of God. *See also* abundance; unfolding; word of God
  in Christ   5–9, 75–6, 79–3, 92–3, 124–5, 127, 132–3, 137–8, 171, 180, 183, 186–90, 196, 198, 201–4, 209, 211, 212 n.31, 214, 222–3, 227, 230–5
  in scripture   140–2, 159, 164–6, 168
Gilbert, Margaret   122 n.37
God. *See also* abundance; knowledge of God; Trinity
  as God of Israel   5, 7, 75, 77, 82, 85, 87, 113, 129, 140, 165, 177–9, 207–9
  as object of doctrine   3, 7, 21, 45, 54, 58, 92, 94, 96, 108 n.46, 112, 137 n.84, 236
Godly Play   53
Gore, Charles   76 n.1
grammar   75 n.1, 115, 204, 209
Great Ejectment / Ejection   27
Gregory of Nyssa   104
Guarino, Thomas   202
Guest, Mathew   62 n.60, 64 n.65
Gunstone, Pete   69 n.78
Gunton, Colin E.   76 n.1, 181 n.34, 211 n.30

Haenchen, Ernst   78 n.6
Hampton, Stephen   24 n.36, 24 n.38
Hanson, Anthony Tyrrell   33
Hardy, Daniel W.   130 n.67, 165, 167, 210 n.25
Harkianakis, Stylianos   181
Hartog, Paul   153 n.34
Harvey, Anthony E.   119 n.32, 122 n.37, 138 n.85
Harvey, Jennifer   157–9, 163
Hauerwas, Stanley   131 n.72
Hays, Richard B.   83 n.20
Healy, Nicholas M.   5, 130 n.68, 167 n.80, 205 n.2, 206 n.9
Heard, James   55–6
Hefling, Charles   12 n.9, 27 n.52
Helmer Christine   12 n.9, 89 n.30, 97 n.7, 131 n.72
Henry VIII   6, 23
Henson, Hensley   23, 100–1
Herbert, George   100
heresy   48, 181, 202, 209
Heyduck, Richard   12 n.9, 87 n.25, 97 n.5
Heywood, David   60 n.57
Hidalgo, Fernando Daniel   172 n.5
Hinze, Bradford   203 n.1, 207 n.14
Hodge, Charles   152 n.31
holiness   79, 101, 167, 189, 239. *See also* sanctification
Holland, Henry Scott   104
Holmes, Steve   96 n.2
homophobia   18, 147, 175, 227
Hooker, Richard   23, 27, 99–101, 182, 212 n.32
Horsley, Teddy   53
Hughes, Ann   27
Hunsinger, George   116 n.20
Hunt, Cherryl   47 n.10
Hurtado, Larry   78 n.7, 83, 89 n.32, 184 n.42
Hütter, Reinhard   116 n.20, 162

idolatry   132, 177, 188, 211, 227
imagination   16, 36, 49, 54–7, 61, 88, 112, 119–20, 125, 132, 161, 165, 168, 178, 193, 199
  of God's love   7, 95, 103–4, 107–9, 121, 222, 226, 229, 235–6, 240–1
  of salvation   49, 68–70

of scripture   141, 146, 152, 154–9, 174–5
of tradition   8, 129, 190, 197, 221 (*see also* construal)
imperialism. *See* colonialism
improvisation   5, 7–8, 55, 87, 111, 125–32, 137–9, 160, 171, 182, 187–8, 204, 224, 226, 230–2, 236–8, 240–1
inattention   34, 134, 214–15
incarnation   4, 12 n.10, 13, 48, 70–1, 113–14
infallibility   187
Inkpen, Mick   53
insincerity   174, 195. *See also* integrity
integrity   195–7, 200. *See also* insincerity
intellectualism   7, 50, 95–101, 123, 192, 225–6, 230–2
Inter-Anglican Standing Committee on Unity Faith and Order   66
Inter-Anglican Theological and Doctrinal Commission   66
interviewing   48–50, 119 n.33, 225, 239
intimacy   8, 36, 82, 204, 218, 221–2, 223, 225
invention   21, 25, 91, 95, 129, 156, 163 n.59, 171, 179, 219 n.66. *See also* creativity
Irenaeus   152–5, 176
Islamophobia   220, 227
Izzard, Eddie   17 n.4

James (apostle)   129
James I   24
Jenkins, Timothy   40–1, 43–4, 99 n.12, 173 n.10
Jennings, Willie James   34, 80 n.10, 82, 117 n.25, 204, 219–22
Jenson, Robert   150 n.23
Jerome, William   23 n.31
Jerusalem, council of   81, 128, 162 n.55
Jervell, Jacob   77 n.5
Jesus. *See also* Christology; discipleship; gift of God; incarnation; word of God
  ascension   80, 154
  crucifixion   5, 49, 75–8, 86–7, 89 n.33, 93, 149, 154, 161–2, 205, 206 n.9
  as Lord   4, 39, 79, 89, 115–16, 119–20, 122–3, 130, 188, 213
  as Messiah   84–6, 88–9, 113, 208
  resurrection   5, 7, 49, 75–88, 89 n.33, 93–5, 149, 154, 161–2, 166 n.73, 168, 171 n.3, 177, 205
  in scripture   8, 39, 76, 83–4, 89 n.33, 114, 116–17, 141–2, 149–53, 154 n.38, 156, 160–2, 166, 175, 185, 207, 227
  unknown   218
Joanna (apostle)   77–8, 85–6, 88
job   215–16
Joel (prophet)   83
John, Eeva   60 n.57
Johnson, Luke Timothy   129 n.65
joining. *See* intimacy
Jones, L. Gregory   167 n.80
Joshua son of Nun   118
journeying   5, 8–9, 77, 90, 102, 108 n.46, 111, 132, 138, 141, 153–4, 156, 159, 165–70, 190–1, 203, 205, 218, 224–5, 231, 233, 235
Jowett, Benjamin   30
joy   78, 96, 201, 204, 215
Judaism   78, 82–5, 102, 207–10, 220–1, 227
Judas   190

Keener, Craig S.   81 n.12
Kellison, Rosemary B.   176 n.16, 228 n.89, 229 n.91
Kelly, J. N. D.   86 n.24, 90 n.36, 93 n.45
Kerr, Nathan   81 n.14
Kinzig, Wolfram   86 n.24
Kirschbaum, Charlotte von   214
knowledge of God   4, 7, 10, 99, 101–11, 124–5, 132–4, 136–7, 234, 240
Knox, Ronald   31 n.67
Konolige, Kit and Frederica   17 n.3

Lake, Peter   27 n.48
Lambeth Conferences   33 n.80, 34, 37, 40, 66, 143 n.4, 200 n.85
Lampe, G. W. H.   28 n.54
Lash, Nicholas   108 n.47, 118 n.27, 186, 222 n.80
Laud, William   25, 29
Laudianism   25–7
leadership   20 n.19, 31 n.65, 57, 88, 94, 103, 201

Ledger-Lomas, Michael 29 n.58
Le Guin, Ursula 49, 51
Leith, Jenny 43 n.130, 54 n.44, 105 n.37, 163 n.60, 214 n.41
Leonard, Graham 70
Levine, Amy-Jill 88
lex orandi 43 n.128
liberalism 31, 36, 46–7, 50, 100
Lindbeck, George 7, 11, 14 n.15, 111–18, 131, 133, 142–3, 193, 204, 206–10, 220–1
listening. *See* attention
literal reading 47, 141, 149–54, 156, 161
Litton, E. A. 21
Liturgical Commission of the Church of England 66, 69, 239
liturgy 12, 19, 25, 37–8, 41, 43, 48–9, 51, 53, 57, 66, 69, 86, 87 n.25, 89, 99, 117, 155–6, 181, 205–6, 227. *See also* worship
Living in Love and Faith 9, 239
Lloyd, Vincent 109
Lois, grandmother of Timothy 91, 142–3, 147
Long, Thomas G. 142 n.2
Longley, Clifford 70
Lord's Prayer 53–4, 112, 160
Loughlin, Gerard 75 n.1, 87 n.26, 130
Louth, Andrew 162
love 4–5, 7, 9, 35, 80 n.10, 82, 95, 99, 101–11, 112 n.3, 121, 124–5, 131, 136–42, 145–6, 156, 159, 168, 170–1, 188, 190, 198, 201, 203, 211, 212 n.31, 218, 222–3, 232–6, 238–9, 242. *See also* abundance; bodies; imagination
  as hermeneutical criterion 154, 175

McCabe, Herbert 70 n.80
McClendon, James Wm., Jr. 13 n.13, 91 n.40
MacCulloch, Diarmaid 17 n.2, 23 n.31, 24 n.39, 24 n.40, 29–30
McGrath, Alister E. 76 n.1, 77 n.4, 115 n.16, 153 n.32
McIntosh, Ian 60 n.57
McIntosh, Mark 105, 107–8
Maciuceanu, Andra Olivia 172 n.5

McMichael, Ralph 37 n.98, 76 n.1
Maiden, John G. 31 n.67, 65 n.68
Mallock, W. H. 155 n.40, 192 n.66, 195 n.72
Maltby, Judith 19, 25 n.41, 26–7
Mandelbaum E. 119 n.28
Manning, William T. 17 n.3
marginalization 8, 52, 58, 72, 88, 109, 141, 147, 163, 169, 223–4, 227, 232 n.94, 236, 241
Markschies, Christoph 86 n.24
Marshall, Bruce 115 n.16
Martin, Jessica 26
'Mary', woman with cerebral palsy 123–5
Mary Magdalene 76–7, 85–6, 88
Mary the mother of James 77–8, 85–6, 88
Mascall, E. L. 22 n.27, 62 n.61, 97 n.7, 99 n.12
Matthews, W. R. 13 n.11, 97, 181
Maughan, Stephen 32 n.73, 33 n.77, 33 n.81
Maurice, F. D. 90
Messy Church 53. *See also* Church (messy)
metaphor 46, 68, 217
Methodist Church 11, 21, 97 n.7, 196
Michael Ramsey Centre for Anglican Studies 11
middle distance 123, 226
Middleton, Robert Dudley 30 n.61
Milbank, John 179
Milton, Anthony 22–3, 26 n.43, 29 n.58, 100 n.21
misogyny 85, 88, 98, 109, 136, 147, 157, 204, 214, 217, 219, 225, 227
mission 3, 31–3, 57, 67, 81 n.14, 119, 213
Mitchell, Basil 122 n.37, 210 n.28
money 3, 5, 58, 79, 92–3, 98, 132, 136, 190, 200, 222, 235, 239
Montagu, Richard 25
Moss, Claud Beaufort 21
Mowat, Harriet 123–5
Muers, Rachel 22 n.25, 196 n.73, 214 n.40
Murray, Paul 196–7
Myers, Ben 20–21

Newman, John Henry 28, 29 n.58, 30, 97, 129 n.66, 179–80, 186–7
Ngidi, William 34
Nicaea, Council of 122, 177–9, 181
Nichols, Aidan 31
Nixon, Naomi 60 n.57
Nussbaum, Martha C. 126 n.53

Oakley, Ann 49
Ochs, Peter 209 n.22, 209 n.24, 215
Oliver, Simon 132 n.77
Origgi, Gloria 122 n.37
Orr, James 13 n.13, 97, 181 n.36
orthodoxy 26 n.46, 39–40, 71, 177, 181–5, 232 n.94
Owen, D. R. G. 20 n.18
Owens, Carol 55 n.45

Page, Sydney H. T. 104 n.30
Papanikolaou, Aristotle 105 n.37
Parker, Matthew 24
Parochial Church Council 54–5
pastoral care. *See* caring
patience 38, 142, 163–3
Patterson, Neil 65 n.68
Paul, Ian 160 n.52
Paul of Tarsus 77–8, 80, 85, 91, 101–4, 129, 141–2, 188–9, 227
Peake, F. A. 37 n.100
Pelikan, Jaroslav 24 n.38, 30 n.60, 86 n.24, 87 n.25, 89 n.30, 89 n.32, 90 n.36, 91 n.40, 98 n.8
Pentecost 77–8, 80–1, 83, 172
Percy, Martyn 19–20, 22 n.26, 37, 57 n.52
Perera, Sanjee 33 n.83
persuasion 92, 102 n.25, 120–1, 173, 191–2, 194–6, 227, 229
Peter (apostle) 77–8, 81–5, 88–9, 129
Petrenko, Ester 103
phronēsis 125–30
Pieper, Franz 212 n.33
Plant, Stephen 214 n.40
Platt, Jane 53 n.39
Plekon, Michael 138 n.85
Podmore, Colin 65 n.66
politics 3, 5, 20, 28, 37, 54, 58, 90, 93, 103–7, 136, 212, 222, 235. *See also* power

polycentricity 80–6, 91–3, 170–1, 184, 187, 202, 222
populism 99
postliberalism 11, 205 n.4, 209 n.22. *See also* Frei, Lindbeck
Powell, Edward 23 n.31
power 19, 37, 55, 85, 123 n.41, 215, 222, 224–5, 229, 232
  of the church 4, 21–2, 24, 42, 52, 57–8, 64, 72, 75, 78, 88, 235, 239
  colonial/imperial 32, 36, 90, 109, 156 n.42, 158 (*see also* colonialism)
  of doctrinal theologians 16, 39, 44, 64, 92–4, 135, 169, 187, 199, 229, 231–2, 234
  of the state 6–7, 23, 28
Pratt, Mary Louise 32 n.75
prayer 3, 26, 36, 50–1, 53–4, 78, 83, 86, 90–1, 102, 105–6, 117, 130, 133, 140, 155, 162–3, 181, 201, 214–15, 222, 232–3, 242. *See also* liturgy; Lord's prayer
preaching 3, 29, 47 n.10, 50, 53, 65, 86, 107–8, 117, 145, 155, 159–60, 175, 213, 238, 241. *See also* proclamation
Prevot, Andrew 163 n.58
Price H. H. 119 n.28
privilege 22, 35, 58, 75, 88, 98 n.10, 133–5, 147, 169, 199, 215, 224–5, 231–2, 242. *See also* Whiteness
proclamation 3, 5, 7, 70, 75, 77, 78 n.8, 80–2, 85–8, 90–6, 113–14, 131, 168, 181, 213. *See also* preaching
proposing 7, 100, 131, 133, 138–9, 151, 156, 183 n.40, 195, 229
proselytizing 81. *See also* conversion
providence 13, 32, 136, 165, 186, 189, 219
provisionality of doctrine 167, 211 n.28, 211 n.30
Puritanism 25, 27, 99

Quash, Ben 100, 164 n.65, 165–7
queer theory 147, 217–19
Quilty-Dunn, J. 119 n.28

racism 5 n.2, 17–18, 33–6, 98, 109, 135–6, 147, 157–9, 204, 220–1, 227. *See also* Whiteness

Radner, Ephraim   81 n.12, 101 n.24,
    133 n.78, 187 n.55, 189–90,
    200 n.85, 201 n.86, 206, 207 n.14,
    208 n.20, 209
Ramsey, Michael   18 n.10
reception. *See* recognition
Receptive Ecumenism   196–7, 199 n.84
receptivity   191, 196–8
recognition   8, 14, 77, 79, 83, 89, 92, 136,
    161, 192–5, 198, 200–2, 204–5, 222,
    228–30, 236
re-construal. *See* construal
Reddie, Anthony   18 n.11, 98 n.10,
    232 n.94
Reformation   6, 17, 22–5, 29–30, 65,
    155 n.40
regula fidei   8, 90, 151–6, 159, 176
repair   185 n.46, 209, 219
repentance   3, 5, 8, 43, 57, 78 n.8, 105,
    111, 141, 144, 158, 170–1, 187–8,
    203, 206–7, 210, 214, 223, 228,
    234, 236
reproduction (of church)   4, 5 n.2, 6, 16,
    134–5, 138, 168, 204–6, 218–19,
    230, 234
Rescher, Nicholas   173 n.9
resolution of disagreements   8, 21, 41,
    174, 176, 182, 191–4, 198, 227
resourcing   7, 9–10, 131–8, 168, 227, 230,
    233 n.95, 234–41
ressourcement   132
restoration   6, 26–9, 36
retrospective inevitability   26–7,
    128 n.64, 176 n.16, 177–80. *See also*
    circularity
revelation   77, 102, 112–13, 124,
    138 n.85, 146, 166, 211 n.30
Rogers, Alasdair   175 n.13, 194 n.68
Rogers, Andrew   47 n.10
Rogers, Eugene F., Jr.   125 n.52
Rose, Marika   60 n.56, 93 n.45, 227 n.87,
    228 n.90
rule of faith. *See regula fidei*
Rush, Ormond   129
Rwandan genocide   206
Ryan, Greg   196 n.74
Ryle, Gilbert   118–19
Ryrie, Alec   17, 23, 24 n.39, 24 n.40,
    25 n.42, 27 n.48, 29

sacrifice   217–18
salvation. *See* soteriology
sanctification   68, 82, 100–6, 112, 125,
    130, 136, 141, 143, 153, 168, 222.
    See also holiness
Sanneh, Lamin   80–81
Sapphira   84
Sarisky, Darren   153 n.34
Saul of Tarsus. *See* Paul of Tarsus
Scharen, Christian   54 n.44, 64 n.64
Schlink   89 n.30, 91 n.40
scholasticism   28, 96–7
Schwitzgebel, Eric   118 n.28
Scriptural Reasoning   196 n.73,
    199 n.84
scripture. *See also* abundance; authority;
    disagreement; figural reading;
    imagination; Jesus; literal reading;
    love as hermeneutical criterion;
    settlements; *sola scriptura*; Spirit;
    word of God
  canon   161 n.54, 177
  in church   3, 5, 47 n.10, 83–56, 93,
    140, 152, 169
  in Church of England   29–30, 34,
    37–8, 41, 46–7, 50–1, 53–6,
    68, 238
  and doctrine   14, 107, 151–6,
    168–9
  features   145–8, 155, 160, 174, 180,
    230
  objectivity   8, 140–56, 159, 164–5,
    180
  re-reading   8, 11, 75, 83–5,
    128–9, 156–63, 197, 203 n.1,
    209, 210 n.27, 212, 221, 228–9,
    236, 240
  scintillation   164–8
  in worship   41, 55
second order   7, 113–18
separation   8, 171, 182–6, 188–90,
    201
  unavailability of   186
settlements   25–6, 36–7, 41, 121, 127,
    129, 137, 140, 178, 180, 220–1,
    223, 226–7, 229, 235, 241. *See also*
    Elizabethan settlement
  scriptural   8, 121, 137, 142–8, 150–1,
    156–9, 165, 173–6

unsettled 141, 148, 159, 161–3, 166–7, 169–70, 190, 202, 204, 210, 216, 223–4, 236
sexuality 9, 18, 135, 158, 195 n.72, 199 n.83, 239
Sharma, Sonya 62 n.60, 64 n.65
Shell, Alison 19
Shepherd, Nick 60 n.57
Shuger, Debora 99, 100 n.20
Silas, companion of Paul 85
Simpsons, The 54
sin 3–4, 8, 17–18, 75, 84–6, 93, 111, 125, 127, 188, 211, 217–18, 233. *See also* ableism; abuse; colonialism; exclusion; failure; homophobia; Islamophobia; marginalisation; misogyny; racism; slaver; supersessionism; transphobia; violence
  sinfulness of church 4, 21, 116, 135, 141, 144, 204–9
singing 3, 43, 50–1, 53, 55–7, 69–70, 86, 119, 140, 155–6, 205, 215
slavery 17, 31–2, 219–21
Slee, Nicola 53
Slocum, Robert Boak 19 n.13, 41 n.125
Smith, Claire S. 91 n.40
Society for the Propagation of the Gospel 32 n.71
sola scriptura 56, 144
Sonderegger, Katherine 20, 76 n.1, 133, 140, 151 n.27, 165, 168
Song, Robert 62 n.60
soteriology 13, 49, 56, 68–9, 86, 220
Spirit 56, 125, 127, 129, 130, 154–6, 183, 196, 198, 202, 209, 211, 214–15, 222, 238–9, 242. *See also* journeying; Pentecost; sanctification
  and church 76 n.2, 80–3, 86, 137, 140, 170–1, 186–91, 203–4, 208, 227, 233
  and Jesus 5, 7, 77, 83, 87, 107, 138, 168, 188
  and scripture 8, 84, 105, 136, 138–41, 143–4, 151, 162–7, 169, 177
spiritual discipline 96, 141, 152, 154, 156, 168

spirituality 13 n.10, 19, 50, 52, 60, 104–6, 124
Stanley, Brian 35 n.90
Stephen (apostle) 80
stipulation 96 n.1, 106, 217
story 46, 48, 68, 78, 83–4, 87–8, 92, 94–5, 107, 113, 150, 184, 207
Stout, Jeffrey 9
Strauss, David Friedrich 71
Strong, Rowan 31, 37 n.98
suffering 7–8, 109, 169, 175, 204, 209–10, 214–19, 221, 223
Sullivan, Francis A. 89 n.30
summarizing 7, 75, 87–90, 92–6, 104, 107, 109, 152, 154–5, 168, 197, 201–2, 230
supersessionism 82, 85–6, 136, 204, 207–10, 220–1, 227
Sweeney, James 45 n.1
Swinton, John 123–5
Sykes, Stephen 17, 20, 37–44, 98 n.8, 126 n.54, 172
systematic theology 13, 20, 28 n.54, 48–9

Tanner, Kathryn 20, 79 n.9, 99 n.12, 117 n.23, 126 n.53, 134 n.80, 171 n.2, 172, 182 n.37, 186 n.47, 198 n.80, 199 n.84, 228 n.88, 229 n.91, 229 n.92
Taylor, Charles 5 n.3, 126 n.56
teaching 3, 5, 7, 51, 75–7, 79–80, 89 n.31, 90–6, 103–4, 131, 168, 186, 201, 235, 237. *See also* catechesis
technicality 4, 71–2, 93, 96–7, 137 n.84, 181–2, 240
Temple, William 107, 237 n.1
Test Acts (1673, 1678) 27
Theological Education Institutions 6, 9, 59–61, 63–5, 234, 237, 240–1
Thiel, John E. 128 n.64
Thirty-Nine Articles 23–4, 26, 28–30, 40, 195 n.72, 206 n.10
Thiselton, Anthony 119, n.28, 119 n.29, 131 n.72, 199 n.83
Thompson, David M. 27 n.52
Thornton, Ed 66 n.70
Ticciati, Susannah 108 n.46, 112 n.3, 113 n.6, 216 n.47

Tietz, Christiane 214 n.40
Tilling, Chris 104 n.31
Timothy, companion of Paul 91, 141–3, 145, 147
Tonstad, Linn Marie 5, 96 n.1, 98 n.10, 106 n.44, 135 n.82, 204, 217–19, 222
Townes, Emilie 5
tradition 10, 21, 37, 128–9, 134, 138–9, 176–80, 211, 217–19, 227 n.87, 228 n.89. *See also* apostolicity; articulate tradition
transphobia 175, 227
Trible, Phyllis 175 n.14
Trinity 10, 13, 106–8, 137 n.84, 154–5, 204, 217
TRS UK 62 n.59
trust 8, 90, 119 n.30, 121–3, 169, 208, 211–13, 242
truth 8, 41, 86, 91, 102–3, 114–17, 120, 129–30, 132, 137–8, 145, 182–3, 187–90, 199 n.83, 200–2, 212 n.31, 214, 223, 228, 237 n.1. *See also* correspondence
Twelftree, Graham H. 83 n.20
Tyacke, Nicholas 24 n.40, 25 n.43

understanding 191, 198–201
unfolding 75, 79, 80–3, 93, 111, 126–7, 138, 165, 183, 186–8. *See also* gift of God
universities 61–4

Valentinians 152–3, 176
Vanhoozer, Kevin J. 87 n.25, 97, 113 n.7, 126 n.53, 131 n.71, 143–4, 147, 152 n.29, 172 n.6
Vatican II 207
via media 22–3, 25
Village, Andrew 46–7, 50, 60 n.57
Vincent of Lérins 202
violence 109, 115, 156 n.42, 181, 208, 217, 227
Virgin birth 48
Volpe, Medi Ann 104, 164 n.63, 179 n.28

Wainwright, Geoffrey 98 n.8
waiting. *See* patience

Walker, Arthur 48 n.16
Walls, Andrew 81
Walsham, Alexandra 27 n.51
Ward, Graham 20 n.15, 54 n.44, 86 n.24, 90 n.39, 97 n.4, 104 n.32, 117 n.23, 132 n.76, 186 n.47, 187 n.55, 217
Ward, Kevin 16 n.1, 31 n.69, 32 n.74, 33 n.78, 33 n.79, 34 n.84
Ward, Pete 57, 63 n.64, 70
Warner, Rob 64 n.65
warning 7, 131–4, 138, 236
Watkins, Clare 45 n.1
Webster, John 14, 20 n.15, 89 n.30, 98 n.10, 106 n.39, 142–4, 147, 151 n.27, 152 n.29, 177, 179 n.26, 210
Wenham, David 160 n.52
Wesley Study Centre 11
Westcott, Brooke Foss 155, 212 n.33
Westminster Confession 26
Westra, Liuwe H. 89 n.33, 90 n.36
White, Peter 25 n.43
Whiteness 17–18, 22, 31–6, 37 n.99, 44, 50, 62 n.60, 98, 136, 156–9, 219–20, 222 n.80, 225
Whitgift, John 24
Wigg-Stephenson Natalie 94 n.47, 98 n.9, 118 n.26
Wiles, Maurice 70
Williams, Anna 96 n.3
Williams, Ferelith Eccles 53 n.43
Williams, Rowan 19, 23, 26 n.46, 38 n.108, 39 n.112, 76 n.1, 88 n.29, 99–100, 129 n.66, 181 n.35, 183–5, 212
Winner, Lauren 205–6
wisdom 7, 84, 96 n.3, 103–4, 129, 130 n.67, 133, 138, 203–4, 215–17, 235, 240–1. *See also phronēsis*
Witherington, Ben, III 102 n.25, 103
witness 3–4, 7, 75, 77–82, 84–6, 88, 91–5, 97, 113–14, 130 n.68, 137, 151, 170–1, 207, 226, 234–6
Woodhead, Linda 37
Woods, Eric 69 n.78
word of God 77–8, 80, 83, 86, 94, 104, 151, 166, 169, 201–2. *See also* abundance; church; gift; unfolding

World Missionary Conference, 1910 34–5
worship   3–5, 7, 37–44, 50, 53–7, 60, 69–70, 75, 77–9, 84–6, 89, 91–5, 97, 99, 101, 105, 112, 119, 137, 170–1, 206, 213, 226–7, 234–6. *See also* idolatry
Wright, N. T.   178

Yeago, David   114 n.14, 177–9

Young, Frances   14 n.14, 84 n.22, 86 n.24, 87 n.25, 89 n.31, 90 n.34, 104 n.33, 126 n.53, 153 n.33, 155 n.40, 176 n.17

Zacchaeus   158
Zahl, Simeon   134 n.81
Ziegler, Philip   210 n.27
Zimmerman, John D.   65 n.69
Zurara, Gomes Eanes de   117 n.25, 219–20, 222

www.ingramcontent.com/pod-product-compliance
Lightning Source LLC
Chambersburg PA
CBHW072129290426
44111CB00012B/1832